There is history precisely because no primeval legislator put words in harmony with things.

JACQUES RANCIÈRE, *The Names of History*

History, Theory, Text

Historians and the Linguistic Turn

ELIZABETH A. CLARK

HARVARD UNIVERSITY PRESS

Cambridge, Massachusetts, and London, England   2004

For Randall Styers
In remembrance of
things past, and for
time regained

Publication of this book was aided by a grant from Duke University

Library of Congress Cataloging-in-Publication Data

Clark, Elizabeth A. (Elizabeth Ann), 1938–
    History, theory, text : historians and the linguistic turn / Elizabeth A. Clark.
      p. cm.
    Includes bibliographical references and index.
    ISBN 0-674-01516-9 (cloth : alk. paper) — ISBN 0-674-01584-3 (paper : alk. paper)
    1. Historiography.   2. History—Philosophy.   3. Christian literature, Early—
History and criticism.   I. Title.

D13.C5827 2004
907'.2—dc22   2004047358

Acknowledgments

I wish to thank many colleagues who have helped me with *History, Theory, Text*. Ten of them—in addition to the three anonymous readers for Harvard University Press—heroically read the entire manuscript and offered helpful suggestions and criticisms: Lewis Ayres, Kalman Bland, Bart Ehrman, Mary McClintock Fulkerson, Dale Martin, Albert Rabil, Randall Styers, Kenneth Surin, Terrence Tilley, and Janell Watson. Scholars at the National Humanities Center in 2001–2002 offered their expertise on particular points; I especially thank Tista Bagchi, Thomas Brady, Gaurav Desai, Kristen Hanson, Keith Simmons, and Orin Starn. Others who lent both assistance (sometimes unknowingly) and good cheer include Sarah Beckwith, Judith Bennett, Edward Bleser, Daniel Boyarin, Virginia Burrus, Averil Cameron, Stanley Chojnacki, Jan Willem Drijvers, Dyan Elliott, Valeria Finucci, Malachi Hacohen, Gail Hamner, Barbara Harris, Cynthia Herrup, Hans Hillerbrand, Andrew Jacobs, Patricia Cox Miller, David Miller, Linda Orr, Paul Strohm, Mark Vessey, Annabel Wharton, and Rowan Williams. I also thank audiences (at the American Society of Church History, Cardiff University, the College Theology Society, the Challenge of the New Historiographies Conference [Smith College], the *Confessions* Conference [Villanova University], Indiana University, the North American Patristics Society, Rice University, Syracuse University, and the University of Uppsala) for their comments on papers and lectures that went into the making of this book. Professors and graduate students in history of Christianity studies at Duke University pushed me to clarify some points. Former Duke graduate student Michael Rackett offered valuable research and bibliographical assistance. The National Humanities Center (at which I was a Henry Luce Senior Fellow) and Duke University provided me with time and resources that made this book possible, while librarians at those institutions (especially Jean Houston, Eliza Robertson, Michael McFarland, and Roberta Schaafsma) and at Union Theological Seminary cheerfully met my quite exorbitant demand for books and articles. Joel Elliott at the NHC provided excellent daily computer support for a technologically challenged writer. I thank my editor at Harvard University Press, Margaretta Fulton, for encouraging this project and seeing it through. Some of this book was written in the New York home of Walter Frisch and Anne-Marie Bouché, whom I thank for making available to me a congenial space for work.

Some points I discuss in various chapters of this book have received fuller treatment in a few of my journal articles. I have profited from response to them.

Last, this book is dedicated to Randall Styers, whose good company, intelligent conversation, adventurous spirit, and urban tastes have added much pleasure to the last fourteen years of my life.

Contents

Preface   *ix*

Introduction: An Overview   *1*

1   Defending and Lamenting History   *9*
"That Noble Dream": Ranke, His Legacy, and His Critics
Ranke in America
Epistemological Problems
Historians Besieged?

2   Anglo-American Philosophy and the Historians   *29*
Karl Popper, C.G. Hempel, and Their Critics
Arthur Danto
Anglophone Historians and Philosophers in the Later Twentieth
    Century
Historians' Appeals to Philosophy

3   Language and Structures   *42*
Structuralism and History
Structural Linguistics: Saussure and Beyond
Claude Lévi-Strauss and Structural Anthropology
Four Critiques
The Legacy of Structuralism

4   The Territory of the Historian   63
     French Historiography
     Microhistory and Its Critics
     British Marxist Historiography

5   Narrative and History   86
     Narrative at Mid-Century: The Anglophone Tradition
        and Its Critics
     Narrative at Mid-Century: The French Tradition
     A "Revival of Narrative"?
     History, Narrative, and Ideology
     The Utility of Narrative?

6   The New Intellectual History   106
     The "History of Ideas": Arthur O. Lovejoy and His Critics
     All History as "Thought": R.G. Collingwood and His Critics
     The New Shapes of the History of Ideas
     From France to America: Dominick LaCapra

7   Texts and Contexts   130
     Literary Theorists and the Text
     Derrida and Gadamer: Deconstruction and Hermeneutics
     Contextualism
     Critiques of Contextualism
     Textualism in Interpretive Anthropology and Its Critics

8   History, Theory, and Premodern Texts   156
     Late Ancient Christian Studies
     Historians and the Premodern Text
     Patristics, History, and Theory

     Abbreviations and Frequently Cited Books   187

     Notes   193

     Index   319

Preface

This book aims to provide an instructive, historically oriented, and user-friendly survey of some important moments in the late nineteenth- and twentieth-century debates surrounding history, philosophy, and critical theory (a term that I do not narrowly restrict to the Frankfurt School). I hope to convince historians that partisans of theory need not be branded as disciplinary insurrectionaries; rather, they raise in new guise issues of long-standing intellectual discussion. More particularly, I wish to persuade scholars of Western premodernity (and especially those of ancient Christianity) that the texts they study are highly amenable to the types of literary/philosophical/theoretical critique that have excited—and indeed, have now transformed—other humanities disciplines under the rubric of post-structuralism. I do not attempt the impossible task of covering *all* possible topics or participants in these debates, but limit my discussion to particular writers and movements I (and others) deem especially significant; I regret my failure to treat some of those favored by my readers.[1] In addition, several issues are beyond my competence to address: thus I leave historians of modernity to debate whether *their* materials should be considered "texts" of a literary nature or "documents" producing social, economic, and other data (or both, depending on the mode of reading);[2] and scholars of various other ancient religions, Eastern as well as Western, to discuss how theory does or does not illuminate their materials. Although my own discipline of late ancient

Christian studies—earlier, and sometimes still, known as patristics, the study of the Church Fathers' writings[3]—is at the forefront of my concerns, I hope that scholars of premodern texts across a variety of academic specializations will find this book useful. While my discussion through Chapter 7 is designed for readers with a variety of disciplinary interests, Chapter 8 offers some "case studies" that aim to model how attending to theoretical considerations can illuminate the study of premodernity.

Two final matters: a working definition of what I mean by "theory" and a comment on how I understand the term "history." Rey Chow defines theory in ways that well suit the purposes of this book: "the paradigm shift introduced by post-structuralism, whereby the study of language, literature, and cultural forms becomes irrevocably obliged to attend to the semiotic operations involved in the production of meanings, meanings that can no longer be assumed to be natural." To the question of what theory has accomplished, she answers, "systematic unsettling of the stability of meaning, [an] interruption of referentiality."[4] Chow's emphasis on theory's embeddedness in this "linguistic turn" is central to my argument. More broadly, medievalist Paul Strohm describes the work of theory: "Refusing an assimilation to the text's self-representations, theory justifies itself . . . by offering a standpoint of appraisal grounded somewhere outside that range of possibilities afforded by the text's internal or authorized commentary"; theory, then, is "any standpoint from which we might challenge a text's self-understanding."[5] These notions of theory will inform the chapters that follow.

As for "history," throughout I differentiate history, a discipline of the modern academy, from the past, an entity that no longer exists as it once did when it was the present and that is available only through its perilously reconstructed traces. History, as Gareth Stedman Jones argues, is an enterprise that takes place in the present and is constructed entirely "in the head."[6]

Introduction: An Overview

Some of my fellow historians are sounding the death knell for their discipline. Peter Novick, at the end of his impressive study, *That Noble Dream: The "Objectivity Question" and the American Historical Profession,* solemnly proclaims that "[a]s a broad community of discourse, as a community of scholars united by common aims, common standards, and common purposes, the discipline of history" has "ceased to exist."[1] Georg Iggers in his survey, *Historiography in the Twentieth Century,* entitles one chapter "The 'Linguistic Turn': The End of History as a Scholarly Discipline."[2] Joyce Appleby, Lynn Hunt, and Margaret Jacob in *Telling the Truth about History,* pronounce that there can be "no postmodern history."[3] And Keith Windschuttle provocatively titles his castigation of theory's influence on the historical profession *The Killing of History: How Literary Critics and Social Theorists Are Murdering Our Past.*[4] What are these solemn obituaries *about,* we may ask?[5] Why are these historians crying "murder"?

The present book offers no obituaries. Although conservative historian Henry Ashby Turner Jr. posits that obituaries are not in order simply because there is no "corpse," his claim is grounded in the belief that "[t]he overwhelming majority of America's historians still strive to uphold the standards of Rankean methodological objectivity in their works."[6] I claim, rather, that the alleged assaults upon the historical discipline by philosophers and theoreticians presage a "resurrection" of intellectual history, including the historical study of early

Christian texts. For textually oriented studies of premodernity, the lament for "the end of history" is groundless. Indeed, critical theory has provoked lively discussions elsewhere in the humanities and provides intellectual historians, including students of early Christianity, with new conversation partners.[7]

I offer this book as one step toward remedying for premodern, textually oriented studies the "disciplinary blindness" for which Allan Megill has castigated the historians' profession.[8] Because the historical discipline did not catapult directly from Ranke's *"wie es eigentlich gewesen"* to its recent confrontations with French-inspired theory, probing the long intervening debates over the status of history clarifies how the discipline arrived at its present contested position. Even the "dead ends," I posit, reveal something about why certain approaches have been (or should be) abandoned. It is this passage with which the following chapters are principally concerned: the route by which we got from "there" to "here."

This book begins with an exploration of the debates between and among historians and theorists in recent decades, moves back to consider some important moments in the prehistory of these debates, and returns to the present to consider the placement of premodern studies within the recently invigorated subfield of intellectual history. While Novick in *That Noble Dream* surveyed the *professional* development of the historians' guild in twentieth-century America, this book, by contrast, centers on the *conceptual* field of history and focuses on *intellectual* debates between and among (largely) French and Anglophone historians, philosophers, and theorists. The world of German historiographical scholarship, earlier so crucial, remained a latecomer to this particular discussion; the theoretical issues that recently rose to prominence in German academia center mainly on hermeneutics, modernization theory, the Holocaust, and the writings of Jürgen Habermas.[9]

Chapter 1, "Defending and Lamenting History," sets the terms of the argument. I claim that the current debates have, in different guises, troubled the intellectual world of historians for much of the twentieth century. Here, I elaborate both the epistemological problems surrounding a discipline that investigates a vanished past and the moral questions pertaining to historians' interests and values; since this past is not "there" for comparison with historians' claims concerning it, appeals to a correspondence theory of verification are precluded.[10]

Chapter 2 moves back to earlier twentieth-century Anglo-American philosophers' exploration of truth claims regarding history. Somewhat counterintuitively, attempts to construe history as a scientific discipline in the English-speaking world emanated less insistently from historians themselves than from analytical philosophers of history, a small but lively subgroup in mid-twentieth-century Anglophone philosophical circles. These philosophers, believing that relativist historians such as Charles Beard and Carl Becker had too readily conceded history's claims to objectivity,[11] offered their own expertise in exploring history's ability to yield certain knowledge.[12] Yet technical discussions of historical causation and explanation by twentieth-century philosophers were of little interest to historians, more puzzled than illuminated by philosophical subtleties. Abandoning the debate, they left to analytical philosophers an open and largely uncontested field for the theoretical investigation of history-writing.

This tale, however, has no comedic plot: the philosophers do not triumph. When their attempt to construe history as a quasi-science failed, philosophers who retained an interest in historiography turned to other disciplines—chiefly, to literature—to seek history's proper affiliations. Did not historians, like the creators of literature, employ narrative and tell stories? Was not narrative the distinctive characteristic of history, even lending it explanatory and persuasive force? Although some may judge that this second attempt to style the discipline of history as narrative came closer to the mark than did the interpretation of history as a quasi-science, it too faltered. Why?

One explanation holds that historians who had labored to escape from an older belletristic history with its rhetorical adornments had no wish belatedly to reembrace it. As Hans Kellner claims, from the early nineteenth century onward, successive generations of historians—from the romantics to the positivists, social and economic New Historians, and quantitative historians—eagerly abandoned rhetoric and charged their disciplinary forefathers (in a repetition of a "primal scene") with hopeless implication "in the toils of linguistic forms and illusions."[13] Such historians, wary of narrative's links to an outdated rhetorical style of historiography, deemed theorists' comparison of history and literature vacuous.[14] Yet, I shall argue, the assessment of history as "like literature" (if not as narrative, then as rhetorical argumentation) characterizes the fields of classical and early Christian studies better than does the categorization favored by *both* social-scientific and structuralist historians. The turn to narrative, however, rejected by most historians, also was questioned by theorists such as Roland Barthes, Hayden White, and various practitioners of Althusserian-derived ideology critique, who argued that traditional narrative, in its concern for unity, coherence, and closure, served as a prime medium of ideology. On this view, narrative historiography was no more "neutral" than narrative literature. These issues are explored in Chapter 5.

If Anglo-American philosophers had hoped by their endeavors to bolster the status of history, French philosophers and theorists influenced by structuralism, in contrast, largely denigrated or restricted history's claims, as I detail in Chapter 3. This divergence surely relates to what variously counted as philosophy in the Anglo-American and French worlds throughout the twentieth century.[15] Nonetheless, it is significant that *both* the Anglophone and the French approaches, so different in other respects, were motivated by the critics' desire either to present *themselves* as scientific, or, less grandiosely, to render history as scientific as possible. Both, indeed, engaged in a kind of formal analysis, however different they remained in other respects.[16] Although structuralism's influence was already on the wane by the late 1970s, several aspects of its program continued to influence historical studies in various disciplines: among others, its denaturalization and semiotic interpretation of culture, its privileging of discontinuity over continuity, and its attention to the self-referring quality of language. These features remained important as structuralism evolved into post-structuralism.

The minimal contact between the Anglophone and French historical, philosophical, and more widely intellectual worlds in the early and middle twentieth century continues to puzzle.[17] For example, although structural linguistics, which revolutionized French intellectual life, was introduced to America in the 1940s, its influence was largely restricted to the fields of linguistics proper, literature, and exegetical disciplines such as biblical studies. In America, structuralism failed to leave its mark on philosophy, history, and theory more generally, as it had in France. Although the Anglophone world could boast an important semiotician of its own, Charles Sanders Peirce, his dense writings made little impact on the larger world of humanities scholarship. Thus English and American academic worlds remained for the most part immune to the major intellectual current that informed scholarship in mid-twentieth-century France. As Peter Brooks notes, in

France post-structuralism took hold in a context in which the contributions of structuralist thought were already well accepted; in the United States, by contrast, structuralism's failure ever to transform disciplines across the human sciences left post-structuralism on these shores uncontextualized.[18]

It is likewise striking how little Anglophone *or* French philosophical reflection on history during this period was produced by practicing historians. For them, the field was tainted by the specters of Hegel and other speculative or idealist philosophers whose company no self-respecting academic historian would wish to keep.[19] As Hayden White notes, the "transformation of history from a general area of study, cultivated by amateurs, dilettantes, and antiquarians, into a professional discipline seemed sufficient justification for the severance of historiography from the endless speculations of the 'philosophers of history.'"[20] These failures to ground history's epistemological credibility appeared less significant to historians than to philosophers and theorists until the last decades of the twentieth century, when many historians became disturbed by what they perceived as attacks by colleagues in more theoretically oriented disciplines: hence, the "history–theory culture wars."[21] For my purposes, a prime significance of these "wars" is that they assisted the reconfiguration of intellectual history in a way that, I argue, is beneficial for the study of premodern texts. A more theoretically oriented intellectual history—unlike the old "history of ideas"—offers an especially welcoming disciplinary home for students of premodernity.

In the forefront of these debates stood revised understandings of language in relation to the external world, that is, questions of reference and representation, initially spurred by the revolution in linguistics occasioned by the earlier work of Ferdinand de Saussure. Although Saussure analyzed the relation between signifier and signified within an intralinguistic (that is, intramental) world, a relation that he famously proclaimed to be "arbitrary," his views were expanded by later linguists, philosophers, theorists, and anthropologists who developed a semiotic approach to nonlinguistic reality; among these, Roland Barthes, Claude Lévi-Strauss, and Clifford Geertz have been prominent, as I discuss in Chapters 3 and 7.

The implications of the "linguistic turn" for the historical profession, however, have been unsettling. If the "real" is known only in and through its discursive construction,[22] as established by an intralinguistic system of differences, how could historians assume (as they customarily had) the adequacy of words to refer to things? Could they continue to operate with what linguists call "nomenclaturist" assumptions? If language does not refer in a one-to-one fashion to things in the "real world," how could historians argue that their language about the past corresponded to "what had actually happened"?

Even the most prominent historians and historical schools of the twentieth century have paid scant attention to these issues. Chapter 4 examines the work of several *Annalistes,* microhistorians, and British Marxist historians, and argues that although they probed new sources and fashioned novel interdisciplinary techniques (developments I explore in detail), they did not much attend to the philosophical and theoretical questions here to be considered; that task was left to relative "outsiders" to the historical profession, such as classicist Paul Veyne. The discipline of history, however, has recently returned to good favor in France after a period of occlusion by structuralism, and some theoretically informed historians, such as Roger Chartier and Michel de Certeau, offer models of a sophisticated history that could be contemplated with profit by historians of premodernity.

In Chapter 6, I explore the present reconstitution of intellectual history from its earlier incarnation in the writings of Arthur O. Lovejoy and his followers. The older history of ideas, in which disembodied ideas appeared to waft through time, has been replaced by a more contextually and materially grounded intellectual history, often aligned with cultural history. Long despised in favor of social history, a reenvisioned intellectual history now differentiates itself from its earlier instantiations by its emphasis on discontinuity, ideology, and power. I here register the immense influence of Michel Foucault on historical studies, along with the work of Roger Chartier, Michel de Certeau, Dominick LaCapra, and others who have importantly contributed to a revisionary intellectual history.

Chapter 7 addresses a central point of debate within current intellectual history—the relation of texts and contexts. What constitutes a "text" is now a fraught question, as is the once-simple query, what constitutes "reading"? Anthropologists and cultural critics (among whom Clifford Geertz is preeminent) undertook a semiotic "reading" of nonlinguistic entities; simultaneously, French literary theorists and philosophers (Roland Barthes, Julia Kristeva, Jacques Derrida, among others) were expanding traditional definitions of text. In the Anglophone world, Quentin Skinner and J. G. A. Pocock proposed a contextualist model of historical interpretation based on spoken (not literary) language that sought (at least for Skinner) to uncover authorial intent—a model that in turn was attacked as insufficiently attentive to the differentiation of speech from writing. Also central were debates over whether nonlinguistic realities, such as the rituals that anthropologists study, should be understood as "texts." Although textual scholars found it exciting to fancy themselves anthropologists encountering "native informants" in the works they studied, recent theoreticians of history argue that this expansion of the textual elides *both* the status of practices *and* the particular work performed by high literary and philosophical writings. Moreover, as debates between and among Dominick LaCapra, Roger Chartier, Carlo Ginzburg, and Robert Darnton suggest, different reading strategies are required for high and for low texts. Texts, indeed, have acquired a new caché among historians—a point of interest to my specific area, the high literary and philosophical texts of late ancient Christianity.

Chapter 8 offers examples of various premodern historical studies that engage recent debates concerning theory and suggests ways in which repositioning late ancient Christian historical studies as a subdiscipline of the newly refurbished intellectual history well suits the type of texts on which practitioners of this subdiscipline work. First, summing up points of discussion from earlier chapters, I claim that such histories should acknowledge that, as intellectual constructions, they differ from "the past," vanished and now available only through "traces," and that no historical construction is "politically innocent" but is driven by the problems and questions set by the historian in the present: recent discussions of relativism and objectivism are here pertinent. Learning from both structuralism and post-structuralism, such studies look less to historical continuity (and hence to the nostalgia for the past that such histories often encourage) than to discontinuity, noting both breaks in the larger historical order and the gaps, absences, aporias, and contradictions in texts. They eschew "grand narratives" that often mask ideological presuppositions, as well as categories such as "experience," if understood as a foundational court of appeal. They implicitly or explicitly acknowledge that a correspondence theory of verification is untenable, and that their own *representations* are not to be confused with *reference*. They recognize that contexts are often multiple or unknown, and are variously constructed by different readers. Analyzing texts that are frequently of a high literary, theological, or philosophical status and hence ripe for rhetorical and ideological analysis, such studies look both to the site of the text's production and to the text's own productivity. Last, they acknowledge that whatever an author's intentions may have been, such intentions—even if discernible—do not necessarily inform what texts "mean" to readers.

Having acknowledged these assumptions, I note how studies of late ancient Christianity have moved from their earlier home as a sub-branch of "theology" through an encounter with the social sciences to its present state, which remains less attentive to the theoretical issues raised in this book than I and some others might wish. I next signal some points that stimulate theoretical reflection in the writings of medievalist Gabrielle Spiegel and of scholars of ancient historiography, before turning to my own field of late ancient Christian studies. Late ancient Christian texts, I argue, are ripe for the sorts of rhetorical and ideological analysis with which this book is concerned. I offer small samples of my own work, in which I argue (for example) that textual aporias may signal both textual and extratextual difficulties encountered by the author, and that ideology critique is helpful in analyzing texts concerning early Christian women. Last, I examine how postcolonial discourse theory can illuminate texts pertaining to situations of power in the Roman Empire, for which Andrew Jacobs's book, *Remains of the Jews: The Holy Land and Christian Empire in Late Antiquity,* affords an excellent model. In sum, the study of early Christian texts stands to benefit handsomely from close attention to critical theory. The following chapters, I hope, will suggest why.

CHAPTER ONE

Defending and Lamenting History

This chapter details nineteenth-century German historians' attempts to establish an objective, factual, and "scientific" brand of historiography, follows the passage of this approach to America, and signals several important criticisms of its construal. At the forefront of discussion are problems involved in historians' study of a vanished past and debates over the meaning of historical "objectivity" and "relativism." Recent critique, informed by theories loosely grouped under the rubric "post-structuralism," has unsettled the historians' profession. Various aspects of these debates are considered more extensively in the chapters that follow.

"That Noble Dream": Ranke, His Legacy, and His Critics

In the title of Peter Novick's justly acclaimed book, *That Noble Dream: The "Objectivity Question" and the American Historical Profession,*[1] the "noble dream" refers to the aspiration for historical objectivity that motivated several generations of American historians, taking their cue (or so they believed) from Leopold von Ranke.[2] The nineteenth-century German debate over defining relations between the natural and the human sciences focused on history, and Ranke stood as prince of historians.[3] Yet both nineteenth-century historicism (the claim that peoples, institutions, and nations are best understood by considering their historical development)[4] and Ranke's famous phrase, *"wie es eigentlich gewesen"* ("as it actually happened") have

been variously interpreted.[5] Uncontested, however, is Ranke's emphasis on the necessity for research based on the study of documents:
where there are no documents, he claimed, there can be no history.[6] A
philosophical approach to history was anathema to him.[7] Although
classicists and ancient historians had refined the methods of source
criticism for some decades before Ranke, he was the first to apply
these techniques to *modern* historical documents.[8] He insisted that
historians of early modern and modern history must go to the archives to find documents, the primary sources from which they could
then construct an objective, factual historical narrative. Seeking to
"extinguish himself" before the facts, he urged students and colleagues to embrace the "supreme law" of history—namely, to offer "a
strict presentation of facts, no matter how conditional and unattrac-
tive they may be."[9] Ranke's enthusiasm for archival research is well
known: the libraries of Vienna, Venice, and Rome aroused in him, he
confessed, "archival greed."[10]

Yet critics have registered important caveats. First, work by modern
historians of historiography—Arnaldo Momigliano in particular—
trace the impulse to a scientific history farther back than Ranke: as
monumental as the latter's influence proved to be, he was not the first
to advocate scientific history.[11] Moreover, that Ranke read his archival sources (to cite Anthony Grafton) "as transparent windows on
past states and events rather than colorful reconstructions of them"
now seems evident. Many of his footnotes are woefully incomplete, as
Grafton has shown on the basis of Ranke's *Nachlass*, and all were
added *after* he had composed his books and essays. The secretaries he
employed in his later years testified to the difficulty in locating references—some of which proved not to exist—for what he had already
written.[12] The "image" of Ranke that has prevailed, however, is that
of a meticulous workman.

Astutely perceiving that his source-critical techniques must be
passed to the next generation of historians, Ranke devised the seminar method of instruction. Based on the scrutiny of source documents, this then-novel training device was introduced in German
universities and later disseminated, notably to America, by budding
historians who had studied with Ranke and his disciples in Germany.[13] Historian Herbert Baxter Adams, writing in 1887, provides a
colorful glimpse of the newly introduced seminar method at Johns
Hopkins University:

There the student appears, fortified by books and documents borrowed from the university library, and prepared with his brief of points and citations, like a lawyer about to plead a case in the court room . . . Authorities are discussed; parallel sources of information are cited; old opinions are exploded; standard histories are riddled by criticism, and new values are established. This process of destruction and reconstruction requires considerable literary apparatus, and the professor's study-table is usually covered with many evidences of the battle of books.[14]

One important, if perhaps underappreciated, result of Ranke's pioneering endeavor was the development of library collections of primary sources, which contributed to the democratization of the historians' profession by making expensive books available to students from the less-privileged classes.[15]

To be sure, Ranke's exaltation of documentary history met with challenges aimed to deflate even within Germany.[16] Although enthusiasm for his historical methods waxed high by midcentury, countervoices also could be heard. Most extreme of these now-heralded figures was Friedrich Nietzsche, whose pamphlet "Thoughts Out of Season: On the Use and Abuse of History" appeared in 1874.[17] Nietzsche's "lament" over history—unlike that of recent traditionalists—stemmed from his disgust at the "excessive" dominance of history in his day. His thoughts, he declared, were "out of season" with his contemporaries' high evaluation of history.[18] It was not, to be sure, that Nietzsche hated "the past": his love of ancient Greece, especially the Greece infused with the Dionysiac spirit, is well known.[19] Whereas the Greeks, he claimed, enjoyed a robust "unhistorical sense," modern men had become "wandering encyclopedias."[20] Life and action had been paralyzed, sickened, indeed "mummified" by an overdose of the historical spirit.[21] Nietzsche ridiculed the cramped and "mouldy" work of antiquarian historians in particular.[22] The stultifying historical education served up to youth in his day, he believed, served only to dampen their instincts.[23]

To Nietzsche, historians' fervent defense of "objectivity" meant trivializing the past to fit the present; they deemed "subjective" any opinion that veered from the canonical judgment.[24] To be sure, he agreed that historians must make a "loving study" of the data, but beyond that, a creative vision, an artistic spirit, is needed to form a "harmonious whole" from what otherwise were simply events stemming from "blind chance and lawless freedom."[25]

Nietzsche posited two means of escape from the stultification of history: either to embrace the "unhistorical," to learn to forget;[26] or, conversely, to become "super-historical," to turn away from the transitory to art and religion, which he believed lent human existence an eternal character.[27] Nietzsche doubtless preferred the second option—but given his scorn for the masses' "herd mentality,"[28] it is unlikely that he envisioned many embracing his preference. That would be left for the Zarathustras.[29]

More moderate (and influential) nineteenth-century German critics of Rankean history include Wilhelm Dilthey, who fostered the hermeneutic turn in the human sciences. On his seventieth birthday, Dilthey reflected that it had been his life's work to compose "a critique of historical reason," to study "the nature and conditions of historical consciousness."[30] In this he took inspiration from Ranke, whose source-critical techniques and lively narrative style made him (to Dilthey) "the master of modern historical narrative," "the embodiment of historical insight as such."[31]

Dilthey's notion of history differed, however, from Ranke's in important respects. Although, like Ranke, Dilthey understood history to be an empirical science, he rejected historical positivism.[32] After history belatedly freed itself from metaphysics, Dilthey argued, it fell captive to the natural sciences, emulating a positivism inappropriate to history; in Dilthey's view, the human sciences, such as history, unlike the natural/physical sciences, should embody purely *human* values and interests.[33] While explanation *(Erklären)* is the province of the physical sciences, he famously declared, understanding *(Verstehen)* is the concern of the human sciences:[34] "[w]e explain nature, we understand mind."[35] "Understanding," however, did not betoken a clairvoyant and empathetic entry to the mind of the other, but an "elucidation of functional and structural relations" of the mental world.[36]

Moreover, arguing that presuppositionless knowledge was impossible, Dilthey endorsed Wilhelm von Humboldt's claim that "in order to understand, we must already in some sense have understood."[37] Here, Dilthey signals the "hermeneutic circle": some criterion of judgment must be operative before the historian selects and abstracts his or her material.[38] And not only written texts call for a hermeneutical approach, he declared: life itself needs exegesis.[39]

Yet against those, like Nietzsche, who complained of the "burden of the past," Dilthey upheld the centrality of historical understanding.[40] While Schleiermacher had defended religion against its "cultured despisers," Dilthey countered the recent despisers and detractors of history.[41] Since humans are historical beings, he argued, they should accept the value of historical understanding—not lapse into the voluntaristic subjectivism that he hints led Nietzsche to madness.[42] Since history is the means by which humans live and work, to cast it off, as Nietzsche advised, would mean renouncing knowledge of humanity itself.[43]

Thus within Germany, the positivism of Rankean history, with its alleged cramping of human imagination and devotion to "scientific" modes of explanation, found its critics.

Ranke in America

In his presidential address of 1909 to the American Historical Association, George Burton Adams urged colleagues to heed "the call of our first leader," who had proclaimed that "the chief duty of the historian is to establish *wie es eigentlich gewesen.*"[44] The customary American interpretation of Ranke's phrase has been that it enjoins historians to provide an objective report of "what actually happened" in a past taken as unproblematically transparent.[45]

Although recent interpreters of Ranke have explored his theological commitments[46]—his search for God's guiding hand in a "universal history,"[47] his Christian idealism[48]—this is not the image of Ranke held by American historians in the early twentieth century. The latter overlooked Ranke's idealist vision and appropriated only his emphasis on the critical study of documents, which came to serve as a credo for a "scientific" history.[49] As Adams remarked in his presidential address, Ranke taught historians that any hint of "philosophy of history" should be left to "poets, philosophers and theologians."[50]

Countervoices, such as those of Dilthey and Nietzsche, had little influence on Anglophone (or, for that matter, French)[51] historiography. Crossing the language barrier was only one, albeit a significant, problem. Although Charles Beard was exceptional among American historians in urging colleagues to study Dilthey, Troeltsch, and other German theorists, his efforts, as Novick notes, were "a total failure."[52] Writing in 1937, Charles Beard and Alfred Vagts rued the thirty- to forty-year time lag between the production of historiography in Germany and its arrival in America.[53] And with the advent of Nazism and

German historians' enchantment with the Third Reich, Anglophone historians had even greater reason to ignore German historiography.[54] An irony that will become apparent below is that German counter-voices such as Nietzsche often were introduced to a later generation of American historians through French *theorists* and the American counterparts they inspired[55]—although, to be sure, the hermeneutic tradition of German philosophy arrived in America without a detour through France.

The creed of historical objectivity, however it entered the American historical profession, contained several interrelated propositions.[56] In his "Noble Dream" essay of 1935 Charles Beard lists the following before leveling his critique: (1) "that history . . . has existed as an object or series of objects outside the mind of the historian" (that is, the past is "real"); (2) "that the historian can face and know this object or series of objects and can describe it as it objectively existed"; (3) "that the historian can . . . divest himself of all taint of religious, political, philosophical, social, sex, economic, moral, and aesthetic interests" (that is, there should be a sharp separation of fact and value); (4) "that the multitudinous events of history as actuality had some structural organization through inner (perhaps causal) relations, which the impartial historian can grasp by inquiry and observation and accurately reproduce or describe in written history" (that is, that historical facts are "found," not "made," and that the past itself, not just the historian's description of it, exhibits a recognizable structure); and (5) "that the substances of this history can be grasped in themselves by purely rational or intellectual efforts, and that they are not permeated by anything transcendent."[57] As Beard derisively noted, this objectivist theory of history "condemns philosophy and throws it out of doors . . . [I]t ignores problems of mind with which philosophers and theologians have wrestled for centuries."[58] For Beard, historical objectivism was intellectually and philosophically defunct.

The "objectivist creed" entailed several corollaries. Its partisans, Novick observes, tend to assume a correspondence theory of verification, believe truth to be "one, not perspectival," and consider historians, as historians, to be disinterested judges who eschew advocacy.[59] Objectivist historiography, Peter Burke adds, deems politics and events the proper subjects of historical study and narration its natural historical medium; assumes that history, based on documents, official records, and archives is written "from above," through the eyes of great men; and explains events by appealing to the thoughts of the historical actors.[60] Novick concedes that historians in recent years have offered more nuanced assumptions; they now more likely claim (for example) that interpretations are tested by facts, not derived from them. These modifications, however, require minimal adjustment of objectivist presuppositions.[61]

Many historians, past and present, deemed the quest for objectivity fundamental to their recognition as professionals. Eager to dissociate themselves from the amateur productions that abounded in nineteenth-century Anglophone historiography, historians made a bid for academic respectability through their quest for a scientific history modeled on German scholarship.[62] In addition, the professionalization of history was thought to require a repression of philosophical or metahistorical theory—a repression that itself constituted a kind of unacknowledged politicization.[63] (That "the cult of Research" *also* constitutes an ideological stance went largely unacknowledged.)[64] Nonetheless, as Novick notes, even by the 1940s there were only a few universities in America where the German model of research was embraced in practice: Johns Hopkins, the University of Chicago, and Cornell. Elsewhere, even at Ivy League universities, historians modeled themselves more on British dons—who largely had not yet adopted German historiographical methods—than on German researchers.[65] (British historian George Macaulay Trevelyan, for example, urged his colleagues to resist being drilled into "so many Potsdam Guards of learning.")[66]

What did the objectivist model entail in historical practice? Hayden White elaborates:

> The "historical method"—as the classic historiographers of the nineteenth century understood the term—consisted of a willingness to go to the archives without any preconceptions whatsoever, to study the documents found there, and then to write a story about the events attested by the documents in such a way as to make the story itself the explanation of "what had happened" in the past. The idea was to let the explanation emerge naturally from the documents themselves, and then to figure its meaning in story form.[67]

Decades ago, historian E. H. Carr wittily deflated the assumptions of this objectivist historiography:

> This was the age of innocence, and historians walked in the Garden of Eden, without a scrap of philosophy to cover them, naked and unashamed before the god of history. Since then, we have known Sin and

experienced a Fall; and those historians who today pretend to dispense with a philosophy of history are merely trying, vainly and self-consciously, like members of a nudist colony, to recreate the Garden of Eden in their garden suburb.[68]

Whence did these assumptions regarding historical objectivity arise? Novick claims that they were grounded in early modern notions of scientific objectivity, and in the Cartesian postulate of "an Archimedean point upon which knowledge could be grounded." The paradigmatic shifts in science and philosophy that occurred during the early and mid-twentieth century found little resonance in historical practice. For evidence, Novick looks to the introduction in the early twentieth century of relativity theory (more precisely, quantum mechanics) in physics, the assumptions of which portended the demolition of the epistemological foundationalism that historians had sought in the sciences. Physicists' theories regarding uncertainty and indeterminacy, and their claim that the position of the observer must be taken into account in measuring space and time, cast doubt on the model of the omniscient observer assumed by classical theories of knowledge.[69]

Philosopher Raymond Aron, for example, writing in the mid-1930s, argued that Einstein's theory had forever changed the assessment of the role of the observer and had forced the abandonment of notions of absolute time and space.[70] Moreover, Aron averred, the theory of relativity found a counterpart in historical relativism: since the past that has disappeared "attains existence only in minds, and changes with them,"[71] there is no stability of the historical object. In the same era, *Annaliste* Marc Bloch urged historians to learn from Einstein and others that they could achieve only epistemological probability, not certainty, and that measurement is relative.[72] Such claims, however, did not noticeably change historians' conception of their task. As Carr observed, while physicists in his day were sounding more like historians, many historians still aspired to models of objectivity that had informed nineteenth-century science.[73]

Concurrent with these scientific developments, Novick notes, avant-garde literary and artistic experiments that employed multiple perspectives and voices stirred the cultural world.[74] Yet these developments had as little effect on the historical profession as had those in theoretical physics; no one tried to write history à la James Joyce.[75] The model for historical narrative remained that of the nineteenth-

(not the twentieth-) century English novel.[76] In short, the historical profession became mired in scientific and literary paradigms that were rapidly being abandoned by practitioners of those disciplines.

As the following chapters will trace, for the better part of the twentieth century historians either ignored or rejected the assistance that philosophers and theorists offered in their attempt to render the historical discipline scientific, or, at the least, distinctive as a form of knowledge. The provocations of philosophers and theoreticians in more recent decades thus have an instructive prehistory.

Epistemological Problems

What historians do worst, Novick concedes, is reflect on epistemology.[77] As "spontaneous epistemological realists,"[78] historians have been hard pressed in recent years to provide compelling responses when challenged by philosophers and theorists. Troubling questions pertaining to historical representation are not readily broached, nor is the problem occasioned by historians' fusion of representation (the historian's rhetorically structured depiction) and referentiality (the actual past realities: "outside the text")—what Robert Berkhofer calls the "referential illusion." In Berkhofer's view, traditional historians create an illusion of realism by conflating their rhetorically structured representations with "the actual."[79]

Although virtually all historians now admit that the remains of the past are fragmentary, that our knowledge of it is partial, that *all* written records (including documents) are conveyed in language, such considerations have only slightly upset the epistemological equanimity of those whom Berkhoffer calls the "normal historians." The concession by such "normal historians" that they cannot fully capture past experience and that their accounts are partial, hence more than one story needs to be told, is viewed as sufficient.[80] More extreme, G. R. Elton registers "suspicion" that "a philosophic concern with such problems as the reality of historical knowledge or the nature of historical thought only hinders the practice of history."[81]

On these points, philosophers and theorists retort that historians' appeals to methodology and techniques of historical research do not save the day: "grubbing in the archives" does not ensure the truth of the product.[82] Historians thus beat a hasty retreat when confronted with Roger Chartier's seemingly innocent (but truly lethal) question—

a question that Chartier directed especially to Appleby, Hunt, and Jacob's *Telling the Truth about History:* "What are the criteria by which a historical discourse—always a knowledge based on traces and signs—can be held to be a valid and explicative reconstruction . . . of the past reality it has defined as its object?"[83] "The pertinent question," he writes elsewhere, "is what criteria permit us to hold possible the relationship that historical writing institutes between the representing trace and the practice represented."[84]

The Past and the Present

Critics of traditional historiography argue that since the past, at least in written form, is preserved in the present only as text, there can be no appeal to a "past" aside from this linguistically constituted record.[85] "What historian has not had the daydream of being able, like Ulysses, to body forth the shades for questioning?" mused Marc Bloch decades ago—but alas, he conceded, those ethereal shades leave, at best, only "tracks."[86] Others, rejecting his daydream, pointedly asked if it is not the very *disappearance* of the past that authorizes the quite different fact of its being written?[87] Since it is not an epistemological possibility for historians—or anyone—to grasp "the past" in an unmediated fashion, realist historiography deludes when it represents the structures of interpretation as if they were the "actual past."[88] As Michel de Certeau puts it, historians, like psychoanalysts, can attend to "a return of the past" only through the discourse of the present.[89]

A major but often unacknowledged problem with historical knowing is that the past is not an object of sense perception that can be experienced empirically in the present. Any view of the past that assumes it exhibits the same features as perceivable things misconstrues how history is constituted; thus historians' disagreements cannot rightly be compared with those of differing eyewitnesses to an event, as historians sometimes claim, for nothing in the practice of history corresponds to eyewitness observation.[90] Rather, as Gareth Stedman Jones puts it, history "is an entirely intellectual operation which takes place in the present and in the head."[91] The nonperceivability of the past carries with it a correlate: the abandonment of a correspondence theory that often assumes that verification can be made by direct sense-perceptible confrontation.[92] Since the historian cannot perceive or confront the past, objectivity and truth in matters historical must be gauged in some other way.

The "pastness of the past" sharply informs historian and political philosopher Michael Oakeshott's notions of historical practice. Oakeshott argued that the historian can only infer, not retrieve, a vanished past. Reentering a past that has disappeared is an impossible feat.[93] The historical fact must be recognized not as "what really happened," but as "what the evidence obliges us to believe." The consequences of Oakeshott's recognition are several. First, history is not "out there," but is something that historians create.[94] Moreover, since historians neither rethink the thoughts of the dead nor relive their lives, but rather bring questions of the present to bear upon the "remains," they necessarily understand the past in ways that people of the time did not.[95] This recognition, however, is not to be rued; some even deem it an *advantage*.[96] Oakeshott's theory foreshadowed recent historiographical debates concerning "presentism."

Presentism

The debate over presentism focuses on the proper distance the historian should assume from the vanished object of study. For traditional historians, the historian's placement in the present constitutes a problem that he or she should seek to overcome. For post-structuralist-inspired historians, on the contrary, the historian's placement in the present is an issue to be registered, perhaps even celebrated: these are "histories which have come out," in Keith Jenkins's phrase.[97]

Traditional historians, such as G. R. Elton, argue against presentist claims; for him, "the past must be studied in its own right, for its own sake, and on its own terms."[98] For such historians, only questions that interested past authors or their readers—that is, questions from *their* world—are permissible. Present-day concerns are not to intrude upon the historian's investigation of the past, for then ideology would overtake objectivity.[99] Indeed, the attack on presentism often focuses not so much on the present *per se* as on particular social and political values that the critics dispute and that are labeled "interests"—often the concerns of feminist and Marxist historians, historians of color, and those investigating the history of sexualities in times past.[100] (And this list might well be updated with the addition of postcolonial theory.) These historians, it is alleged, allow their personal convictions to intrude into work that should be free of interests; they have forgotten that the past must be allowed to "speak for itself."

Presentism is not a new issue, as some critics imply. Presentist assumptions were acknowledged as inescapable, and even defended, by historians and philosophers working far earlier than the "culture wars" of the late twentieth century—Benedetto Croce,[101] Carl Becker,[102] Frederick Jackson Turner,[103] Raymond Aron,[104] and John Dewey[105] come to mind.[106] Likewise, the founders of *Annales,* Marc Bloch and Lucien Febvre, were emphatic that history-writing grows out of present questions and concerns.[107] Historians of our own time likewise challenge the "anti-presentists." As Dominick LaCapra pointedly comments, "In the sort of historicism that is still prevalent among professional historians, one attempts to understand the past in its own terms and for its own sake, as if the past had its own terms and was there for its own sake. Today it is difficult to escape the idea that values at least affect one's choice of problems and that theoretical assumptions have something to do with the way one construes facts."[108]

Some, such as David Harlan, adopt an even more assertive posture, arguing that presentist history performs a *more* genuinely historical function, by raising up texts "from the graveyard of dead contexts and helping them take up new lives among the living." For Harlan, a presentist stance provides a means for scholars to pay their respect, as well as fulfill their historical responsibility, to the dead.[109] Indeed, Harlan urges, historians must adopt some such stance if they do not wish their discipline to remain what it regrettably is at the moment, in his view, "the great reactionary center of American intellectual life." History is here taken seriously as a form of "moral reflection"—albeit of a quite different variety than the moral lessons that some eighteenth- and nineteenth-century historians believed the past contained.[110]

Objectivism

Objectivity, Novick argues, persisted as a shared ideal in the profession only through the ideological and social homogeneity of the historians' community.[111] To be sure, Charles Beard and Carl Becker had earlier challenged the profession's conservative political outlook, thus prefiguring the later breakdown of ideological consensus among historians.[112] Yet that consensus was not much disturbed either by those relativists, by the entry of Jews to the historical profession in America at midcentury,[113] or, slightly later, by that of labor historians.[114] Jews and labor historians did not constitute an epistemological challenge to the discipline of history, however much they represented a different social clientele with research programs sometimes different from those favored by mainstream male historians of Anglo-Saxon descent.[115]

Historians of a traditional cast have recently proclaimed that the field has suffered a decline from objectivity, but their opinions vary as to what this "decline" entails and who is responsible for it. Some years ago, Arnaldo Momigliano blamed Marxists and radicals, along with historians who warmed to psychoanalysis, existentialism, and theology.[116] On Novick's more recent reconstruction, by contrast, it was the arrival of feminist historians and historians of color in the 1960s and 1970s that unsettled the historians' guild—and not only because these newcomers to the field did not fit socially among an almost exclusively male and white peer group.[117] More important, these scholars brought a different perspective to historical work: here, social and epistemological factors meet.[118] As Joan Scott expresses it, "women cannot just be added on without a fundamental recasting of the terms, standards and assumptions of what has passed for objective, neutral and universal history," for that view of history "included in its very definition of itself the exclusion of women."[119] The newcomers challenged the dominant assumption that the historian should be a disinterested judge, that facts are independent of interpretations, that the meaning of events remains unchanged with the passage of time. Their social position, in other words, entailed a different epistemological perspective on the historian's task. They read Foucault. They read Said. Everybody (in Novick's reconstruction) read Thomas Kuhn on paradigm shifts. Objectivity was under attack.[120]

In the view of traditionalists, these differing epistemological assumptions represented "interests," negatively construed. Thus Geoffrey Elton laments the "corruption" of historical writing by "strident" feminist historians—a result of their "bigoted idleness."[121] Oscar Handlin denounces historical studies of "femininity, ethnicity, and population" as "frantic scratchings for substance," "doomed to futility."[122] Gertrude Himmelfarb dismisses Marxist history as "a continuation of politics by other means."[123] Historians, she argues, should rather engage in "self-sacrifice," in "a continual extinction of personality."[124]

Replying to the charges of presentism and "interests," the newcomers remained unapologetic: if interest is at stake, it is so for all historians, however often traditionalists fail to acknowledge their own social and political positioning. Thus Reinhart Koselleck argues that the discipline of history "always performs a political function, albeit a changing one."[125] Or as Keith Jenkins has put it, "[h]istory is never for itself; it is always for someone."[126] On this view, what separates the traditionalists from the alleged offenders is their divergent answers to the question, "Who is this history *for?*" As Hayden White advises:

> if one if is going to "go to history," one had better have an address in mind rather than go wandering around the streets of the past like a *flaneur*. Historical *flaneurisme* is undeniably enjoyable, but the history we are living today is no place for tourists. If you are going to "go to history," you had better have a clear idea of which history, and you had better have a pretty good notion as to whether it is hospitable to the values you carry into it.[127]

Indeed, what is alleged as a vice by conservative historians is touted as a virtue by the accused. Traditional historians, the latter charge, fail to acknowledge their own biases that for centuries were rationalized as "normal" (and hence not worthy of mention): the acquisition and maintenance of power by white males of a certain class. Feminist and black historians, and those who deal with postcolonial history and theory, claim that they are merely unmasking the sexist and racist assumptions that undergird much traditional scholarship.

Bonnie G. Smith's book, *The Gender of History: Men, Women, and Historical Practice,* illuminates how "the development of [historians'] modern scientific methodology, epistemology, professional practice, and writing has been closely tied to evolving definitions of masculinity and femininity"—a view, she notes, that goes "against the grain of professionalism itself." The modern notion of scientific history, Smith argues, did not arise by "parthenogenesis"; professionals *became* professionals "by differentiating themselves from a low, unworthy, and trivial 'other'"—namely, from women historians who wrote for the marketplace and whose efforts were labeled "amateurism." Analogous to Foucault's question how an author is created, Smith asks how a historian is created, how is he gendered a masculine "original," in contrast to the women historians with whom such men often collaborated, who were labeled mere "copyists" or even "falsifiers"?[128]

Joan Scott summarizes the issue:

> The proliferation of Others' histories has not so much "politicized" the discipline (a charge usually leveled by the defenders of the orthodox) as it has exposed the politics by which one particular viewpoint established its predominance. As such, it has raised questions about difference and power: how have differences among groups been constructed to organize and legitimize social and economic distinctions? How has the exclusion of some stories from the record of the past perpetuated inequalities based on attributions of difference?[129]

Relativism

Frequently the charge against those who entertain theoretical challenges to history-writing is that of relativism.[130] The least sophisticated form of this charge holds that if post-structuralist claims were seriously considered, there would be no way to privilege one historical interpretation over another, since every belief would be equally good.[131] Thus—so runs the caricature—if historians make the slightest concession to epistemological skepticism, "then all is lost, history will slide into fiction, Holocaust deniers will rise up everywhere, and we will have to fight the Second World War all over again."[132] Marxist historians, for their part, worry that postmodernism's "*jouissance*-like exultation in the pleasures of a free-wheeling relativism" damages historians' ability to speak for political progressivism.[133] (To be sure, non-Marxist historians also fault postmodern history on similar grounds: thus Gertrude Himmelfarb acidly comments that postmodern historiography recognizes "no reality, only the pleasure principle—history at the pleasure of the historian.")[134] To such allegations Hans Kellner retorts that "to challenge the ideology of truth is not to champion lies, falsify documents, or suppress information; it is to assert the constructed nature of the human world."[135]

What might cognitive relativism mean for an historian? This question was faced by earlier critics of historical positivism, who understood that a thoroughgoing historicism inevitably implied relativism. Writing in 1959, Hayden White posited that historicism is inextricably bound to relativism: "to interpret the whole of reality . . . in historical, that is to say relative, terms."[136] Earlier, Charles Beard and Carl Becker were often classified as relativists or skeptics in their challenge to the notion of scientific history.[137] Even philosophers such as Maurice Mandelbaum who stood *against* historical relativism claimed that if historians reject "transcendent" values—holding rather that knowledge is value-charged and historically conditioned, and that epistemological validity must be understood "with reference to the conditions under which it was formed"—then relativism is inevitable.[138] Since many historians (as well as theorists) *do* believe that values are conditioned and nontranscendent, and that knowledge is value-charged, it is hard to escape Mandelbaum's conclusion.

To be sure, more positive "spins" can be put on the notion of relativism. Richard Rorty argues that "there is nothing to be claimed about either truth or rationality apart from the descriptions of the familiar procedures of justification that a given society—*ours*—uses in one or another area of inquiry." From Rorty's viewpoint, the "anti-relativism" of traditionalists represents less a philosophical position than "the need to preserve certain habits of contemporary European life," and, in disguise, represents "the fear of the death of our community."[139] To claim that we work from our situated communities and networks surely does not imply that "every community is as good as every other."[140] Rorty suggests that changing the label from "relativism" to "ethnocentrism," understood as a purely negative critique that abandons a correspondence theory of truth, puts the issue in a better light.[141] Historians who endorse the historical nature of justification have often welcomed Rorty's views.[142]

Twentieth-century cultural anthropology contributed its own distinctive interpretation of relativism to the discussion. By midcentury, the *cultural* relativism long accepted by anthropologists—Lévi-Strauss calls it "one of the foundations of cultural anthropology"[143]—was seen to entail a *cognitive* relativism as well.[144] Addressing fellow anthropologists, Clifford Geertz urged critics to cast out their demonic fear of "cultural relativism": "the norms of reason were not fixed in Greece."[145] "Anti-relativists" should not worry, he joked, that "if something isn't anchored everywhere nothing can be anchored anywhere"; "[i]f we wanted home truths, we should have stayed at home."[146] Nor, Geertz concluded, need anyone fear that "reality is going to go away unless we believe very hard in it."[147] Geertz's admonitions seem equally appropriate reminders to traditional historians

who worry that their discipline may vanish if they abandon epistemological positivism, correspondence theories of verification, objectivism, and anti-relativism.

Historians Besieged?

The above issues have occasioned much contention in recent historiographical discussions. Historians now largely concede that they only
partially capture the past's fullness and must diligently labor to build
up an explanatory context—the historian's version of Geertz's "thick
description."[148] Despite such concessions, there seems no easy escape
from the epistemologically problematic nature of the historian's enterprise. Since it is the historian who offers explanations for events,
posits causes and effects, fills in the gaps of and provides meaning for
the historical record, how is the truth of an account to be assessed?[149]
Should, or should not, the historian strive to align "the structure of
interpretation" with "the structure of factuality"?[150] Traditional historians, however, more likely rest content if they can ascertain the relative plentitude or paucity of documents: are there enough to make a
case, to tell a story?

Such historians, grounded in an epistemological foundationalism,
have offered few convincing rejoinders to philosophers' and theorists'
critiques of this assumption. Some appear to believe that time-honored appeals to objectivism and realism are still credible, with only
slight modification.[151] Others perhaps fear to test their philosophical
skills against those whom they suspect (with good reason) are more
adept than they in theoretical debate. As I argue in Chapter 4, even
noted pioneers of twentieth-century historiography—*Annalistes*,
microhistorians, and Marxist historians—retained traditional, and
largely unexamined, epistemological assumptions.

In larger perspective, these debates can be seen as contests over
"who controls the past."[152] In narrower perspective, historians perceive that they are under attack. No longer, with Leopold von Ranke,
can they picture themselves as heroes laying claim to the "virgin" archive, the "princesses in need of rescue";[153] or, with Lucien Febvre, as
storming the "sleeping necropolis" to call back to life the frozen,
sleeping princess, "History."[154] No: now it is *historians* who are under
siege. The scene has changed even since circa 1970, when J. H. Hexter
could wittily report that although *other* disciplines were experiencing

their "St. Bartholomew's Day" massacres, their *"auto-da-fé,"* their "major holocausts" at professional meetings whose corridors "are littered with slaughtered reputations . . . and made horrid by the screams of the maimed and the moribund," history had to date escaped such battles. Although Hexter feared that such "massacres" *could* develop within the historical profession, he hazarded that they would involve political disagreements.[155] "Theory" was nowhere in sight. That, however, was 1970. Since then battle has erupted, and Hexter himself joined it.

As historian Beverley Southgate writes, "To have the bedrock of one's discipline questioned, is to be unsettled; and when stability is threatened, aggression usually follows."[156] Thus the discourse of traditional historians abounds in metaphors of besiegement. Microhistorian Carlo Ginzburg rails against the "skeptical war machine,"[157] while Lawrence Stone summons Gertrude Himmelfarb[158] (and presumably other historians) "to stand shoulder to shoulder against the growing army of enemies of rationality."[159] Robert Frykenberg fulminates against post-structuralist "regiments and warlords" marching forth with their "weapons of choice" (allegedly borrowed from Marxism); the past has become a site of "battle," on which, he claims, "human consciousness and culture are no more than booty."[160] Georg Iggers calls on historians who still believe that history is a *Wirklichkeitswissenschaft* not to "surrender" their intellects, as have "postmodernists."[161] J. H. Hexter compares deconstructionist-inspired historians to "Atilla the Hun in the throes of indigestion."[162] Theoretically attuned historians, for their part, likewise depict the traditionalists as "circling the wagons,"[163] as crying "murder,"[164] as fighting "a last-ditch stand to preserve the foundational premises of the normal history paradigm."[165] And if metaphors of embattlement do not suffice, critics who object to the alleged obfuscation and jargon of post-structuralist critique can resort to charges of a moralizing and psychologizing order. Thus postmodernist colleagues are described as "deeply disillusioned intellectuals." Even worse, they are lazy: the authors of *Telling the Truth about History* claim that whereas those passionate for knowledge (presumably, historical realists) will climb the more than three hundred steps to the Lyon archives, "the relativist might not bother."[166]

Such indictments, predictably, annoy theoreticians who fault historians' failure to comprehend their claims. Thus Jacques Derrida registers impatience that he has been caricatured as "against history," *tout court,* when he critiques "metaphysical" and "linear" concepts of history.[167] Deconstructive understandings of history, he suggests, can help to rescue "lost heritages" from being melted down "into the anonymous mass of an unrecognizable culture, to '(bio)degrade' in the common compost of a memory said to be living and organic."[168] Many of his works (including his critique of Foucault's *Madness and Civilization*) offer arguments based on a precise reading of texts in their appropriate historical contexts[169]—a point to which historians surely should not object. Deconstruction, it has been argued, "insofar as it insists on the necessary non-coincidence of the present with itself, is in fact in some sense the most historical of discourses imaginable."[170]

More patiently, Joan Scott, whose approach to history-writing is inspired by deconstruction, again explains her practice: "My argument is not that reality is 'merely' a text, but rather that reality can only be attained through language."[171] Other nontraditionalists revert to sarcasm. Thus Robert Berkhofer: "It is a good thing that historians know a fact when they see one in practice," for their efforts to theorize about them might well suggest otherwise.[172] And F. R. Ankersmit offers a psychologizing (and condescending) analysis of traditional historians' reaction to theoretical critique, positing that when theorists "confront historians with these sad and disappointing facts about their discipline, it is only natural that historians tend to project their own frustrations about the uncertainties of their discipline onto theorists. In short, historical theorists are historians' obvious target if they wish to work off their all too understandable professional inferiority complexes."[173]

Jibes and caricatures in themselves, however, do not assist the reconceptualizing of history. Although that task may seem formidable, why (asks Beverley Southgate) should the call for historians to set forth more explicitly the philosophical underpinnings of their subject constitute a particularly threatening assignment? It is not only Hayden White, he reasons, but historians of yore, such as Herbert Butterfield and Edward Gibbon, who issued such calls to self-awareness.[174] What would it mean (asks Patrick Joyce) for historians to acknowledge that "the events, structures and processes of the past are indistinguishable from the forms of documentary representation, the conceptual and political appropriations, and the historical discourses that construct them"?[175] Could historians accept Franklin Anker-smit's thesis that a historical narration does not convey any technical knowledge, but is simply a "proposal to look at the past from a certain point of view"?[176] Could they endorse his (seemingly counter-intuitive) claim that historiography is "the postmodernist discipline *par excellence,* since in historiography (historical) reality yields to the depictions of itself so that we are left with mere appearances, that is, with representations mirroring an ever absent past reality"?[177]

In the following chapters, I delimit the historical and intellectual background to the present debates. In particular, I hope to convince readers of the advantageous position in which *intellectual* history stands in the early twenty-first century—and the benefits that might accrue to the practitioners of a premodern, textually oriented history if they were to seize the moment.

CHAPTER TWO

Anglo-American Philosophy and the Historians

Analytical philosophy of history constitutes a subdiscipline of linguistic philosophy that dominated the Anglophone philosophical world for much of the twentieth century. Exploring how "words 'hook onto' the world,"[1] linguistic philosophy aimed to solve (or dissolve) philosophical problems either by reforming language or by better understanding its ordinary use.[2] Since (in Ludwig Wittgenstein's famous phrase) philosophical problems arise from a "bewitchment of our intelligence by means of language,"[3] philosophers hoped that by attending to ordinary language use, they could provide a "therapy" to dispel the pseudoproblems haunting the history of philosophy.[4] In the course of this exploration, early versions of linguistic philosophy associated with the Vienna Circle and logical positivism, which had aimed at a rigorously scientific analysis of language, acquired a "softer" Wittgensteinian hue. Likewise, Anglophone philosophy of history gradually abandoned its scientific aspirations for more humanistic approaches to history that, eventually, centered on the role of narrative.

Analytical philosophers of history in the 1940s and 1950s embraced a positivist model that privileged law-governed types of explanation and attacked their idealist counterparts, such as R. G. Collingwood, who claimed the uniqueness of historical knowing.[5] How could history be classified as a science, they asked, if it did not conform to an (allegedly) universal mode of explanation shared by all sciences?[6] Their efforts to clarify and defend the scientific status of history, however, went largely unappreciated by historians.[7] Late in the century, some historians turned to other philosophical arenas, appropriating philosophical props from Hilary Putnam and from popular forms of pragmatism in order to shore up traditional historiography. None of these appropriations, I argue, was ultimately satisfactory, at least in the form in which they were adopted.

Anglo-American philosophy's appeal to a scientific approach to history that assumed the unity of the sciences resonated with the quest favored by many structuralist-inspired French social scientists and by French historians of the *Annales* school in the mid-twentieth century, as I detail in Chapters 3 and 4. French and Anglophone scholars at midcentury, so different in other respects, sought a common goal in the unity of the sciences, including history. That these assumptions would largely be abandoned by century's end is manifest in Chapters 6 and 7.

Karl Popper, C. G. Hempel, and Their Critics

Karl Popper, initially inspired by philosophical currents emanating from the Vienna Circle and logical positivism, as well as from Kantianism, undertook a rigorous analysis of historical explanation. His books, *Logik der Forschung* (1935), *The Open Society and Its Enemies* (1945), and *The Poverty of Historicism* (1945), went through several editions and modifications, making more complex the process of tracing out the evolution of his thought. His views on history developed largely while he was working on the latter two books between 1942 and 1945.

Popper believed that the discipline of history was not characterized so much by its reliance on causal explanation as by description and interpretation, which provide differing perspectives on a subject. Although he argued that the logic of casual explanation was the same in history and the sciences, it held a very reduced place in historical work. History, like all disciplines, explains by a deduction (a "prognosis") from general laws, subject to "initial conditions" that usually are understood by historians as the cause of events. Yet historians only assume such laws, Popper argued; they do not themselves formulate them. The logic of explanation, in which explanation is firmly tied to prediction, must be the same for the natural and the social sciences.[8] But what did Popper mean by "prediction"?[9]

Popper argued that a faulty understanding of prediction in the natural sciences had misled social scientists as to its meaning within their own disciplines. Natural scientists, he claimed, usually do not "predict" a natural event, which is no more foreseeable than history; rather, they create controlled experimental conditions under which they test the particular prognosis, attempting to rule out hypotheses and events, not to specify outcomes. Prediction, then, does not entail forecasting the future or "prophesying," but only testing hypotheses—an enterprise in which social as well as natural scientists engage.[10] Historians, in other words, proceed on no different grounds from natural scientists, *if* the latter's operation is correctly understood.

Historians, nonetheless, must remain content with the particular and the nonrepeatable; those who yearn for an "unchanging world" governed by law and prediction, Popper scathingly concluded, suffer from an emotional defect. Since history's interest lies in single, specific, nongeneralizable events, it could not count as a law-governed science.[11] No discipline could qualify as a science unless it contained falsifiable propositions, an unobtainable requirement for history. Indeed, it was impossible that laws could be established for history, he averred, and only a misguided historicism would seek to find them.[12] To philosophers he praised the historical method, which he described as "trying to find out what other people have thought and said about the problem in hand: why they had to face it: how they formulated it: how they tried to solve it."[13] By the end of his work, Popper had made natural science look more like history than history like science.[14] Malachi Hacohen argues that "Popper began by insisting on causal nonhistorical social science, but ended up with noncausal science," and deems his insistence upon contingency "poststructuralist."[15] For Popper, history is not, and did not aim to be, a science.

Popper's view of causal explanation was appropriated but greatly modified by Carl G. Hempel in his landmark essay of 1942, "The Function of General Laws in History."[16] Whereas Popper rejected positivism and all attempts to establish historical laws, Hempel embraced both positivism and the search for a "law-governed" history. Whereas Popper deemed historians to be little concerned with causal explanation, Hempel placed causal explanation at the center of his investigation of history. Hempel argued that history was not methodologically autonomous: since all science is united, the structure of explanation for both human and nonhuman phenomena must necessarily be the same.[17] General laws ("universal hypotheses") in history, Hempel argued, have analogous functions to those in the natural sciences, although in history they generally are derived without much reflection from other fields, such as psychology; history has no explanatory laws uniquely its own.[18] Explanations that rely on historians' "empathy" with their subject matter, however, are to be categorically rejected.[19]

Since causal explanation in natural science involves a prediction that is a deduction from natural laws subject to original conditions, Hempel explored this link (or its lack) in historical explanation. He concluded that historical explanation is less rigorous than scientific in that it attempts merely to show that "the event in question was not 'a matter of chance,' but was to be expected in view of certain antecedent or simultaneous conditions." Nonetheless, since history cannot supply a sufficiently full account of the initial conditions and universal hypotheses that govern its explanatory system, it offers neither a causal nor a probabilistic type of explanation. Unlike science, it can offer only "explanation sketches," that is, drafts of explanations that, with elaboration, could make explicit the laws they implicitly contain—*if* historians pursued their work more rigorously.[20] Hence history in Hempel's view can at best be deemed a "rudimentary science."[21] Hempel's theory, which assumed that both historical and scientific explanation proceeded by hypothesis and deduction, came to be called "covering-law" theory.

Hempel's plea for a law-governed historical practice, however, was soon challenged by both historians and philosophers. Critics noted, for example, that Hempelians tested their "laws" either by devising hypothetical experiments or by noting recurrences of an event in the present; such tests, however, were not transferable to the particular and nonrecurring events of history.[22] Others observed that history does not operate within a closed deductive system in which explanation is linked to prediction; historical objectivity can be understood only in an "everyday," not in a strictly scientific, sense. Moreover, historians' conclusions, unlike scientists', are not "detachable," that is, the results of their research cannot be separated from the research process itself.[23]

In addition, critics alleged, the attempt to impose one model on all disciplines in the name of the unity of science was misguided in its neglect of disciplinary particularity.[24] Historians should resist infatuation with nomothetic models; they need not "mutilate research into human affairs by remodelling the social sciences into deformed likenesses of physics."[25] Nor should historians pretend that they offer "weak" versions of scientific explanation, since historical explanation works by "thickening up" or "tightening up" a narrative.[26] Rejecting notions of reference and truth that ill fit the discipline, historians need only settle on a notion of objectivity appropriate to the field, and to do this, they need not pretend to be philosophers.[27] Early-twentieth-century philosophers' attempt to construe disciplines such as history as scientific represented (in Richard Rorty's view) "a brief moment of megalomania."[28]

Under the impact of such arguments, covering-law theory was abandoned: history was not to be claimed as a law-governed protoscience. Historical understanding did not equate with prediction in a Hempelian sense. Generalized hypotheses would not be viewed as potential laws, but as mere "guides"—a "Virgilian function of hypotheses," quipped Louis Mink.[29] Rejecting Hempel's nomothetic imperative, philosophers now looked for other philosophically acceptable ways to describe the historical discipline and its notion of explanation.[30]

So strong was the impact of Hempel's thesis that philosophers of history for years afterward sought to work within his assumptions while modifying them to ameliorate their presumed defects, such as were suggested above. A minor modification was offered by Patrick Gardiner, who suggested that since history employs generalization (events are not "absolutely unique"), it operates with some sort of explanatory laws, albeit ones different from those offered by covering-law theory. Gardiner's proposal that historical explanation rested on appeals to purposive behavior and agents' "dispositions," however, advanced a much looser theory of explanation than Hempel's.[31] Aiming for greater precision, W. H. Walsh posited that historical explanation involves a process of "colligation," in which the historian locates dominant concepts that help render detailed facts intelligible, traces connections between events, and constructs a "significant narrative" from the material.[32] Here, explaining is linked to describing[33]—a nontechnical notion of explanation that probably suited many historians.

It was William Dray, however, who offered a frontal "humanistic counterattack" on Hempel's theory.[34] Dray argued that the covering-law model was so misleading that it should be abandoned, not just "loosened up."[35] Developing a position that somewhat resembled Walsh's notion of colligation, Dray claimed that historians do not appeal to laws, but rather seek to explain "how-possibly," a quite different procedure from scientists who explain in a more technical manner "why-necessarily."[36] "Explaining what" for historians, Dray argued, usually involves a process of summarizing, collating, and weighing various factors. While covering-law theory assumes a simplistic view of explanation ("whenever x then y"), historical explanation proceeds by gathering together related pieces of data that, taken collectively, explain on the model of "x, y, and z amount to a q = 'what it really was that happened.'" Although this procedure lacks philosophical or scientific rigor, Dray conceded, it better represents how historians actually work than does Hempel's nomological theory.[37] The retreat from science was now patent.

Arthur Danto

The most prominent Anglo-American philosopher of history for the generation of the 1960s and beyond was Arthur Danto. Danto raised the question of what philosophy could be said to do, just when it appeared that science had "covered everything."[38] Arguing against a law-governed notion of historical explanation, Danto assured historians that they were no more epistemologically disadvantaged than were researchers in other disciplines: why should the nonobservability of the phenomena under investigation count against history any more than it does against theoretical physics? Persons may espouse a thoroughgoing skepticism about *all* knowledge if they so choose, Danto argued, but history does not constitute a special problem in this respect.[39]

Insofar as Danto's target was the (in his view) excessive skepticism evinced by some earlier twentieth-century historians, he aimed to provide an account of how historians can, to some extent, apprehend "history-as-actuality."[40] Charles Beard and other relativist historians, he quipped, had implied that documents stand "as a statement-proof curtain between ourselves and a past we could not as much as mention." Do not such skeptical historians harbor "an old platonic attitude, which considered it a scandal that pictures of beds were not themselves real beds, much less Real Beds"?[41] Perhaps historical relativists such as Beard had secretly yearned for the certainty that a correspondence theory of truth seemed to offer—but whose unverifiability prompted their despair about the possibility of historical knowledge.[42] Danto, in contrast, urged historians not to degrade their discipline simply because they do not have "perfect knowledge" of a subject. We do not demand perfect knowledge of the Empire State Building or of an apple; why should we expect it of history?[43] Yet some historians might well retort that Danto's comparison trivializes the problems of representation at issue: after all, that apple—assuming it's not a Real Apple—is an object of perception in the present, while "the past" is not.

Danto put a distinctive edge to his claim that historians cannot have perfect knowledge: since humans (as "temporally provincial") do not know the future, which governs how past events are seen, they cannot presume to have perfect knowledge of how events of their own time—the present—will come to be understood. It is precisely because events *are* past that historians can accord them significance.[44] Historians redescribe events whose significance is hidden from the persons who live through them, since the latter do not know how things will turn out. Rebutting an example given by Descartes to demonstrate the frailty of historical knowledge, Danto argued that historians know the last years of the Roman Republic in a way that Cicero's slave girl did not: since she did not realize that these were the last years of the Republic, she remained oblivious to the historic significance of the time through which she was living. That could be known only in the future.[45]

Danto's interest in the status of the future in historical narration, however, held little interest for historians, as is evidenced by the types of historical statements he raised for consideration. For example, historians rarely worry over such sentences as, "Newton, author of the *Principia* was born at Woolethorpe on Christmas Day, 1642." (This sentence appears problematic to philosophers of Danto's persuasion, since no one could have uttered this statement at the time of Newton's birth in 1642, but only after 1687, when the *Principia* was published.)[46] That philosophers from the time of Aristotle had argued over the status of future events was of no interest to historians in their work *as historians*—although, to be sure, if they ventured outside their discipline to philosophy of history, they might enjoy entertaining problems such as these.

Moreover, critics observed, it was not the practice of historians to focus attention, as Danto did, on "the sentence" as the bearer of historical truth—a topic that occupied various contemporary Anglophone philosophers. As Hayden White pointedly commented, "narrative is not a large sentence."[47] Likewise, Jerzy Topolski observed that historians do not deal with single sentences, but with texts in which those sentences are embedded as part of a historical narrative; it is at this level, not at that of single sentences, that debates among historians occur.[48] Danto's attention to "narrative sentences," in F. R. Ankersmit's view, did "next to nothing" for historiography.[49]

In retrospect, Danto conceded that the midcentury debate, including his own *Analytical Philosophy of History,* was a "skirmish in the wider wars of the time which concerned competing views of ordinary language and the relationship to language of analytical philosophy."[50] Perhaps all that Danto succeeded in showing, Leon Goldstein posits, was that "the denial of the past is radically incompatible with strongly entrenched habits and beliefs"—but "history does not need this kind of help from ordinary language. It does that much for itself."[51] The attempt to establish truth claims for history conceived as a science, it appears, was abandoned by analytical philosophers and historians alike.

It should nonetheless be noted that even some analytical philosophers of history who rejected covering-law theory endorsed historical objectivism. The most "humanist" of Hempel's critics, William Dray, worried that history would lack "epistemological respectability" if its claims always had to be qualified by concessions about the historian's point of view.[52] Maurice Mandelbaum, for his part, endorsed a correspondence theory of verification that assumed a naturally given fit between and among the mind, language, and external reality.[53] And Danto's proposition that such a theory is "intuitively correct" and relatively unproblematic for historians assumes a similar view of language in relation to reality.[54] Danto appears to have combined a positivist view of knowledge of the past with a reduced expectation, cheerfully accepted, of what historians can realistically claim to know.[55] Such assumptions would be strongly challenged by European, especially French, theorists and philosophers.[56]

Within the Anglophone world as well, the utility of linguistic philosophy for historians was questioned. In 1961, reviewing the first issues of the new journal *History and Theory,* historian J. G. A. Pocock asked "how far a philosophy which consists essentially in the logical analysis of explanations is of value in defining the historian's problems and the means by which he attempts to solve them . . . If philosophy of history is an enquiry into the logical character of historical explanation, what it produces is not necessarily a reproduction or reconstruction of 'what historians do'."[57] Philosophy may offer *criticism* of the historians' enterprise, but it provides no means of directly *explaining* it. From his vantage point of 1961, Pocock noted the failure of the Popper-Hempel account of historical explanation and historians' subsequent turn to narrative: "[w]hat the historian cannot explain in the strict sense, he narrates."[58] Narration thus stands in when the scientific explanation of history fails—a topic to which I turn in Chapter 5.

In the end, Anglo-American linguistic philosophers' attempt to "improve" the status of history as a discipline was abandoned by philosophers and rejected by historians. As Peter Novick concludes, "Earlier, historians had sought to win autonomy for the historical profession from speculative philosophy of history . . . Now historians sought to maintain that autonomy in the face of what seemed to them epistemological supervision by analytic philosophers of history."[59] In retrospect, it seems obvious that questions that engaged analytical philosophers were not those that counted with historians—and vice versa. Could Anglo-American philosophers *other* than philosophers of history offer greater assistance to historians?

Anglophone Historians and Philosophers in the Later Twentieth Century

Most contemporary historians, to be sure, do not attempt to justify their epistemological assumptions—yet given recent theoretical critiques, some believe that they should.[60] Favorite philosophical courts of appeal are either Hilary Putnam's notion of "practical" (or "internal") realism, or a popular version of pragmatism (that is, to Dewey or Rorty, not to Peirce).[61] What do historians hope to gain by these appeals?

Hilary Putnam

In the mid-1970s and after, Hilary Putnam renounced "metaphysical realism," a "God's Eye point of view" that implied a correspondence between human minds and the external world, between words and things, and that deemed the world to be independent of our representations of it[62]—"a magical theory of reference," he later quipped.[63] Metaphysical realism failed, Putnam argued, because "to single out a correspondence between two domains [that is, mental concepts and the external world] one needs some independent access to both domains"—an access that humans do not have, or, more precisely, an access that a correspondence theory of verification assumes but is unable to prove. That such a theory survived for over two thousand years signals not its truth but rather "the naturalness and the strength of the desire for a God's Eye view," a view "from Nowhere."[64] If objects are theory-dependent, then the attempt to define truth as "a 'correspondence' between items in a language and items in a fixed theory-independent reality" must be abandoned.[65]

"Internal realism"—the view that Putnam developed to replace metaphysical realism—attempts a middle ground: the mind neither copies nor invents a world.[66] Asking questions about the world is understood to take place *within* a theory of description. Our beliefs can be said to cohere, Putnam claims, "with our experiences *as those experiences are themselves represented in our belief system*"; they are not understood to be in "correspondence with mind-independent or discourse-independent 'states of affairs.'"[67] There can be "*objectivity for us*, even if it is not the objectivity of the God's Eye view."[68]

Putnam bases this reduced version of objectivity on a notion of rational acceptability.[69] From an internal realist perspective, he argues, facts are "something that it is rational to believe," given the tradition and culture in which we stand.[70] Although humans can never be certain that they have even approximated the "epistemically ideal conditions" that would enable them to speak of truth pure and simple, they may justifiably speak of "truth within the theory" or of "warranted assertibility."[71] "Truth" is here understood as an idealized version of rational acceptability, that is, that which is *most* rational to believe, given our time, place, and circumstances.

Certain of Putnam's claims resonate with those customarily attributed to "popular pragmatists" and to Wittgenstein.[72] Like pragmatist Richard Rorty, Putnam argues that humans can successfully muddle through life without *any* metaphysical theory of truth.[73] Like John Dewey, he holds that we can speak of objective right or wrong, but only from within a framework that attends to the circumstances of acts, the mores of the culture we inhabit.[74] Moreover, like an assortment of pragmatists, Putnam appeals to the notion of a community of users who share a conceptual scheme that governs how signs apply in particular ways; if the community of users agrees on a descriptive scheme, we can "say what matches what" since objects and signs are both *internal* to the scheme. In this context, Putnam endorsed Wittgenstein's notion that practice fixes interpretation and that public norms constituting a "form of life" are necessary for language and thought.[75] How historians have appropriated Putnam's philosophy for their own enterprise, I shall suggest below.

Richard Rorty and Other Pragmatists

A second court of philosophical appeal by contemporary historians is a popular form of pragmatism. Of the older generation of pragmatists, John Dewey still attracts historians, despite his chastisement of historians' unreflectiveness and failure to reveal their conceptual framework and assumptions. Dewey scoffed at the Rankean notion that historians should seek to present events "as they actually happened." Such a statement, he claimed, is meaningless, except in its admonition "to avoid prejudice, to struggle for the greatest possible amount of objectivity and impartiality, and as an exhortation to exercise caution and scepticism in determining the authenticity of material proposed as potential data":[76] here, the *epistemological* ideal of traditional historians is transformed into a *moral* maxim.

Richard Rorty is the contemporary pragmatist most often cited by historians who seek philosophers' sanction for their work. Rorty accepts Putnam's theory of internal realism as "uncontroversial," "true but trivial,"[77] and agrees that a correspondence theory of verification should be abandoned, along with the desire for "a God's eye view of things."[78] "What would we lose," he asks, "if we had no ahistorical theory-independent notion of truth?" To those of a Rortian persuasion, the answer appears to be "nothing." To quest for a theory of reference, Rorty argues, is to ask for "some transcendental standpoint outside our present set of representations from which we can inspect the relations between those representations and their object"—a standpoint not available to us.[79] Indeed, epistemological problems can simply be sidestepped since justification need rest on nothing more than "social practices and human needs."[80]

Philosophers of a more analytical stripe would doubtless deem

Rorty's (or pragmatism's) claim too "loose." Arthur Danto, for example, protested that pragmatism's "naturalization" of language, which turns theories about *meaning* into theories of *use,* "collapse[s] the concept of truth onto the concept of success" and thus fosters relativism.[81] Rorty would likely respond by positing that "success in use" *is* an adequate criterion for truth, and that what Danto and others label "relativism" might well be assigned a more positive valence.[82]

Historians' Appeals to Philosophy

Despite philosophers' objections to the "looseness" of Putnam's, Dewey's, and Rorty's positions, historians have found them welcome courts of appeal, yet in sometimes mistaking the philosophers' arguments, they weaken their case. For example, the authors of *Telling the Truth about History* (Appleby, Hunt, and Jacob) appeal to Putnam's notion of practical realism, which they claim means that human perceptions of the external world do to some extent correspond with that world, thus enabling historians to "connect words to things by using words." Yet for internal realism, things are not knowable outside their conceptualized form; correspondence theories in their classical sense are precisely what internal realism rules out. Likewise, when Appleby, Hunt, and Jacob redefine historical objectivity as "an interactive relationship between an inquiring subject and an external object," they seem to lapse into the metaphysical realism that Putnam rejected, covertly invoking a correspondence theory of verification.[83] Other commentators, such as Chris Lorenz, eager to appropriate Putnam's notion of internal realism, seem not to notice that doing so aligns them with the very post-structuralist historiography that they otherwise denounce.[84]

Similarly, historian James Kloppenberg, critiquing Novick's *That Noble Dream,* elaborates a "moderating" position that appeals to Dewey's pragmatism. Elsewhere declaring that the "deconstructive method makes writing history impossible,"[85] Kloppenberg here argues that pragmatism presents a "fruitful alternative" to both objectivism and relativism that Charles Beard and Carl Becker would have endorsed; historians might profitably heed pragmatists' claim that (for example) all human inquiry arises out of communities of inquiry that control the terms of the discourse. Likewise, Kloppenberg posits, pragmatism offers a model of testing that helpfully combines a scientific method of verifying facts and a hermeneutic method of interpreting the past. A pragmatic model of truth encourages historians to devise hypotheses and propose "warranted interpretations," which stimulate inquiry and result in "useful" but "tentative" knowledge. Introducing a note of jocularity to his otherwise severe critique of Novick, whom he thinks capitulates to post-structuralist claims, Kloppenberg concedes that some readers will find his historical perspective "Dewey-eyed."[86] Despite Kloppenberg's claim to espouse a "middle position" between objectivism and relativism, he (like Appleby, Hunt, and Jacob) suggests that there is a mind-independent world in which historians can "verify facts." How this process of verification between mind and world works, he does not specify.

In my view, such claims by historians are not brought into satisfactory alignment with the philosophical theories they appropriate. Hard-line metaphysical realists such as Gertrude Himmelfarb provide more coherent, internally consistent (though, I think, ultimately misguided) approaches.[87] Given the generally unsatisfactory nature of historians' appeals to philosophy, some critics (such as Martin Bunzl) suggest that historians should forget philosophy and concede that history involves only "weak" forms of interpretation.[88]

Not only did the early-twentieth-century effort to construe history as a science fail; neither internal realism nor pragmatism's warranted assertibility has much helped historians with "what they do"—at least in the form in which they have appropriated these positions. Should historians abandon the attempt to "think" their discipline? I would argue not. Although traditional historians might advise members of their guild to continue their practice without *any* explicit philosophizing,[89] I suggest in Chapters 6 and 7 that historians of premodernity might derive assistance from some recent forms of post-structuralist theory. A post-structuralist form of intellectual history that attends to texts and writing would accord well with the epistemological implications of internal realism.

CHAPTER THREE

Language and Structures

Structuralism and History

Structuralism, I here argue, challenged historians in ways that have been productive for reconfiguring intellectual history, despite its reputation (justifiably earned) as an anti-historical movement. Largely deaf to the concerns of Anglo-American analytical philosophy[1] and outrightly hostile to existentialism and phenomenology, French structuralists during the mid-twentieth century waged a campaign against "humanism," "the subject," and "reference" that could not but take history as a primary opponent.[2] Insofar as structuralists did not seek temporal antecedents and casual chains, but rather looked to the function of phenomena within a larger system, their procedures might appear as diametrically opposed to those of historians.[3] Yet, as I hope to show, various structuralist theses helped recast the discipline of history in the mid- to late-twentieth century. In France, unlike the Anglophone world, "post-structuralism" truly came "after" structuralism, absorbing as well as modifying its themes.

François Dosse, in his impressive two-volume study of structuralism's rise and decline in France, claims that its success was unprecedented in the history of French intellectual life, serving as "the *koine* of an entire intellectual generation" of the 1950s and 1960s.[4] Structuralism's popularity, Dosse argues, correlated with French intellectual and political developments of the era: it stood simultaneously as a critique of Enlightenment values, as a protest against the rise of governmental technocracy under Charles de Gaulle, as "antimandarin trench warfare" against aging Sorbonne scholars, and as a rejection of both Sartrean existentialism and phenomenology, whose demise it hastened. Reacting to a feared erosion of the humanities' place in French education, structuralists attempted to align themselves and their disciplines with science.[5] Another effect of structuralism, Michel Foucault claims, was "to unsettle Marxist dogmatism" as well as phenomenology.[6] Yet, by the mid-1970s, its influence had faded considerably: in 1975, Roland Barthes could ask, "Who is still a structuralist?"[7]

Notions of discontinuity and of the demotion of the subject or referent (for example, Foucault's "dissolving of 'man'")—soon to find a home in structuralism—earlier marked linguistics (the arbitrariness of the sign), quantum mechanics, and broader cultural movements reflected in Impressionist and Cubist painting.[8] In their search for universal and invariant structures, structuralists across the disciplines gave priority to synchrony over diachrony, form over content, the signifier over the signified, space over time, the text over the author, and the unconscious over the conscious.[9] In Foucault's view, the common property of all the so-called structuralists was their denial of fundamental and originary significance to "the subject."[10] "The goal of all structuralist activity," Roland Barthes claimed, "is to reconstruct an 'object'" in such a way as to make evident the rules of its functioning.[11] Such goals were advocated in the quest for a united science.[12]

Given this constellation of priorities, it does not surprise that history—at least in its traditional form, and for some, in *any* form—became a focus of attack. "War was declared," Dosse writes, "against historicism, the historical context, the search for origins, diachrony, teleology and the argument was made in favor of permanent invariables, synchrony, and the hermetic text"[13]—an assessment that some structuralists themselves thought exaggerated, as I detail below. In structuralism's heyday, however, many structuralist theorists shunned history as a discipline. Claude Lévi-Strauss relegated history to the status of "myth," "the last refuge of transcendental humanism."[14] Linguist Algirdas Julien Greimas argued that structural linguistics must be "achronic"; context and content—so important to historians—was of no concern to linguists.[15] Jacques Lacan proclaimed that history was "the thing that I detest for the best reasons";[16] although history may have seemed "very important" at the time of Bossuet or Marx, he conceded, it was no longer.[17] Louis Althusser, for his part, deemed history a "fall" from science.[18]

To be sure, structuralists might tolerate history of a structuralist sort—insofar as that was a conceivable reorientation for a discipline committed to diachronic explanation. Historians such as Fernand Braudel and (early) Michel Foucault passed the test; more traditional historians, devoted to diachrony, change over time, and causal explanation, did not.[19] Indeed, in the view of Roland Barthes, Marxists committed to history (that is, to preserving "the subject" as the center of agency, to direction in history, or to a unified explanation for historical development) stood as the primary resistance to structuralism.[20]

Of the many fields that structuralism touched, I here explore the importance of two in particular for the study of history: linguistics/semiotics and Lévi-Straussian anthropology. While linguistics provided the model for structuralist analysis in other fields, Lévi-Strauss stands as a major structuralist thinker who attempted both to apply the model of language to culture (and quite differently from Clifford Geertz, whose theories will be explored in Chapter 7) and to relate structuralism to the discipline of history. As I argue, although structural linguistics doubtless put one nail in the coffin of correspondence theories of verification, structuralism was not nearly so damaging to historical work, conceived in a new mode—described in Chapter 6—as has often been claimed. Indeed, since many of its themes were carried over into post-structuralism, echoes of the structuralist project will reverberate in all the chapters that follow.

Structural Linguistics: Saussure and Beyond

All commentators agree that linguistics provided the primary inspiration for structuralism, whose foundational principle held "that all manifestations of social activity . . . constitute languages, in a formal sense."[21] A variety of disciplines appropriated the linguistic model: anthropology, literary criticism, psychoanalysis, and to some extent philosophy (as practiced in France, not an argumentative discipline).[22] In 1945, philosopher Ernst Cassirer compared the importance of "the new science of linguistics" to "the new science of Galileo which in the seventeenth century changed our whole concept of the physical world."[23]

The work of Swiss linguist Ferdinand de Saussure (1857–1913), later considered the pioneer of structuralism, decisively broke with the historical and philological orientation of the linguistics of his day.[24] Emile Benveniste describes the older orientation:

> History as the necessary perspective and successivity as the principle of explanation, the splitting up of language into isolated elements and the investigation of the laws of evolution peculiar to each one of them—these were the dominant characteristics of linguistic doctrine . . . The novelty of the Saussurian point of view was to realize that language in itself [that is, the system of language] does not admit of any historical dimension, that it consists of synchrony and structure, and that it only functions by virtue of its symbolic nature.[25]

Saussure abandoned the tradition of linguistics that viewed languages as naturally developing organisms evolving according to a teleological model. He joked that most philosophical conceptions of language up to his day naively implied that nomenclature originated with "our first father" Adam's assigning names to the animals.[26] Against "nomenclaturism," Saussure argued that signs do not "naturally" link names to extralinguistic things, but arbitrarily link concepts (*le signifié,* the signified) and sound images (*le signifiant,* the signifier).[27] Saussure elevated the arbitrariness of the link between the sound image and the concept to "the first principle of linguistics."[28] Yet since the arbitrariness of signs operates within a fixed system of language *(langue),* he posited, what otherwise would be "chaos" is limited by this regimentation.[29]

As unions of sound images ("signifiers") and concepts (the "signified"), signs acquire their meaning chiefly through their difference from each other within a language system.[30] Language, Saussure proposed, can be imagined as the two sides of a sheet of paper that necessarily exist together: the "thought" side is the recto, and the "sound" side the verso. Although linguists would primarily concern themselves with the linguistic system *(langue),* humans, employing language to express their own purposes, introduce an accidental and individualizing feature of language, the speech act *(parole)*—the "executive side" of language, as Saussure put it.[31] Individuals' particular speech *(parole),* however, was not his main concern, nor was writing (as compared to speech) of special significance to him.[32]

Saussure's theory of the sign ostensibly relates only to inner-mental phenomena; although he noted that a linguistic community connects arbitrary signs to the external world,[33] he did not dwell on issues of reference or on the correspondence between language and the domain of the extramental. Early in the study of Saussurean linguistics, however, the implications of the arbitrariness of the sign were more broadly construed. Emile Benveniste, for example, writing in 1939, already recast Saussurian "arbitrariness" as relating not to the signifier (sound image) and the signified (concept), but to the signifier and an extramental referent, that is, the sound image and "things."[34] Benveniste argued that although Saussure *believed* he was exclusively investigating signifiers and signifieds within an inner-linguistic system, he had actually introduced a third term, "reality," "by a detour." Benveniste provided an example: when Saussure discussed the words *boeuf* and *ochs,* he was not merely illustrating the difference between signs in two different languages, but was referring them to an external reality, the animal itself.[35] In Benveniste's view, Saussure, by introducing the notion of "reality," even via a "detour," had signaled the philosophical problem of mind's relation to world. Perhaps someday, Benveniste posited, linguists would fruitfully explore the question of how Saussurean linguistics construes the mind/world problem—but for the moment, it would be best to leave it alone![36] Indeed, the technical aspects of Saussure's research held less appeal than its implications for explorations of linguistic and nonlinguistic representation and of cultural signs.[37]

To be sure, some professional linguists, challenging the implications that others drew from Saussure's work, accused nonlinguists of misunderstanding its technicalities and "theoretical stakes" and of imagining linguists' descriptive statements to be "breathtaking metaphysical pronouncements." These linguists held that Saussure's theories applied only to systems of language, not to extralinguistic realms.[38] Yet, I argue, Saussure's own work encouraged such elaborations insofar as he posed that language is only *one* system of signs among others that constitute social life, and noted that others (such as symbolic rites, forms and gestures of politeness, and military signals) awaited exploration. He envisioned linguistics as part of a larger semiological science, but such a field (perhaps to constitute a branch of social psychology, he suggested) was yet to be created.[39] Thus even though Saussure himself did not develop these topics further, he assumed that future scholars might study nonverbal signs.[40]

Roland Barthes was one such critic who elaborated Saussure's teachings in the arena of culture. Barthes hailed as revolutionary Saussure's "epistemological challenge." Whereas the semiologies of hermeneutics, Barthes argued, stop at signification (they go for "the Gold of the Signifier") and assume that "the signified *certifies* the signifier, just as, in good finance, gold certifies currency," for Saussure neither the Gold nor the Sign is to be trusted: there *is* no "certification."[41] Barthes inverted Saussure's notion that linguistics constituted a part of semiology: for him, semiology was rather to be grounded in linguistics. All signs, Barthes posited, should be read as linguistic, that is, all culture could be understood as "a general system of symbols."[42] Barthes's free interpretation of Saussure elicited the wrath of traditional linguists, who deemed his semiological analysis of fashion (*Système de la mode* [1967]) "a *tour de force*" in its complete misconstrual of Saussure.[43]

On the basis of this enlarged understanding of Saussurean linguistics, later theorists posited that the "real" is known only in and through its discursive construction, established through an intralinguistic system of differences.[44] Traditional historians, by contrast, had customarily assumed the adequacy of reference, of words to things; they had largely (and often unconsciously) operated with these "nomenclaturist" assumptions. The notion of the arbitrariness of the sign deeply challenged the correspondence theory of truth: if words relate only to each other, how could language be deemed to refer to the world?[45] And how could historians argue that their discourse about the past matched up with "what really had happened"?[46]

Thus both "the arbitrariness of the sign" and the extension of Saussurean linguistics to a semiology of culture would suggest new approaches to history in later decades.

Claude Lévi-Strauss and Structural Anthropology

Anthropologist Claude Lévi-Strauss likewise drew models from structural linguistics. His interpretation of culture as linguistically structured, his "de-naturalization" of the study of humans in their respective cultures, and his attack on history and existentialist philosophy for their assumptions regarding "human nature" proved important in the debates over history. Yet, as I explore in Chapter 7, Lévi-Strauss's notion that cultures are structured like languages rests on a different linguistic model from Clifford Geertz's reading of cultures as "texts" —and in that difference lie some important considerations for historians.

In Edward Said's provocative analogy, if Saussure is acknowledged as the "father of semiotics," then Claude Lévi-Strauss stands as "its tacitly recognized Prospero."[47] By his own account, Lévi-Strauss found the key to a revolutionary, "scientific" anthropology in structural linguistics,[48] which he thought might teach anthropologists "to understand phenomena by considering them as manifestations of an underlying system of relations," and to identify their oppositions.[49] In 1960, when Lévi-Strauss assumed the first chair in social anthropology at the Collège de France, he paid tribute to Saussure as the scholar who had come closest to defining the field of social anthropology in his prediction that linguistics stood as part of a science—semiology—yet to be born, and in his claim that at the heart of social life stands "the life of signs."[50] Anthropology, like linguistics, he proposed, found its true subject matter in discontinuities.[51] Later, Lévi-Strauss confessed that from linguistics he had learned to recognize "the role of unconscious mental activity in the production of logical structures," namely, that no intrinsic meaning attaches to the component parts, but arises only from their position in relation to each other.[52] As with language, so with myth: its users might actually be hampered in their ability to communicate if they knew the laws, structures, and modes of its operation.[53] The science of mythology that he hoped to encourage would, like structural linguistics, look to differences, oppositions, and contrasts—to the *relations* between terms, especially to their transformational relations—for only by such procedures could myths be understood.[54]

In his early exploration of kinship systems, as in his later analysis of mythology, Lévi-Strauss appropriated ideas from structural linguistics. In his first book, *The Elementary Forms of Kinship* (1949), he argued that his analysis of kinship systems stands "close to that of the phonological linguist," and that the incest prohibition "is universal like language."[55] In systems of marriage and through the incest prohibition, women, like language, function as signs "to be communicated."[56] Anthropologist and linguist share a common task of studying communication and human integration, of exploring the workings of the mind.[57] And in the preface to *The Elementary Forms of Kinship*, Lévi-Strauss warmly thanks linguistics scholar Roman Jakobson "for theoretical inspiration."[58] Indeed, it was Lévi-Strauss's meeting with Jakobson at the New School for Social Research in New York, when both were exiles from their native lands during the Nazi regime, that set the course for his work.[59] Later, Lévi-Strauss declared himself to be Jakobson's "disciple" and testified that Jakobson was "the most dazzling teacher and lecturer" that he had ever encountered.[60]

In subsequent works as well, Lévi-Strauss confessed the stimulus that linguistics—especially phonology—had provided for his understanding of kinship systems and the incest prohibition.[61] He "de-biologized" the understandings of kinship he had learned at university by taking clues from structural linguistics.[62] Like the phoneme, he argued, the incest prohibition is not only universal (and thus part of "nature"), but also provides an entry to culture and communication, to a network of exchanges.[63] In the bonds of alliance found in kinship structures, the "dominance of the social over the biological, and of the cultural over the natural," is ensured.[64]

In essays dating from the 1940s and 1950s, Lévi-Strauss repeatedly emphasized the scientific nature of his enterprise. In "Structural Analysis in Linguistics and Anthropology" (1945), he lauded the "scientific" status of linguistics—the only social science, he posited, that could claim to be one. He predicted that structural linguistics would "play the same renovating role with respect to the social sciences" that nuclear physics had for the physical sciences.[65] Years later, he voiced his hope that "when the last trumpet sounds," anthropology might wake to find itself in the heavenly halls among the natural sciences, rather than in the "purgatory" of the social sciences.[66] Thus it is no surprise that he pointedly subtitled his massive four-volume study of North and South American Indian myths, *Introduction to a Science of Mythology*.[67]

Structuralism fueled Lévi-Strauss's alleged animus against history— although, as I shall argue, this "animus" has been exaggerated. To be sure, Lévi-Strauss had rebelled against the historical orientation of his own teachers, particularly those of philosophy, who merely studied (he alleged) how what came later emerged from what came before.[68] Philosophies of history from Hegel onward that viewed other societies as if they were earlier stages of their own were especially anathema to him.[69] Even Rousseau, the "father of anthropology," had distinguished the historical approach from the anthropological, observing that "[w]hen one wishes to study men, one must look close at hand; but to study man, one must learn to look into the distance."[70]

Once his academic interests shifted from philosophy to linguistics, Lévi-Strauss also rejected the priority of diachrony and the view of history as "progress"; a culture's contribution consists rather in its "difference from others," he posited.[71] He also adopted the structuralist principle that researchers should first define their object and take an "inventory of its internal determinants" before reconstructing the process by which the object of study came into being,[72] a procedure that suggests the secondary status to which history could be assigned.

Lévi-Strauss's alleged anti-historical bias emerges especially in his essay "History and Anthropology" [1945][73] and in his attack on Sartre in "History and Dialectic" [1961],[74] yet even here his critique is nuanced. In "History and Anthropology," Lévi-Strauss criticized Bronislaw Malinowski, Margaret Mead, and other anthropologists for their "over-estimation of the historical method," and blamed historians for popularizing the functionalist approach.[75] To be sure, he conceded, both history and ethnography concern themselves with societies different from those inhabited by the researcher, and both seek to make the experiences of those "others" accessible to people living in a different place and time. Historians of the past, he suggested, can even be called "amateur ethnographers." Although history and anthropology "journey" together, they proceed with different orientations: history works from the explicit to the implicit, while anthropology, from the particular to the universal.[76]

Nonetheless, Lévi-Strauss conceded that history should "have its rights," and in his inaugural lecture at the Collège de France he denied that he was "against history."[77] These views he elaborated throughout his four volumes on mythology; far from rejecting history, he there declared, "structural analysis accords history a paramount place, the place that rightfully belongs to that irreducible contingency without which necessity would be inconceivable."[78] The problem with the so-called historical method of interpreting myths, he explained, rested in its contentment with merely discovering, locating, and dating themes.[79] Structuralist interpretation of myths, however, does not completely disregard history, for by classifying variants in myths so as to bring out the sequence of transformations, it raises historical problems—but problems that history on its own cannot solve. Even the native peoples whose myths he studied were in a relation to history, he claimed, since their entire elaborate mythological system was devised "for one purpose only: to come to terms with history and, on the level of system, to re-establish a state of equilibrium capable of acting as a shock absorber for the disturbances caused by real-life events."[80]

This relation, however, can be seen as negative, insofar as myth, in Lévi-Strauss's view, is an instrument "for the obliteration of time."[81] Playing on themes of Marcel Proust's monumental novel, Lévi-Strauss posits that if through myth time past could be kept alive for the benefit of what would come later, then "time would be obliterated."[82] Valorizing the subject matter to which he devoted so much of his life—the mythology of preliterate peoples—prompted Lévi-Strauss's reevaluation of Western notions of time and history.

One major difference between traditional history and ethnography, Lévi-Strauss emphasized, is that "history organizes its data in relation to conscious expressions of social life, while anthropology proceeds by examining its unconscious foundations."[83] The role accorded to the unconscious differentiates the disciplines—not the fact, as some might assume, that historians, unlike anthropologists, work from documents. The forms that the unconscious imposes on content, he argued, hold for all persons across time, and for other institutions and customs. Yet history remains valuable: by examining institutions in the process of transformation (that is, historically), scholars learn to appreciate how structures underlie the succession of events. The work of historians as well as that of anthropologists elucidates Marx's comment that "men make their own history, but they do not know that they are making it." In fact, Lévi-Strauss allowed, "good" history books are "saturated with anthropology," and cites as an example Lucien Febvre's study of Rabelais, *The Problem of Unbelief in the Sixteenth Century.* Attentive to psychological attitudes and logical structures, to that which "eluded the consciousness of those who spoke and wrote," *this* kind of history holds much appeal for anthropologists.[84] Likewise, Erwin Panofsky's art historical studies, he claimed, proved that an excellent structuralist could also be an excellent historian.[85]

In later life, Lévi-Strauss declared that "nothing interests me more than history—and that has been the case for quite a while!" What he particularly valued about history, he then claimed, was its randomness, its unpredictability. And he proudly reminded his interviewer that Lucien Febvre had taken such an interest in his early work that he had invited him to lecture in the Sixth Section of the Ecole pratique des hautes études, the historians' bailiwick. Moreover, it was precisely to avoid historians' criticisms, he claimed, that he had contrasted the "cold societies" that anthropologists study, in which different notions of time and history prevail, with the "hot" societies" filled with rapidly occurring events, beloved by historians.[86]

Despite his self-proclaimed embrace of history, there is much in the writings of Lévi-Strauss that led critics to view his work as anti-historical. For example, historian François Furet, writing in 1967, argued that the intellectual Left in France, "demoralized by history" (that is, by revelations concerning the Stalinist era and France's oppression of Algeria), had attempted "to find the truth of man" in a "plebiscite of the 'savage.'" Lévi-Strauss had turned "man" into a natural object; his books could be labeled "a commentary without hope on the nothingness of man."[87] Furet's critique is grounded in a humanism that Lévi-Strauss and other structuralists indeed opposed. That critique, as we shall see, surfaced particularly in Lévi-Strauss's attack on Sartre's humanistic existentialism. Although Lévi-Strauss appears less resolutely "anti-historical" than his critics allege, is he "anti-humanist"?

While in his inaugural lecture, *The Scope of Anthropology,* Lévi-Strauss proclaimed that he wished to "spread humanism to all humanity,"[88] it was not (apparently) the humanism advocated by Jean-Paul Sartre, which was undergirded by a strong sense of the "subject" and of history. As his declaration indicates, Lévi-Strauss was not anti-humanist, pure and simple: certain sorts of humanism he could espouse. In a brief essay published in 1956, "Les Trois Humanismes," he praised classicists and historians who had contributed the first works of ethnology in their studies of Greco-Roman and other earlier cultures. Here, he did not hesitate to call ethnology a third stage in humanism—albeit one that utilized the human and natural sciences in a way that earlier aristocratic and bourgeois humanisms had not.[89] In a 1979 interview, he claimed that he opposed only the type of humanism derived from the Judeo-Christian tradition, the Renaissance, and Cartesianism, which makes man into "an absolute lord of creation."[90] This type of humanism, he alleged, promoted humans' self-absorbed destruction of other forms of life.[91]

In "History and Dialectic" (1962), however, Lévi-Strauss vigorously attacked Sartre's brand of humanism.[92] Sartre's worldview, as expressed in his *Critique de la raison dialectique,* he argued, was excessively narrow; the book could stand as "a first-class ethnographic document" that unconsciously revealed the mythology of the modern West.[93] Sartre's definition of "man" in relation to history leaves no way to understand peoples "without history."[94] Moreover, Sartre wrongly imagines that savages (as Lévi-Strauss customarily calls the peoples whom anthropologists investigate)[95] lack complex thought and are incapable of analysis and demonstration.[96] Although Lévi-Strauss agreed with Sartre's claim that "man" has meaning only insofar as he views himself as meaningful, he suggested that Sartre should learn from the addendum, derived from Marx and Freud, that *"this meaning is never the right one."* Metaphysical claims about "the meaning of man"—superstructures—are merely *"faulty acts* which have 'made it' socially." What Sartre calls history, he alleged, is simply a different kind of myth, from which any "man of science" should distance himself. Since shortly *our* history will look like myth, he advised Sartre's advocates not to be "tormented by transcendence."[97] Elsewhere, Lévi-Strauss claimed that Sartre's philosophy, far from providing an insight into universal features of the human mind, was provincially rooted in his own time and place, undergirded by a "mythology" derived from the French Revolution.[98] One would have to be both egocentric and naïve to think that "man" can be identified with just one time or place, he argued; rather, the "truth about man resides in the system of their differences and common properties."[99] In contrast to Sartre's humanism, Levi-Strauss elsewhere argued, anthropologists practice a technique of distancing or marginalizing themselves—*dépaysement*—from their own culture.[100] In sum, for Lévi-Strauss, Sartre's type of historical consciousness does not provide the best access to the human.[101]

Even in his sharp critique of Sartre in "History and Dialectic," however, it is not history *tout court* that Lévi-Strauss faults. Biographical and anecdotal history, to be sure, although rich in detail, operates at a very low level and remains "unintelligible in itself," he claims, although other kinds of history might meet approval. In "History and Dialectic," Lévi-Strauss argues that history is a discipline "complementary" to anthropology (history examines the range of human societies across time, while anthropology examines them across space), yet he accords it no "special privilege."[102] As Lawrence Rosen explicates the debate, chronology for Lévi-Strauss is "important not as a statement of actual continuity or development, but as an indication of how the mind groups, codes, and imposes meaning upon a set of constituent units drawn from the uninterrupted sequence of events."[103] In retrospect, Lévi-Strauss admitted that the "pretensions" he had railed against were not so much those of historians but of some philosophers of history who replace the ever-elusive and unforeseeable reality of historical evolution with an ideological system.[104]

In subsequent years, Lévi-Strauss continued to fault the kind of humanism and devotion to the "subject" that existentialism implied. He is not, he proclaims, against "consciousness"—to achieve it had always been his aim. But philosophy had become so ingrown that it could imagine no other object of study than consciousness itself. Rather, philosophers who yearned for some "private area inaccessible to scientific knowledge," some form of mysticism, should learn from the social and physical sciences not to limit the object of their study to the apprehending subject. If structuralism aims to reintegrate humans into nature, then the subject must be disregarded—"that unbearably spoilt child who has occupied the philosophical scene for too long now, and prevented serious research through demanding exclusive attention." Existentialism he caricatured as "a self-admitting activity which allows contemporary man, rather gullibly, to commune with himself in ecstatic contemplation of his own being," thus cutting himself off from both scientific knowledge and the human reality that historical and anthropological perspectives might afford.[105]

Indeed, in Lévi-Strauss's description of "good" historiography, we note several issues that resonate with post-structuralist historiography. For example, he recognized that since historical "episodes" can be broken down into multitudinous smaller units, the historian might have reason to doubt which of these expressed "what really took place." Likewise, Lévi-Strauss understood that historical facts are not "given" but are constituted by the historian; insofar as historians select only a few out of a vast total, their accounts are always incomplete and necessarily partial—and if partial (in both senses) and written by individuals who did not experience the events, then history is always "history-for."[106] Moreover, history represents a discontinuous, rather than a continuous, set of events, with different "codings of *before* and *after*"; events significant for one code are not for another.[107] Given such concessions, the view that Lévi-Strauss stood against history *tout court* must be modified. The points here noted, we shall see in Chapter 4, were pondered by the French "New Historians" and reflected in their histories. Likewise, Lévi-Strauss's notion of culture as something to be "read" via linguistic theory will again be considered in my discussion of Clifford Geertz in Chapter 7.

Four Critiques

Of the various critiques of structural linguistics and Lévi-Straussian anthropology, four are especially important for the argument of this book: those of Paul Ricoeur (in "Structure et herméneutique" [1963]),[108] Jacques Derrida (in *Of Grammatology* [1967]),[109] Perry Anderson (in *In the Tracks of Historical Materialism* [1983]),[110] and Pierre Macherey (in *A Theory of Literary Production* [1966]).[111] If 1966 fairly can be declared "the structuralist year,"[112] it is significant that major critique appeared both before and during the movement's heyday, soon to be followed by others.[113]

Paul Ricoeur

In various ways, Ricoeur positioned himself against structuralist linguistics—a system, he declared, that has "no outside," but is "an autonomous entity of internal dependencies" that violates linguistic experience. Structuralism's preference for *langue* over speech, he argued, casts aside history and intention; no way remains open for language to "take hold" of reality. Ricoeur preferred philosophies that broke "the closure of the sign," that is, that accommodated an extra-linguistic referent. He saw his own work as "blowing the whistle" on structuralism's central thesis, that language had no "outside," but only "relations immanent to the system."[114] Moreover, he deplored the erasure of the subject implied in structuralism; through his notion of "discourse," Ricoeur wished to accommodate both the speaking and the listening subject and a "world" that discourse opened up.[115] With manifest satisfaction Ricoeur welcomed Noam Chomsky's generative grammar, which, he declared, signaled "the end of structuralism conceived as a science of taxonomies, closed inventories, and already settled combinations."[116]

Nonetheless, Ricoeur argued that structuralist analysis was a necessary stage between a naïve and a critical interpretation, which he identified with a "depth-interpretation" that (borrowing Heideggerian categories) opens up a world. It prevents interpreters from imagining that "understanding" *(Verstehen)* involved an intuitive grasping of intention, and when applied to social phenomena, provided an escape from older notions of causality based on antecedents and consequents.[117] While rejecting structuralism as a universal system, he acknowledged particular structuralist analyses as helpful.[118] Lévi-Strauss's application of structuralism to myth he deemed problematic, however: if that author believed that myth's function was to overcome such oppositions as birth and death, did not his analysis presuppose that there actually *were* such existential conflicts?[119]

In his critique of structuralist anthropology, Ricoeur especially faulted Lévi-Strauss for concerning himself only with "savage thought"—of little use in recovering "signifying intentions."[120] Ricoeur argued that Lévi-Strauss in *The Savage Mind,* far from relegating "savage thought" to a prelogical stage of humanity, assumes that it is "global" in range and "homologous" to *all* thought. For Ricoeur, this can only be labeled "thought which is not thought," for it does not uncover intentional meaning, itself dependent on a "historical act of interpretation which inscribes itself in a continuing tradition."[121] To be sure, exploring "savage thought" is a perfectly legitimate enterprise, Ricoeur conceded, but Lévi-Strauss failed to note the conditions and limitations of its validity—for example, that the "savage thinker" is tightly constrained by materials already available, by "signs already used," by "an odd and limited repertoire." Working only with "debris," the *bricolage* model of savage thought affords no access to higher forms of creative thought such as philosophy. Ricoeur suggested that early Hebrew culture might provide an alternative model of primitive thought, in that it brimmed with inventive possibilities and was amenable to historical interpretation. Whatever the utility of structural linguistics for understanding the operations of the "savage mind," Ricoeur concluded, they are of little use for philosophical thought, a more distinctively human activity. Ricoeur accuses structuralism of being an "absolute formalism, "a Kantianism without a transcendental subject."[122]

Responding to Ricoeur, Lévi-Strauss accepted the description of his work ("a Kantianism without a transcendental subject") as a compliment, not as a criticism,[123] but rejected the proposition that he should also have analyzed myths of the Hebrew Bible or of ancient Greece. These have been excised from their original social setting and reworked by redactors who had other purposes in view, he argued; they have already been submitted to an intellectualizing and historicizing operation. Scholars now are unable to recover the social setting in which such myths originally appeared—appealing to their present location in the Bible constitutes a *petitio principii*. Hence the ethnologist has no context in which to assess such "historicized" myths.[124] Ricoeur had mistakenly imagined that the materials of the Hebrew Bible present an unreworked form of savage thought, when they are in fact *texts* that are a product of a literate and literary culture. (The insistence that "texts" are already "worked over" will inform the views of later theorists, such as Dominick LaCapra and Roger Chartier, as I discuss in Chapter 7.)

Although Lévi-Strauss here again acknowledged history's importance, he also argued that it stands as but one "code" among many and suffers from the inexactness and frailty of all human knowledge. He himself preferred to concentrate on the synchronic, which can be more solidly grasped than the diachronic in anthropological study.[125] Against critics such as Ricoeur, Lévi-Strauss argued strenuously throughout his works that the preliterates who told these myths engaged in a form of abstract thought and that the purpose of myth is analysis.[126] Their mental equipment is not inferior to ours, nor is its logic so opposed, as Ricoeur and others have assumed.[127] The debate between Lévi-Strauss and Ricoeur provides a classic instance of structuralism confronting humanistic phenomenology.

Jacques Derrida

Derrida's critique of structural linguistics in *Of Grammatology* unsurprisingly concentrates on Lévi-Strauss's demotion of writing in favor of speech. Derrida argued that if, as Saussure posited, signs are "unmotivated," then there can be no natural subordination or hierarchy among orders of signifiers, that is, writing cannot be subordinated to speech. Indeed, Saussure's principle forbids writing to be seen as an "image" of spoken language, since it is not the property of the sign to be an "image." How can there be an "image" of a phoneme? The very word implies visibility.[128]

For Derrida, in contrast, "writing in general" covers the whole field of linguistic signs, including the phonic. To be sure, this is a different notion of "writing"—"archi-writing"—than the "vulgar concept" that the word is usually taken to denote. Archi-writing, for Derrida, contains both "the possibility of the spoken word" as well as the "graphie," the written word. Thus speech itself, for Derrida, is already a kind of writing.[129] The science of signs that Saussure had pre-

dicted for the future is here labeled "grammatology."[130] Derrida's attack on the demotion of writing in structural linguistics would inform
his specific critique of Lévi-Strauss.

At the Baltimore conference on "The Languages of Criticism and
the Sciences of Man" in 1966, Derrida had praised Lévi-Strauss for
his challenge to the dominance of Western culture and his "reduction" or "neutralization" of time and history.[131] In *Of Grammatology,* however, he faults the "phonologism" that Lévi-Strauss
adopted from linguistics for its implied exclusion or abasement of
writing.[132] To score his point, Derrida dissects a chapter of *Tristes
tropiques* entitled "The Writing Lesson," in which Lévi-Strauss recounts how an illiterate Nambikwara chieftain pretended to read so
as to lend authority to his division of gifts among some hostile neigh-
bors.[133]

Reciting this tale afforded Lévi-Strauss the opportunity to mark the
"strangeness" of writing. Although misguided moderns may imagine
that the introduction of writing beneficially preserves knowledge and
acts as an "artificial memory," Lévi-Strauss demoted its claims. First,
he observed, since writing was invented only somewhere between
4000 and 3000 B.C.E., it cannot be the cause, but only the result, of
the world-historical neolithic revolution. Moreover, the invention of
writing did not result in a simple progress of knowledge, which "fluc-
tuated more than it increased" until the birth of modern science. The
only phenomenon with which writing correlates, Lévi-Strauss posited, is the creation of cities, which entailed the division of castes or
classes: thus the "primary function of written communication is to facilitate slavery." Even today, he added, combating illiteracy encourages increased governmental control of the citizenry.[134] In interviews
for French radio in 1959, Lévi-Strauss concluded that since human ascendancy over nature had been established by the subjection of one
human to another, the tale of human progress remained equivocal.[135]

Lévi-Strauss's demotion of the status of writing would have been
"anathema-enough" to Derrida, but even worse could be said. In a
typically close reading of *Tristes tropiques,* Derrida noted that "The
Writing Lesson" is preceded by a chapter entitled "Family Life,"
which lauds the gentle innocence of the Nambikwara. In this tribe,
Lévi-Strauss claimed that fathers show "tender concern" for their
children; men deeply desire and admire women; the sexes cooperate
to provide for themselves and their children; "couples embrace as if

seeking to recapture a lost unity." He senses in them "an immense kindness, a profoundly carefree attitude, a naïve and charming animal satisfaction"; all in all, the family life of the Nambikwara offers a "moving expression of human love."[136]

Such sentiments doubtless accord well with Lévi-Strauss's expressed gratitude to and admiration for the peoples he studied.[137] His words, however, were taken by Derrida not merely as romantic fluff, but worse: positioned to immediately precede the chapter on writing, Lévi-Strauss leads his readers to assume that the Nambikwara enjoyed this "goodness and sweetness," without violence or hierarchy, before the introduction of writing.[138] Here is a prime expression of Western "logocentrism," Derrida argued, of the "fall into evil from the innocence of the [spoken] word," a notion of "fall" borrowed from classical theology. Did not the very notion of *bricolage* (with which Levi-Strauss had described "savage thought") imply a descent from some earlier plentitude? Had not Lévi-Strauss, devoted to combating ethnocentrism, incriminated himself in a theory of "descent" by privileging speech over writing?[139] For Derrida, Lévi-Strauss's disprivileging of writing not only reveals his highly restrictive notion of writing, but also forbids an ethics to these peoples—since, for Derrida, to have an ethics demands not just "the presence *of the other*" (as in speech), but also "absence, dissimulation, detour, differance, writing."[140] The ethnographic ideal of "distancing," Derrida implies, might better accord with writing than with speech. The debate between Lévi-Strauss and Derrida reveals the gap between various theories that take speech as their linguistic model and post-structuralist literary theory, in which writing trounces speech. Derrida's focus on the distinctiveness of writing and texts will invite different ways of thinking about history, as I detail in Chapter 7.

Perry Anderson

Marxist historian and theorist Perry Anderson offers a third critique of Lévi-Strauss's appropriation of structural linguistics that centers on the difference between practices and language.[141] Marriage and kinship structures, Anderson observes, are poorly analogized to language: whereas no one alienates vocabulary to his or her interlocutor, but can freely reuse the words as many times as the speaker wishes, fathers cannot reclaim their daughters after the wedding. Anderson here signals the freedom and "inventivity" of speech, unlimited by material constraints, whereas persons, goods, and powers remain "subject to the laws of natural scarcity." Moreover, Anderson argues, in class society, linguistic structures change much more slowly than those of economics, politics, or religion; hence language provides an inadequate model for the latter. And last, "the subject of speech is axiomatically *individual*," yet the relevant subjects in economics, culture, politics, and the military are in the main collective (nations, classes, and so forth), which exhibit agency in a way that can profoundly affect structures.[142] For these reasons, in Anderson's view, language affords a poor model for anthropologists.

Lévi-Strauss, I suspect, would counter that Anderson mistakenly assumes that he was working from the *parole* side of language with its freedom for invention and endless, individualizing elaboration, not from the model that Lévi-Strauss found in the linguistic system, the structure of language *(langue)*. Although Anderson is doubtless correct that a linguistic model could be understood to weaken the notion of causal explanation in history,[143] this objection would not disturb non-Marxist historians, such as many *Annalistes,* who decades ago abandoned a focus on causality. Non-Althussserian Marxist historians, by contrast, fault structuralism for allegedly erasing, or at least constricting, notions of individual agency, subjectivity, purpose, and causality, which they deem essential for charting a teleologically oriented notion of class struggle within history. These competing approaches are detailed in Chapter 4. Anderson's critique well represents the Marxist concern that linguistic models not obscure the distinctive role of material practices. Could language and concern for material practice be better combined? Pierre Macherey's work represents one version of how this might be done.

Pierre Macherey

Pierre Macherey's critique of structuralism at the movement's height in the mid-1960s underscored several themes that soon would emerge in post-structuralist analysis. As a literary critic with intellectual allegiances to both Althusser and Freud, Macherey employed a "symptomatic reading," making it possible to explore the gaps, absences, and contradictions in literary texts that revealed their ideological nature.[144] Here materialist, literary, and post-structuralist concerns find an expression that is suggestive to historians who wish to situate their textual work within a theoretical but materialist frame.

In Macherey's view, structuralist criticism of literature (including myth, Lévi-Strauss's territory) differed little from traditional literary criticism in that both rested on "a mechanical theory of reflection" that posited a "unique and self-sufficient" model, rather like Plato's scheme of archetype and image. In both types of criticism, Macherey concluded, meaning was assumed to be already "in" the work—a point that manifests structuralism's deviation from Saussurean linguistics. In structuralist analysis, each work is seen to have a "message," a "secret," that the analyst attempts to isolate, decode, and transmit. On this model, literary analysis would seek to uncover the text's inherent rationality, and the critic's comments would simply restate what the work itself, understood in its "true" meaning, had already said.[145] In this respect, Macherey argued, Lévi-Strauss and other structuralists operate with a traditional psychology that looks to intention. Structuralist criticism, like traditional literary criticism, he concluded, shows its link to ideology in its endorsement of the "fallacies" of the secret, depth, rules, and harmony.[146]

By way of contrast, Macherey proposed that it was the critic's task to bring out the "*difference* within the work by demonstrating that it is *other than it is.*" The work exists in relation to what it does not say, to its absences. The question that must be asked is: "In what relation to that which is other than itself is the work produced?"[147] Within each literary text, Macherey proposed, there are signs of an "internal rupture" that disallow its being considered "a coherent and unified whole," as both structuralist and traditionalist literary critics assume.[148] (In this claim, Macherey appears to fault Lévi-Strauss and other structuralists for not staying true to the theme of *discontinuity* that Saussurean linguistics implied.) To make a work an object of knowledge, a "production" rather than merely an object of "consumption," the critic must transform it by his or her analysis.[149] The critic must also ask what the preexisting conditions are that make the work possible.[150] Macherey's concerns resonate with those of theoretically oriented historians, such as Michel Foucault and Roger Chartier, discussed in Chapter 6. And Macherey's claim that the gaps, absences, and inner disparities in a literary work relate to ideology links literary to materialist concerns, as I discuss in Chapters 5 and 8.

The Legacy of Structuralism

What is lasting about structuralism, François Dosse asks? He answers: the concern for rigor, the desire to find "meaningful wholes," and the message that "communication is never entirely transparent to itself." Even after structuralism's heyday, structural semiotics continued to entice scholars whose work was to explicate religious texts.[151]

For historians, I claim, several features of the structuralist program remain important, including its denaturalization of culture, its privileging of discontinuity over continuity, its semiotic interpretation of culture, its injunction to break down and rebuild the object of study, and its attention to the self-referring quality of language. From around 1970 onward, the new attention in historical studies given to language, as I suggest in Chapter 4, is an indirect but highly important legacy of structuralism. Perhaps most significant, structuralist linguistics, with its view of the "arbitrariness of the sign" as elaborated by theorists after Saussure, called into question any natural relation between linguistic signs and external reality, thus rendering problematic the correspondence theory of verification with which traditional historians had (often unconsciously) operated. The precedence given to speech over writing in various forms of structuralism, however, will be critiqued by intellectual historians in a new mode, as I explore in Chapter 6. And an outgrowth of the emphasis on language, the concern to consider almost anything a "text" ripe for hermeneutic decipherment, is critiqued in Chapter 7.

CHAPTER FOUR

The Territory of the Historian

This chapter[1] illustrates some major shifts in twentieth-century historiography through an examination of the work of *Annalistes,* microhistorians, and British Marxist historians, whose innovative approaches inspired a history—largely a social history—concerned with "mental tools" and material bases, with the dissident and the forgotten. Nonetheless, a lingering positivism, accompanied by inattention to the theoretical and philosophical issues discussed in this book, marks much of their writing. Even these highly distinguished "practicing historians," I conclude, cordon off the "territory of the historian" from critiques offered by philosophers and theorists. Scholars of premodern Western history, I argue in Chapter 8, while gleaning much regarding historical practice from the historians here surveyed, are well positioned to appropriate such philosophical/theoretical critique. New directions in intellectual history, attentive to such critique (as I detail in Chapter 6), will offer some models.

French Historiography

The Annalistes *and Their Predecessors*

The movement that developed around the journal *Annales* is inarguably the most important in twentieth-century French historiography. Founded in 1929 as *Annales d'histoire économique et sociale* by Lucien Febvre and Marc Bloch as a counter to historical positivism, *Annales'* influence has, over the decades, reached far beyond France.[2]

Historical positivism in France, commentators note, itself emerged in opposition to an older belletristic history. Marking French historians' desire to compete more successfully with Germany (albeit a generation later) on the historiographical front than France had on the battlefields of 1870, history (Jacques Revel posits) "became the repository of a humiliated nation's pride, and its instruction was to contribute to the civic rearming of the nation."[3] In order to rival German historiography, French historians abandoned the literary style for a more allegedly scientific model. "Method" was now the order of the day, and Ranke's influence—the Ranke of facts, archives, and documents —was to dominate.[4] In their eagerness to prove themselves scientific, French historians ignored the critiques of positivism developed by Dilthey and other German scholars.[5]

In France, historical positivism was encapsulated in Charles V. Langlois and Charles Seignobos's *Introduction aux études historiques* [1898] and Seignobos's *Méthode historique appliquée aux sciences sociales* [1901], books used in the training of historians for several decades.[6] Langlois and Seignobos rued the slowness of their discipline to become "methodical," a fact they blamed on history's origins as a form of literature.[7] Their new scientific history, by contrast, eschewing philosophical speculation, would be grounded in the careful utilization of documents.[8] Thus they advised budding historians to reach for "the real sense of the text," for "truth," for "knowledge pure and simple," rather than for pleasing effect or edifying example.[9] French students, like German historians, should concentrate on the collection of facts and learn a "contempt for rhetoric, for paste diamonds and paper flowers"—although developing "a pure and strong, a terse and pregnant style" was not a misguided goal. Such a history, Langlois and Seignobos proclaimed, would be "very hygienic for the mind," curing it of credulity.[10] It was from historical positivism of this type that Bloch, Febvre, and, later, Henri-Irénée Marrou sought to break free.[11]

To be sure, Bloch and Febvre had predecessors who encouraged historiographical innovation, for example, Henri Berr, founder in 1900 of the journal *Revue de synthèse historique,*[12] and François Simiand, who sought to link history more closely with the social sciences. Simiand relentlessly attacked traditional historiography—of which Charles Seignobos stood as the symbol—for its "idolization" of politics, the individual, and chronology, and for its pretensions to exactness and impartiality that its practitioners imagined eschewed tendentiousness and moralism.[13]

Nonetheless, although the early *Annalistes* ventured new historiographical approaches, they often ignored the epistemological issues attending historiography, a failure perhaps partially attributable to philosophy's then-absence from the educational curriculum of French historians.[14] Speculative philosophy of history remained anathema to them, as it had to their positivistic predecessors.[15] Nowhere do the *Annalistes'* proposals for reform focus on the issues that engaged philosophers of history;[16] these would be left to "outsiders," such as Paul Veyne.[17] As André Burguière argues, although the legend developed that *Annales* had provided a new historiographical method, no methodological rupture in fact divided earlier positivist historians from the *Annalistes*.[18] Nonetheless, the *Annalistes* addressed the topics of historians' "interest" and of "presentism" in ways that stimulated debate among historians and theorists throughout the century.

Concerns of Annales *History*

In a 1937 editorial in *Annales,* Bloch and Febvre set forth their goals for the journal: to attempt a "total" history undertaken in an interdisciplinary manner; to refuse both "rhetorical historiography and one of an erudition without limit"; to champion a history based on the precise questions framed by the historian; to attend to both concrete reality and "deeper" phenomena.[19] These general *desiderata* were elaborated in distinctive approaches to the study of history.

First, for the early *Annalistes,* history as a discipline is organized in the present and reflects historians' present concerns; the present was a "motor for the writing of history."[20] In response to the positivist demand that historians should "submit" to documents, Febvre claimed that "[t]here is no history; there are only historians"—that is, it is the historian (not documents) who poses questions and hypotheses.[21] "History is a way of organizing the past," he wrote, "so that it does not weigh too heavily on the shoulders of men . . . It consults death in accordance with the needs of life."[22] Taking cues from the present, Bloch argued, differentiates historians from "antiquarians"; "the study of the dead," he argued, must be joined to that of the living.[23] More recently, this presentist stance has been championed by Jacques

Le Goff, François Furet, and André Burguière.[24] The degree to which historians should be motivated by present interests, however, remains a heated debate in other quarters of the discipline.

Second, *Annales* historiography rejected "event history," which they thought was an amateurish and superficial approach to history. This rejection was sometimes viewed as a revolt by "dispossessed" historians against the Sorbonne's iron control of historical scholarship.[25] Febvre and Bloch imposed on *Annales* (in Michael Bentley's words) "a tone calculated to *épater les bourgeois,* especially bourgeois professors."[26] The revolt against "short-time-span" history likewise countered the previous generation's obsession with documents.[27] "Event history" was now scornfully dismissed by *Annalistes* as offering a mere "theatre of appearances."[28] In Emmanuel Le Roy Ladurie's colorful caricature, "the narrative history of events and the individual biography"—a history that leaps "from massacre to boudoir or from bedchamber to anteroom"—had been sentenced to death by the new preference for "the quantifiable, the statistical and the structural."[29] Bloch himself, however, remained resolutely humanist, unlike later *Annalistes* who abandoned the "human subject" to study topics such as demography and climate.[30] In Bloch's famous analogy, the "good historian is like the giant of the fairy tale. He knows that wherever he catches the scent of human flesh, there his quarry lies."[31]

The critique of *histoire événementielle* was reflected in the movement's decided animus against political history.[32] For a second generation of *Annalistes*, chronological succession as the prime determinant of historical causality was replaced by an investigation of structural and functional relations; longer time spans and larger socioeconomic entities formed the subjects of inquiry.[33] Fernand Braudel, who made famous *la longue durée,* argued that the consideration of longer time spans recaptured an earlier historiographical tradition, which he saw being revived in studies of the history of religion and classical antiquity, especially archeology.[34] In a move calculated to illustrate the demise of event history, Braudel moved the event of Philip II's death to the concluding pages of *The Mediterranean;* the history of kings was here displaced by the history of the sea.[35]

The enthusiasm expressed by Braudel and others for the long term spawned the interest in serial history that characterized *Annales* historiography at midcentury: history of the long term would be based on statistics.[36] Quantification would enable historians to unearth the social lives of "little people," offering a means to cheat "the silence of the poor."[37] The popularity of quantification has been correlated with the new availability and seeming wonders of computers; less positively, it represented a resurgence of the old dream that historical knowledge could be completely objective.[38] In his inaugural lecture at the Collège de France in 1973, Le Roy Ladurie illustrated the benefits to demographic history of studying series in his discussion of the very slow, indeed "immobile," rate of population growth in France between 1300 and 1700. Social science techniques, he concluded, had raised history from its "semi-disgrace" of previous decades to become "the little Cinderella of the social sciences."[39] Critics, however, soon alleged that serial history overlooked the symbolic dimension of culture[40] and merely replaced an older narrative history with a "newer, more technologically-advanced form of positivism."[41]

Still another mark of *Annaliste* history was its reorientation of the historian's task away from the *description* of events and toward the *analysis* of problems.[42] Reversing the practice of traditional historians, the "new historians" argued that the choice of problem must precede that of relevant time span.[43] To identify a problem meant, in effect, that historians *created* the objects of their study: the historical object was not "there," awaiting the historian's gaze.[44] Questions asking "why," not "what" or "how," dominated—especially those that concerned the material basis of existence, the masses rather than the elites, society, culture, demography, and *mentalités*.[45]

Another feature of *Annales* historiography was its practitioners' eagerness to appropriate the intellectual spoils and methods of other disciplines. This embrace of interdisciplinarity, especially with the social sciences, has been variously interpreted: as a retreat from an idealist historiography that encouraged historians' mental "empathy" with their subject,[46] or as a renewed attempt to unify the social sciences, this time around history.[47] A change in the journal's name—in 1946, *"Civilisations"* was added to *"Economies"* and *"Societés"* in its subtitle—rendered visible the editors' interdisciplinary intent.[48]

Reflecting on *Annaliste* history, Braudel noted that from its early days, the concern to build "a community of the human sciences" as auxiliaries of history was dominant. Febvre, Bloch, and others, he claimed, took as their task to raid other disciplines, "return with the booty," and "set forth again on the quest of discovery, demolishing obstructing walls at each occasion."[49] Some fields of study traditionally associated in France with the education of historians, such as geography, were at the forefront of the interdisciplinary effort; Febvre himself, for example, wrote a *Geographical Introduction to History*.[50] Significantly, although Febvre and his colleagues urged historians to attend to language, they appear to be familiar only with a prestructuralist, historicizing type of linguistics. Despite the new approaches to history that the early *Annalistes* pioneered, their attachment to a traditional linguistics doubtless contributed to the profession's belated recognition of the implications of structural linguistics for history-writing.[51]

After Febvre, historians interested in quantification and serial history appropriated work in economics as well. Bloch, for his part, chastised colleagues for their inattention to archeology.[52] Le Roy Ladurie championed the climate as a new topic of research: "history without people," he joked.[53] Braudel called for mathematicians, geographers, and other social scientists to help in constructing *longue durée* history, focusing on the formulation of models.[54] Somewhat later, *Annalistes* interested in *mentalités* looked to ideology critique, psychoanalysis, structural semantics, and discourse theory.[55] More recently, interdisciplinary exploration has centered on historical anthropology, politics divorced from an older narrative "event history," and the "history of attitudes."[56] As anthropological interests prompted historians to reflect on their distance and difference from the subjects of their inquiry, discontinuity became a hallmark of the New History.[57]

More generally, *Annales* historiography endorsed the acknowledgment of the historian's own social placement. The vision of "Others," of "the vanquished," promoted (in Paul Ricoeur's words) a "suspicion concerning the guardianship of history by the inventors and the beneficiaries of the discourse pronounced on the front-stage of history"[58]—a view later registered in Michel de Certeau's counsel that historians must look to the social place of their own historiographical operation.[59] Nonetheless, this emphasis on the historian's "social place" did not satisfy more committed Leftists such as Louis Althusser. Althusser faulted *Annales,* a journal he deemed obsessed with the "temporal rhythms" of a society, for failing to critique hierarchical relationship. For Marxists, the *Annalistes'* emphasis on "ways of life" suggested a "myth of immobility" that gave scant attention to class struggle.[60]

Mentalités

Mentalité history, especially favored by later *Annalistes,* focused on the "intellectual mechanisms, sentiments, [and] behaviors of humans who have preceded us."[61] Hans Kellner argues that *mentalité* history in its present form stands as a reaction of *third*-generation *Annalistes* against the serial and quantitative history favored by the "elders" of the previous generation: "it cost too much," Kellner continues, "to renounce a world of ideas and human expression."[62] In effect, *mentalité* history returned to the unfinished work of the first-generation *Annalistes.*[63]

Mentalité history, to be sure, has been differently inflected: while Fernand Braudel defined it as "the important locus of slow change and inertias," Ernest Labrousse saw it as the "history of resistances" to dominant ideologies,[64] and Michel Vovelle as "the study of the mediations and of the dialectical relationship between the objective conditions of human life and the ways in which people narrate it, and even live it."[65] That *mentalité* history might appear "imprecise," overly adaptable, Jacques Le Goff argued, in fact constituted part of its attraction.[66]

Lucien Febvre had made famous the notion of the "mental tools" *(outillage mental)* available to individuals within past cultures: what could or could not be thought?[67] Febvre's book on Rabelais, *Le Problème de l'incroyance au XVIe siècle: la religion de Rabelais* (1943),[68] attempted to locate the "mental tools" of his protagonist's society. Elsewhere, Febvre noted the birth of a new historical subject: the emotions, "affect," as they appeared in social life. We do not have, he rued, a history of love, death, pity, cruelty, or joy—indeed, these were yet to come. Febvre nonetheless offered tips on where historians might look for material: to philology (especially its examination of word-roots), iconography, and literature.[69] His hope, and his advice, were prophetic.

The decades after Febvre saw an explosion of innovative studies of the "mental tools" of past societies. As distinguished from an older "history of ideas," which focused on elites and "high" literary and philosophical texts—an "outmoded spiritualism," in Jacques Le Goff's view[70]—the history of *mentalités* has been described as an "intellectual history of non-intellectuals."[71] It focused on common people, "collective attitudes," the "everyday automatisms of behavior," and "the impersonal content" of thought.[72] Le Goff exhorted historians of *mentalités* to consider "where and by what means such mentalities were produced," how they were created, popularized, and diffused. *Mentalité* history attended more carefully than had its predecessor to the social, economic, and political embeddedness of ideas. Where did the "social locus" reside in the creation and popularization of particular mentalities? Which groups or professions served as intermediaries in their diffusion?[73]

Thus the third generation of *Annalistes* turned away from a history dominated by "structures" and economics, toward *mentalités*. Here, the importance of Jacques Le Goff, Emmanuel Le Roy Ladurie, Jacques Revel, Pierre Nora, and others has been noted. They transposed anthropological interests into an historical framework: the "Other" might be found in the past, as well as in distant lands.[74] The rapprochement of anthropology and history was signaled by Lévi-Strauss himself, who in 1971 appeared on the *Annales* radio program, "Mondays on History," to proclaim that "the great book of history is also an ethnographic essay on past societies."[75]

Given the focus on "the material" in *mentalité* history, its popularity among historians of religion is striking: the afterlife, the devil, saints, sorcery, death, relics, and pilgrimage became favored subjects for these scholars.[76] Holding together such concerns within a critical and materially oriented historiography could prove difficult. Some critics in fact posit that the history of *mentalités*, allegedly an exercise in defamiliarization, lapsed into nostalgia for "the emotions, beliefs, and mental universe of our ancestors."[77]

Last, and important for my argument, even though the *Annalistes* ventured on new historiographical approaches and problems, for the most part they ignored the epistemological issues attending the writing of history: philosophy was not in their province.[78] The question of how history might make truth claims was no more satisfactorily addressed by these innovative historians than by Anglo-American analytical philosophers.[79] Only a few French historians, such as Paul Veyne, attended to Anglo-American philosophers' interests in narrative, albeit within a different philosophical framework.[80] I turn next to Veyne and other "non-*Annalistes*" whose work assumed greater importance in later historiographical discussions.

"*Non*-Annalistes"

Not all historiographical developments in twentieth-century France were associated with *Annales,* nor even with scholars classified as historians. The interest in philosophy of history exhibited by Henri Marrou and Raymond Aron, for example, little concerned the *Annalistes;*[81] the former pursued a critical historiography that engaged the German discussion of "understanding" and "explanation," largely absent from French historiography.[82]

Aron's studies of existentialism and phenomenology informed his reflections on philosophy of history. After Germany's defeat of France in 1871 and its continuing ascent, he claimed, Frenchmen lost faith in the future, without which there can be no philosophy of history. Aron faulted both the *Annalistes* for their "hostility" to "theories of historical knowledge," and Marxist historians for "historical absolutism."[83] Alleging that historians had paid dearly for their indifference to philosophical problems, Marrou argued that Aron's "critical philosophy of history" had occasioned a "Copernican revolution" in its insistence that the mind of the investigator be taken into account in the formulation of history more fully than had traditional historians.[84]

Aron and Marrou, to be sure, shared certain historiographical concerns with the *Annalistes.* Like the latter, Marrou emphasized that history is a matter of constructing, not discovering. Moreover, his critique of the misinterpretation of documents in positivist history, his downplaying of "event history," and his insistence that contemporary historians (not documents) set the questions converged with themes of *Annales* historiography.[85] For these "non-*Annalistes,*" as well as for *Annaliste* historians, history was distinctively conceptual rather than event-driven.[86]

By the 1970s, French historians committed to structuralist and quantitative historiography had yet another "outsider" in their midst, Paul Veyne. Veyne's *Writing History (Comment on écrit l'histoire),* published in 1971, bore an unusual subtitle, *Essay on Epistemology*—unusual not just for an historian of antiquity, but for *any* historian. Although Veyne, like the *Annalistes,* claimed that historians "invent" their subjects and bring to the fore what people of the time were not able to see,[87] his interest in epistemology (albeit not of a high technical order) and in narrative theory was unusual, indeed, unfavored, at that time among French historians.[88]

For Veyne, "History" (with a capital "H") stands largely as a regulating idea, a heuristic principle.[89] Substantively, he claimed, it provides "knowledge through traces," most of which concern ordinary, everyday matters—"things that would be as banal as our lives if they were not different," he ironically observed. What lends the historian's profession its characteristic flavor, he quipped, is its "astonishment at the obvious."[90]

Since history is "knowledge through documents," and documents cannot be identified with the event, Veyne argued, then history cannot be construed as *mimesis*. Moreover, there can be no scientific explanation in history, since neither prediction nor deduction form part of its procedures. Any "rigor" history possesses cannot derive from science (history has "no threshold of knowledge, no minimum of intelligibility"), but only from "the level of criticism" that historians bring to bear on their subjects.[91] Historical explanation, then, is not scientific, but rests entirely on historians' organization of their material around plots and descriptions of circumstances.[92] Any historian who imagines that history exhibits causes reveals himself or herself to be (in Veyne's witty but ungenerous phrase) a "survival of the paleoepistemological era."[93]

In an anti-Braudelian move, Veyne rejected the *Annales'* emphasis on *histoire global, la longue durée,* and collective mind sets.[94] A worthy partner to history, Veyne thought, was not to be found in the social science disciplines, as the *Annalistes* posited, but in literature. Describing history as a "mutilated knowledge" marked by gaps and absences, Veyne proposed that history differed from the novel on one point only, that the events it related were "true."[95] Even more alarming, Veyne added, historians cannot even pride themselves on being exemplary humanists who offer models of the Good or the Beautiful for emulation; they can claim nothing more distinctive for history than that it concerns "the interesting." For Veyne, history is "one of the most harmless products ever elaborated by the chemistry of the intellect." Insofar as history devalues what it treats and eradicates passion, the history of our own nation soon appears just as boring as that of any other; in this respect, Veyne deemed the existentialists of his era foolish in their mistrust of history on the grounds that it is depoliticized. History rather is "an intellectual activity that, through time-honored literary forms, serves the aims of mere curiosity." When historians are asked why they pursue their particular topics, they should respond in the words of the mountaineer who, when asked why he wished to climb Mount Everest, tersely replied, because "it is there."[96] Such sentiments shocked *Annalistes* (and others) who thought that "interest" did not provide a sufficient rationale for historical work.[97] "Curiosity," Michel de Certeau later observed, is not enough to justify the historian's practice.[98]

Another important intervention in historiography offered by Veyne was his early, and influential, advocacy of Foucauldian historiography. In this, he stood outside the then-reigning *Annaliste* approach. In 1978, appended to an abridged version of *Comment on écrit l'histoire,* Veyne published an important essay, "Foucault révolutionne l'histoire," in which he argued that Foucault was "the first completely positivist historian," a claim doubtless meant as a jab to Marxist historians, among others.[99] Admitting his own misguided approach in *Bread and Circuses* and seeking to dispel misconceptions of Foucault's theories, Veyne argued that Foucault's revolutionary historiographical move was to discount the notion that historians study "natural objects" such as madness or the State—or "History."[100] Rather, Foucault, as "the consummate historian" who insists that everything is historical, teaches his readers to look to practices: in what practice will people assume and do one thing, and in what other practice will that very thing be unthinkable? Imagining that there is an "eternal" concept of the governed, the rulers, and so forth prevents access to what is particular and exceptional about a practice; here, "the eternal phantoms that language arouses in us" need to be eliminated.[101] Historians should look to the *relation* of practices, how neighboring practices determine the object studied; in this regard, relations among practices can be understood as structures, that which gives to matter "their own objective faces." Representations and utterances thus form part of practices; consciousness does not explain them.[102] Foucault's genealogical history, Veyne argues, fulfills the aims of traditional history in that it examines societies, economies, and so forth, doing so not in terms of centuries, civilizations, peoples, but of practices.[103] As one of the first ancient historians to press the utility of Foucault's writings for historians (considered further in Chapter 6), Veyne rendered an important service to the profession.

Veyne's interest in epistemology, his linking of history to literature, and his explication of Foucault's importance for historians foreshadowed some later critical approaches to history. The fact that *Com-*

ment on écrit l'histoire (1971) and "Foucault révolutionne l'histoire" (1978) did not appear in English translation until (respectively) 1984 and 1997, however, suggests a certain failure in historians' ready appreciation for his work.

The Post-Structuralist Return of History in France

That history was accorded a return to favor in late-twentieth-century France, it has been postulated, may in part relate to the aftermath of the revolts of workers and students in May 1968: those moments of high drama forced the recognition that it had not been "structures" that took to the streets, but intentional human subjects.[104] "May 1968 exhumed what structuralism had repressed," Dosse observed—in particular, "history."[105] Now, even the hard sciences could be imagined as "historical": did not the "big bang" theory of the universe's origin imply that there were "events"—and if astrophysics recognized events, could the social sciences lag far behind?[106]

A new variety of history, which recuperated structuralist concerns, was embraced in the 1970s by the third generation of *Annalistes*.[107] The formerly despised "event history" acquired a new focus in its attention to historical traumatism and rupture.[108] History (with its events and movement) and structures could reunite, as essays published in *Annales* after 1968 made evident.[109] In 1971, André Burguière boldly asserted that historians could even claim "certain rights of paternity" to structuralist approaches, insofar as historians had learned from Marxism "to define a society or period in terms not of a series of events but of an operational system, namely, the mode of production." "A little structuralism takes us away from history," he concluded; "a great deal of structuralism brings us back."[110]

François Dosse, helpfully signaling some important moments of history's recuperation, notes the influence of Mikhail Bakhtin's writings, transmitted largely through Julia Kristeva after her arrival in Paris in 1965. Bakhtin's notion that the literary text is "polyphonic" and "dialogic" implied that texts were not hermetic, but were woven through with history: thus was the notion of intertextuality introduced to France.[111] Historians of a new generation soon learned to listen for those divergent voices in their texts and to give greater attention to the language of the agents they studied.

A third important development in post-1968 French historiography was Michel Foucault's turn from structuralism toward a history based on archival research.[112] His "return" to history, however, abandoned older notions of continuity, progress, and (at least for this middle period of Foucault's work) "the speaking individual" or the "unified subject."[113] Here, concerns of structuralists and those of historians appeared to meet. Foucault's immense importance for the development of a new type of intellectual history is explored in Chapter 6.

An illuminating example of historiographical change is furnished by the ever-evolving interpretations of the French Revolution.[114] A Marxist interpretation that centered on class analysis (the Revolution was deemed "bourgeois," a stage in the demise of feudalism and a prelude to capitalism) largely held sway in France from the 1930s through the 1960s. By the late 1970s, however, a different model emerged, spurred by François Furet's *Interpreting the French Revolution* (1978). Furet viewed the Revolution largely as a cultural phenomenon—he explored the "mental representations of power," the "network of signs," that governed political life—and stressed the novel political ideology that emerged during the Revolution's course.[115] And two manifestations of the "linguistic turn"—rhetorical analysis and deconstruction—inform a more recent study of the French Revolution, William E. Sewell Jr.'s *A Rhetoric of Bourgeois Revolution* (1994). Sewell explores the rhetoric (and its self-deconstruction) of an important revolutionary-era treatise that reveals, he concludes, "the simultaneous power and uncontrollability of all inventive political language."[116] Sewell is nonetheless insistent that the social not be erased; text production, he argues, counts as "action in a social world."[117] Here, social history and the new intellectual history (as explored in Chapter 6) appear to meet.

Microhistory and Its Critics

Like some third-generation *Annalistes,* French and Italian microhistorians, who investigate small episodes and the "little people," rejected what they deemed a mechanistic or deterministic form of history-writing that emphasized statistics, generalization, quantitative formulation, the *longue durée,* and "immobile history."[118] By the 1980s, Jacques Revel comments, macrohistorical approaches that demanded maximal aggregation were being questioned; historians more readily acknowledged that many aspects of history were not amenable to such analyses. Reconstruction might rather come from the "bottom up."[119]

Microhistorians argue that macrohistorical approaches do not capture the "lived experience" of people, "the day-to-day problems of survival." Microhistory, by contrast, permits a reconstitution of "real life," attempting through narrative reconstruction to provide a "thick" description of an event.[120] Working from inquisition and trial records, and other sources that purport to speak in the voices of the time, microhistorians seek to locate the history of the often forgotten, to display (in Natalie Zemon Davis's happy phrase) "the social creativity of the so-called inarticulate."[121] To be recaptured were ordinary people's freedom of choice, their ability (in the words of Peter Burke) "to exploit the inconsistencies or incoherences of social and political systems, to find loopholes through which they can wriggle or interstices in which they can survive."[122] Here, quantification assists microhistory, Carlo Ginzburg and Carlo Poni concede, insofar as it provides a way to unearth the lives of the otherwise unrecognized; quantitative methods and qualitative approaches could be profitably combined.[123] Moreover, the "detective story" quality of much microhistorical writing, its anthropological/ethnographical approaches, and its focus on tales of love gone astray,[124] "heresy" of grander or smaller dimensions,[125] lesbian nuns,[126] fake and missing husbands,[127] exorcism manias,[128] village festivals,[129] and massacres of cats[130] lent considerable excitement to the historian's enterprise.

Microhistory, historian Giovanni Levi argues, provides a more cogent approach to historical work than does Geertzian interpretive anthropology. Microhistory possesses a superior ability to define and measure public signs and symbols in their social particularity, rather than "homogenize" them, as Geertz and his followers within the historical profession are alleged to do. Levi deems Geertzian history "a cultural history without social analysis"; it erroneously assumes that charisma and the symbolism of power speak the same to everyone in socially differentiated societies. In this respect, Levi concludes, microhistory's attention to "conflicts and solidarities" produces a "thicker description" than does interpretive anthropology. Levi also claims that their approach to historical scholarship openly displays (rather than obscures) the research procedures involved, including its documentary limitations. In microhistorical writing, readers participate in the dialogic construction of the argument insofar as they are permitted to engage the research procedures and grasp their difficulties.[131] This claim resonates with other calls that historians should explicitly state their interests and the problems they encounter in their research.

Microhistorians' contribution to the revival of narrative history is further elaborated in Chapter 5.

Two works of microhistory are frequently singled out for discussion: Carlo Ginzburg's *The Cheese and the Worms: The Cosmos of a Sixteenth-Century Miller* and Emmanuel Le Roy Ladurie's *Montaillou: The Promised Land of Error*.[132] Ginzburg's book tells the story of an Italian miller, Domenico Scandella (called Menocchio) who ran afoul of the inquisition when the religious and cosmological views he openly propounded were deemed heretical. Working from inquisition records, Ginzburg shows how Menocchio's theories combine themes derived from "high" literary culture with those from oral and popular culture. Le Roy Ladurie, also working from inquisition records, details the Catharist enthusiasm of a French village (Montaillou) in the early fourteenth century. Here, too, themes of popular culture intersect with those of literary culture. Le Roy Ladurie also highlights the role of social status in the drama that played out in the Church's effort to eradicate dualistic "heresy" from France. These works are microhistorical in that they deal with a particular case that is raised up by the historian to provide a window onto larger societal issues of the time.

In Germany, some aspects of microhistory find a counterpart in *Alltagsgeschichte*.[133] Precisely what *alltags* encompasses has been debated: it has been taken to signal the investigation of the history of life routines, of the workday, of the masses, of private life, of what seems spontaneous and unreflective (or, more negatively, of false consciousness or ideology).[134] Like microhistorians, *Alltagsgeschichte*'s practitioners reacted against serial and structural historiography by emphasizing individuals' experiences and the operations of power, and by demoting universalizable hierarchies of explanation, particularly those derived from economics.[135] Among the future *desiderata* of *Alltagsgeschichte*, in historian Wolfgang Hardtwig's view, are a deeper investigation of the history of consciousness, a wider conceptualization of culture, and a decentering of perspective so that a plurality of questions and methods is brought into play.[136] Yet, to the best of my knowledge, no book of *Alltagsgeschichte* has achieved the international fame of *The Cheese and the Worms* or *Montaillou*.

Criticisms soon surfaced: microhistory resembled "fairy tales"[137] and rested on "an excess of invention";[138] the personal quality of its subject matter encouraged a too-easy identity with the people represented and their emotions, obscuring the "otherness" of the past.[139] It promoted nostalgia for premodern times, rather than looking to the present and future.[140] It focused on idiosyncratic cases and individuals, eschewing the "typical," so important to social historians.[141] Moreover, did not microhistorians assume that they find "raw" (rather than "worked-over") stories in their sources?[142] Trial records and inquisition testimonies cannot, in any case, be considered "neutral" witnesses, as some microhistorians imply.[143]

Some critiques were especially biting. Simon Schama, for example, who himself had alarmed the historians' guild with his experimental histories,[144] scathingly referred to microhistory as "the pigmification of historical scale." In Schama's assessment, the "microcosmic view" amounts to "a neo-pointilliste heresy of immense positivist vulgarity." Historians should return to evaluating evidence, he acidly advises, rather than practicing their beachcombing skills on "the casually washed-up detritus of the past." The anthropologist's "thick description" has here, he alleged, been turned into "thin understanding."[145]

A second critique of microhistory, attentive to issues of power, turns a sharp eye on microhistorians' often apolitical reading of sources. Anthropologist Renato Rosaldo's review of Le Roy Ladurie's *Montaillou* stands as a salient example.[146] Rosaldo faulted the "innocent tone" Le Roy Ladurie had adopted in regard to his source, an inquisition record: the inquisitor, Jacques Fournier, appears as "more an instrument for gathering data than a man bent on making the guilty confess their heresies." By removing "the context of interrogation from the 'documentary' findings thereby extracted," Le Roy Ladurie has excised the text from "the politics of domination." Another problem: the interrogated peasants gave their testimony in Occitan, which was translated into Latin by scribes attending the inquisitor, and the proceedings are now paraphrased for readers in modern French; does not the social hierarchy embedded in this linguistic mix contain grounds for suspicion, Rosaldo asked? To the "ethnographic reader," Le Roy Ladurie's inattention to such issues suggests that he is "peculiarly insensitive to power relations and cultural differences." A false polyphony resonates in his work, in that the voices of the peasants are made to seem of equal power with the author's.[147]

Moreover, Rosaldo continued, ethnographers would suspect the "textualization" of peasant life in *Montaillou*; peasants here emerge as "articulate and insightful about the conditions of their own existence," remarkably "like us" in their concerns (especially sex).[148] The "shepherd-hero" of the book, Pierre Maury, is portrayed as existing in an ahistorical time that runs from the Neolithic period to his own century in a "democratic, freedom-loving" world. *Montaillou* becomes "an ancestral national community" with which French readers of the twentieth century can identify.[149] Rosaldo, in effect, urges the maintaining of ethnographic distance, rather than indulging in nationalist nostalgia. Anthropological techniques, in sum, have not been carefully appropriated by the author of *Montaillou*.

Moreover, microhistorians have not engaged the epistemological issues confronting historians any more fully than have *Annalistes*. Microhistorians' manner of collecting and criticizing evidence has been deemed not just traditional, but "positivistic."[150] Carlo Ginzburg names this approach "the evidential paradigm":[151] starting with "facts," the historian works up an hypothesis.[152] Lynn Hunt notes that despite the microhistorians' novel enterprise, they still "brim with confidence in the historian's power to evoke, recapture, and, yes, tell the truth about the past, even while raising questions about the way the sources work to distort and distract our vision of what happened."[153] The most vocal positivist among microhistorians, Ginzburg proudly claims his "realistic" or "positivistic" notion of truth— although he does not demonstrate how this "realistic truth" is to be guaranteed aside from an appeal to careful philological work. He declares himself against "every kind of skeptical attitude," which he labels a "very silly ideology," and denigrates Derrida's writing in particular as "one of the cheapest intellectual things going on," as "a kind of cheap nihilism."[154] With such dismissals, Ginzburg apparently assumes that he has sidestepped the problems that philosophers have posed for historians.

British Marxist Historiography

Although, like the *Annalistes,* British Marxist historians favored "history from below," their "below" was more firmly centered on class struggle and human agency.[155] They endorsed a historiography that owed nothing, and in some cases was violently opposed, to structuralist-inspired historiography, as is manifest in their focus on the ethical individual, human agency, and "experience."[156] Epistemological concerns, however, are no more evident here than in *Annaliste* historiography or in microhistory. As Nicholas Dirks notes, the very historians who are the "most political and critical" seem unconcerned with epistemological questions, and perhaps for a good reason: such concerns "might lead to the suspension of the reality effect."[157]

The movement of "history from below," historian Raphael Samuel testifies, took shape during the late 1940s and early 1950s in the Communist Party Historians' Group, which counted Christopher Hill,[158] Eric Hobsbawm, and E. P. Thompson among its members.[159] The revisionary nature of their work—their choice of subject matter, their overt championship of the oppressed—nonetheless joined with traditional assumptions regarding language and representation.[160]

Without doubt the most famous book produced by a British Marxist historian is E. P. Thompson's *The Making of the English Working Class* (1964). Called "the greatest literary *tour de force* in recent historiography," *The Making of the English Working Class* launched "history from below" for a generation or more of historians.[161] Like Christopher Hill, Thompson believed that conservatives should not be allowed to run off with "the past"; radical resources lay in the early English working-class tradition that could inspire demands for social justice in the present.[162] He sought to rescue his heroes—the Luddites, weavers, artisans, and others who had "made" the English working class—"from the enormous condescension of posterity."[163] Throughout, Thompson favors "bottom up" explanations and scathingly depicts the decline of social conscience among nonconformists (who might have been expected to do better), offering sobering evidence regarding Methodists' collusion with and exploitation of child labor.[164] The key theoretical issue at stake in the book is the relationship between agency and determination, and Thompson embraces the side of agency.[165]

In the late 1950s and early 1960s, Thompson broke with the Marxist orthodoxy of that period. His suspension from the Communist Party in 1956 coincided with the Soviet repression of the Hungarian revolution.[166] Disillusioned with the Stalinist version of Communism, as were many others, Thompson embraced a "socialist humanism."[167] Yet, he alleged, the ideology of Stalinism had reproduced itself, long after its high moment, in Althusserian theory.[168] In Thompson's acrid debate with Louis Althusser, the assumptions of British Marxist historiography ran up against those of French structuralist Marxism. This debate invites further elaboration, as it reveals the largely anti-theoretical stance of British Marxist historiography, particularly in its appeal to "experience."

The Thompson–Althusser Debate

Althusser favored a type of history that attended to "epistemological breaks," in the tradition of the anti-empiricist and anti-positivist historians of science Gaston Bachelard and Georges Canguilhem, and the historian of mathematics Jean Cavaillès.[169] Althusser perceived a major break between an earlier humanistic, Hegelian-inspired Marx, and a later scientific Marx: the Marxist tradition, in effect, could claim no unified picture of its founder to guide its teleological narrative.[170] In his *Essays in Self-Criticism* (1974), Althusser argued (on the basis of the discovery of Marx's early manuscripts) that circa 1845, Marx turned from philosophical critique to the "scientific denunciation of errors as errors." Espousing the standpoint of the proletariat, Marx abandoned his earlier amalgam of "German philosophy, English political economy and French socialism."[171]

Marx, Althusser claimed, was the founder of a new science: History. Prior to Marx, history had occupied itself with "ideological conceptions derived from the religious, moral or legal-political sphere"—in short, with philosophies of history that were centered on "man," "the economic subject," and so forth. Against this notion of history, Marx proposed a different conceptual history that focused on the "mode of production, social formation, infrastructure, superstructure, ideologies, classes, class struggle."[172] For the writing of history, the notion of "epistemological break" meant, in Althusser's view, that commonsense notions of human "experience" should be ruled out as unscientific.[173] Socialist humanism, with its emphasis on human individuality, ethical commitment, human agency, and "experience" did not sit comfortably with structuralist-inspired versions of Marxism.[174]

Thompson disputed Althusser's reading of Marx. Thompson's Marx remained humanistic throughout in that he put "real men and women at the centre of socialist theory and aspiration."[175] Thompson accused those who started from concepts, not real people—namely, Althusser—of "elitism," "ideology," and "idealism." (History, in Thompson's view, is not "a factory for the manufacture of Grand Theory.")[176] In Althusser's approach, Thompson charged, "the problems of historical and cultural materialism are not so much solved as shuffled away or evaded; since the lonely hour of the last instance never strikes, we may at one and the same time pay pious lip-service to the theory and take out a licence to ignore it in our practice."[177] And it was not only Althusser who received Thompson's critiques: so did British Leftist historians Perry Anderson and Tom Nairn, whose sympathies with other approaches to Marxism Thompson deemed resonant with Stalinist ideologies. Thompson acidly advised these historians to "leave their Parisian journals for a moment and encounter the actual personnel of the labour movement."[178]

Thompson focused on the role of the "experience" of the working class, presumably hoping that this concept would provide an escape from what he deemed Stalinist formalism. His appeal to "experience" (which he later defined as "social being's impingement upon social consciousness,"[179] or "the dialectic between social being and social consciousness")[180] elicited heavy criticism.[181] If to Thompson, French theory's denial of a unified subject reeked of Stalinism, those who had listened to theory from across the Channel deemed *his* position redolent of the "commonsense" approach of British historians who wished to associate Marxism with an appeal to "the real." As Antony Easthope comments, "More than any other academic discourse, the writing of history is the one most contaminated by unexamined Englishness and its ideology of the real."[182]

But more could be faulted about Thompson's appeal to "experience." Perry Anderson, for example, argued that Thompson offered no way to distinguish "valid" from "invalid" experience, and associated "experience" with the very non-Marxist notions of "morality and affectivity," with "lessons" and with "moral examples, to be learnt and handed on for ethical imitation." Since the concept of experience, Anderson argued, carries no explanatory force, it provides limited assistance to an historian. In addition, Anderson deemed Thompson's misconstrual of structuralism's background and of Althusser's own commitments (he was a partisan of Maoist China, not of Stalinist Russia) was shameful for a distinguished historian.[183] Anderson himself ventured a far more knowledgeable and nuanced critique of structuralism and post-structuralism than Thompson.[184]

A trenchant review of Thompson's anti-Althusserian *The Poverty of Theory*, entitled "The Necessity of Theory," was offered by a (then) Althusserian sympathizer, Paul Q. Hirst. Hirst focused on Thompson's unargued assumption that the "experience" of the subject is able to capture "reality." For Hirst, Thompson's appeal to "experience" assumed that knowledge and its object are united in a knowing subject, a unified "Man."[185] "How convenient!" Hirst retorted. "How providential that reality should make the world in empiricism's image and give us confirmation of the fact." The "I," Hirst countered, is "by no means singular or stable (although by no means without effects)"; hence the solidity of "experience" as something the subject possesses is deemed problematic.[186]

More critique of "experience," emanating from different quarters, followed: Thompson had failed to register that experience is a construct devised through the culture and the language available to his working-class people, and although experience may be based on real processes, it does not simply reflect them; Thompson fails to tell readers *how* experience is constructed.[187] Historian Joan Scott argued that Thompson had not registered that "experience" is something that has already been worked over—and, she pointedly asked, why do some people's "experiences" (men's) count for more than those of others (women's)?[188] In light of such critiques, Thompson's retort that "experience" does not wait outside the philosopher's door until invited in, but "walks in without knocking" in the form of death, crises of subsistence, unemployment, and genocide, skirts the intellectual issues raised by his critics.[189]

Eric Hobsbawm

A lack of theoretical engagement also attends the essays of the distinguished Marxist historian Eric Hobsbawm. In the course of his productive career, Hobsbawm delivered numerous public lectures in which he championed the utility of Marx's theories for historians: Marx allows for "subjects" and their agency (Hobsbawm is adamant that Marxist theory does not entail "economic determinism"),[190] and for human progress, measured by the increasing control humans have wrested from nature. For Hobsbawm, Marx is sensitive to "what human beings can do as the subjects and makers of history as well as what, as objects of history, they can't."[191] With its hierarchy of social phenomena (base and superstructure), its acknowledgment of internal tensions within society, and its insistence on the historicity of social structure, Marxist theory better accommodates historical change than do more static structuralist-functionalist models of society. In sum, Hobsbawm is convinced that "Marx's approach is still the only one which enables us to explain the entire span of human history."[192] Here we have, once more, a humanist Marx, unlike the Marx of Althusser.

Like other British Marxist historians, Hobsbawm combines political passion with a wariness of what he calls "'postmodernist' intellectual fashions," characterized in denigrating stereotypes: postmodernism denies the distinction between fact and fiction, holding that "'facts' are simply intellectual constructions."[193] He praises the authors of *Telling the Truth about History* for arguing that "what historians investigate is real,"[194] and Richard Price for "deliberately avoiding references to Barthes, Bakhtin, Derrida, Foucault *et al.*" in his book, *Alabi's World*. Postmodernist approaches, in Hobsbawm's view, have "convulsed and undermined" anthropology-ethnography and (to a lesser extent) history by raising "doubts about the possibility of objective knowledge or unified interpretation, that is to say, about the legitimacy of research as hitherto understood."[195] Historians must defend "the supremacy of evidence" against those who would presumably deny it—those (among others) "who see themselves as representing collectivities or milieux marginalized by the hegemonic culture of some group (say, middle-class white heterosexual males of Western education)."[196]

For Hobsbawm, a major problem with "postmodernist" approaches is their "profoundly relativistic" stance: "if there is no clear distinction between what is true and what I feel to be true, then my own construction of reality is as good as yours or anyone else's."[197] Relativism, he alleges, leaves no room for privileging one account over another. (Hobsbawm's formulation stands close to the caricature mocked by David Harlan, as I described in Chapter 1.)[198] He gives one brief concession to the theorists: "If their [historians'] texts are fictions, as in some sense they are, being literary compositions, the raw material of these fictions is a verifiable fact."[199] Here, the concession to the literary nature of all texts is overridden by the implicit epistemological claim that historians have some (unexplained) means of verifying their "raw material." Hobsbawm seemingly rejects the critique that the "raw material" to which he appeals does not constitute "evidence" until the historian makes it such. Moreover, Hobsbawm clearly holds a different view of what language as a mediating factor means than do post-structuralists.[200]

As this chapter illustrates, even the most celebrated historians of the twentieth century display little concern for the epistemological problems attending the writing of history, and sometimes attack those who even raise such issues for discussion. Although analytical philosophy of history tried, and failed, to contribute a satisfactory theoretical assessment of history's status, and structuralism seemed at best lukewarm (and often hostile) to the claims of history, historians themselves contributed even less to the examination of epistemological issues attending historical work. That task would be left for theorists and more theoretically attuned intellectual and cultural historians, as I detail in Chapters 6 and 7.

CHAPTER FIVE

Narrative and History

Historians in the late nineteenth century, as I observed above, rushed to dissociate their discipline from literature, arguing that while literary and rhetorical structures might supply "aesthetic forms" for historical writing, they did not affect its scientific substance.[1] Some decades later, *Annalistes* and other historians jettisoned narrative as a concomitant of "event history," deeming it suitable only for popularizing amateurs, not for academic historians whose task was analysis. Yet the links between history, narrative, and rhetoric continued to tantalize both critics of the *Annalistes* (such as Paul Ricoeur) and some late-twentieth-century historians who heralded, in Lawrence Stone's celebrated phrase, a "revival of narrative."[2] Such resuscitative efforts, however, were challenged by theorists, among whom Roland Barthes and Hayden White are prominent. These theorists countered that narrative is not a "neutral" form into which content is stuffed, but is ideologically freighted. Narrative, they claimed, serves to impose coherence, continuity, and closure on the messiness of life and of the historian's sources; the historian then smoothes over the gaps and absences to create an "effect of the real." This chapter examines these debates, with special attention to the claims of various analytical philosophers of history, and to Paul Ricoeur, Roland Barthes, Hayden White, and their supporters and detractors. Critique of the ideology embedded in narratives, as I argue in Chapter 8, is a mental tool of considerable assistance in analyzing early Christian narratives written by men.

Narrative at Midcentury: The Anglophone Tradition and Its Critics

Analytical philosophers of history, acknowledging the failure of law-governed theories, turned to narrative as a form they deemed more characteristic of historians' actual practice. "When philosophy of history finally joined in the linguistic turn in Anglo-Saxon philosophy," F. R. Ankersmit posited, "it did so under the guise of narrativism."[3] The interest in narrative was represented in such works as W. B. Gallie's *Philosophy and the Historical Understanding,* Arthur Danto's *Analytical Philosophy of History,* and essays by Louis Mink.[4] It is significant that in the Anglophone world, it was analytical philosophers who encouraged the discussion of narrative among historians, while—as we shall see—in France, interest in narrative in relation to historiography developed under a quite different aegis, namely, that of literary criticism and discourse analysis.

Writing in the 1950s and 1960s, Gallie argued that historical explanation rests on the ability to follow a narrative.[5] The characteristic function of history's stories, he claimed, is to "unstick" problems of understanding and explanation.[6] Critics swiftly challenged Gallie's thesis, noting that *Annalistes* had already denounced the association of history-as-story with "event history";[7] that the ability to "follow a story" characterizes the reading, not the writing, of history;[8] and that historians' attention to social and historical rupture disturbs the coherent unity that history-as-story seeks to present.[9]

Of the analytical philosophers of history, Arthur Danto provided the most comprehensive statement of history-as-narrative. The thesis of Danto's major book, *Analytical Philosophy of History* (1965), is brief: "History tells stories." The historical significance of events, he argued, can be discovered only in the context of a story. Although historians do not reproduce the past, they nonetheless organize it through stories that provide historical significance for events;[10] the scattered bits of "history-as-record" become evidence when they are supplied with a narrative. Danto claimed that stories "explain" insofar as they plot the change of a subject through time, yet he conceded that this nontechnical, everyday form of explanation was not distinctive to history.[11]

To illustrate his claim, Danto cited history books written as grand narratives of the Battle of Hastings and the Thirty Years War.[12] Academic historians, however, retorted that only amateur, not scholarly, histories employed grand narratives. (As Emmanuel Le Roy Ladurie condescendingly put it, narrative history still survives "in our cultural supermarkets," thanks to the mass media.)[13] Paul Ricoeur, celebrated for his own work on narrative theory (elaborated below), deemed the history-as-story approach "naïve" insofar as it remained within the realm of "event history." "It is when history ceases to be eventful," he countered, "that the narrativist theory is truly put to the test."[14]

Philosopher Louis O. Mink's essays pertaining to narrative and history, dating largely to the 1970s, better attended to historians' actual practice. Reaching conclusions similar to Hayden White's, Mink explored how narrative history borrows conventions from fictional narrative and shares the "artifice" of narrative form, while distinguishing itself by its truth claims.[15] Mink sympathized with historians' wariness of narrative: having earlier eschewed covering-law models, they now feared being dragged back "to an old-fashioned and belletristic history, written at the second remove from the sources by novelists manqués."[16] Nonetheless, Mink argued that narrative is not only the historian's natural medium, but is "a primary and irreducible human capacity . . . so primary, in fact, that the real wonder is that the historians were so late in discovering it."[17]

These assessments of the historiographical operation were not widely shared by historians or even by many philosophers of history, although their critiques issued from diverse standpoints.[18] Did not the claim that stories are explanatory stretch the meaning of explanation?[19] Was not narrative tainted by its association with a now-scorned objectivist historiography?[20] Did not narrative history's hidden assumptions and buried causal structures obscure its lack of falsifiability and standards of proof?[21] Why did philosophers focus only on the finished product of historians' work, the narrative "superstructure," when the substance more properly lies in the "infrastructure" of research?[22] How could narrative claim to report things "as they actually happened" when by its nature it both contextualized from a different perspective and imposed a linear structure on simultaneously occurring events?[23] Was not history an "epistemic" (not a "literary") endeavor, whose task is to assess disagreements, not to tell stories?[24]

Annalistes, we have seen, rejected narrative as connoting an "event history" that concerned itself with politics, military exploits, and diplomacy,[25] a history (as Marc Bloch phrased it) that had "grown old in embryo as mere narrative, for long encumbered with legend, and for still longer preoccupied with only the most obvious events."[26] Elaborating this critique, François Furet argued that *Annalistes* deemed narrative "a somewhat lazy mode of writing history" marked by a failure to frame questions.[27] Fernand Braudel simply mocked the enterprise: "The historian is naturally only too willing to act as theatrical producer. How could he be expected to renounce the drama of the short time span, and all the best tricks of a very old trade?"[28] More recently, Jacques Le Goff blamed the media for promoting the history of "the event": this "cadaver"—which ignores the *longue durée,* focuses on politics, delights in anecdotes about "great personnages," and ignores structures—should not, in his view, be resurrected.[29] At best, Le Goff conceded, "event history" might be permitted a "return" if it adopted "a profoundly renovated problematic," an agenda based on problems, open to the social sciences, and not confined to narrative.[30]

Indeed, once the "New Historians" associated with *Annales* were firmly established, they retrieved modes of historiography that had earlier been deemed reactionary, including narrative; Emmanuel Le Roy Ladurie's highly popular *Montaillou* stands as case in point.[31] A more extended defense of narrative emanated from two fronts in the mid- and late twentieth century: on the French side, by literary theorist Paul Ricoeur and historian Paul Veyne, and by historians of various nationalities who heralded its "revival." The nuanced and complex assessments of narrative by Roland Barthes and Hayden White receive fuller treatment below.

Narrative at Midcentury: The French Tradition

Narrative theory in France during the 1960s and 1970s did not develop among analytical philosophers, but among structuralist-inspired scholars of literature who aimed to construct a "poetics" that would "make explicit the system of figures and conventions that enable works to have the forms and meanings they do."[32] Poetics, according to one of its leading proponents, Tzvetan Todorov, is a science that concerns itself not with "actual literature," but with "that abstract property that constitutes the singularity of the literary phenomenon: *literariness.*"[33] Moreover, the works to which French narrative theorists directed their attention were of a far more complex literary structure—for example, Proust's *A la recherche du temps perdu*—than the less ornate, popularizing historical texts from which Anglophone philosophers had drawn their examples.[34] French literary theorists' interest in narrative stimulated its appropriation by such philosophers and historians as Paul Ricoeur and Paul Veyne.

A renowned defender of narrative historiography, Ricoeur largely accepted the premises of a traditional historiography: a pre-structuralist view of language, a commitment to historical objectivism, and an assertion of history's ability to make truth claims.[35] His main target was the then-dominant *Annales* historiography with its emphasis on structure. Such an emphasis, he claimed, detracted from human agency—an unsurprising critique, given Ricoeur's grounding in phenomenology, which focuses on the agency of the individual.[36] In effect, Ricoeur transposed the narrative themes of analytical philosophy of history into a phenomenological framework:[37] "the meaning of human existence is itself narrative," he declared.[38]

History, Ricoeur argued, has a narrative character—indeed, it would not be history if there were no connection to the basic human ability to follow a story. Even those histories that seem distant from the narrative form remain bound to a narrative understanding, since narrativity is the guarantor that the representation "contains" meaning.[39] History from beginning to end lay for him in the recital of a tale.[40] In Hans Kellner's assessment of Ricoeur, narrativity is "that which turns straw into gold."[41]

Moreover, Ricoeur argued that narrative constitutes a form of explanation, not merely of description: this was his challenge to logical positivism and covering-law theory, which he faulted for a reductionist notion of explanation on the model of the natural sciences. Explanation ("why?") and description ("what"?) coincide to the extent that a "narrative that fails to explain is less than a narrative."[42] In this, Ricoeur saw himself as trying to overcome the dichotomy between "explanation" and "understanding" in Dilthey.[43] Ricoeur applauded W. B. Gallie's thesis that understanding history is analogous to following a story.[44] Modifying William Dray's theory, Ricoeur posited that when historians "explain," they are not "placing a case under a law," but "gathering together scattered factors and weighing their respective importance in producing the final result."[45] To these claims, Ricoeur added Louis Mink's argument that historians' conclusions are "exhibited by the narrative order," not demonstrated in a strict scientific sense.[46]

Unlike some analytical philosophers of history, however, Ricoeur untied narrative from the history of events and agents. Claiming that even forms of historical writing seemingly removed from narrative historiography are bound to a "narrative understanding," Ricoeur bravely took as his test case Fernand Braudel's *The Mediterranean and the Mediterranean World in the Age of Philip II.*[47] Even in this resolutely structuralist history, Ricoeur argued, there are quasi-events, quasi-plots (such as the decline of the Mediterranean arena and the shift of history toward the Atlantic and northern Europe) and quasi-characters (not least of which is the Mediterranean itself), which Braudel had worked into a scheme of emplotment. Although narrative and history understand time differently, Ricoeur acknowledged, emplotment in historical writing nonetheless has a chronological dimension and thus shares in the episodic quality of narrative.[48]

Having conceded these differences between narrative and history, Ricoeur claimed another benefit of narrative: it can serve a moral purpose: "to save the history of the defeated and the lost." Narrative helps to redeem the history of suffering. Yet quite apart from this salvific function, he concluded, "[w]e tell stories because in the last analysis human lives need and merit being narrated."[49]

Nonetheless, Ricoeur believed that there is no simple identity between history and narrative. Among their differences is that historians are also concerned with justification. They not only recount, they also try to prove the superiority of their favored explanation and they seek warrants for their claims. Unlike novelists, historians explain by conceptualizing, appealing to universals, making objective truth claims, and addressing readers who, far from suspending disbelief, are "distrustful" and expect authentication of historical stories.[50] Historians, in other words, expect readers to operate with a hermeneutic of suspicion.

Ricoeur's theses on narrative, however, were wedded to a phenomenological philosophy that was roundly attacked by many twentieth-century theorists. Although his phenomenological emphasis on "experience" has been positively understood as a sign of the moral character of his theory,[51] it earned the scathing critique of poststructuralists. J. Hillis Miller, for example, faulted Ricoeur's embrace of phenomenology as committing him to a realm of "lived experience" quite apart from its linguistic construction, and to a copy theory of language. "[W]riting as though structuralism were still the major alternative narrative theory," Miller charged, Ricoeur bypassed post-structuralist critique and the deconstructive forms of narrative theory that were flourishing in his native France in the early 1980s, the very years in which he was writing his magnum opus.[52] In Miller's estimation, Ricoeur's theory of narrative is *passé*.

Ricoeur's focus on narrative was matched at a less philosophical level, but with more deflationary critique, by ancient historian Paul Veyne. As detailed above, In *Writing History: Essay on Epistemology* (published in 1971, but not translated into English until 1984), Veyne attacked the *Annalistes'* infatuation with social science, and positivistic history more generally.[53] He claimed, in contrast, that the discipline with which history can best be compared is literature or literary criticism. The one difference between history and the novel, he argued, is that history relates to "true events" and thus can be characterized as a "true novel."[54]

In Veyne's view, historical explanation depends entirely on historians' organization of their material around plots and description. The facts that will interest them relate to their predetermined plots.[55] Historians, he claimed, create a "deceptive continuity" by bringing coherence to the gaps and absences in the sources—if they even notice such.[56] Moreover, what historians often count as explanation simply depends on a story's being told in a coherent and comprehensible way—a patently unscientific enterprise.[57] Better narrations are simply those that explain more. "History," he concluded, "is what the conventions of the genre make of it, unknown to us."[58] By 1978, under the influence of Foucault, Veyne expressed a revised notion of plot: "the history of the practices in which men have seen truths and of their struggles over these truths."[59] Here, plot is organized around the historicization of practices, not around "natural objects." Discourse analyst Régine Robin especially credits Veyne (and Michel de Certeau) with forcing the question of language on a somewhat reluctant historical profession.[60]

In such ways did a French philosopher (Ricoeur) and a theoretically minded historian (Veyne) argue for history's tight connection with narrative.

A "Revival of Narrative"?

More recently, historians who rejected the structuralist emphases of second-generation *Annalistes* embraced narrative once more, a move some calculated would win back lay readers put off by analytic and quantitative approaches.[61] In addition, narrative historiography, they argued, accorded well with historians' current interests in such topics as disease, death, sex, marriage, work, leisure, and ritual.[62]

The most celebrated defense of narrative among English-speaking historians was mounted by Lawrence Stone, whose 1979 essay, "The Revival of Narrative: Reflections on a New Old History," inspired a protracted debate between and among historians and theorists.[63] Stone's targets were structural history (with its analytical approach and its focus on "circumstances," not "man"), Marxist economic history, French ecological/demographic history, and American cliometric history. The move to narrative, Stone claimed, signaled the rejection of the attempt to find scientific explanations for historical change, and of determinist models of explanation that failed to ask the larger "why" questions. Granted, the "new" narrative history could not simply resurrect traditional modes. Rather, it often focused on the poor and obscure, employed sources such as criminal records, and explored, via anthropological approaches, "symbolic meaning."[64] Although the subject matter, types of evidence, and interdisciplinary influences here differ from those of the "old" narrative history, the epistemological and other philosophical questions earlier put to narrative history went largely unregistered.

Critiques of Stone's "revival" abounded. Some thought that narrative should be left in its grave; others scoffed that since historians—even certain *Annalistes*—had never abandoned narrative, why speak of a revival?[65] Still others asked whether Stone had rested his case on works of history that could not rightly be labeled narratives.[66] Countering the latter point, Hans Kellner argued that even though not all historians write narratives, their histories are nonetheless "founded on a narrativity that guarantees that what they represent will 'contain' meaning."[67]

Compromise was attempted. Peter Burke, for example, argued for an integration of narrative and structural approaches. Conceding that structural historians have shown how poorly traditional narrative history deals with economic and social frameworks and with "ordinary people," he also noted the countercharge leveled by narrative historians that structural analysis is "static" and "unhistorical." Could not a new kind of narrative be crafted, Burke asked, that took account of structural issues as well as the chronological flow characteristic of narrative "event history"? Might not historians devise narratives "thick" enough to deal adequately with structures as well as with people and events?[68]

One popular example of the "revival of narrative" is furnished by microhistory, as suggested in Chapter 4. While rejecting the grand narratives of nation-building and politics, microhistorians argued that narrative is nonetheless indispensable for attending to the "spaces" and internal inconsistencies in documents, to fragmentation, and to plurality of viewpoints—typically post-structuralist emphases.[69] Did not the court depositions and inquisitorial records, so favored by microhistorians, seem themselves to narrate?[70] With its anthropological approach, arresting themes, and detective-story style, microhistory, its practitioners claimed, was just what the historical discipline needed to win back a general readership.[71]

In addition to the critiques of microhistory noted in Chapter 4, a further point needs to be registered: microhistorians' enchantment with anthropology obscures the fact that they deal with texts, not with native informants.[72] Microhistorian Giovanni Levi, for example, claimed that his massive documentary evidence resembled "field research . . . much as if we had been loitering on the central piazza of Santena for twenty-five years, hearing what went on in every family." For Levi, the only significant complication attending his materials stems from their gaps, imprecisions, and obscurities; the historian has no control over the chance selection of the documents that remain.[73] Nowhere does Levi note that the comparison of written documents with face-to-face conversations with native informants might be problematic.

Likewise Carlo Ginzburg, while admitting that archival sources and fieldwork notes differ, dismissed the notion that the literary and ideological character of sources such as inquisition records pose particular problems for historians; of more concern to him was the tendency of archival sources to fragment people's lives, revealing them only at moments of (for example) birth and death.[74] The inquisitors' records he employed (most notably in *The Cheese and the Worms*), he alleged, encapsulated oral speech and thus resembled anthropologists' records; he rued that archival files "cannot be a substitute for tape recorders."[75] Nowhere has Ginzburg registered Dominick LaCapra's point that these documents supplement, not just represent, the realities to which they refer.[76] Ginzburg, who called post-structuralist concerns "trash," claimed that his task was simply to "get the right meaning of a text."[77]

To be sure, more textually oriented microhistorians, such as Natalie Zemon Davis, have been attentive to the ways in which the records themselves are literary.[78] Particularly in *Fiction in the Archives: Pardon Tales and Their Tellers in Sixteenth-Century France,* Davis explored how the literary construction of the pardon tales creates a sense of the real.[79] Throughout, Davis aimed to let the "fictional" elements of the letters of remission stand at the center—thus disavowing the usual historical procedure of stripping away the "fiction" to get at the "facts."[80] Here, Davis hinted, the literary magic performed by the pardon accounts is analogous to history-writing itself as a type of "fiction in the archives." Her attention to sources as texts is a welcome aspect of Davis's scholarship for historians of premodernity.

History, Narrative, and Ideology

Narrative "revived" among some historians only to be challenged from a different quarter, by theorists. The latter, unlike many historians, largely agreed that historical writing was aligned with literature, yet they viewed this alignment as more problematic than did the pro-narrative historians and analytical philosophers considered above. Historical narration, they suggested, is not a neutral genre, but is deeply implicated in ideological construction.[81]

Roland Barthes

Nearly forty years ago, literary theorist Roland Barthes challenged historians to admit that narrative history did not substantially differ from the "imaginary narration" of the novel or drama.[82] It probably was no accident, he claimed, that the novel and history as a discipline, both relying on narration, developed at the same time.[83] Writing in the heyday of *Annales* historiography, Barthes noted with seeming approval history's abandonment of narration and chronological organization and its turn to structures. "Historical narration is dying," he announced, "because the sign of History from now on is no longer the real, but the intelligible."[84] Lending appeal to Barthes's structuralist approach, Hans Kellner suggests, was its "demythologizing power" that raised suspicions of realism.[85] After Barthes's retreat from structuralism in the late 1960s, however, his work found a warmer reception among historians.[86]

Barthes broached his critique of narrative historiography in a now-famous essay published in 1967, "The Discourse of History." Although in historical discourse, Barthes argued, the recipient of the text (the reader) is rarely in evidence, the signs of the utterer or sender (the historian) are more patent—even when the historian has "objectively" vacated his account so that the "history seems to be telling itself all on its own." This "objectivity," Barthes noted, was naively referred to by Fustel de Coulanges as "the chastity of History."[87]

Further, Barthes characterized historical discourse as a form of ideological elaboration insofar as it is the historian who organizes language to fill out an otherwise absent meaning. "Facts" have only a linguistic existence, Barthes argued, yet historians often write as if they were a copy of something situated in an extralinguistic domain of the "real": "what happened" is first seen as external to discourse, but then becomes confused with the historian's narration. For Barthes, historians' accounts are better understood as acts of authority lending credibility to their descriptions. The "realistic effect" of historical discourse, he claimed, is produced by sheltering the "real," never more than an "unformulated signified," behind "the apparently all-powerful referent."[88] Narration, he concluded, is thus instituted as "the privileged signifier of the real."[89]

Barthes elaborated his notion of the "effect of the real" (or "the reality effect") in a second essay published the following year (1968).[90] Building on his earlier work that questioned the neutrality of narration (he had argued that Realist literature is "loaded with the most spectacular signs of fabrication"),[91] Barthes now detailed the subtle ways in which novelists strive to convince readers that "reality" suffuses their works. Pondering Flaubert's description of a sitting room in his short story, "Un Coeur simple," Barthes exmined Flaubert's mention of a barometer, unrelated to the plot and seemingly devoid of meaning (unlike the piano, which signifies "bourgeois culture"). What is the "signification of this insignificance?" Barthes asked—and answered, to communicate a sense of reality. Such details signify nothing, but say "we are 'the real.'" Granted, the ancient literary practice of *ekphrasis* also relied on description, but its details were not intended to convey reality (northern lands could be populated with such fanciful items as lions and olive trees) as are those in Realist fiction. Barthes linked the historical development of the Realist novel (such as Flaubert's) with the advent of the reign of "objective" history, also manifested in such diverse phenomena as photography, journalistic reporting, exhibitions of antiquities, and tourism, and invited historians to contemplate this "time-honored aesthetic of 'representation.'"[92] Barthes's purpose (so Hayden White argued) was "nothing less than the dismantling of the whole heritage of nineteenth-century 'realism'—which he viewed as the pseudo-scientific content of that ideology that appeared as 'humanism' in its sublimated form."[93]

Moreover, with Barthes, ideology critique shifted from its earlier political framework within Marxist, specifically Althusserian, analysis to that of semiology.[94] Yet, as commentators readily observed, it did not shed its Leftist connotations in the transfer. Through an idiosyncratic appropriation of Saussurean semiology—one studded with references to Marx's *The German Ideology*—Barthes wedded linguistic theory to ideology critique.[95] Myth (for practical purposes identified with ideology), Barthes argued, is constituted as a system of signs, whose purpose is to transform "history into nature."[96] In his essay "Myth Today," he "read" a magazine photograph of a Negro soldier in full French uniform saluting. The myth the photo conveys, Barthes posited, is that France is a great nation, that all its sons regardless of color serve her faithfully, that France is not (really) a colonialist power. The photo "naturally" conjures up these associations, "as if the signifier gave a foundation to the signified." A semiological reading of the photograph, Barthes claimed, illustrates how "historical intention" is transformed into "natural justification"—a process that he ascribes to "bourgeois ideology."[97] To his late years, Barthes remained convinced that all ideology critique should rest on semiology.[98]

Barthes's claims were roundly denounced by the practicing historians who bothered to consider them. Arnaldo Momigliano's response perhaps typified their view: history-writing, he protested, differs from other types of literature in "its being submitted as a whole to the control of evidence. History is no epic, history is no novel, history is not propaganda because in these literary genres control of the evidence is optional, not compulsory."[99] Momigliano's contention, in turn, was viewed as reactionary by scholars who by the 1980s had digested the arguments of Hayden White, Paul Veyne, and ideology critics.[100] In John Thompson's explanation of the link between narrative and ideology, stories of the past told by the dominant classes "create a sense of belonging to a community and to a history which transcends the experience of conflict, difference and division"; they "justify the exercise of power by those who possess it" and "serve to reconcile others to the fact that they do not."[101] That history resembled literature was now not merely a comment on style or writing technique; the ideological dimensions of narrative placed it under suspicion.

Hayden White

Hayden White's *Metahistory* (1973) likewise challenged the view that history operates in a manifestly different mode from literature.[102] Reacting to the familiar tag that history is both an art and a science (as White rather acidly put it, mid-nineteenth-century art and late-nineteenth-century social science),[103] and acknowledging that recent analytical philosophy of history had addressed the scientific aspect of history-writing, White opted to examine history as an art, in particular, to explore its linguistic protocols.[104] Designed as a study of four nineteenth-century historians committed to some form of realism (Michelet, Ranke, Tocqueville, and Burckhardt), who are read in relation to four nineteenth-century philosophers of history (Hegel, Marx, Nietzsche, and Croce), *Metahistory* posited that their work culminated in an "Ironic" (and still dominant) historiography, characterized by "skepticism in thought and relativism in ethics."[105]

White believed that his characterization of these works offered considerable specificity: rather than labeling them simply (for example) liberal or conservative, he pried apart and recombined their epistemological, aesthetic, ethical, and linguistic levels to offer a more nuanced description.[106] Implicitly rejecting the structuralist predilection for binaries, White posited that these histories variously combined four modes of linguistic prefiguration (Metaphor, Metonymy, Synecdoche, and Irony), four theories of truth (Formism,[107] Mechanism, Organicism, and Contextualism), four archetypal plot structures (Romance, Tragedy, Comedy, Satire), and four "strategies of ideological implication" (Anarchism, Radicalism, Conservatism, and Liberalism).[108] White presumably imagined that the specificity at which he aimed through his reconfigurations would appeal to professional historians.

Borrowing from literary theorists Northrop Frye and Kenneth Burke, White argued that it is not only the "write-up" stage of historical work in which language plays a role, as historians often claim. Rather, histories contain a deep structural content of a linguistic nature, which provides the paradigm for historical explanation. What kind of story will the historian write: Romance, Tragedy, Comedy, or Satire?[109] The differences in historians' conclusions when working from the same data, White claimed, can be attributed to the different ways in which they prefigure the historical field; these differing prefigurations entail metahistorical presuppositions and varying "strategies of explanation, emplotment, and ideological implication."[110] Moreover—and here White broached a larger historical argument that would be roundly attacked—these tropes distinguished whole modes of historical thought in this period:

> The theory of tropes provides a way of characterizing the dominant modes of historical thinking which took shape in Europe in the nineteenth century . . . For each of the modes can be regarded as a phase, or moment, within a tradition of discourse which evolves from Metaphorical, through Metonymical and Synecdochic comprehension of the historical world, into an Ironic apprehension of the irreducible relativism of all knowledge.[111]

In sum, White claimed that every work of history has embedded within itself a metahistory insofar as the author has already chosen, well before the so-called writing stage, the tropological mode in which the book is to be composed. And this prefiguration is not some incidental embellishment, but shapes the entire narrative from start to finish. Choosing a mode of emplotment consciously or unconsciously commits an historian to a philosophy of history.[112] The historian's interpretation involves a "web of commitments" that constitutes a metahistory; he or she must make an aesthetic choice (of "narrative strategy"), an epistemological choice (of "explanatory paradigm"), and an ethical choice (of how to draw out a representation's ideological implications).[113] Moreover, White implied, it is not only nineteenth-century narrative histories that are amenable to his analysis; so are the narrative devices of *Annalistes* and cliometricians. Narrative's "unfailing ability to make sense out of things, and to present them in a form that seems natural," marks contemporary as well as earlier histories, in Hans Kellner's elaboration of White's theory.[114]

White acknowledged that some contemporary historians (for example, the *Annalistes*) had rejected narrative—but they did so less on theoretical grounds than because of narrative historiography's association with the history of politics and of dramatic events. White puzzled over the grounds of their objection: do they imagine that dramatic events did not happen in history? Or does the fact that the events were "dramatic" for some unknown reason rule them out as a proper subject for historical investigation? The *Annalistes'* arguments against narrative history, White concluded, are "jejune."[115]

Although Dominick LaCapra ventured that "[n]o one writing in this country at the present time has done more to wake historians from their dogmatic slumber than has Hayden White,"[116] historians themselves paid little heed to such acclamations: they objected that *Metahistory* did not concern the kind of historical practice in which they engaged. For them, the work stood as a philosophy of history, extraneous to the real work of historians. (As LaCapra wittily notes, any reference to "metahistory" constitutes "the kiss of death" for "working historians"; it stands as "the nefarious Mata Hari of historiography.")[117] White was denounced as an ahistorical structuralist, and faulted for obscuring the research that constitutes the "real stuff" of history.[118] In part, such objections were prompted by White's overly rigid schema of tropes (Metaphor, Metonymy, Synecdoche, Irony) as linked to historical periods.

Even as sympathetic an analyst as Hans Kellner concedes that White did not satisfactorily resolve his ambivalence about whether the tropes constituted a set of stages of mind's self-knowledge, or "a spatial 'grid' of linguistic possibilities always already inherent in natural languages."[119] (White, however, later retreated—albeit not completely—from linking the tropes to periods of world history.)[120] A second problem Kellner notes is that White's static and overly rigid scheme of tropes implied to some readers a determinism that White himself ostensibly rejected.[121]

Given historians' mistrust of White's emphasis on language,[122] *Metahistory* more often than not was simply ignored. Those unsympathetic to White's project so misrepresented his views—he became the symbol of "nihilistic relativism"—that historians might well feel justified in their disdain.[123] Thus it should not surprise that distinguished historian Lawrence Stone, writing in 1979, thanks another scholar for calling *Metahistory*—published in 1973—to his attention.[124] And, as Roger Chartier admitted, the French felt no compulsion to attend to Hayden White at all[125]—whether one attributes this inattention to the lack of philosophical interest evinced by the *Annalistes,* to the failure of French historians to cross the language barrier, to the predilection of French theorists to work with more complex literary writings, or to the recognition that France had had its own, earlier counterpart to Hayden White in Paul Veyne.

Theorists, too, added their critiques: White had insufficiently elaborated the notion of irony and overplayed its links to realism in nineteenth-century historiography,[126] appropriated the wrong type of literary rhetoric (rather than that used by ancient and Renaissance writers) to illumine his project, misrepresented historians as beginning from an "unprocessed historical record,"[127] abandoned historians' concern for truth claims,[128] and reduced history to texts, omitting contexts, institutions, politics, and other matters to which historians must attend.[129] In the view of Marxist theorist Fredric Jameson, *Metahistory* needed "reintegration into the social history of culture as a whole"—presumably, situated in a more materialist understanding of culture.[130]

Although burdened with an unnecessarily elaborate theory of tropes, *Metahistory* nonetheless raised many issues that, if read in context, might resonate better with both historians and theorists. F. R. Ankersmit summarized why historians should heed *Metahistory:*

> Precisely by focusing on and by problematizing the historian's language, White demonstrates not the impossibility of getting hold of past reality, but the naivete of the kind of positivist intuition customarily cherished in the discipline for how to achieve this goal. More specifically, what these positivist intuitions proudly present as historical reality itself is more a spectral illusion that is created by the historical discipline itself. Surely there is a historical reality which is, in principle, accessible to the historian. But historians have forgotten about this historical reality and mistaken the product of their tropological encoding of the past for the past itself. Within this reading, White, rather than the practicing historian criticizing White, is the realist who reminds us of the difference between reality itself and what is mere intellectual construction.[131]

Hans Kellner suggested another positive feature of *Metahistory:* refusing to privilege either class or libido, White had encouraged historians to look for new theoretical tools. With this refusal of privilege, White had challenged the dominance of Marxist and psychoanalytical interpretations that variously posited stories of "beginnings" (economic infrastructure or unconscious psyche, respectively). In contrast, Kellner argued, White's turn to Nietzsche (famed for his critique of "origins") precluded such appeals.[132] White stands one of the first of his generation to recover Nietzsche—but a Nietzsche whose emphasis on will and human freedom stands in stark contrast to the more pessimistic image of Nietzsche "on sale in modern markets."[133] These emphases, it should be noted, distance White from some poststructuralists, with whom he is often incorrectly aligned. In Kellner's view, White's desire to keep human subjectivity as "the foundation of human intellectual projects" provided the driving force to his work.[134]

In an interview conducted in 1993, White was invited to reassess *Metahistory*. He had aimed, he averred, "to deconstruct a mythology, the so-called science of history." But in retrospect, he readily admitted the book's limitations, advising readers not to take his theory of tropes literally.[135] Without renouncing the ascriptions to his work of "formalism" and "structuralism," White claimed that he now preferred to call himself a "cultural historian" and to describe rhetoric as "the theory of the politics of discourse."[136] Acknowledging that very few praised *Metahistory* at the time of its publication (in addition to its theoretical defects, it was "intimidatingly long, . . . very tiresome, repetitive"), he registered pleasure that a new generation finds it useful for quite different work (he appeared bemused that some students imagine it was written "yesterday"). He confessed how much he had recently learned from Roland Barthes ("the most inventive critic of his time"), Jacques Derrida (who "shows us how to analyze all the kinds of binary oppositions that we take for granted"), Louis Mink (concerning narrative), and Foucault (concerning texts and authors).[137] As White moved beyond *Metahistory*, he took greater care to distance himself from the labels of arch-relativism and nihilism ascribed to him.[138] He clearly distinguished "events" (as something given) from "facts" (as constructed entities).[139] Although inaccessible to us, past events, he claimed, leave their "traces" in the form of documents, monuments, and in present social practice.[140] Would he now consider himself a postmodernist? "No!" was his resolute response. He was no "subjectivist," that is, someone who believes that facts can be manipulated for aesthetic effect.[141] Yet his concessions show how far he had moved from a more narrow structuralism to entertain poststructuralist concerns.

After *Metahistory*, White continued to explore the rhetoric of historical writing, the chief means, he argued, by which a historical work convinces readers to accept it as a realistic and objective account of past events.[142] When in the nineteenth century historians allegedly eschewed rhetoric in favor of "scientific" approaches, he argued, their abandonment of a florid for a plainer style merely signaled a shift in rhetorical registers. They were then forced to bury their rhetorical devices beneath the surface of what they represented as a literal discourse. When the linguistic encoding of historical work was obscured, history could then purport to "serve as a custodian of realism in political and social thinking."[143]

Historians' aversion to White's "tropes" unfortunately obscured some helpful aspects of his work, for example, his explorations of the relation between narrative, ideology, and power.[144] As Ankersmit has observed, by the time that White composed the essays that constitute *The Content of the Form,* the tropes had been almost entirely replaced by "the politics of interpretation" and attention to the ideological function of language.[145] White now defined ideology and its work thus:

> a process in which different sorts of meaning are produced and reproduced by the establishment of a mental set toward the world in which certain sign systems are privileged as necessary, even natural ways of recognizing "meaning" in things and others are suppressed, ignored, or hidden in the very process of representing a world to consciousness.[146]

In these essays, White argued that it was not "merely" a question of the literary forms and tropes that history-writing shares with literature: ideology intrudes as a consideration. Narrative, White insisted, is not "neutral," but "entails ontological and epistemic choices with distinct ideological and even specifically political implications"—implications that often run in socially (as well as intellectually) conservative directions.[147] There is, he concluded, no "politically innocent historiography."[148] He criticized the "revivalists of narrative" for their tacit assumption that narration is a neutral form into which content is stuffed.[149] Narrative, White countered, is driven by the desire to have real events manifest "the coherence, integrity, fullness, and closure of an image of life that is and only can be imaginary";[150] individuals are taught to live "an imaginary relation to their real conditions of existence."[151] Full-blown historical narrative (unlike annals and chronicles) aims "to moralize the events of which it treats," performs this operation especially by providing closure to its story, and allows continuity, not discontinuity, to govern the discourse's articulation.[152] Far from being "merely a form of discourse that can be filled with different contents" and that "adds nothing to the content of the representation," narrative for White "already possesses a content prior to any given actualization of it in speech or writing."[153] White believed that by exposing the origins of historiography in "literary sensibility," he was drawing out the ideological aspect of historical discourse.[154]

Thus narrative, in White's rendition, is inextricably bound to issues of authority: no wonder that dominant social groups have always wished to control their culture's authoritative myths and have championed the notion that social reality can be both lived and understood as a story.[155] White noted that despite their manifest differences, Lévi-Strauss, Lacan, Althusser, Foucault, Derrida, and Kristeva all share the view that historical narrativity is a representational practice "by which society produced a human subject peculiarly adapted to the conditions of existence in the modern Rechtsstaat."[156] Just as the belletristic, narrative style of nineteenth-century historiography contributed to block a more visionary politics,[157] White argued, so the mid-twentieth-century repudiation of narrative suggests a "sickness unto death" with stories invoked by the powers-that-be to justify the sufferings and sacrifices imposed on ordinary citizens.[158] A commentator sums up White's claim: narrative history is "an overwhelmingly political mode of disciplining the past."[159]

From White's essays on ideology, an entire generation learned to reflect on the ways that narrative works to conceal the contradictions in and discords of society by framing a unifying story that emphasizes continuity.[160] Further, cultural critics influenced by him came to agree that narrative serves conservative political ends by justifying "the exercise of power by those who possess it," and by attempting "to reconcile others to the fact that they do not."[161] As Sande Cohen argued, by imposing the form of story on its material, narrative "reproduces a culture of common language, common society, or common reality in the face of uncommon language (codes), class society, and uncommon realities (chasms between cultural worlds)."[162] Far from promoting the claims of literary rhetoric, as his critics charged, White taught Anglophone historians and theorists to attend to ideology's "work."

The Utility of Narrative?

Given the two-fold charge that history is an inferior intellectual enterprise that simply "told stories" and that narrative is ideologically suspect, what useful ends might a "return to narrative" accomplish? Some simply rejected the association made by White and others between narrative and ideology. Louis Mink, for example, questioned whether "narrativizing and moralizing are necessarily or universally linked,"[163] while philosopher William Dray argued that the formal properties of narrative are value-neutral: there is no "'content of the form.'"[164] Literary theorist Barbara Herrnstein Smith similarly rejected the notion that narrative necessarily harbors a repressive political purpose, arguing that storytelling can serve multiple functions: "to reflect reality or to supplement it, to reinforce ruling ideologies or to subvert them, to console us for our mortality or to give us intimations of our immortality."[165] Even theorist Jean-François Lyotard, famed for rejecting grand narratives, defended the telling of "little stories," claiming that people have a political right to a narrative voice.[166] More broadly, some (like Hans Kellner) might argue that any historical study with a thesis has a certain (if reduced) "narrativity" contained within it.[167]

Some historians and theorists deem the debate over narrative to be political, not philosophical—and their views perhaps constitute a different kind of "theory of narrative." By the mid-1980s, for example, Joan Scott could argue that defending narrative had simply become a successful rallying cry for conservative historians who rejected various strands of post-structuralist critique.[168] Likewise Hans Kellner: the debate is "not really over narrative and 'science,'" but "about power and legitimation within the profession, not how best to present or conduct research."[169] Narrative, in effect, had entered the "history-theory culture wars," as described in Chapter 1. The appeal to narrative as a "neutral" form into which content is poured was powerfully critiqued by theorists. Yet, as I argue in Chapter 8, the ways in which theorists called attention to the ideological dimensions of literature are provocative for those who work on premodern texts, the primary aims of which are variously to persuade, exalt, denigrate, and denounce.

CHAPTER SIX

The New Intellectual History

Although intellectual history enjoyed a heady moment in Anglophone historiography, associated especially with the writings of Arthur O. Lovejoy and the founding in 1940 of the *Journal of the History of Ideas,* this "queen of the historical sciences" was presently dethroned by the ascendancy of social and economic history.[1] For two decades and more, social history reigned supreme. By the late 1970s, however, a challenge to its dominance began to emerge in the form of a new cultural history equipped with a theoretical apparatus whose concepts— "*mentalité, episteme,* paradigm, hermeneutics, semiotics, hegemony, deconstruction, and thick description"—might well bewilder many social and economic historians.[2] These theoretical currents, however, have not merely reinvigorated *intellectual* history, but have contributed to its "dizzying" success, as the writings of Michel Foucault, Michel de Certeau, Roger Chartier, and Dominick LaCapra (among others) testify.[3] Intellectual history in this new mode provides a welcoming home for late ancient Christian studies, as for premodern studies more generally. That this revivification of intellectual history alarmed traditional political, social, and economic historians does not surprise. Geoffrey Elton, for example, scorned intellectual history's promotion "from the scullery to the drawing room," claiming that it did not "count" as history since it was "removed from real life."[4] To these more recent turf wars I shall shortly return. First, however, I wish to signal the importance of Lovejoy and of R. G. Collingwood for twentieth-century Anglophone historiography. Despite the ignominy into which their names have fallen—now often invoked to represent everything misguided in intellectual history—I claim that their work, when given a more sympathetic reading, still instructs.

The "History of Ideas": Arthur O. Lovejoy and His Critics

The history of ideas achieved prominence in twentieth-century America under the aegis of Arthur O. Lovejoy. Although some equated the history of ideas with history of philosophy, Lovejoy rejected this identification, arguing that historians of ideas (unlike those of philosophy) *dismantle* systems of thought into "unit-ideas," which are then traced through various eras and disciplines.[5] Which categories or imagery, particular turns of reasoning, or "sacred" words, he asked, were favored by writers within a period or movement?[6] How were "new beliefs and intellectual fashions" introduced and appropriated—and how did old ones lose their power to inspire? How, in particular, did images circulate from one intellectual arena to another, from (for example) English landscape gardening to French and German Romantic literature? Lovejoy prodded historians to explore more than one nationality or language group, and to attend to the less distinguished writers of an era.[7] Long before "interdisciplinarity" became a byword in academia, he argued that no one field could supply adequate answers to a problem: "Ideas are commodities which enter into interstate commerce," he quipped.[8] Although Lovejoy was willing to entertain the "non-rational" as a topic of historical investigation, he nonetheless focused on "thought," best exemplified in his famous study of "the Great Chain of Being."[9]

These seemingly modern desiderata—interdisciplinarity, broader linguistic and international scope, an expanded literary canon—were not, however, themes for which Lovejoy would be remembered: intellectual history was branded as idealist and elitist, oblivious to broader social, cultural, economic, and political currents.[10] His work fell prey to criticism soon after the publication of *The Great Chain of Being* in 1936. He had, critics alleged, failed to register the extent to which present interests govern historians' approach to the past,[11] and had obscured historians' need to decide *which* values of the past were to be sympathetically understood ("the Romans' or the Britons'? the Roman Catholics' or the Protestants'?")[12] He was faulted for flattening out the continuity of "unit-ideas" through time;[13] for "atomistic" assumptions and decontextualized approaches.[14] Some philosophers, alluding to Lovejoy, bluntly charged that historians were intellectually incompetent to expound "ideas" and should abandon the business.[15] Lovejoy's more positive contributions were often overlooked in historians' rush to dissociate themselves from what they perceived as an old-fashioned "history of ideas."

All History as "Thought": R. G. Collingwood and His Critics

R. G. Collingwood—deemed by Bernard Williams "the most unjustly neglected of twentieth-century British philosophers"[16]—provided another stimulus to Anglophone intellectual history. His claim to fame (or infamy) within the profession rests chiefly on his book, *The Idea of History*, delivered in part as lectures in 1936 and posthumously published in 1946.[17] Although, as with Lovejoy, his work is more often noted for its rejection than its affirmation, some aspects of it, I claim, foreshadowed concerns of contemporary intellectual history. Collingwood sharply criticized a positivist historiography that was oblivious to problem-solving, and resolutely championed the notion that historians' present situatedness must be highlighted in their investigations.

Traditionalist historians, Collingwood alleged, consult works that they deem authoritative and, utilizing a "scissors-and-paste" method, stick them together.[18] By contrast, Collingwood argued that all history should be problem- or question-oriented: the historian must ask, what *question* was the writer of the past trying to answer? He deemed his own specialization, the archeology of Roman Britain, particularly deficient in this respect; these archeologists, he alleged, customarily dug at random to see what turned up, rather than framing a problem to be solved. Collingwood labeled such work "pseudo-history," bereft of purpose,[19] and judged "scissors-and-paste" historians as lacking the critical skills requisite for their task.[20]

Collingwood also attacked positivist historiography. Taking its cue from natural science, positivist historiography assumed that history is the study of events inhabiting a "dead past" that await the historian's classification. Positivist historians' claim that they deal with "facts," by which they assume "something immediately given in perception," Collingwood deemed misguided. Although visual perception may be pertinent to certain branches of the natural sciences, he countered, it is not applicable to historians' establishment of "facts." He argued to the contrary that only when events "are no longer perceptible do they become objects for historical thought." Hence Collingwood faulted all theories of history based on analogies with perception[21]—a point later scored by other philosophers and theorists of history.

Like the Italian historian Benedetto Croce,[22] whom he cites with large sympathy, Collingwood believed that the writing of history invited the historian to enter into the minds of past humans, for "mind is the proper and only object of historical knowledge." *All* history, including that of action, is for Collingwood constituted as the history of thought.[23] Historical knowledge he defined as "the knowledge of what the mind has done in the past, and at the same time it is the redoing of this, the perpetuation of past acts in the present"[24]—a definition that demands elaboration.

For Collingwood, actions have an "inside" and an "outside." The "outside" consists of events, the passing flux of bodies and movements; the "inside" comprises the thought lying behind the deed. Historians' explication of an action requires uniting the "inside" of thought with the "outside" of event. Causation, he posited, is located in the mind of the agent, whose thought historians must relive in their own minds[25]—a heavily criticized claim which can, nonetheless, be more sympathetically interpreted.[26] In his autobiography, Collingwood argued for the benefits of this agenda.

For Collingwood, the historian's rethinking of the past does not perform a simple recapitulation, but is always undertaken in the new context of the present, which "incapsulates" remnants of the past. For example, an historian might try to rethink the thought that lay behind the words and deeds ascribed to Lord Nelson at the battle of Trafalgar (namely, "Shall I take off my decorations?"). Such words and deeds, however, are always considered in a different context, the present of the historian, for whom Nelson's answer ("In honour I won them, in honour I will die with them") does not resonate—on the contrary, the historian may rather be pondering, "Shall I go on reading this book?"[27] If historians take contextual change seriously, Collingwood urged, they, as part of the process to be studied, will register how their present standpoints condition their work.[28] Einstein's theories of relativity render philosophical claims about the eternity of problems or concepts "baseless," however often historians conveniently overlook this point.[29] Some of Collingwood's claims, in fact, were deemed entirely *too* presentist by his critics.[30]

Concluding his autobiography, Collingwood revealed the context in which he came to endorse presentism: his unhappy realization of the British government's complicity with Fascism in Spain, Germany, and Italy; official whitewash had duped the British public. Scholars who now—the autumn of 1938—claimed "scientific detachment" from present-day concerns were themselves complicit with Fascism, Collingwood declared; for his part, he would henceforth fight such ideas "in the light."[31] Collingwood's open acknowledgment of his political commitments is a characteristic now vaunted by many contemporary theorists—as are his concerns to develop a problem-oriented historiography and to register the historian's placement in the present.

The New Shapes of the History of Ideas

Lovejoy's grandiose sweep of disembodied ideas through time brought the history of ideas into disrepute with social and economic historians. As I have suggested, their critique entailed an ungenerous reading of Lovejoy's work. Nor should *all* intellectual history be branded with guilt by association, for contemporary intellectual historians have taken pains to dispel the identification of their field with a history that is "idealist," divorced from material reality, and neglectful of context.[32] The new intellectual history, by contrast, explores the material embeddedness of ideas and their relation to power; it acknowledges the historian's present situation and interests.[33] It appeals to climates of opinion, literary movements, ideologies and their diffusion, and to an anthropologically infused notion of culture.[34] Intellectual history's refurbishing, I submit, has been impressive.

Nonetheless, some social historians and intellectual historians of a more traditional stripe remained chary of intellectual history's move to encompass "theory."[35] Richard J. Evans's otherwise moderating book, *In Defence of History,* illustrates the point. Evans's plea that diverse historical approaches should be tolerated gives way to scarcely disguised scorn when he discusses recent currents within intellectual history.[36] Since, Evans alleges, intellectual historians have few texts on which to work (and these rarely augmented by new discoveries), their only option is reinterpretation. Unlike other historians, intellectual historians use their sources "as interpretative vehicles for ideas, not as clues to an exterior reality."[37] Evans faults the recent literary turn in intellectual history,[38] accusing Hayden White in particular of trivializing questions of evidence, overestimating the role of interpretation, and implying that history works on the model of literary criticism. Both White and Frank Ankersmit, in Evans's view, "assert that all the world's a text" and that every historian, in effect, must be an intellectual historian since "text" is all that can be studied.[39] (The polyvalent senses of "text" are explored in Chapter 7.)

Such comments suggest that no armistice has been reached in the "turf wars" among historians. Now, social and economic historians are alleged to be *victims* of theory's onslaught, while (in Evans's view) "cultural history, intellectual history and even the history of high politics have received a fillip from the new theories and approaches of the late 1980s and 1990s."[40] This "fillip," I later argue, is one that has been entirely to the benefit of historians of premodernity.

German Influences

Although French historians and theorists, and those influenced by them, surely are in the forefront of the reconfiguration of intellectual history, I first note some important German contributions.[41]

Although Hans-Georg Gadamer cannot properly be classified as an historian, his theories have decisively influenced not only German, but also French and Anglophone, historiography. Rejecting the assumption that historians can study the past without that engagement reflecting their present situations, Gadamer countered that historical understanding always develops within particular traditions of knowledge that involve presuppositions and "prejudgements" on the part of the interpreter.[42] Appropriating Heidegger's emphasis on the finitude and temporality that mark the human condition, Gadamer argued that the notion of "prejudice" (*Vorurteil,* that is, "fore-meaning") should be rehabilitated by historians to signal that they recognize their own situatedness.[43] (For Gadamer, there can be true as well as false "prejudices,"[44] which stand as "the positive enabling condition of historical understanding commensurate with human finitude.")[45] Gadamer deemed historicism's quest for objectivity a naive illusion that forgets its own historicity.[46] Here, Gadamer cleverly bests historicists, who, while affirming the historicity of everything else they study, fail to register their *own* historicity.[47]

Gadamer argued that scholars, as finite beings, bring their own "horizon" with them in posing questions to texts of the past;[48] human finiteness precludes the illusion that historians' work escapes the mark of their own "present." Since it is the historian who chooses these questions, the process of historical reconstruction always concerns his or her own time. Although historians strive to uncover the views of the past authors they study, their own comprehension nonetheless affects the outcome of their investigation. The writing of history involves a "fusion of horizons" *(Horizontverschmelzung)*, that of the historian and that of the past, both of which are always in motion; the text's "otherness" throws the reader's present into relief, transforming both past and present.[49] In this respect, Gadamer's theory has been compared to Collingwood's notion that the question addressed to the text, which the historian tries to reconstruct, cannot stand entirely within its own original horizon, since this horizon is "always already enveloped within the horizon of the present."[50] Gadamer claimed that his major work, *Truth and Method,* was meant to prove "the constant process of mediation by means of which societal tradition perpetuates itself in terms of linguisticality."[51] Although Gadamer has been criticized for excessively emphasizing tradition and the authority of the past, here it is his presentist concern that stands at the fore.[52] These claims resonate with the views of many contemporary intellectual historians—although his understanding of "text" is grounded in a hermeneutical tradition that many theorists now find problematic, as we shall see in Chapter 7.

A second German contribution, this of the late twentieth century, to a new intellectual history is *Begriffsgeschichte* (history of concepts).[53] *Begriffsgeschichte* strives to remedy the defects of the older history of ideas by attending to how language is used in specific situations and how the meaning of words and concepts is reconfigured by later generations; thus *Begriffsgeschichte* encompasses reception history *(Rezeptionsgeschichte)*.[54] Ideas are here understood not as unchanging constants, but as linguistic entities to be historicized[55]—yet, in contrast to social history, *Begriffsgeschichte* concerns itself primarily with words and texts. Nonetheless, its proponents argue, analyzing conceptual change provides a means for studying the transformation of social conditions, for linguistic concepts and political structures mutually inhere.[56]

In 1996, Reinhart Koselleck, the major theoretician of *Begriffsgeschichte,* completed his monumental eight-volume edition of *Geschichtliche Grundbegriffe.*[57] Koselleck's project aimed to examine "the dissolution of the old world and the emergence of the new [from the eighteenth century onward] in terms of the historicoconceptual comprehension of this process."[58] Insofar as *Begriffsgeschichte* measures and investigates the "differences among or convergence of old concepts and modern cognitive categories," Koselleck argued, it serves as "a kind of propaedeutic for a historical epistemology."[59]

How far this movement accords with a linguistically oriented approach to history has been differently assessed: Donald Kelley envisions *Begriffsgeschichte* as a bridge between the older history of ideas and the new linguistically influenced intellectual history,[60] Gabriel Motzkin takes it to counter "the resolute anti-historicism of contemporary linguistics,"[61] and J. G. A. Pocock posits that it might serve to link German and Anglophone scholarship on the history of political speech and writing.[62] Whether this "bridge" is possible remains in doubt, since surprisingly few Anglophone historians read German,[63] and since even Pocock's approach to discourses fails to reconceptualize texts in a way satisfactory to recent theorists.[64] The "new" French intellectual historians and those who have learned from them, by contrast, are deeply attentive to texts and textuality.

The New History of Ideas in France: Michel Foucault, Michel de Certeau, Roger Chartier

The reinvigoration of intellectual history owes much to French theorists and historians Michel Foucault, Michel de Certeau, Roger Chartier, and to American intellectual historian and literary theorist Dominick LaCapra. Their attention to language and rhetoric, to the gaps and absences in texts, to how difference is created, is instructive for historians seeking to reconfigure intellectual history.[65] Students of premodern disciplines have appropriated many themes from these thinkers, as I later suggest in Chapter 8.

MICHEL FOUCAULT

Classifying Foucault as an historian may seem dubious, both because he resisted all classifications of his work[66] and because historians, viewing him as "anti-disciplinary," often discount his standing in their guild.[67] Even his sympathizers label him an "anti-historical historian."[68] (Foucault once remarked with a touch of sarcasm, "I am not a professional historian; nobody is perfect.")[69] His influence on the reconstrual of intellectual history, nonetheless, has been immense.

Despite the popularity in France of Foucault's *The Order of Things* (1966),[70] many historians found both it and *The Archaeology of*

Knowledge (1969) too schematically abstract, not to mention questionably accurate.[71] What could "a discourse about discourses" possibly mean for historians?[72] What could historians hope to derive from this "most unrelenting offensive against historicist theories of history,"[73] from this structuralist-inspired writer who compared texts as historical objects to tree trunks?[74]

Foucault, however, fashioned himself as a professor of "the history and systems of thought."[75] In *The Archaeology of Knowledge,* he espoused the hope that he had been able to do for the history of ideas what "Bloch, Febvre, and Braudel have shown for history," and suggested that he was perhaps "a historian of ideas after all," albeit a "presumptuous" one.[76] He was not, he elsewhere conceded, so much interested in how ideas evolved as in "trying to discern beneath them how one or another object could take shape as a possible object of knowledge."[77] In *Madness and Civilization, Discipline and Punish,* and the volumes on the history of sexuality, historians found material they could better appropriate for their own projects.[78] In such works, Foucault owned, he had endeavored to write a history of the politics of "truth," linking it to knowledge production and systems of power.[79]

To be sure, Foucault created a *new* history of ideas, an "archaeology," which concerned itself with discourses and the rules that govern them—that is, with the structures of discourse—not with chronology, influence, or authorial creativity.[80] There were rules "internal" to discourse, Foucault argued ("the principles of classification, ordering and distribution"), as well as systems for "the control and delimitation of discourse," systems of exclusion, which function on the "exterior" and concern power and desire.[81] Foucault's work after the *Archaeology of Knowledge* stressed more fully that "discourse" did not mean "language" apart from the situations of its production or its material grounding in institutions and disciplines. This approach he shared with French literary theorists of the 1960s and 1970s who specialized in "discourse analysis"; their explorations of textuality similarly emphasized the materiality of language and the conditions of its production.[82] Foucault's elaboration of "discourse" and "discursive formations" was welcomed by these literary scholars—but not by many historians.[83]

Foucault argued that the older history of ideas had been governed by what he deemed "magical" concepts: influence, crisis, sudden realizations.[84] In their quest for origins and precedents, traditional historians of ideas had worked with "childish" notions of history, "harmless enough amusements for historians who refuse to grow up"—but which had, nonetheless, hampered a proper understanding of the historian's task. History, he argued, should not be construed as a repetition of what the sources "said," but as a discourse that "rewrites."[85]

Two aspects of Foucault's early work in particular alarmed historians: his denial of the referential quality of language, and his attack on "man," often taken to foreclose the writing of history.[86] Yet, as we have seen, twentieth-century French intellectuals who had engaged structuralism—as most Anglophone historians had not—commonly denied the referentiality of language. In *The Order of Things,* Foucault attempted to historicize this development, arguing that already in early modernity, signs and reality, words and things, were seen as incommensurate with each other. Cervantes's *Don Quixote,* "the first modern work of literature," in which "words wander off on their own . . . no longer the marks of things," heralded this development.[87] Later, Foucault's reading of Nietzsche reinforced his view that language, opaque by nature, does not refer.[88] Rather, words seduce us into believing that there are "natural objects" such as "madness" and "sexuality"—but their lure, he advised, should be resisted.[89] And although Foucault's claim that "to speak is to do something" might remind readers of speech-act theory, his qualification—it is always "to do something other than one thinks"—shows that he was operating with quite different presuppositions, ones that deny the transparency of expression.[90]

Nor did Foucault's pronouncements about "man" as "a kind of rift in the order of things," "a new wrinkle in our knowledge," "a recent invention" in European culture, invite historians to join his conversation.[91] Although calling into question "the subject" was common among French theorists of his day,[92] Foucault's pronouncements (such as "[h]umanism is the Middle Ages of the modern era")[93] sounded extreme—or perhaps simply bizarre—to many. "Man," he concluded, emerged only after the fragmentation of language from things; as a recent blip on the canvas of history, "man," following God's demise, would soon expire.[94] His dismissal of "man," with the concomitant eclipse of humanistic history, led some to cry "murder."[95] Historians protested that if "man" does not exist to exert agency, there can be no history. If the "Cartesian ego" were to be toppled from its pedestal, would not the discipline of history meet a similar fate?[96]

The question of "man," Foucault rejoined, like that of "the au-

thor,"[97] constituted an inquiry about the *rules* of the concept's formation and function, that is, it stood as a question about the workings
of language. To those who imagined that he was denying that "people existed," Foucault caustically remarked, "Let us hold back our
tears."[98] By the phrase "the death of man," he later explained, he signaled that the human sciences had never discovered a "human essence": "man" had eluded researchers.[99] He advised historians to
abandon their attempts to "provide a privileged shelter for the sovereignty of consciousness."[100] And in his later work influenced by Nietzsche, Foucault continued to reject the search for origins or for transcendental subjects.[101]

Historians feared that their interest in analyzing change would be
damaged by Foucault's synchronic approach.[102] Foucault, however,
denied that "structure" and "development" need be pitted against
each other in historical analysis. He suggested that historians should
consider transformative ruptures and shifts, rather than "change," so
often associated with models of individual creation, consciousness,
and evolution. He suspected that a political reason informed historians' reluctance to consider his approach to history, but did not specify
what that politics might be; one might speculate that it involved a
conservative embrace of tradition and historical continuity.[103]

Throughout his writings, Foucault focused on gaps, ruptures, and
shifts of meaning. This approach to history, he acknowledged, owes
much to Marx,[104] and differentiates his own work from that of traditional historians of ideas, who more often searched for continuities.[105]
The very purpose of history, he declared, is to seek "to make visible all
of those discontinuities that cross us."[106] He posited that if a way
could be found to introduce into "the very roots of thought . . . notions of chance, discontinuity and materiality," he would be able to
connect his interest in intellectual systems with more traditional historical practice.[107] In this, Foucault stands as heir to historian of science Georges Canguilhem, whose emphases on discontinuity, chance,
risk, and error he adopted.[108] Historians' recent turn from a quest for
continuities to an analysis of rupture and discontinuity is heavily indebted to Foucault.[109]

Likewise, Foucault's interest in "de-familiarizing" past phenomena
jolted the "familiarizing" schemes of conventional historiography.[110]
Study of the past, Foucault argued, reinforces its *dissimilarity* with the
present and assists the recognition of our own historical distinctive-

ness.[111] His approach to history has been variously compared to Cubist painting, which "dehumanizes" the objects of representation,[112] to ethnology with its "distancing" technique,[113] and to Brecht's "estrangement device."[114]

Foucault's challenge to the presumed "naturalness" of such concepts as madness and sexuality has been of signal importance to the reconceptualization of history. How, he asked, did "madness" (for example) come to be understood under the rubric of psychiatry, rather than in the ways familiar in centuries past?[115] Concepts such as madness and sexuality he deemed "metaphysical," and believed they could be categorized differently in other times, places, and practices. (His friend and commentator Paul Veyne provides an example: eating human flesh is called "cannibalism" only in a certain context.)[116] In Roger Chartier's view, Foucault's denaturalization of such objects may well be his revolutionary contribution to history; he taught historians to ask how the subjects they study are constituted by the very way in which these subjects are demarcated and by what they exclude.[117]

Likewise, Foucault prompted historians to explore the conditions of possibility for ways of thought that become dominant in an historical period: what are thinkers of a given era *prohibited* from saying, what is the "unspoken" that attends their writing?[118] Especially in *The Order of Things*, Foucault explored how an epistemological field, an *episteme*, develops.[119] On what basis, he asked, do certain kinds of knowledge arise within various historical eras? His grandiose claim, however, that for any given culture and era "there is always only one *episteme* that defines the conditions of possibility of all knowledge"[120] met with sharp criticism: it provided no explanation of change between *epistemes*, each of which seemed "to emerge *ex nihilo*."[121]

In his later work, Foucault retreated from his structuralist-inspired claim that discourse was a rule-governed system.[122] A heightened concern for practice now emerged in his writings, although, to be sure, he had emphasized even in *The Archaeology of Knowledge* that discourse exists not in some ideal realm, but as a practice linked to social, economic, geographical, and other conditions.[123] The archaeological method was not dropped—it remained useful in highlighting discontinuities and shifts in meaning—but was subordinated to "genealogy," a method that, Foucault thought, gave a better way of dealing with practices. The genealogist, in Hubert Dreyfus and Paul

Rabinow's words, "is a diagnostician who concentrates on the relations of power, knowledge, and the body in modern society," whose task is "to destroy the primacy of origins, of unchanging truths."[124] The genealogist sees at the historical beginning of things not "the inviolable identity of their origin," but dissension and disparity.[125] Connecting nonlinguistic practices with linguistic discourses, Foucault alleged, distinguished *his* approach to history from the older history of ideas.[126]

"Genealogy," a Nietzschean concept, better accommodated the emergence of new forms of power and conflict without enlisting an unchanging transcendental subject, and allowed greater scope for change. As early as his 1970 lecture, "The Discourse on Language," Foucault had signaled the utility of genealogy, which, he then wrote, studies the formation of processes of discourse, and asks about the power that constitutes "domains of objects, in relation to which one can affirm or deny true or false propositions."[127] Now, practices, power, the body come to the fore more prominently.[128] Genealogy's role, Foucault claimed, is to record the history of humanity's "morals, ideals, and metaphysical concepts, the history of the concept of liberty or of the ascetic life."[129] Arnold Davidson explains that whereas archaeology, for Foucault, works with the interdiscursive relations of knowledge, genealogy refers to "the extradiscursive dependencies between knowledge and power."[130] Foucault's turn from "archaeology" to "genealogy" also marked his turn to the body; genealogy's task, he wrote, is "to expose the body totally imprinted by history and the process of history's destruction of the body."[131]

Although Marxists (particularly centering on Foucault's earlier writings) accused him of insufficient attention to material reality,[132] their allegation was sharply challenged by Paul Veyne, who argued that Foucault, "the first completely positivist historian," was truly a "materialist" in that he sought to "eliminate the last non-historicized objects, the last traces of metaphysics." Those who reduce Foucault's highly material history to "intellectual process" have completely misunderstood him, Veyne concluded.[133] When accused by Marxists of "idealism," Foucault retorted that Marxist thought belonged, "like a fish in water," to the nineteenth century.[134] And he stressed that in *The History of Sexuality* volumes, he understood his project to be a "history of bodies"[135]—surely material entities. Moreover, his notion of discourse was intended to link power, knowledge, and institutional

forms; for Foucault, discourse connotes not "language" in some neutral sense, but a "strategic field" that is linked to force and is productive of effects.[136] Yet insofar as Foucault's notion of discursive practice, especially in his earlier works, "did not refer to the activity of a
subject but to the rules to which it was subjected,"[137] Marxists of a
certain stripe might deem his materialism weak.

Moreover, in Foucault's late writings on sexuality and ethics, "the
subject" returned.[138] In these works, he averred, he was concerned to
explore "the relation between 'telling the truth' and forms of reflex-
ivity," that is, how the self is shaped through discourses and practices
that install a particular regime of truth.[139] In lectures given at the
Collège de France in 1982, Foucault discussed "the hermeneutic of
the subject," materials incorporated into *The Care of Self (Le Souci
de soi)*, published in 1984.[140] In these lectures, he explored how the
"self" became an object of intense concern in philosophical writers
of later antiquity. In his later works, Foucault relied heavily on the
framework that Pierre Hadot had devised for studying the "spiritual
exercises" of ancient philosophers; indeed, Arnold Davidson claims
that Hadot was as important for Foucault's later writings as Georges
Canguilhem was for the earlier.[141] Although "man" in the traditional
sense did not "return" in these late writings, Foucault's focus on notions of the "art of living," "subjectivation," "truth-saying," "conversion," and "bio-techniques" surely heralded a resurgence of "the
self."

MICHEL DE CERTEAU

As intellectual historians, both Michel de Certeau and Roger Chartier
are distinguished by their emphasis on the social and institutional
space of historiographical production, including the historian's own
"place" of writing.[142] Both affirm that all historiography implies some
philosophy or theory of history, whether acknowledged or not.[143]
While attuned to theoretical developments in structuralism and post-
structuralism, as "practicing historians" they sought ways to reconfigure history that does not relinquish the "real" of the past.

Michel de Certeau, Jesuit and historian/theorist of early modern
mysticism, is an important voice in this reconfiguration. Unlike idealist historians who privilege their connection with objects of the past,
de Certeau emphasized historians' placement in the present, in relation to the "state of the question."[144] The "essence of the historical,"

he wrote, is "a return of the past in the present discourse."[145] Yet between the present ideas of the historian and the documents, the archival sources, lies an absence, the reality that "no longer is":[146] themes of absence, loss, and death mark de Certeau's work. Far from focusing on "origins," de Certeau argued that historical writing attends to the successive stages of the historian's loss.[147] This loss it tries to deny "by appropriating to the present the privilege of recapitulating the past as a form of knowledge."[148] Like psychoanalysis (a practice with which de Certeau was very familiar), history stands as "a return of the past in present discourse";[149] "[t]he dead souls resurge," he wrote, "within the work whose postulate was their disappearance."[150] Historiography for de Certeau can thus be understood as a form of mourning, a burial rite that attempts to exorcise death through its insertion into discourse.[151] (Christianity, for example, was instituted by the loss of a body—that of Jesus as well as the "body" of ancient Israel;[152] the women who come to mourn at Jesus' tomb [Mark 16:5–7] are confronted with a "lack.")[153] The literary fiction produced by history, de Certeau argued, aims "to deceive death," to veil absence.[154]

Two important themes emerge from these considerations. First, the alterity of the past remains, in that the historical text stands as a semantic operation destined to "speak the *other*."[155] Second, by such emphases, de Certeau signaled that "historiography is a form of writing," not of speech; the "voice" has vanished.[156] Indeed, it is the death of speech, he argued, that authorizes writing:[157] "After Death, Literature," he entitled one chapter.[158] *Writing* is that which produces history.[159]

De Certeau recognized diverse approaches to history. A "less descriptive" history (presumably *Annaliste*), he claimed, "ponders what is comprehensible and what are the conditions of understanding"; here, models and series claim attention.[160] This analytical historiography does not offer itself as "the story of 'what happened,'" but transposes "the real" onto created models.[161] A second type of history, by contrast, seeks to capture past experience, hoping to "revive" the traces of humans now gone.[162] Although Certeau embraced some themes of analytical historiography, he nonetheless favored the "resuscitation" of the dead as an aim for historiography. Unlike his predecessors' attempts to "familiarize" those dead, however, Certeau left them in their alterity. Moreover, countering the anti-narrative stance of analytical history, de Certeau argued that narrative is a "necessary form for a theory of practices" and cannot simply be renounced—even Foucault, he alleged, employed narrative.[163]

Appropriating Foucault's turn to discontinuity as an historiographical *desideratum,* de Certeau posited that the making of history entails the production of difference.[164] Such histories do not offer the reality of the past, he claimed, but serve as a present-day instrument of distanciation by constructing a discourse about the absent.[165] In his view, history's function is to measure deviations—and not just those of the quantitative type with which serial historians work.[166]

How do historians locate deviation? By "prowling" in the margins and on the frontiers, in "zones of silence" such as sorcery and madness.[167] De Certeau's particular margins and zones of silence centered on late medieval and early modern mysticism, a phenomenon that he sought to historicize.[168] His research on the seventeenth-century French mystic Jean-Joseph Surin convinced him that he must abandon any felt proximity between such mystics and himself: what he encountered was, rather, distance. They were to him—even as a Jesuit—strangers and (in a sense reminiscent of Lévi-Strauss) savages.[169] Yet mystics' denaturalizing of language that removes it from the representation of things makes them an interesting object of study for de Certeau in light of twentieth-century philosophy.[170] Apophatic mysticism, de Certeau suggested, should give historians pause that their "cannibalistic" discipline can replicate, let alone better explain, the religious traditions they study. The historian, like the mystic, must remain humble in the face of the Absent.[171] De Certeau here suggests a homology between the mystics' experience of the inaccessible and absent God, and the historian's search for a vanished past—both of which quests resonate with psychoanalysis's "desire for the impossible."[172]

De Certeau emphasized that historians must look to historical *practice* to discover the distinctiveness of their discipline, since historical discourses cannot be understood independently from the practices that produced them.[173] Chief among these is the "split structure" *(structure dédoublée)* of historical writing, constituted by *both* the citation, which displays the research and lends reliability to the historian's work, *and* the historian's discursive narrative, which transforms the quoted elements into something else.[174] "Split structure," de Certeau argued, serves to separate historical writing from "literature," despite their other similarities.

De Certeau underscored other disciplinary conventions and requirements of historical practice, such as the social location of its practitioners in institutions and academies.[175] Groups, not individuals, he argued, produce a disciplinary discourse and the space in which it flourishes.[176] The disciplinary institution also organizes a discourse's silence, that is, disciplines prohibit as well as enable what can be said.[177] Moreover, de Certeau questioned those historians who deemed authorial "place" (including class, race, gender, and religion) irrelevant to the writing of history: is not a different epistemology needed, he asked, than that which assumes that such specifications are irrelevant for the "truth" of a work?[178] To be sure, historical discourse frequently tries to hide all vestiges of "the social and technical apparatus of the professional institution that produces it," camouflaging the real conditions—socioeconomic, institutional, and technical—of its production.[179] As an example, he noted that *Annalistes* who faulted Marxist historiography—and de Certeau learned much from Marxist writers[180]—constructed histories that, socially marked by their own (bourgeois) position, obscured class conflict.[181] Historians, in de Certeau's view, should own up to such deceptions of historiography.

These themes distinguish de Certeau's vision of historiography from those of both Barthes and Foucault. With Barthes, de Certeau posited that history as "manufactured" stands as a performative operation.[182] Likewise with Barthes, de Certeau emphasized the narrative quality of historical writing. Nonetheless, he distinguished historical narration from fiction: there *is* a "real" both of past society and of the historian's operations in the present. Reference to the "real" is not obliterated in historical writing, he argued, even when the latter is no longer organized around the theme of "what happened." In de Certeau's view, Barthes had too readily identified history with fiction; relying on older, narrative works rather than on current histories, he assumed a "univocality of the genre" that ill suited the current discipline. Moreover, Barthes had overlooked the specific practices that establish historical writing in relation to the past it considers—presumably, the "split structure" that provides strategies of accreditation as well as rhetorical elaboration.[183]

In addition, de Certeau argued against Barthes that historical analysis, unlike literature, cannot be separated from the situation of its production. A historical work approaches texts as indications or clues to action, attempting to relate what was said to what was done, to examine the conditions that made the text possible. The historian tries to recreate the process of religious, social, or other economy out of which the work developed and of which it is a "partial symptom." What made possible those traces or products that today remain? What was "the other" that stood as the "condition of possibility" for that which the historian now analyzes?[184] In this way, the historian attempts to learn both "what is no longer" and "what once made possible" these remaining traces.[185] By exploring such questions, historians position their works differently from fiction, whatever the similarities.[186]

De Certeau is no less critical of Michel Foucault, whom he nonetheless greatly admired.[187] The daring of Foucault's attempt "to invent a discourse that can speak of non-discursive techniques," he observed, resembles the nerve of a driver whose car is perched "at the edge of a cliff" with nothing beyond but the sea. Foucault's commitment to a history that explored distance and difference inspired de Certeau, as did Foucault's technique ("micro-technique," in de Certeau's phrase) of first isolating some practices to serve as his historical object, and then, in a second step "turning them over" to shed light on whole systems. Indeed, de Certeau notes the homology between Foucault's own historiographical technique and his discussion of the panopticon in *Discipline and Punish*: from the center all else is scrutinized.[188]

De Certeau nonetheless criticized Foucault's historiographical procedures. More generally, he argued that the human sciences, especially those marked by structuralism, were not as "innocent" as they made out, for they too were conditioned by a philosophy.[189] As for Foucault in particular, he, like the surveyor in the panopticon, cannot be "seen" in his work: he has obscured the research process that established it.[190] He has not enabled his readers to follow how he obtained his results or to situate him as historian/author.[191] Moreover, in *Discipline and Punish*, Foucault had encouraged readers to imagine that disciplinary apparatuses possessed a seamless coherence. In response, de Certeau queried, do not the panoptical procedures serving as "a weapon" against and a control of "heterogenous practices" render the process too "monotheistic"? What became of the "polytheism" of the practices that were warred against, which may have been "dominated but not obliterated"?[192] Luce Giard, an important commentator on de Certeau, here posits that in contrast to Foucault's "pessimism," de Certeau championed the "rising from within of an inventive lib-

erty, productive of a thousand small ruses," whose "micropowers" in-
sert themselves into the interstices of the social order.[193] And, in Wlad
Godzich's view, whereas Foucault was unable to account for the shifts
from one *episteme* to another, de Certeau's careful attention to the
"emergent" and "residual" forces at work[194] provides a better picture
of how hegemonic forms of knowledge established and maintained
themselves. De Certeau, such commentators suggest, provides an excellent model for historians.

ROGER CHARTIER

Roger Chartier's particular historical expertise lies in plotting how
printed texts circulated and were appropriated by different reader-
ships in the early modern and modern eras.[195] In his explorations of
how through time and in diverse social situations readers relate to
texts, he provides a culturally specific approach to the history of reading. What happens to works when they are placed in a different cultural matrix, with different readers, from that for which they were
originally intended? Here, Chartier faults *Rezeptionästhetik* for its alleged neglect of the material forms that embody the text.[196] "Authors
do not write books," he insists—"they write texts that others transform into printed objects."[197]

While acknowledging that social-scientific approaches to history no
longer dominate the field, Chartier nonetheless argues that history
should remain within the social sciences[198]—but with a difference.
The form of social history with which he is concerned might be
reconstrued as "a cultural history of the social." Such an approach
asks how social identities are constructed through struggles over representation.[199]

In Chartier's view, the "new" intellectual history can claim a vener-
able predecessor in early *Annales* historiography, viewed as a protest
against the old "history of ideas" in which ideas were imagined to
float beyond time and space in disincarnate minds, detached from institutions.[200] Yet the later *Annaliste* turn to *mentalités,* Chartier argues, neglected (in a way that cultural history as he conceives it does
not) "the modalities of appropriation," the "processes for constructing meaning," and the "connections among practices and representations."[201] Throughout his writings, Chartier emphasizes the need for
historians to focus more closely on practices, and he lauds those who
do so, such as de Certeau (with whom he shares a special affinity) and
Louis Marin.[202]

Chartier urges colleagues to abandon the dichotomies with which social and intellectual historians have customarily functioned—a too-ready contrast between high and popular culture,[203] production and consumption (especially as relates to reading, viewing, and listening), reality and representation. He would like to erase the distinction between "documentary" and "literary" texts, since *no* text enjoys a "transparent relationship with the reality that it apprehends."[204] Reducing literary works to the status of "documents," he argues, destroys their specificity and ignores the ways in which they transform ordinary discourse and practices.[205]

Chartier, however, resists what he considers too great an emphasis on language (for him, "discourse") in the construction of history. Although he recognizes that the texts on which historians rely are not identical with the event recounted, which is "gone,"[206] and that history shares rhetorical tropes and narrative structures with other "figurative discourses," he aims to link, not collapse, discursive and nondiscursive practices.[207] For Chartier, the logic of practices pertaining to institutions and domination is not reducible to that hermeneutic logic that constructs discourses.[208] Rejecting what he calls "the tyranny of strictly linguistic approaches" among historians, he critiques those (such as Keith Baker) who, in his view, obscure real actions and practices.[209] Chartier, by contrast, insists on the social determination of discursive construction, which "necessarily refers back to the objective social positions and properties external to discourse that characterize the various groups, communities, and classes making up the social world."[210] He faults the "uncontrolled use of the category of text" in the name of preserving the irreducibility of experience.[211] And in a move that would surprise many American scholars, Chartier associates historical writing overly influenced by the "linguistic turn" with America, particularly with Hayden White. In Chartier's view, the "linguistic turn" goes too far in taking language as a closed system of signs, detached from intention and individual control, and understands reality as constituted by language, thus rendering history problematic.[212]

As an early modern historian, Chartier has far more materials at his disposal with which to construct a realm of practice than do historians of earlier eras. Nonetheless, Chartier acknowledges that historians know about practices largely through texts (as emerges in his critique of Robert Darnton for allegedly ignoring the textualization of the practices *he* describes in "The Great Cat Massacre": this debate is examined in Chapter 7). His views on texts in relation to practices, on texts and documents, on the materiality of books, and on reading practices seem relevant to historians of premodernity as well as to those of later eras.

From France to America: Dominick LaCapra

For over twenty years, Dominick LaCapra has advanced and defended intellectual history in a new mode. "If intellectual history is anything," he writes, "it is a history of the situated uses of language constitutive of significant texts."[213] The dominance of social and cultural history in recent decades has, in his view, regrettably led to a denigration of the study of complex texts. Defending intellectual history from charges of its inherent conservatism and elitism, LaCapra argues both that "high" cultural texts often provide revolutionary impetuses to change, and that even seemingly conservative texts can be read against the grain for "radical" purposes:[214] "high culture may itself harbor forces of resistance and criticism that are most effective socially when they connect with aspects of popular culture."[215] In part, he suggests, texts of high culture may retain this critical force because they are incidental to the functioning of the commodity system.[216] Often, he alleges, interpreters of canonical texts "eliminate, domesticate, or radically marginalize" their noncanonical or contestatory features."[217]

Deeply attentive to the "linguistic turn," LaCapra urges scholars not to settle for a smattering of "social science jargon" that merely dresses up "commonsense"—a *New York Review of Books* level.[218] Contemporary literary and critical theory will serve them better: language "is not a purely transparent medium that may simply be looked through (or bracketed) in the interest of (re)presenting the object or findings of research." Although the "linguistic turn" troubles the work of historians, LaCapra concedes, attention to its themes would warn them not to approach the object of their study "in a purely objectified manner, and provide unproblematic, 'sun-clear' reports about its nature," nor understand language as merely "instrumental."[219]

The model of the historian's work that accompanied the earlier professionalization of the discipline, LaCapra argues, assumed that he or she gathered and analyzed archival information, a process different from "reading and interpreting texts or textualized phenomena."[220]

Documentary-style historiography of this type "tries to exclude interpretation or to see it only in the guise of bias, subjectivity, or anachronism . . . [I]t strives for an unchanging representation of changing 'particulars' that would itself transcend the historical process."[221] The documentary approach, LaCapra alleges, is grounded in a positivism that has been roundly attacked by post-structuralist thinkers such as Derrida and Foucault; it represents "a reductive equalization of all texts and artifacts into a homogeneous body of documentary 'information.'"[222]

The documentary approach that reigns supreme in history, in LaCapra's view, "diverts attention from the way 'documents' are themselves texts that 'process' or rework 'reality' and require a critical reading that goes beyond traditional philological forms of *Quellenkritik*." Reading texts as if they were "simply sources of information"—as most professional historians do—leads LaCapra to question, acidly, whether historians are even trained to read. Their approach fails to recognize texts as "important events in their own right" and to ask the more "'rhetorical' question of how texts do what they do."[223]

Thus the argument sometimes advanced by social and economic historians that *they* work on "documents" giving access to "the real," unlike "texts" of a more literary nature, should be rejected: *all* historians, in LaCapra's view, work on texts.[224] To be sure, there are different sorts of texts: documentary approaches attempt to situate "the text in terms of factual or literal dimensions involving reference to empirical reality and conveying information about it," while "worklike" texts supplement reality "by adding to or subtracting from it," and thus bring into play, in a way that documentary approaches do not, "the roles of commitment, interpretation, and imagination."[225] Still, they are all "texts."

The documentary approach to sources—even literary and philosophical sources—taken by the majority of historians, LaCapra argues, contributes to the marginalization of intellectual history. Attempting to adjudicate the dispute by blandly proclaiming that "history has many mansions" fails to palliate, since "social history tends to occupy many of the mansions and intellectual history a number of the shacks."[226] Just as social and economic historians sometimes denigrate intellectual history, so LaCapra labels the work in which many historians engage, "grubbing in the archives."[227]

Certainly, LaCapra affirms, the task of gathering and analyzing information and testing propositions is one that historians across sub-disciplines accept as a given. His objection is rather to the model of "reading" here in play—a model that he thinks might better be called "the denial or repression of reading," in which the historian takes context as decisive and relegates texts to subordinate status.[228] Against this model, LaCapra urges intellectual historians to abandon the notion of "context" as "a simple explanatory concept," and rather to ask how texts and contexts come into relation with each other.[229]

There is no reason, LaCapra argues, why rigorous research and the striving for accuracy should not be coupled with the recognition that "language helps to constitute its object, historical statements depend on inferences from textualized traces, and the position of the historian cannot be taken for granted." Such concerns should not be dismissed as appropriate only for metahistorians. In no way does a concern for language compromise the demand for exhaustive research, a "thorough knowledge" of the relevant secondary literature, and "meticulous care" in documenting one's claims.[230]

Once research is coupled with the reading and interpretative practices that LaCapra advocates, the distinction between "documents" and "texts" would largely collapse: "[d]ocuments would be read textually, and the manner in which they construct their object in an institutional and ideological field would be a matter of critical scrutiny, while the documentary dimensions of texts would be posed as an explicit problem and elucidated." To take cues from deconstructionist reading practices that invite suspicion of contextual reductionism, to note carefully "the important resistances to meaning and the internal contestations or tensions in texts," in no way diminishes the necessity for careful work.[231]

Nor does the adoption of such reading practices obscure "reality." Here, the admonition of LaCapra's critic, James T. Kloppenberg, that intellectual historians (and LaCapra in particular) should not "lose sight of the importance difference between Emma Bovary's fiacre ride and Rosa Parks's bus ride,"[232] seems beside the point: no one, certainly not LaCapra, is "losing sight." Derrida's famous claim that "there is no outside-the-text," in LaCapra's interpretation, does not "eliminate all meaning or reference," but rather situates it "within a network of instituted traces."[233] It rejects an appeal to a "'context' outside the text that escapes involvement in such a network of traces."[234] And Derrida's notion of dissemination that encourages readers to "rewrite" a text, raising up submerged possibilities that authors underexploited or failed to explore, should stimulate historians to read more creatively—although historians will doubtless continue to distinguish "what may be ascribed to the past and what is being added in the present."[235]

LaCapra's conception of the intellectual historian's task, I posit, provides a helpful charter for the reconsideration of early Christian history; his approach to "text" is considered further in Chapter 7. In that chapter, I turn to a set of questions that confronts contemporary intellectual historians in particular: what constitutes a "text" and how do "text" and "context" relate in contemporary discussions of history? Intellectual history's celebration of "texts" stands to benefit studies of premodernity whose remains are often constituted by high literary and philosophical texts that invite analyses informed by contemporary theory. The specificity of such texts, I argue, needs to be preserved against those who would "textualize" the nontextual world *and* those who would imagine that we transparently locate practices "as they really were" in texts. On this model, premodern studies might rejoin a refurbished intellectual history.

CHAPTER SEVEN

Texts and Contexts

What, indeed, is a text?—an entity that once had an assuring solidity and concreteness, indeed a kind of identity that allowed it to serve as a model of whatever was comprehensible in both culture and nature. What happened to that text that used to lay before the scholar in a comforting materiality and possessed an authority that the "context" in which it had arisen and to the existence of which it attested could never have? Where is this context which literary historians used to invoke as a matter of course to "explain" the distinctive features of the poetic text and to anchor it in an ambience more solid than words? . . . The text-context relationship, once an unexamined presupposition of historical investigation, has become a problem . . .[1]

Thus did Hayden White, writing in 1982, signal the problematic status of text and context in recent theory. While historians, unlike White, have largely operated with a "precritical" concept of text (solid, concrete, authoritative)[2] and have assumed an easy differentiation between texts and contexts, they have also often insisted on the distinction between "texts" (the more literary sources on which most intellectual historians work) and "documents" (the data of social, political, and economic history). Differentiating texts from contexts, and "texts" from "documents"—not pondering revisionary notions of "text" in literary theory—historians might insist, is the proper territory of the historian.[3]

These traditional assumptions, as White suggests, have been called into question by recent debates troubling literary and political theory, interpretive anthropology, and history.[4] What might Derrida mean by his aphorism, "there is no outside-the-text," or Quentin Skinner and J. G. A. Pocock by their notion of *context* as linguistic? Should cultural phenomena such as rituals and festivals be seen as "texts," as Clifford Geertz posited? Do written texts constitute an extension of oral discourse? Or do "text" and "context" signal not entities in themselves, but simply different ways of reading? What, at the end of the day, might count as a text—or as a context?

This chapter surveys the reconfiguration of notions of text and context by mid- to late-twentieth-century theorists across the human sciences, with a special focus on literary theory, contextualism in the disciplines of political theory and history, and interpretive anthropology. To be sure, historians may reasonably object—and have so objected—that *their* texts are not profitably subjected to the minute literary scrutiny appropriate to (for example) symbolist poetry. Yet, I would argue, there is much to be learned from recent discussions of writing—and its institutional embeddedness[5]—concerning the productive quality of texts, their intertextual references and multiple meanings, their aporias, gaps, and contradictions. Such considerations give pause to an overly quick appropriation of Skinner's and Pocock's contextualism and Geertz's "world-as-text" model, or of an easy assumption that texts merely constitute an extension of oral speech. Scholars of premodern texts, I argue, would benefit from registering theorists' critiques of such claims.

Literary Theorists and the Text

"Text" was already a matter of discussion among structuralist literary theorists, who (as I signaled in Chapter 5) developed the notion of "poetics" to deal not with the content or interpretation of literary texts as a whole, but with types of discourse, literary genres, and modes of enunciation—an exploration of *how* texts do their work, *how* they achieve meaning. Over the years, some structuralist theoreticians moved in directions we would now call post-structuralist. Gérard Genette, who pioneered structuralist literary theory and narratological criticism in France, provides a good example of this transition. In his recent work, Genette redefines "poetics" to mean "transtextuality," "all that sets the text in a relationship, whether obvious or concealed, with other texts."[6] Borrowing the notion of "palimpsests" (in which "on the same parchment, one text can become superimposed upon another, which it does not quite conceal but allows to show through") from scholars who study ancient and medieval manuscripts, he explores different ways in which texts transform or imitate other texts. The process by which older writings are launched "into new circuits of meaning" he describes as a form of bricolage, which makes "new things out of old." Genette defines his revised approach as "open structuralism," by which he indicates his focus not on the internal relations of a "closed" text, characteristic of early structuralism, but on texts in their relation to each other.[7] Other theorists, as we shall see, emerged as "post-structuralists" in varying ways.

Roland Barthes, Jacques Derrida, and Julia Kristeva, among others, understand texts as "tissues of quotations"[8] ("citations, references, echoes, cultural languages . . . antecedent or contemporary . . . cut across [them] through and through in a vast stereophony"),[9] as dialogues among various "voices."[10] Positing that all texts are supplements, "substitutive chains" of allusions and references to other texts with which they interact,[11] Derrida argues that there is no pure originary text that has not been "touched" by other texts.[12] Text, he claims, is "no longer a finished corpus of writing, some content enclosed in a book or its margins, but a differential network, a fabric of traces referring endlessly to something other than itself, to other differential traces."[13] Insofar as reading can be understood as a form of rewriting, Derrida calls it a "disseminating" activity that, following "the logic of the supplement,"[14] "adds to" as well as "substitutes for" what is read.

Rejecting earlier critics' desire to uncover a text's unity and harmony, these theorists, by contrast, explore the ways in which texts incorporate within themselves seemingly contradictory and heterogeneous elements, aporias, and "splicings" that trip readers up so as to invite a more complex reading; here, the very notion of "interpretation" is reinterpreted. Also abandoning older assumptions of authorial intention and creativity, such theorists view texts as "productive,"[15] enjoying autonomy and power in their own right.[16] As John Mowitt puts it, "[t]ext thus becomes a way of naming what a certain model of reading produces when it approaches texts (in the 'precritical' sense) as though the discourses which comprise them obstruct as much as facilitate expression."[17] The product of the reader's interaction with the text that evokes multiple meanings these writers call "textuality."[18]

Roland Barthes, for his part, famously distinguished "work" from "text": the work is something that can be held in the hand, contained within the covers of a book, while the text is "held in language." While the work is monist, Barthes quipped, "the text could take as its motto the words of the man possessed by demons (Mark 5:9): 'My name is Legion: for we are many.'"[19] Especially in disciplines such as scriptural exegesis in which "theological monism" has reigned supreme (that is, where a single interpretation has been deemed correct and authoritative), the new construal of text calls for a fundamental change in the understanding of reading: readers, "collaborating" with the text, themselves become in effect writers.[20] Barthes viewed readers as the "space" that holds together the allusions constituting the text,[21] "producing" rather than "consuming" it, disentangling rather than deciphering it, "liberating" it from any one fixed meaning.[22] To look to "authorship" as the decisive clue to meaning, he argued, is misguided in that it constitutes an attempt "to impose a limit" on the text. Writing, by contrast, in its refusal to assign an ultimate meaning to the text, is an "anti-theological activity," for "to refuse to fix meaning is, in the end, to refuse God and his hypostases—reason, science, law." Barthes's aphorism, "A text's unity lies not in its origin but in its destination,"[23] signals with elegant economy the shift in emphasis from the author to the reader in contemporary literary theory. Barthes mocked traditional literary criticism with its devotion to "objectivity," "good taste," "clarity," its "deafness to symbols," and its assumption that the subject is a "solid whole."[24] He called rather for a new science of literature, one in which language itself would be the subject, and in which he would no longer have to bear the critics of his day who could not tolerate "that language should talk about language."[25]

Just as the notion of text has here been revised, so has the notion of author. Whether one proclaims "the death of the author" with Barthes, or asks, with Michel Foucault, "What Is an Author?,"[26] much late-twentieth-century criticism questions the assumed authority of writers and the discernibility of their "intentions"; such assumptions, theorists now claim, served mainly to limit and circumscribe a text's meaning. To conceive of the author as "the eternal owner of the work," Barthes argued, makes readers into "simple usu-fructaries."[27]

In an early and much-cited essay, Foucault asked, "What Is an Author?" When and how did the "authority" of a work become linked to "authorship"? Whereas in early antiquity, the anonymity of epics and other works did not stand against their celebration, in later times, when authors circulated in a "system of property," the ability to identify an author who "owned" a text served to validate its worth. With this shift, the "author-function," as Foucault called it, changed. Now, readers sought to identify—or construct for themselves, in Foucault's view—a rational being called an "author," to whom motives, creative powers, and designs could be attributed.[28] He proposed that the attempt to discern an author in order to assign "authority" to his work began in the early Christian period. As an example, Foucault cited Jerome's catalog of Christian writers, *On Illustrious Men,*[29] observing that Jerome, in order to discern the authorship of a text, formulated the same questions that later literary critics put to the texts they explored: for example, is the work of the same quality and style as the author's other known works? Are the teachings of this text in agreement with views that the author posits in other works?—and so on. Yet a distinctive feature of early Christianity's authorial assignment, Foucault wryly noted, was the "saintliness" of the presumed author: sanctity was the decisive characteristic that lent credence to an author's work.[30]

Today, instead of asking who the real author is, and with what authenticity or originality does he or she speak, Foucault rather asked, "What are the modes of existence of this discourse? Where has it been used, how does it circulate, and who can appropriate it for himself? What are the places in it where there is room for possible subjects? Who can assume these various subject-functions?"[31] Just as Foucault believed that "man" was an elusive entity who had escaped his pursuers, so "the author" appeared not so much as an identifiable human whose temporal and geographical placement, motives, and intentions were crucial to a work's interpretation, but as a "function" that granted authority to writing.

Such theorists also challenge the customary differentiation of text from context. For Derrida, whose critique of contextualism will be considered at length below, that "there is no outside-the-text" implies that the text is no longer a "snug airtight" entity unto itself.[32] Countering numerous misinterpretations of his phrase, he insists that, far from suspending reference, it "embraces and does not exclude the world, reality, history."[33] He had never wished, he claims, "to transform the world into a library by doing away with all boundaries."[34] (Thus to object that "the world is not made up of printed words" quite misses Derrida's point.)[35] To the contrary, challenging common assumptions about reference should not suggest that there is "*nothing* beyond language . . . Deconstruction is not an enclosure in nothingness, but an openness towards the other"—including the "other of language." It asks *why* we read a literary text in a particular way, inviting readers to explore the hidden philosophical and political assumptions that inhabit institutionally sanctioned ways of reading, to open themselves "to the search for that which remains absent and other than oneself."[36] "Outside" and "inside" are here called into question.

Yet another thinker who contributed to a reformulation of the notion of text is Paul Ricoeur, who argued that discourse itself is an "event": "something happens when someone speaks."[37] He acknowledged his early interest in speech-act theory, so popular in Anglophone philosophical circles in the 1960s and 1970s.[38] In an influential essay of 1971, Ricoeur explored the ways in which "meaningful actions" might be viewed as "texts." Do not events, like texts, "leave marks"? Do not actions have social dimensions that become detached from the agent to carry on a life of their own, and do they not have relevance beyond the immediate situation of their enactment? Are not actions—like texts—"addressed" to a large audience that gives them ever new interpretations? The model of reading, Ricoeur posited, offered a good paradigm for the social sciences, providing a new approach to earlier debates, especially associated with Wilhelm Dilthey, about the relation between "explanation" and "understanding."[39] The application of the notion of "text" to phenomena of the nonlinguistic world, as we shall see below, is a primary characteristic of Clifford Geertz's interpretive anthropology.

Derrida and Gadamer: Deconstruction and Hermeneutics

Another aspect of Derrida's approach to texts emerged during his encounter with Hans-Georg Gadamer, staged in Paris in 1981. As noted earlier, Gadamer in *Truth and Method* (1960) strongly faulted historians' reliance on authorial intention as a "seduction of historicism";[40] since historians can never "repristinate" a text to its original meaning, he advised them rather to explore its *Wirkungsgeschichte* ("effective history") and the possibilities it opened for the future.[41] If uncovering the author's meaning were the quintessence of interpretation, he asked, how could so many competing ones co-exist?[42]

Nonetheless, Gadamer at the same time claimed (somewhat contradictorily) that there was a "clear hermeneutic demand" for a text to be understood in terms of the situation in which it was written. Moreover, in both *Truth and Method* and in his encounter with Derrida, Gadamer posited that hermeneutics takes as its model the notion of "conversation" between reader and text.[43] Claiming that the "essence of language is conversation," Gadamer defined hermeneutics as "the art of grasping what someone has really wanted to say."[44] The German tradition of *Geisteswissenschaften* (broadly, the human sciences) in which Gadamer stands, commentators note, has customarily employed an "intentional hermeneutics."[45] Elsewhere, Gadamer wrote that the "culminating form of human social life . . . in its final formalization is a speech community."[46]

In the Gadamer-Derrida debate—misnamed, since Derrida curtly replied to Gadamer that his entire paper was problematic[47]—Gadamer argued at length that texts were meant to be readable, to be understood without difficulties; moreover, he posited, understanding required a forgetfulness of language. In the midst of his lecture, however, Gadamer abruptly cut short this line of argument, insisting that these claims did not apply to the *literary* text. The latter differs from ordinary texts, he now asserted, in that it does not refer to spoken words; in it, language itself comes to the fore. Even here, however, Gadamer characterized the literary text with such words as "sonority," "melody," "sound"—all features of speech, not of writing.[48] But earlier, in 1967, he had argued that in writing the audience remained so remote from the author "that the art of grasping the sense of the text takes on the character of autonomous production"[49]: a view that, although not Derridean in its claim that there is "a sense" embedded in the text, nonetheless accords more productivity to the text.

Derrida's critique of Gadamer's usual elision of writing and speech—characteristic of the German tradition of hermeneutics—centers on its association with the phenomenological notion of a prereflective "lived experience," which Derrida deems a "metaphysical" concept.[50] (Indeed, in *Truth and Method,* Gadamer had claimed that his goal was to illustrate "the linguistic nature *of the human experience of the world.*")[51] Insofar as both structuralists and post-structuralists rejected the phenomenological appeal to "experience" (assumed as something transparently given, not "always already" touched by interpretation), Derrida's critique does not surprise. Elsewhere, while acknowledging Heidegger's influence on his own philosophical formation, Derrida denied that he had ever shared the philosophical commitment to the "phenomenology of presence."[52]

That the linguisticality *(Sprachlichkeit)*[53] central to Gadamer's hermeneutics is based on the model of speech—an association consonant with Gadamer's phenomenological predilections—is, to Derrida, one of its major faults. Derrida elsewhere argues that privileging voice over writing presumes the simultaneous presence of speaker and listener to one another, whereas writing assumes the absence of the author, an absence that necessarily renders equivocal the text's meaning.[54] Even in speech, Derrida asks, does one ever know, as Gadamer so easily surmises, that one has been "perfectly understood"?[55] Moreover, as Derrida elsewhere insists (and as I shall presently discuss), there are multiple contexts in which written words can be understood, making more complex the relation of text to context.

Commenting on the debate, Fred Dallmayr offers an admittedly schematic characterization: Gadamer is aligned with "understanding, immanence, continuity, and truth" (characteristics valued by the tradition of hermeneutics), and Derrida with "non-understanding, rupture, and artistry" (traits commonly associated with post-structuralism). Dallmayr partially attributes this disconnection to the "different Heideggers" that were appropriated by Gadamer and by Derrida. Gadamer (befitting his hermeneutic allegiances) focused on the early, existentialist Heidegger of *Being and Time* who analyzed "being-in-the-world" *(Dasein),* while Derrida favored, in addition, works of the later Heidegger, in which "meaning" and "being" had become problematic concepts—and in which Nietzsche loomed large.[56]

Derrida's extended critique of the elision of speech and writing, however, appears in his debates with speech-act theorists, to be considered below.

Contextualism

More broadly, contextualism refers to historians' customary appeal to the explanatory force of extratextual political, economic, and social phenomena; more narrowly, it is associated with the work of political theorist and historian Quentin Skinner and historian J. G. A. Pocock.[57] Although Skinner and Pocock investigate context in a way that privileges the linguistic, their notion of "linguistic" rests on a model of speech that entails different assumptions than those held by the literary theorists discussed above. Although Skinner's and Pocock's attention to linguistic context inspired a new approach to intellectual history, its utility for students of premodern texts, I believe, is diminished by this model.

Quentin Skinner

Quentin Skinner is an historian of the early modern and modern periods, whose work on political theory investigates the linguistic conventions attending the determination of meaning and the argumentative uses of ideas as "weapons" or "tools" in the social and political vocabularies of particular historical periods.[58] The scholar's task, he argues, is to locate the world of thought available to authors in their time and place, to extract the "intellectual treasure" that reveals the questions, values, and contexts of the past.[59] Skinner rejects the notion that political theorists address perennial problems (none such exist), ideal types, or unchanging unit-ideas, for such assumptions reduce the "radical contingency" of intellectual history and render it agentless, as if "ideas get up and do battle on their own behalf."[60]

Three aspects of Skinner's work are of particular importance for my argument. First, borrowing from speech-act theory, especially as developed by J. L. Austin,[61] Skinner takes speech (not writing) as his linguistic model. In his late works, he argues explicitly against a Derridean claim for the precedence and peculiarities of writing, on the grounds that the types of writing *he* analyzes are forms of dialogue and hence are modeled on speech.[62]

Second, Skinner stresses the importance of contexts in determining the meaning of texts. Yet context for Skinner does not always lie in the realm of the social and economic, as many social historians assume:[63] he privileges linguistic, generic, and ideological contexts, attempting to ascertain the range of meanings that particular words would have conveyed to people of the society in which the text was produced.[64] Appropriating philosophers' appeal to the "rational acceptability" of beliefs, he investigates what was considered "rational" for someone at a particular time and place to accept.[65]

Third, Skinner believes—despite his registering of contemporary theoretical debates—that authors' intentions can be extracted from their texts. An author's intention, he argues, means his intention *in* uttering a statement, which can be inferred from "inside" the work itself.[66] In later essays, Skinner refines his point: he does not refer to the *meaning* of a text, for texts may contain meanings that their authors did not intend. He rather asks what "authors were *doing*" in writing their texts:[67] where is the "linguistic action"?[68] In most situations, Skinner claims, unearthing the original intention of statements is relatively unproblematic—after all, even dogs can understand humans' intentions![69]

These three assumptions—that writing is simply an extension of speech, that contexts are readily discernable, and that authorial intention is usually unproblematic to locate—would be challenged by poststructuralist theorists, to whom I shall return below.

J. G. A. Pocock

J. G. A. Pocock, historian of the laws, institutions, thought, and historiography of early modern and modern England,[70] works from similar assumptions, while eschewing some of Skinner's stronger theses. His field of study he describes as composed of speech-acts and the conditions/contexts in which they were performed.[71] Twentieth-century linguistic philosophy's claim that language should be seen as a product of history, he posits, "subverted" traditional political philosophy—a "subversion" that leads him, like Skinner, to question whether the traditional canon of political philosophy ever possessed the internal coherence it is often thought to have.[72] Pocock, again like Skinner, argues that language itself serves as a context,[73] and that speech is the primary form of linguistic reference; texts are, in effect, verbal performances.[74] Pocock, however, engages different conversation partners from Skinner's: Kenneth Burke,[75] structural linguistics,[76] and Thomas Kuhn, with whose help he recasts "political thought" as "the exploration and sophistication of political languages."[77]

While agreeing with Skinner that the interpreter's task is to "present the text as it bore meaning in the mind of the author or his contemporary reader,"[78] Pocock nonetheless rejects the notion that readers can always decipher authorial intention.[79] With the assistance of extratextual data, Pocock postulates, scholars form hypotheses about texts concerning the "(1) intentions and actions [the author] may have performed without our noticing them at first reading; (2) intentions and actions he may have performed without noticing them himself; (3) intentions and actions he might have performed but did not; and (4) intentions and actions he could not possibly have performed or tried to perform."[80] These qualifications pry free from an easy decidability of authorial intention, and resonate with recent interest in the "unsaid" of a text or culture. Linguistic "translations" from one time, place, and idiom to another, Pocock argues, may make authorial intention unclear: later readers function in a situation in which "the matrices, idioms, and languages [of the original text] have been modified." Indeed, Pocock goes so far as to claim that the most interesting acts of translation in interpretive traditions are anachronistic.[81]

Although Skinner's and Pocock's attention to the historical nature of language and its particularity, to the uses of language in argument, and to its "translation" into different historical contexts should stimulate historians' reflection, several of their assumptions—especially Skinner's—have met with sharp criticism.

Critiques of Contextualism

Mark Bevir

Critiques of contextualism issue from different quarters. Philosopher Mark Bevir identifies himself as a postanalytic anti-foundationalist "modern idealist," although his anti-foundationalism is situated in the tradition of analytical philosophy, not of post-structuralism;[82] he openly positions himself against "post-modern sceptics."[83] Bevir faults conventionalists for confusing *meanings* of statements (a hermeneutic category, always concrete, specific, and particular) with the "what is said"—a distinction that audiences, he claims, unproblematically register[84]—although Bevir (unlike Derrida, for example) believes that hermeneutic meaning rests mainly on the author's intention.[85] If, as Skinner and Pocock assume, meaning is dependent upon linguistic convention, how can they account for linguistic changes or for unconventional uses of language? How, on Skinner's theory, could someone (like Mrs. Malaprop) use a word in an innovative way?[86] Is it not rather the case that people often fail to follow linguistic conventions, whether deliberately (as might a creative writer) or inadvertently? Questions of meaning, Bevir concludes, are always individual and intentional, not "conventional."[87]

Dominick LaCapra and David Harlan

Intellectual historians similarly challenge contextualist assumptions, not only Skinner's and Pocock's, but those of historians more generally. Among these critics is Dominick LaCapra, who argues against the adequacy of "contextualization" for historical understanding and explanation.[88] Although historicisms both old and "New," he posits, rely on contextualization as explanatory (as in Geertzian "thick description") and place a premium on its exhaustiveness,[89] they fail to explain *how* historians select the contexts they find pertinent, a task that becomes more problematic for the distant past.[90] The claim that *one* set of contexts is essential must be argued, not assumed, since the notion "that any one or any set of these 'contexts' provides a fully unified framework of interpretation that constitutes a univocal 'key' to the meaning of a text" is highly dubious.[91] Moreover, LaCapra urges historians to ask how a text relates to, transforms, or "reworks" the contexts of its production and reception.[92] Such investigations must be kept to the forefront if context is not to become "a facile pseudo-explanation."[93] In particular, LaCapra fears that contextualism's elision of "great works" with lesser ones diminishes their distinctive character and their ability to *contest* ordinary assumptions, to subvert tradition.[94]

LaCapra critiques Skinner's and Pocock's version of contextualism in particular. He aims first at their appeal to authorial intentions, arguing that newer notions of "text" rule out a "proprietary relation between the author and text," "a unitary meaning for an utterance."[95] Abandoning quests for intention, interpreters should rather explore both the "unthought" of a tradition with Heidegger, and deconstructive reading practices.[96] LaCapra questions whether Pocock's self-proclaimed allegiance to theory runs very deep, insofar as he constantly resorts to contexts of speech;[97] and his suspicion is heightened by Pocock's self-description as a "working historian," since such a historian is committed to reconstructing (not deconstructing) the past.[98]

Historian David Harlan endorses LaCapra's critique of contextualism. Praising Pocock as "the most theoretically sophisticated of practicing historians," Harlan nonetheless claims that both he and Skinner lapse into a "textual fundamentalism" that short-circuits the focus on language to which they are committed.[99] Their interest in the text becomes "purely instrumental," reducing complex texts to mere tokens and documents.[100] Contextualists, Harlan alleges, fail both to acknowledge the difficulty of precisely defining a linguistic context and to register that there is no context that has not already been textualized.[101] Relying on speech-act theory, which assigns chief importance to the context of utterances and assumes that language is relatively transparent, that authorial intention is decisive, and that writing is merely "a sort of frozen speech," leads contextualists astray. Like Martin Luther, they try to dive back through layers of interpretation to ascertain authorial intention: "a Protestant proposal," Harlan suggests. Indulging in some biblical (and Derridean) playfulness of his own, Harlan urges historians to recognize "[t]hat every text, at the very moment of its inception, has already been cast onto the waters, that no text can ever hope to rejoin its father, that it is the fate of every text to take up the wanderings of a prodigal son that does not return." Mindful of their own presuppositions and "prejudices," Harlan suggests, historians might better look to the "effective history" of texts.[102]

Jacques Derrida

Perhaps the most famous critique of contextualism, and one that doubtless influenced LaCapra and Harlan, was offered by Jacques Derrida in his essays on speech-act theory, "Signature Event Context"[103] and "Limited Inc a b c."[104] Contexts, Derrida argues, can never be absolutely determined or "saturated"; the "arbitrariness of the sign" disrupts this certainty.[105] Moreover, the peculiarity of the written sign lies in its *break* with its (original) context; it is "readable" even if the circumstances of its production and authorial intention remain unknown.[106] Determining a context for a text, in any event, is never a politically "neutral, innocent, transparent, disinterested" act nor a "purely theoretical gesture"; it is only a question of *which* politics is implied in its determination.[107] To believe that a reader must locate one particular and exclusive context in order to understand a text, Derrida concludes, is itself a "metaphysical assumption."[108]

So eager is Derrida to correct misunderstandings of his own position regarding context that he goes so far as to translate "il n'y a pas de hors-texte" as "there is nothing outside context." Deconstruction, he claims, can itself be construed as "the effort to take this limitless context into account, to pay the sharpest and broadest attention possible to context, and thus to the incessant movement of recontextualization."[109] Replying to critics who accuse him of holding that context is "always and only *verbal*," Derrida comments that "'there is no outside-the-text' signifies that one never accedes to a text without some relation to its contextual opening." Rather, "[a] deconstructive understanding of history consists . . . in transforming things by exhibiting writings, genres, textual strata (which is also to say—since there is no outside-the-text, right—exhibiting institutional, economic, political [and so on] 'realities') that have been repulsed, repressed, devalorized, minoritized, delegitimated, occulted by hegemonic canons."[110] Arguing that historians (and others) should rethink the text–context relation, Dominick LaCapra concludes that Derrida's famous phrase *also* implies that there can be no separate "inside-the-text," no autonomous realm of linguistic signification.[111]

To illustrate the difficulties of according contextualism an explanatory force, Derrida analyzes that "undecidable" sentence, standing alone in quotation marks amidst Nietzsche's unpublished manuscripts: "I have forgotten my umbrella."[112] What is it, Derrida asks: "a citation? the beginning of a novel? a proverb? someone else's secretarial archives? an exercise in learning language? the narration of a dream? an alibi? a cryptic code?" and so on.[113] Undecidability, however, does not mean that we cannot make *some* determination among possible interpretations;[114] undecidability need not leave the reader with *no* context.[115] Nonetheless, Derrida concludes, Nietzsche's sentence illustrates "the poverty of hermeneutics," which assumes that original meaning is unproblematically retrievable.[116]

Second, Derrida argues, writing should not be considered merely one species of communication—"at least in the limited sense of a transmission of meaning."[117] To posit, as speech-act theorists do, that writing simply "extends" oral or gestural communication, implies that there is "a sort of *homogeneous* space of communication." This assumption Derrida contests: writing cannot be assimilated to the model of speech. It is not just a *simple* absence or distance between sender and receiver that marks writing, as is often supposed; there is an *absolute* absence. The written communication must be repeatable even if there is *no* receiver or sender: "For a writing to be writing it must continue to 'act' even when the author is not present." This, to be sure, decisively cuts writing off from authorial consciousness, "from the father."[118]

Theorists such as Austin err, Derrida claims, in imagining speech-acts only as acts of communication, which require a conscious, intentional, speaking subject from whom no "residue" of meaning escapes. While Austin admits that "infelicities" may mar the communicative process—that the intention of the speaker might not be conveyed to the receiver—he believes that such occasions are "negligible." Derrida counters: can "infelicity" simply be labeled an "accident" if it is *always* possible?[119] (In his debate with John Searle, Derrida wittily asks: if, as Searle claims, he has "misunderstood" Austin, what does this imply about speech-acts?)[120]

A third characteristic of writing that Derrida emphasizes is its "iterability," and argues that performative utterances in speech (such as words customarily pronounced in marrying or in launching a ship) assume their force from a characteristic that they share with writing.[121] By "iterability," Derrida signals not just "repeatability," but also the possible "alterability" contained even within any *one* such instance of writing or speech: from numerous possibilities, readers or listeners select what they believe the sentence/statement might mean in context—as in the case of Nietzsche's umbrella—but their choice does not preclude other possibilities.[122]

These Derridean claims are helpfully elaborated by commentator Geoffrey Bennington. First, he notes, since readers can read in more than one context, attempting to single out the one and only "correct" context, identified with the author's original intention, is misguided. Insofar as no context is ever really closed, the reader could indefinitely posit disparate contexts for sentences such as "I have forgotten my umbrella." Since writing by its very definition is read in a context different from that of the writer, the issue of a work's "origin" decreases in importance. For Derrida, as for other post-structuralist writers, an appeal to authorial intention (even if it were recoverable) settles nothing about a text's meaning, since "every demand to put things back into context is already interested and cannot be neutral." As for readers who claim to take the text "in itself," do they not notice that by their very act of reading they have first extracted the text from its supposed original context and then reinserted it?[123]

Thus contextualism both broadly and narrowly construed, I suggest, appears inadequate as a model of historical explanation and interpretation. For scholars of "high" philosophical and literary texts such as those of early Christianity, whose precise original contexts are often a matter of sheer guesswork, appeal to context as explanatory has definite limitations—although, I concede, perhaps not so many as Nietzsche's famously indecidable sentence might suggest.[124]

Textualism in Interpretive Anthropology and Its Critics

Clifford Geertz: The World as "Text"

What counts as a "text"? Let us aim in a different direction. In the work of Clifford Geertz, much appropriated by historians of religion,[125] "text" serves as a code for interpreting practices, actions, and rituals in the "real" world. "Arguments, melodies, formulas, maps, and pictures," Geertz writes, "are not so much idealities to be stared at but texts to be read; so are rituals, palaces, technologies, and social formations."[126] Somewhat unaccountably, Geertz does not necessarily appeal to the written texts of the literate cultures he studies: as Benedict Anderson notes, in Geertz's 1960 classic work on Indonesia, *The Religion of Java,* he presents his subjects as if they were denizens of a nonliterate society, despite the millenium-long literary tradition of Javanese civilization.[127] Geertz's thesis that culture may be approached as a text lent heightened importance to "texts," while luring textually oriented scholars to don the exotic guise of anthropologists.[128] To be sure, Geertz was not the only proponent during the 1960s and 1970s of considering nonliterary phenomena as "texts"; recall philosopher Paul Ricoeur's attempt to do so, as described above. Thus Geertz's interest in exploring culture as a "text" had its counterpart among scholars in other disciplines.

Convinced that anthropology could (and should) not emulate the criteria operative in the natural sciences, Geertz proposes an interpretive mode of construing anthropology characterized by "thick description."[129] The "culture of a people," he claims, "is an ensemble of texts, themselves ensembles, which the anthropologist strains to read over the shoulders of those to whom they properly belong."[130] He compares ethnographic fieldwork to reading manuscripts, and ethnographers to exegetes, translators, and iconographers.[131] The "hermeneutic circle" is as relevant to ethnographers, Geertz argues, as it is to "literary, historical, philological, psychoanalytic, [and] biblical" scholars.[132] Some interpretive anthropologists, ruing historians' "shallow" appropriation of literary theory (limited to "a narrative perspective"), envisioned that literary theory might have a more significant impact on their discipline.[133]

That this appropriation of "the literary" has little in common with the linguistic models informing structuralism, Geertz makes abundantly clear.[134] In his view, structuralism constitutes "a sort of high-tech rationalism," a "new intellectualism" whose orientation he deems "hyper-logistic." We do not need a "new cryptography," Geertz posits, but an interpretive science that "can determine the meaning of things for the life that surrounds them."[135] Lévi-Strauss, he alleges, views aspects of culture not as "texts to interpret," but as "ciphers to solve."[136] "Thick description" based on careful ethnography, not the codification of "abstract regularities" (his characterization of Lévi-Strauss's work), should be the discipline's goal.[137] Geertz openly declares his skepticism regarding structuralism as a "research program" and his "outright hostility to it as a philosophy of mind."[138] When anthropologist William Roseberry observes that "Geertz takes his lead from Ricoeur rather than from Lévi-Strauss,"[139] he signals that Geertz follows a hermeneutic, not a structural, model.

Nonetheless, Geertz's assessment of Lévi-Strauss softened over the years, as two of his essays, written some twenty years apart, attest ("The Cerebral Savage: On the Work of Claude Lévi-Strauss"[140] [1967] and "The World in a Text: How to Read 'Tristes Tropiques'"[141] [1987]). In "The Cerebral Savage," an analysis of La Pensée sauvage and Tristes tropiques, Geertz faults Lévi-Strauss's structuralist dissolution of "man"; his pretensions to "High Science"; his turn from the study of "customs, beliefs, or institutions" (the usual arena of the anthropologist) to "thought." With high sarcasm, Geertz alleges that since Lévi-Strauss failed to achieve in Brazil the anthropologist's aim of "physical closeness and intellectual distance" with his subjects, he settled for what perhaps "he always really wanted—intellectual closeness and physical distance." "What a journey to the heart of darkness could not produce, an immersion in structural linguistics, communication theory, cybernetics, and mathematical logic can." In the end, Geertz concludes, Lévi-Strauss is an heir to the "universal rationalism" of the French Enlightenment; Rousseau, not Saussure, is his true guru.[142]

Eighteen years later, Geertz continues to fault Lévi-Strauss's "fastidious mandarinism."[143] Still hostile to structuralism, Geertz now more generously predicts that Lévi-Strauss's "work will survive [its] dissolution." He acknowledges that Lévi-Strauss developed a "new language," a semiotic reading of culture that could be employed across a variety of disciplines; he had "cleared an imaginative space" for others to inhabit.[144]

Nonetheless, their "linguistic turns" took different models: Lévi-Strauss inhabits the aesthetic tradition of Baudelaire, Mallarmé, Rimbaud, and Proust (*Tristes tropiques,* Geertz suggests, stands as a counterpart to *A la recherche du temps perdu*),[145] while his own "interpretive turn" looks to Shakespeare, Dickens, and Dostoevsky.[146] Among literary critics, Northrop Frye and Kenneth Burke emerge as Geertz's heroes.[147] His interest in the realist novel resonates with his desire to speak about "experience," social "reality," and "lived life."[148] Does not Geertz resemble traditional literary critics who aim to locate "the unruly meanings of a text in a single, coherent intention," asks James Clifford?[149] The model, in other words, tilts towards Dickens, not Flaubert.[150] Moreover, Geertz's appeal to experience aligns him with phenomenology, a philosophical approach that structuralism (and post-structuralism) aimed to dethrone.

Yet—and important for my larger argument—despite Geertz's approbation of a hermeneutic model for anthropology, it is not literary (that is, written) texts that stand behind his claim: it is speech and therefore a model of proximity and presence—and this despite Geertz's ostensible rejection of the dialogical model of ethnography that sticks close to the speech of anthropologist and informant.[151] Behind, or under, Geertz's appeal to texts there is an appeal to speech, albeit less explicitly acknowledged by Geertz than by Skinner and Pocock.[152] By gaining access to their cultural worlds, he writes, anthropologists seek to "converse" with their subjects.[153] In cautious moments, Geertz labels the fieldwork experiences "text-analogues," a term he claims to adopt in order "to quiet the literal-minded."[154] One wonders if he did not also sense that his notion of text differed notably from that of modernist and post-structuralist literary critics.

For Geertz, anthropological analysis involves not only "sorting out . . . structures of signification," but also "determining . . . their social ground and import."[155] His choice of word—"ground"—is not accidental: for Geertz, language does not float free, or merely relate to other texts, but refers to behavior in a "real," experienced world. Signifiers are to be socially contextualized; symbolic systems, he argues, can be deciphered only by studying behavior and events, for it is through social action that "cultural forms find articulation."[156] Thus for Geertz, anthropological interpretation is "reading"—but a reading of "what happens."[157] Geertz's "texts" remain rooted in everyday realities open to human "experience."[158]

Moreover, the symbols that ethnographers "read," Geertz argues, are publicly available.[159] (With Wittgenstein, whom he acknowledges as one of his masters, Geertz affirms that there is no such thing as a private language.)[160] The "natural habitat" of signs is "the common world in which men look, name, listen, and make."[161] Geertz seeks not "inaccessible interiorities," "but what is made publicly manifest and embodied in words, lives and works."[162] He eschews "hermetic" theories that isolate meaning from practice.[163] In sum, it is society that gives life to signs and symbols;[164] "local knowledge"—not Lévi-Strauss's universal structures—remains the key.[165] The particularity of "local knowledge," however, does not always square with Geertz's phenomenologically grounded appeals to experience and symbol systems that presumably humans share.

Critiques of Geertz and Interpretive Anthropology

Although Geertz's textual model appealed strongly to some humanists, it fared less well with anthropologists and theorists; their critiques, nonetheless, centered on different points. Some anthropologists worried that a "textual" approach would render realist writing impossible and would lead to disciplinary paralysis.[166] Others, working in the period when Gramscian and Marxist analyses flourished, attacked Geertz as inattentive to issues of power, political and economic structures, social differentiation, and exploitation; he had detached "culture" too cleanly from its social, political, and economic grounding.[167] (Pierre Bourdieu asked whether Geertz transformed social connections into communication connections.)[168] Despite the importance of such critiques, I wish here to focus elsewhere, on Geertz's textual model.

Geertz's "text/reading" model of interpretation involved larger questions of representation that rendered it easy prey for philosophers, theorists, and literary critics who suspected that he harbored positivist and objectivist notions of reality: does not (asks Graham

Watson) Geertz presuppose "a reality which obtains prior to and independently of his descriptions of it" and fail to register that facts themselves are products of interpretive procedures?[169] Similarly, James Clifford observes that the Geertzian model of "reading" was based on "the persistence of an ideology claiming transparency of representation and immediacy of experience." This "ideology has crumbled," Clifford declares; ethnography "is always caught up in the invention, not the representation, of cultures." Anthropologists should ask of the ethnographies they read, "How was 'objectivity' textually constructed?"[170]

An exuberant critique of interpretive anthropology is offered by literary theorist David Chioni Moore, who urges anthropology to "cut its (pure-)theory angst . . . and learn to love, at least in theory, interpretation." By "interpretation," however, Moore does not signal the Geertzian variety, which attempts to preserve "the reassuring notion of a transcendental real." The ethnographic realism practiced by most anthropologists, he argues, is simply their disciplinarily particular version of Barthes's "the effect of the real." Given the depth of anthropology's investment in "an objective real," renouncing this investment may be more difficult in anthropology than it was in literary studies, Moore concludes, where "objectivism's death" was "generally greeted with a sigh of relief."[171]

Geertzian Anthropology and the Historians

To be sure, historians writing before Geertz's "interpretive turn" also appropriated anthropology for their work.[172] Natalie Zemon Davis, for example, bridged to good advantage the older functionalist anthropology and the new interpretive ethnography.[173] Interpretive anthropology based on a textual model, however, provided new impetus to this appropriation. Yet Paul Rabinow's wry observation in 1986, that historians were eagerly assimilating Geertz's approach just at the time when anthropologists themselves were questioning it, is telling.[174]

William Sewell Jr.'s *Work and Revolution in France: The Language of Labor from the Old Regime to 1848,* published in 1980, provides an illuminating example of interpretive anthropology's strong appeal for historians. Sewell, a historian of the French Revolution, described his own intellectual evolution: he had been trained as a labor historian to employ quantification and other social scientific techniques, but gradually realized that these approaches gave no access to the *language* of the workers who allegedly "made" the Revolution. Intellectual historians, to be sure, studied language, but they looked to authors (often to ones with developed biographies) and their intentions—an individualistic approach unhelpful for studying collective movements. An anthropological notion of "culture" appeared to provide a better model. In Geertz's writings, Sewell found inspiration for investigating the "language of labor," taking "language" in an extended ("Geertzian") sense to mean "institutional arrangements, ritual gestures, work practices, methods of struggle, customs and actions that give the workers' world a comprehensible shape."[175] Sewell's book electrified the field. Thus it is interesting that for his book published fourteen years later, *A Rhetoric of Bourgeois Revolution: The Abbé Sieyes and "What is the Third Estate?"* which investigates the ramifications of an important literary treatise of the Revolutionary era, Sewell found rhetorical analysis and deconstructive reading practices the most helpful allies.[176] The change of "mental tools" appropriate to a different kind of project—one that examined a "high" literary text—is significant. As I suggest in Chapter 8, since scholars of late ancient Christianity have no data of the sort that Sewell and other scholars of modernity possess, but work almost exclusively on "high" literary texts, the reticence some have exhibited in the face of literary theory is surprising.

Given Geertz's concern for "groundedness" and the "local" quality of knowledge, the paucity of his writings about history *per se* is striking—fewer than those of the allegedly anti-historical Lévi-Strauss, whose view of culture Geertz takes to "annul history."[177] Anthropology, Geertz notes, encouraged historians to abandon their focus on "Kings, Thinkers, Ideologies, Prices, Classes, and Revolutions," and promoted a near-obsession with "charivaris, dowries, cat massacres, cock fights, and miller's tales."[178] Although Geertz claims that there is an "elective affinity" between the two disciplines in their concern for other times and places,[179] the historical approaches that he *rejects* are more readily ascertained than those he favors. He obliquely eliminates Collingwood's approach: anthropologists cannot replicate the feelings or thoughts of anyone else. And the familiar slogan of historians, "the past is another country," he deems irreversible: "another country is quite definitely *not* the past." Such considerations should discourage too easy an identification of interests between history and anthropology.[180] Moreover, the "ecology of learning" has changed, Geertz claims, so that France ("Europe") is no longer the "feeding ground" for historians, while Samoa ("the foreign") supplies the anthropologist: the anthropologist may now explore what is closer to home, and the historian what is more distant. Yet what the two fields continue to share is "the enmeshment of meaning in power" in studying (for example) "the role of symbolic forms" in the construction of the state.[181] These references, however, seem surprisingly few, given the enormous impact of Geertzian interpretive anthropology on the discipline of history. The trade balance appears uneven.

Despite the wide appropriation of Geertz by historians, with whom "thick description" appears to resonate, their critiques nonetheless abound—and from different quarters of the profession. Some fear that historians could too easily appeal to Geertz's textual model to bolster their anti-theoretical tendencies. How ironic it would be, Ronald G. Walters exclaims, if Geertz's chief contribution to historians was to assist them "in creating a kind of old-fashioned ethnographic museum, in which text after text piles up, parts catalogued without a sense of the whole."[182]

For historians, such as Lynn Hunt, who champion the centrality of social theory for historical work, Geertz's "textualization" appears as an "aestheticizing move" that endangers the autonomy of contexts.[183] Although historians readily appropriated Geertz's discursive model of culture, she argues, they took from his work merely the *forms* (such as of festivals and rituals) as ends in themselves, rather than as materials useful for the construction of new social theory. Would historians, Hunt asks, be able to elaborate a general social theory from Geertz's virtuoso reading of culture? The task seems near impossible, for "the more 'thickly described' an event is, the less susceptible it is to being integrated into a generalizable story about cause and effect" that would enable the connections between the social and the symbolic realms. Geertz's attempt to disengage himself from economic and social reductionism through a turn to culture offers no satisfactory model for historians.[184] The burden of Hunt's critique appears to be that Geertz has not preserved "the social" as a contextual realm distinct from and external to the text. Microhistorian Giovanni Levi likewise doubts whether an approach to history that rests on the circular procedure of hermeneutics really explains contextual change.[185]

The New Intellectual History and Geertz

Dominick LaCapra's assessment of Geertz's work is mixed. He acknowledges the utility for historians of Geertz's focus on "the problem of meaning and symbols" and rejection of "crude sociological reductionism." Geertz's "nonreductive emphasis upon the interpretation of symbolic practices has marked a clear advance in the understanding of culture," LaCapra asserts.[186]

This said, LaCapra levels his critique: Geertz's insistence on the autonomy of symbolic forms may lean toward a "precritical idealism"; a stronger dose of ideology critique is needed.[187] A sharper critical edge might derive from a nonfoundational approach to discourse and practice that recognizes the difficulties of "translating" between contexts.[188] In LaCapra's opinion, a Derridean notion of "text" as "a network (or interweaving) of relations among instituted 'traces'" would serve intellectual historians better than Geertz's appeal to "text" or "text analogues."[189]

Roger Chartier likewise challenges the Geertzian model of "text." He warns historians "to guard against unconstrained use of the category of the 'text'—a term too often inappropriately applied to practices (ordinary or ritualized) whose tactics and procedures bear no resemblance to discursive strategies."[190] Historians, Chartier argues, should attend more closely to written texts, querying how readers of different social classes variously appropriate and understand them.[191] They also should focus on how reception shifts the meanings of texts, how works produced within a certain field with its own conventions "escape that sphere and take on a certain density in their pilgrimage."[192]

Intellectual/cultural historians such as LaCapra and Chartier thus call attention to the idiosyncrasies of texts, especially those of "high" culture, and urge a clear differentiation between such works and those practices that Geertz views as "texts." Historians who do not attend sufficiently to these distinctions are the targets of their critique, as the following example illustrates.

Geertzian-Inspired History: Massacring Cats or Texts?

An example of Geertzian-inspired history on which several critics focus is Robert Darnton's essay, "The Great Cat Massacre."[193] Darnton analyzed the symbolic meaning of the "massacre" of many cats by a group of journeymen printers in Paris around 1730 (a "prank" that scarcely clothed their deep anger over degenerating labor conditions), here appropriating anthropological notions of symbol and culture to support his argument. Historians' critiques of Darnton's approach varied, reflecting their own disciplinary positions.[194]

Some social historians, for example, faulted Darnton's inadequate handling of context, a defect allegedly stemming from his dependence on Geertz. Thus Giovanni Levi, warning historians against "Geertzismo," criticized Darnton's work for its reliance on the "hermeneutical circle," an approach that Levi claims obscures context and renders it "immobile." Small episodes, meant to betoken larger cultural attitudes, are inserted into the unchanging context: the symbolism of the cats, the relations between the master and the workers, are placed in an "immobile context," unmodified by the events happening within it. Darnton's "textualization" of events fails to distinguish the extratextual social world from the text. Since ethnography emerges from discussions with living interlocutors (Geertz's Moroccans and Balinese), not with "the dead" in historical texts, can Geertz's model be so comfortably transposed onto historical works, Levi asks?[195]

Roger Chartier—from a quite different perspective, a cultural and intellectual history concerned to preserve the distinctiveness of *texts* —also critiques Darnton's too-ready capitulation to the blandishments of Geertzism.[196] Although Chartier respects Darnton's critique of *mentalité* history (texts need to be "read," not "counted"),[197] he deems Geertz's definition of culture, centered around patterns of meaning expressed in symbols, an unsatisfactory base for an historian.[198] In Chartier's view, Darnton fails to explain how texts give access to the symbolic forms of earlier societies, how symbols are historicized, and how symbol differs from sign.[199]

Most important for Chartier, by appropriating too uncritically Geertz's notion of "text" to name events and rituals, Darnton has obscured—indeed, "obliterated"—the important fact that the story he narrates is a *written* text of a particular genre (*Anecdotes typographiques,* dating to 1762, whose author has been identified).[200] Has not Darnton confused the logic of writing with that of practice? In Darnton's rendition of the cat massacre, readers might not realize that "a real text with a status of its own stands between the observer and this oral or festive supposed 'text.'" The cat massacre is not the cockfight observed by Geertz, for it already exists as a *text*, "invested with its own specific ends." Chartier concludes that Darnton's (and other historians') reliance on anthropology may create new problems "by destroying the 'textuality' of texts that relate the symbolic practices being analysed." The cat massacre has become "a massacre in writing." It is rather the "massacre's" function *in the text* that needs to be unpacked.[201] Any scholar who wishes "to decipher the symbolic system that underlies a text," Chartier concludes, needs

> to take the text as a text and to try to determine its intentions, its strategies, and the effects produced by its discourse; next, to avoid supposing a stable, full value in its lexical choices, but to take into account the semantic investment or disinvestment of its terms; finally, to define the instances of behavior and the rituals present in the text on the basis of the specific way in which they are assembled or produced by original invention, rather than to categorize them on the basis of remote resemblances to codified forms among the repertory of Western folk culture.[202]

Darnton responded to Chartier's (and others') critiques in an essay entitled "The Symbolic Element in History."[203] Rejecting Chartier's overly bookish approach to symbols as "representational," Darnton appealed to anthropologists—Michael Herzfeld, Victor Turner, Edmund Leach, Mary Douglas, S. J. Tambiah, and others—to argue that anthropologists learn from their "native informants" that symbols convey multiple meanings (in Michael Herzfeld's words, "Symbols do not stand for fixed equivalences but as contextually comprehensible analogies").[204] Darnton here amasses examples of multivalent symbols that anthropologists have noted in the rituals and everyday life of the cultures they study. He seeks to defend his interpretation of the cat massacre primarily with anthropological props, arguing that ethnographic material is decisive for understanding the cultural frame of the story. He acknowledges that he is dealing with a written text, and one with various generic precedents, but does not press that fact to the effect that Chartier does: the "textuality" of the material is not registered. Rather, he acknowledges that the story represents a telling moment in labor history: the worsening climate for journeymen and the master's rise to a higher social position.[205]

Most interesting, Darnton repositions his argument (without so signaling to readers) *away* from Geertzian interpretive anthropology *toward* an approach that borrows from semiotics (Peirce informs his rejoinder) and Lévi-Straussian "structures"—although he hastens to add that he does not subscribe to "an elaborate and perhaps outdated variety of structuralism." Nonetheless, he concludes with an analysis of the story in terms of the oppositions it sets up and the mediating terms it enlists.[206] Darnton's rejoinder should interest historians of premodernity for its (unacknowledged) rejection of a purely "Geertzian" approach; Lévi-Straussian semiotics here emerges as of greater assistance.

Nonetheless, Darnton still minimizes the import of Chartier's claim that the *textual* nature of his source has consequences; by appealing to anthropologists' field work that relies on "native informants," he elides with writing the speech that occurs in face-to-face ethnographic work. I question whether such approaches help in deciphering the highly literary texts that constitute the sources for the study of premodernity. Despite Chartier's reliance on an overly rigid and "bookish" notion of symbol, it is nonetheless *his* critique to which students of "high" texts might better attend.

Many issues raised within literary theory, I conclude, have a better claim on the attention of scholars of premodern texts than do contextualism and interpretive anthropology. Both of these, even when adopting a "textual" approach, take as their model of communication face-to-face speech, a model that appears inappropriate to "high" texts that travel across the centuries and are read in different times, places, and circumstances than that of the original author. The vast corpus of premodern literature could be explored to good profit by scholars who attend to the distinctive qualities of texts as elaborated by these theorists. If, with them, we understand "text" as a *way* of reading, how might we explore premodern writings? Chapter 8, after summing up the issues of previous chapters, presents examples that I hope will illuminate present debates.

CHAPTER EIGHT

History, Theory, and Premodern Texts

How might the considerations raised in the previous chapters bear upon the construction of a premodern, textually oriented history, most particularly that of late ancient Christianity? A first question to be asked (with Keith Jenkins and Hayden White) is "for whom" is a particular history written, to what "address" is it being sent? This history is for those who will consider some premodern historical specializations, such as late ancient Christianity, as a subdiscipline of a new, theoretically informed intellectual history. On what assumptions does this history operate? It distinguishes "history," a disciplinary operation, from "the past," whose very disappearance authorizes the historian's work. It recognizes (with Michel de Certeau) the foreignness of the past, that "dead souls" resurge only in present discourse, and (with Dominick LaCapra) that the past is not an entity that was ever there "on its own terms and for its own sake." As both R. G. Collingwood and various *Annalistes* argued, this history is driven by the historian's questions, and understands historical fact to be something created, not discovered. With Arthur O. Lovejoy and the *Annalistes,* it looks for assistance from other disciplines. With Hans-Georg Gadamer, it recognizes that since historians' "horizons" fuse with that of the text, they themselves comprise part of the phenomena to be studied.

Since historians' questions are marked by issues of the present, this history finds unsurprising that (for example) gender studies and postcolonial theory have in recent years been appropriated to illuminate historical work. Here, historical relativism is not taken to mean that "everyone's opinion is equally good," but that scholars should seek to understand the differing cultural and moral views of past and present societies—and to recognize the limited and often provincial quality of their own. The critique of objectivism by this history does not imply that historians need tolerate lazy scholarship or fudged footnotes, or that counterevidence can be conveniently overlooked.

Such a history is less tied than were traditional histories to a quest for origins, causes, and influence, although investigations of inter-textuality and "effective history" offer ways to connect earlier and later entities, as does exploring (with de Certeau, Chartier, Macherey and others) what in the past made possible the traces that now re-main, what were the conditions of their production. It looks less to continuity—too often, an ideologically suspect category—than to dis-continuity,[1] noting (with Foucault) the breaks in the larger historical order, as well as (with Derrida and other post-structuralist theorists) the gaps, absences, aporias, and contradictions in texts. It recognizes (with Lyotard and critics of narrative) that "grand narratives," such as the rise and triumph of Christianity, often cloak ideological as-sumptions. It registers that "experience" is a nonfoundational cate-gory that is always already worked over and to which texts offer no original insight. Since issues of power inform the interpretation of the past, it accepts, with Hayden White, that there is "no politically inno-cent historiography."

This history acknowledges that if the structure of language is an ar-bitrary system, words do not refer directly to extralinguistic entities. Since, in Roland Barthes's phrase, there is "no certification," a naïve correspondence theory of verification becomes untenable; "internal realism," correctly understood, offers more promise. With contex-tualists Quentin Skinner and J. G. A. Pocock, this history investigates linguistic convention and change. But with critics of contextualism, it recognizes that contexts may be either unknown or multiple, are vari-ously assigned by different readers, and largely come to scholars of premodernity in already-textualized form; although historians will doubtless continue to accord an important place to contextualization, it should be one that takes account of these issues. Although its own texts are frequently of a high cultural order, readily amenable to rhetorical and ideological critique, it acknowledges (with Dominick LaCapra) that they sometimes cut across the grain of expected assumptions. It recognizes that writing renders problematic the presumed centrality of authorial intention, both because readers in different times and places "collaborate" with texts to produce new meanings and because "high" texts themselves encourage the proliferation of meaning beyond authorial intention. Thus the textuality and textual productivity of its sources are ripe for investigation. Such might be the assumptions of a textually oriented history of premodernity.

Late Ancient Christian Studies

Late ancient Christian ("post–New Testament") studies, however, has idiosyncracies foreign to other premodern disciplines: it developed under the aegis of a confessional theology and leaped somewhat precipitously from this orientation to that of social history and social theory in the 1970s and 1980s. These studies bypassed structuralism and other intellectual currents that were then informing scholarship pertaining to other ancient religions, the classics, and the New Testament.[2] Overlooking structuralism perhaps contributed to the late entry of post-structuralist analysis to the field; indeed, only recently have younger scholars, especially in the United States, undertaken their own reeducations in various forms of post-structuralist theory.

The rapid passage from theological-philological to social-scientific approaches to texts obscured for many practitioners of late ancient Christian studies (myself included) the benefits attending post-structuralist theory. While the race for social science provided an escape from a narrowly philological and confessionally oriented theological orientation, the field remained largely oblivious to the literary/theoretical currents that were being appropriated by scholars in departments of English, languages, and literature. Overlooked in the rush for realignment was a point not then so obvious: that we do not possess the type of documents on which social historians of modernity work, but high literary/philosophical texts that lend themselves well to theoretical analysis. If scholars in other premodern disciplines find the situation of late ancient Christian studies puzzling, I ask their forbearance.

Yet, I would argue, our attention to grids and groups, networks, liminality, and "thick description" was by no means futile. Encounters with anthropology and other social sciences from the end of the

1960s onward greatly enlivened studies in late antiquity; I would not wish to return patristics to its traditional disposition. Nonetheless, these social-scientific appropriations obscured the fact that scholars of late ancient Christianity deal not with native informants, nor with masses of data amenable to statistical analysis, but with texts—and texts of a highly literary, rhetorical, and ideological nature. Social-scientific, especially anthropological, approaches, however, were far more readily accepted by scholars of late ancient Christianity than was theoretical/philosophical critique.[3] I claim, to the contrary, that Christian writings from late antiquity should be read first and foremost as literary productions before they are read as sources of social data.[4] Joining theoretical to social-scientific and theological-philological analyses will enrich the field.

Late ancient Christian studies would benefit from reenvisioning itself as a form of the new *intellectual* history, grounded in issues of material production and ideology, that has risen to prominence in the late twentieth century. In positioning late ancient Christian studies as a form of intellectual history, I by no means wish to discount the indispensable assistance that archeology, numismatics, epigraphy, and other fields that attend to material culture have contributed to our understanding of past peoples and places; the enormous and learned scholarship in these fields speaks for their importance. My focus, however, in keeping with the themes of this book, is more precise: issues of recent theory that pertain to *texts*.

The humanities, to be sure, is not the traditional location of patristic studies. The importance of the institutional location of disciplinary work has recently been illuminated by two distinguished senior scholars of late ancient Christian studies who have reminisced (in print) on their own educational formations. Both are intellectual pioneers who forged new paths for a generation and more of their students and successors; indeed, their writings changed a field. Their work, as that of all scholars, is marked by both their own institutional formation and their engagement, outside customary institutional expectations, with challenging intellectual issues of their day. Yet their institutional formation, quite obviously, was not that of the North American academy of the early twenty-first century.

Robert Markus, summing up developments within Augustinian studies during the last half century, recollects that when he joined the Dominican order, he was forbidden to pursue philosophy further (the field in which he had already earned a doctorate), but was enjoined by his novice-master to read, for an entire year, *only* the scriptural commentaries of Augustine. Markus muses that one can now hardly "imagine a modern—or postmodern—novice-master taking such a view," and suggests that this feature of his education reveals by way of contrast the enormous transformation of the Catholic Church in the later twentieth century.[5] One could add more: this context for studying Augustine—theological and confessional—would appear almost unimaginable to many contemporary American students.

Likewise, Peter Brown, in a retrospective on *The World of Late Antiquity*, reflects on his intellectual development in the course of his university and post-university education. Reading about Brown "at university," American students might imagine that they are closer to home than with Markus's novice-master. But several moments here give pause (and not just Brown's report of perusing Henri-Irénée Marrou's *Saint Augustin et la fin de la culture antique* while lying in a punt drifting down the river Cherwell on a summer's day . . . presumably without the added baggage of a dictionary): the talking partner who, over tea, so stimulated his mind was Mary Douglas. As Brown notes, books such as *Purity and Danger* "did not circulate among ancient historians," but only among those who studied "small face-to-face societies."[6] Brown's and Markus's self-revelations illustrate well the course through which patristic studies have passed in the last half-century, from a theologically oriented environment to one inspired by social-science methodologies.

My own education—both formal and "self-education"—likewise passed through these developments. "Patristics," in my own graduate education, was a theologically oriented discipline that centered largely on the Church Fathers' Trinitarian and Christological expositions against "heretics." To bring ancient philosophy into relation with theology was as broad a disciplinary reach as I could then imagine would be professionally viable. The social revolutions of the late 1960s merged in the 1970s with social science approaches that were implicitly (and sometimes overtly) aimed at undercutting the dominance of theology in the study of early Christianity—and in the years thereafter, cultural approaches were added in. Social formations, women, the poor, "heretics," and sexuality now were deemed suitable topics for investigation. What was largely missed along the way were precisely the issues on which this book has centered.

Early Christian studies, I suggest, is now poised to attend to the textuality of early Christian writings: the works of Augustine, Eusebius, Tertullian, Gregory Nazianzen, John Chrysostom, and others invite a different kind of reading from the cultural phenomena explored as "texts" by interpretive anthropologists and from the forms of speech analyzed by contextualists. Theology has not been abandoned, but finds a welcome place in this reconfiguration of late ancient Christian studies; the work of scholars such as Virginia Burrus, who read early Christian theological texts through the illuminating lens of critical theory, stands as confirmation of this point. The recent prominence of literary/theoretical studies within humanities disciplines suggests that scholars of ancient Christianity would profit— and have already profited—from entering more fully into conversation with those whose business it is to deal with ideology, rhetoric, and textuality. Indeed, theorists themselves—Jacques Derrida, Fredric Jameson, Jean-François Lyotard—have lately appropriated for their own purposes the rich texts of late Christian antiquity.[7] In my view, students of early Christianity should not cede wholesale the interpretation of our textual treasures to contemporary theorists: we have something to contribute to theoretical analysis as well. Since theorists have now registered considerable interest in writers of late antiquity—Augustine in particular—why should not scholars of this period reach across disciplinary fences to those who have already, and variously, reached across to us?

Historians and the Premodern Text

Critics sometimes allege that theoretically inclined historians seem unable to produce the type of historical writing that they themselves advocate; while they press "extravagant" theories (which appears to mean "French" and "deconstructive"), in the end they exhibit only "cautious truisms," formalist analyses, and "textual prudence."[8] Critics of Joan Wallach Scott, for example, claim that post-structuralist critique has not informed her actual historical practice,[9] while Simon Schama's *Dead Certainties,* which experimented with voice and narrative technique, is faulted for its confusing "cacophony."[10] Given such allegations, it seems imperative for historians who endorse theory's utility to illustrate how the wider intellectual shifts signaled above might impact scholarly writing in their fields. Here, I argue, scholars of late ancient Christianity, as intellectual historians who work with literary texts of a highly rhetorical and ideological nature, enjoy an advantage.[11] Indeed, scholars of other premodern disciplines have already led the way, as I shall illustrate with a few examples from medieval and classical studies.

Gabrielle Spiegel and the "Social Logic of the Text"

How might a premodern historian, reflecting on texts and contexts, understand Geoff Eley's injunction for historians to move both "back, to the contexts of the text's production [note that this does not mean "authorial intention"], and out, to the ways in which its meanings get constructed," that is, to focus on how texts "work."[12] Gabrielle Spiegel's much-cited essay, "History, Historicism, and the Social Logic of the Text in the Middle Ages,"[13] illustrates one attempt to do just that. Yet, I shall note, although Spiegel is in general "theory-friendly," she sometimes appears to balk at the consequences that post-structuralist theory might entail for historical studies.

Spiegel asks, "What, if anything, can the historian contribute to the reconfiguration of both theoretical concerns and interpretive practices signaled by the very notion of postmodernism?"—a question implying that historians are not simply the passive recipients of theoreticians' reflections, but have something of their own to offer. She urges historians to face the semiotic challenge, since the "real" is itself the product of discursive construction, and theorists to resist "the absorption of history by textuality."[14] Abandoning the notion that historical studies reflect the world, Spiegel presses historians to join with literary critics in exploring "the social dimensions of textual production in past times" and the "ideological mystifications" of texts. Yet, with most historians, she distinguishes literature from documents, resists collapsing contexts and texts, and champions human agency. Opting for a social view of language, Spiegel modifies the post-structuralist claim that "language constitutes the social world of meaning" with a Bakhtinian caveat that "social differences structure language."[15] In a manner reminiscent of de Certeau, Spiegel concludes, "In the final analysis, what is the past but a once material substance, now silenced, extant only as sign and as sign drawing to itself chains of conflicting interpretations that hover over its absent present and compete for possession of the relics, seeking to inscribe traces of significance upon the bodies of the dead."[16]

The phrase Spiegel devises to indicate her double concern is "the social logic of the text," a logic that attends to both the text's "site of articulation and its discursive character as articulated 'logos.'" Historians, she argues, should explore the text's mode of production (again, not to be identified with "authorial intention") as well as the "surplus of signification" that readers (whether or not Derrideans) have found, and will find, in it.[17]

In this essay, Spiegel brings various stripes of theory (from Raymond Williams, sociolinguistics, and Bakhtin)[18] to bear upon the texts she analyzes. Her theoretically eclectic reading, accomplished with disparate "mental tools" derived in part from the social sciences, doubtless suits many historians, who resist dissolving the social and economic orders into "texts" and who claim that their historical subjects—however decentered—possessed will and agency that they expressed in surprisingly creative ways.[19] Some historians, however, might counter that Spiegel enjoys a theoretical advantage because the genealogical histories on which she works are more "like" literature than the economic, political, and other documents with which many social historians deal.[20] Even if this were the case, it would suggest that those who study the texts of late ancient Christianity enjoy a similar advantage: while their texts offer only scant materials for social, political, and economic history as historians of modernity construe it, they afford abundant resources for intellectual and cultural history in a new mode.

Spiegel's particular example focuses on two texts of genealogical history (a new literary genre in eleventh- and twelfth-century France) which, she claims, reveal the changing dynastic patterns among Franco-Flemish aristocrats as they challenged the growing power of the monarchy. These genealogical histories can be treated both as consequence *and* as cause of this extratextual development, Spiegel argues, insofar as they helped first "to create a consciousness" of lineage and then "to impose it on the members of the lineage group." Exploring the changed meanings that the legend in the *Pseudo-Turpin Chronicle* accrued as it passed from a clerically rendered Latin prototype to the new environment of the French nobility, and acknowledging that the nobles' political struggle is not detailed in the text itself, Spiegel argues that the "political unconscious" of the text places the work within the "historiography of resistance," in this case, resistance to the expanding power of the French monarchy.[21]

Nonetheless, Spiegel's embrace of post-structuralist theory is qualified: while enjoining historians to entertain theory, she insists that context be kept separate from text, that the social not be absorbed into "textuality," that political and social practices not be treated as "cultural scripts."[22] While the latter admonition might also be endorsed by certain theorists as a rejection (or at least a qualification) of Geertzian-inspired history, her caveats suggest that she more easily appropriates certain types of social theory—as her allusions to Raymond Williams and sociolinguistics suggest—than the types of literary-philosophical theory that were discussed in previous chapters. Thus it does not surprise that critics more decisively influenced by post-structuralist theory question whether Spiegel's sharp and easy differentiation of texts and contexts fits well with her advice to historians to abandon a correspondence theory of verification and their nostalgia for the "real" past. Does she believe that there is some approach to "the social" which is untouched by language?[23] Alun Munslow critiques Spiegel's notion of the "social logic of the text" as a "practical realist compromise with deconstruction," in that she treats texts as if they were material embodiments of speech.[24] The preference Spiegel displays in this essay for social (rather than literary-philosophical) theory, it might be noted, has also been that of early Christian studies for the last several decades.

In recent essays, Spiegel appears to retreat even further from a warm embrace of theory. Although she now appreciatively notes the significance of Derrida's attention to a text's silences, absences, and indeterminacies for historical work,[25] she also insists (allegedly in contrast to Derrida) upon "referents," upon the strong differentiation of history and literature, and upon the "givenness" of literary (as contrasted with historical) texts[26]—a point that surely would surprise some literary theorists discussed above.

Strikingly, in her later work Spiegel deems "unsolvable" the problem of supplying "an adequate epistemology for history" that takes account of the semiotic challenge.[27] Elsewhere, however, she posits that the problem might be resolved by conceding a "middle ground" in which different understandings of language are deemed appropriate to diverse types of texts: thus documentary texts are deemed "instrumental" in their approach to language, while literary texts are considered "self-reflective"[28]—a neat division of labor not likely to withstand philosophical scrutiny.

Nonetheless, several aspects of Spiegel's argument are illuminating for students of late ancient Christianity. Her notion of "the social

logic of the text" provides a stimulating "mental tool" that I appropriate below. Since the materials on which scholars of early Christianity work *are* for the most part literary texts, not "documents,"
Spiegel's fear that "the literary" might overtake and absorb the extratextual is less pertinent. While she worries that a Geertzian program
of reading the social order as "text" diminishes the independence of
the *extratextual* realm,[29] the concern of scholars of early Christianity
might rather be (with LaCapra, Chartier, and others) that amalgamat-
ing social and institutional practices under the rubric of "text" also
diminishes the special properties of high *literary* writings that refuse
"domestication," that address—and contest—even the commonplace
in exceptional ways that subvert as well as reinforce tradition.[30] The
social realm to which scholars of patristic Christianity have access is
garnered largely from *texts,* with limited assistance provided by archeological remains, coins, and inscriptions.

Here, Spiegel's encouragement to ferret out the "political unconscious" of the text is provocative. Literary critics, she avers, have
often been more attentive to the affective, aesthetic, and ethical dimensions of texts, and historians to a text's ideological function, but
under the influence of ideology critique and Foucauldian history, explorations of ideology have become "a virtual obsession" with those
who study discourse.[31] Early Christian texts, I suggest, are especially
ripe for such treatment: the "political unconscious" (taken in the
larger sense of "political") here lies only slightly below the surface
"consciousness" of the text. Moreover, Spiegel's assessment of deconstruction's utility in listening for silences, ruptures, absences, and
displacements[32] is highly pertinent to the reading of early Christian
texts. And surely commendable for all historians is her claim that a
"historiographical practice grounded in an awareness of its own philosophical and practical commitments will not diminish but rather
strengthen our appreciation both of the past as the object of our study
and of the present as the site of our investment in the past."[33] Although Spiegel declines to venture a program by which historians
might respond to "the semiotic challenge," her work offers significant
assistance in rethinking the history/theory divide.

Classicists, Ancient Historians, and Theory

Although numerous classicists and ancient historians have argued
that the texts on which they work must be viewed primarily as literary

products, this view has only slowly and somewhat reluctantly been conceded by scholars of late ancient Christianity.[34] The books of the New Testament, although closer to late ancient Christian studies in content and purpose—that is, in their promotion of Christianity—bear little resemblance to the long, rhetorically ornate texts of second- to fifth-century Christianity, and hence, for my purposes, offer less helpful comparative materials than do many texts of "pagan" antiquity.

The debates attending the study of ancient history replicate in a different register the philosophical and literary critiques detailed in earlier chapters. More than a quarter-century ago, Moses Finley noted the distance between the institutional location and training of classicists and that of historians who study more recent eras. Ancient history, Finley argued, is unique among the various branches of Western historiography in that its practitioners are "not in the first instance historians but men trained in language and literature who call themselves classicists (or Hellenists) and classical philologists, epigraphists and papyrologists . . . [F]or many classicists, history is in effect another discipline."[35]

Finley faulted classicists' ignorance of larger debates occurring within the historical profession. They naively accept the explanations proffered by ancient writers, he charged, instead of posing questions that the texts themselves do *not* ask, exploring that which past societies *fail* to divulge.[36] Such procedures, Finley proposed, would generate new hypotheses and explanatory models for the field.[37] Although Finley was writing before the "linguistic turn" and hence perhaps envisioned social science models, his injunction to search for explanations other than those the text offers, to pose questions *not* asked, are highly pertinent for historians of early Christianity.[38]

To be sure, "writing history" was a different enterprise for the ancients than for our contemporaries: no continuous historiographical tradition stretches from antiquity to the present. As Foucauldian theory might suggest, there is here no natural object "history." Ancient historians, unlike our contemporaries, wrote for nonprofessional audiences for whom epic poetry was the only other narrative genre;[39] thus they were immune both to Rankean concerns and to modern demands for "professionalism." As R. G. Collingwood put it, "the historian was only the autobiographer of his generation and autobiography is not a profession."[40]

Debates about ancient historiography's relation to literature and its implications for notions of historical "truth" resonate with the history/theory debates of our own era.[41] The ancients, many scholars now concede, saw history as a species of literature—a claim that makes ancient history-writing readily amenable to aspects of recent literary critique.[42] Thus T. J. Luce: "History was . . . a literary enterprise above all, the imaginative creation of its author."[43] Or T. P. Wiseman: ancient historians, like novelists, were "fabricators and creators of illusion."[44] Or Glen Bowersock: the ancients would have been unsurprised by recent discussions linking history with fiction or rhetoric.[45] To be sure, traditional classicists dispute such claims; Charles Fornara, for example, while acknowledging the rhetorical overlay of ancient historical writings, faults the "scepticism" of colleagues who attribute "deception" to ancient historians.[46] Such scruples are dismissed by Averil Cameron, writing in another context: modern commentators should shed their worries about "sincerity" and rather look to the function of genres.[47]

A central issue distinguishing ancient from modern historiography concerns the assessment of truth claims. Whereas modern historians point to accuracy in the use of sources as their hallmark, ancient historians concentrate rather on the absence (or presence) of favoritism stemming from political views or social relations that would affect the writer's view of living persons—about the dead, who could no longer hurt or help, there was less concern.[48] In this regard, Sallust's claim that the historian should be "unaffected by ambition, fear or partisan politics" is often cited, as are Tacitus's words that historians should scrutinize their subjects *"neque amore . . . et sine odio"* ("neither with love nor with hate") or *"sine ira et studio"* ("without anger or partiality").[49] According to Lucian of Samosata's "How to Write History"— the only extant systematic historiographical essay from antiquity[50]— the historian should shun fear or hope as motivations, as they preclude the "factual" *(hôs eprachthê)* reporting of events. And in a claim jolting to modern historians, Lucian adds that since writers have no reason to lie about the dead, who can no longer help or harm, we are entitled to accept as true Homer's depiction of Achilles.[51]

Differences between ancient and modern historiography reveal themselves in other ways as well. Two characteristics attending ancient history-writing—the authors' lack of recourse to documents[52] and their extensive rhetorical training[53]—contributed to the free com-

position of speeches deemed appropriate to the characters represented. The desired effect of this practice was to achieve "verisimilitude," that is, to convince an audience that the deed or the speech
might have been done or said as represented.[54] "Verisimilitude," Luce
asserts, for the Greek historians "was equivalent to veracity."[55] Particularly important in this rhetorical context was the role of the *inventio,*
the elaboration of events or speech by the historian, the only test for
which was its probability.[56] A prime example is Thucydides' history of
the Peloponnesian War: despite the author's being hailed as a forerun-
ner of Leopold von Ranke,[57] for sections of his history there remain
no other sources with which to compare his narrative. "[T]his happy
circumstance, coupled with the authorial assurance," A. J. Woodman
claims, has convinced most readers that his history is largely reli-
able.[58] Thucydides likely included so many speeches in his work because oratory played a predominant role in public life; moreover,
Homer had set a precedent by assigning paramount significance to
speeches in the *Iliad* and the *Odyssey.* "Verbatim speeches [that is,
speeches men actually gave] and classical historiography are a contradiction in terms," Woodman trenchantly concludes.[59]

A last disputed point concerns historians' trusting acceptance of ancient oral traditions. Here, Herodotus is the prime suspect. Today,
Woodman posits, Herodotus would be "taken to court for false pre-
tences."[60] Arnaldo Momigliano phrases the matter more gently: although Herodotus has been discredited, he remains "the father of history" because he "determined the paramouncy of oral evidence"—a
practice that obtained "until historians decided to go to the record of-
fice," a method perfected only in the nineteenth century.[61]

Defenders of Herodotus include Charles Fornara, who appeals to
oral tradition's tenacious hold in preliterate societies in order to challenge insinuations that Herodotus invented some of the speeches and
events he recounts; "[s]uspicion of the Greeks, and of Herodotus in
particular, surely cannot reach this far," Fornara exclaims.[62] "Suspicion's" reach is long, however, and Finley in particular scathingly
mocked historians of early Greece for their "touching faith," for "en-
veloping themselves in the warm glow thrown off by the word 'tradition.'"[63] Finley advised them rather to contemplate the ancients' capacity to invent and to believe.[64] Greek and Latin sources should not,
he argued, remain "immune from the canons of judgment and criticism that are applied to all other documentation." Historians of antiquity might rather ponder the ideological functions of memory, such

as shoring up aristocrats' right to rule, enhancing their prestige, and justifying particular institutions.[65]

Such assessments of Greek and Latin historians resonate with those that scholars of early Christianity increasingly make of *their* major historical source, Eusebius. Although Eusebius cited documents to a greater extent than did his predecessors, for many events, his account (like that of Thucydides) is the only source we possess. Moreover, for the sources Eusebius cited that we *can* check, the citations are often mangled and incomplete.[66] Scholars cling to his tendentious account of early Christianity since they have little else on which to rely. But, paraphrasing Moses Finley, we might use Eusebius to better effect by asking how his account shores up claims for the dominance of the proto-orthodox Church, enhances its leaders' prestige, and justifies particular institutions and teachings.

Averil Cameron, in *Christianity and the Rhetoric of Empire: The Development of Christian Discourse,* observes that in the battle between Christians and pagans over who had "the right to interpret the past," Christians, oddly enough, did *not* make the genre of historiography their own; Eusebius's specialized history of the Church apparently failed to "inspire the development of a new and perhaps more pragmatic Christian history." Christian writers' failure to co-opt the genre of history-writing, she suggests, perhaps allowed pagan historians in the fourth century and beyond to continue employing the genre with such ease. But Christians' failure in this respect did not impede them from writing history by other means, such as *Lives* of martyrs, ascetics, saints, and bishops. *Lives,* Cameron argues, "provided a more congenial and flexible genre" than did classical historiography, one that could "embrace all subjects—male, female, high, low—and all literary levels." Such writing, while appealing to educated elites, could also be more broadly disseminated.[67] Cameron's study brilliantly illustrates how issues of rhetoric, power, and genre are intertwined in early Christian discourse, and in this represents the successful deployment of Foucauldian themes for the study of late ancient Christianity.

Patristics, History, and Theory

As a species of intellectual historian, scholars of late ancient Christianity occupy an advantageous position when considerations of theory are at issue. Given the rhetorical and ideological nature of their materials, these scholars may safely assume that their texts lie in a largely unknown and dubious relation to the "reality" of the ancient Church, and should often be approached with a hermeneutic of suspicion and by reading against the grain. If scholars of premodern Christianity adopted Roger Chartier's suggestion that historical work should constitute an exercise in analyzing the process of representation, and that historians should refocus their task to examine the function of ideas in ideological systems,[68] what might their studies look like? Among the "mental tools" that theory offers scholars of patristic Christianity in approaching these tasks are (1) an examination of "authorial function" that calls into question attributions of intention and context; (2) symptomatic and Derridean readings that attend to the gaps, absences, and aporias in texts; (3) ideology critique, especially helpful in unpacking the early Christian writers' representations of various "Others," including women; and (4) postcolonial discourse theory that helps to illuminate the ways in which Christianity and Empire intertwined.[69] I will illustrate some uses of the first two sets of tools briefly, and more fully elaborate the latter two.

Authors, Contexts, Metaphors, and Aporias

Although the authors of many early Christian treatises and letters can be identified with relative assurance, various types of early Christian literature render authorship—and hence issues of context and intention—less certain: they provide excellent material for pondering Foucault's question, "What Is an Author?" For instance, the Apocryphal Acts of the Apostles (writings composed in the second century and beyond in the name of a New Testament apostle) well illustrate both early Christian writers' desire to claim authority for their work by the assignment of prestigious authorship, and some early Christian readers' willingness—however misguided, from later perspectives—to endorse that authority.[70] Similarly, various writings by alleged heretics were passed down through the centuries because they were mistakenly attributed to such acclaimed Church Fathers as Jerome and Augustine.[71] Here, the "author-function" served not just to bolster the prestige of texts, but contributed to their preservation.

As for debates over context, a salient example plaguing early Christian studies in the late twentieth century is found in the Nag Hammadi documents: were they preserved by and for the use of Gnostic "heretics"? or did "orthodox" Christians save them to assist in combating such heretics? or did Pachomian monks who inhabited a monastery near the site of discovery take them to be edifying treatises? Do they (or not) constitute a "library"? Does the careful manner of their burial suggest (or not) a context for their use?[72] The unknown authors and contexts of these texts leave historians without the clues that they claim help them situate and interpret documents of the past.

Early Christian writers also struggled to overcome the contradictions and fill in the gaps in biblical texts. Their own writings, too, reveal problems and aporias that signal for modern readers the textual and extratextual conflicts in which these writers were mired.[73] Here, metaphoric language occasioned difficulties. As Averil Cameron argues, from Christianity's very beginnings, metaphor stood "at the heart of Christian language" and by late antiquity had acquired special prominence.[74] Yet metaphor, whatever its theological utility, could signal trouble for Christian writers, as is well illustrated by theologians' elaborations of divine Fatherhood and Sonship, and of Christian celibates as "Brides of Christ."

The New Testament had referred to Jesus as God's "only Son" (John 3:16) and to the Son as *monogenês* ("only-begotten" [I John 4:9; John 1:18, with disputed variants]). What could such attributions mean? Greek and Roman mythology, to be sure, was replete with stories of gods fathering offspring, but early Christian writers insisted that divine Fatherhood excluded sexual relation.[75] Hence the words "Father" and "Son" were redefined so as to preclude association with the processes of human reproduction. "Begetting" within the Godhead bore no resemblance to the shocking sexual behavior of the Greek and Roman gods, or to the pairings of gendered beings within Gnostic godheads.[76] The fourth-century controversy between pro-Nicene theologians such as Athanasius and those whom they came to typify as followers of Arius rendered the explanatory process even more complex, as the former sought to explain not just how divine begetting was unlike human begetting, but also how "begetting" differed from "making," a term thought to resonate too closely with human craftsmanship.[77] As Virginia Burrus has argued in *"Begotten, Not Made": Conceiving Manhood in Late Antiquity*, Trinitarian formulations erased both the messiness of male sexual functioning *and* the lowliness of female materiality in its "transcendentalization" of the masculine, and in the process provided a potent new image of spiritualized masculinity for late ancient Christians.[78] Trinitarian theology provides a fertile site for the exploration of the difficulties and advantages underlying the appropriation of metaphor.

Nowhere, Averil Cameron argues, did the paradoxical aspects of Christian exhortation emerge more forcefully than in discourses pertaining to virginity and celibacy, themes that "held out virtually limitless possibilities for virtuosity" in the construction of a Christian discourse.[79] A central metaphor favored by the Church Fathers was the ascription of the terms "Bridegroom" to Jesus and "Brides of Christ" to his celibate devotees. The image was doubtless inspired by the description of Jesus as a "bridegroom" in Matthew 25:1–13 and Ephesians 5:22–33, as well as by Christians' interpreting the lovers of the Song of Songs as Christ and either the Church or the individual soul— "Church" and "soul" conveniently of the feminine gender in both Greek and Latin. Yet one might well be puzzled why Christian *virgins* should be described as "Brides of Christ," since with a few exceptions, the "marriage" is never depicted.[80]

A fascinating example that illustrates this dilemma for early Christian writers is afforded by Methodius of Olympus's *Symposium,* a treatise probably composed in the early fourth century[81] and modeled on Plato's *Symposium.* Although the similarities between the two texts are clear (participants at a banquet compete in offering speeches on a common theme), the differences are notable—differences that must necessarily attend the change from a gathering of Athenian male pederasts to one of female Christian virgins, and from an elaboration of love under the metaphor of reproduction to the celebration of sexual abstinence. Although the virgins of Methodius's text are alleged to have overcome feminine disability through manly reason and are depicted as Olympian contenders,[82] they are chiefly described as "Brides of Christ."[83] Yet the virgins are not even metaphorically represented as "reproducers," as Plato had coded his male symposiasts, but are alleged to be "sterile" and devoid of passions.[84] Having made their speeches in praise of virginity, the virgins queue up to enter the divine wedding chamber and receive the Bridegroom's nectar.[85] Yet their toes do not cross the doorway: always betrothed, they never become "wives." At the decisive moment, the Bridegroom (or Methodius) appears to shut the door in their faces. Why?

Here, "the social logic of the text" prompts speculation on social context. We might argue, for example, that restricting access to the divine Bridegroom solely to virgins ran up against a more egalitarian streak of Christian theology that understood *all* Christians, including chaste couples, to be married to Christ:[86] neither maleness nor a "sexually soiled" past precludes a Christian's espousal to Christ, some early Christian authors claim.[87] Moreover, a problem of representation attends the ascription: since the "historical Jesus" in the Gospels is not depicted as married, and thus could serve as a model for virginal living, did not some awkwardness attend his representation as a bridegroom? Even more problematic was the socio-ecclesiastical reality that churchmen of late ancient Christianity faced: Methodius and other Christian authorities forbade consecrated virgins to have any relations with men. In particular, early Christian texts suggest that the sharing of a household by male and female ascetics was a major worry for bishops.[88] The attempts of the Church Fathers to construct Jesus as "celibate Bridegroom" stumbled on the theological and socio-ecclesiastical difficulties of the "marriage"—but was not this difficulty part of the metaphor's appeal?[89] Notions of warm affectivity, tinged with a sexual charge, "hovered over" the metaphor—while it simultaneously encouraged chaste living in the here-and-now.[90] As Georges Bataille once observed, "[m]isunderstanding the sanctity of transgression is one of the foundations of Christianity."[91]

Ideology Critique and the Representation of Early Christian Women

Although many older philological studies detailed the rhetorical devices and style of patristic writings, they did not often explore the *work* that these literary devices perform.[92] Many late ancient Christian writers, to be sure, were highly self-conscious of style (not least when rhetorically decrying the style of their own productions)[93] and enjoyed flailing the "barbaric writing" of opponents.[94] Yet style does not account for the startlingly different conclusions reached by Christian authors addressing the same issue and employing similar rhetorical strategies. Something else is at stake—namely, differing ideologies. Here, some examples are illuminating.

On the topic of Christians' possession of wealth, for example, a comparison of Clement of Alexandria's treatise *Who Is the Rich Man Who Is Saved?* with the anonymous but allegedly Pelagian work *On Riches* stands as a case in point in demonstrating the work of differing ideologies: whereas Clement gladly widens the needle's eye to welcome the rich who generously give, the author of *On Riches* requires a far more rigorous program of renunciation for Christians.[95] In this case, the "social logic" of the text is easy to unpack: Clement, in the company of other early Christian leaders, needed to keep the rich from despairing of their salvation. Despite the rigorous biblical injunctions to renounce wealth, the early Christian churches were dependent on the rich to support their extensive charity and other operations. "Despair," Clement suggests, is an appropriate response only for those who have not contributed generously.[96]

A second example: what could account for the divergence of patristic opinion regarding history's "progress" or "decline"? Has sacred history progressed from the swamp of carnality to the pinnacle of virginity, as Methodius claims, or declined from a Golden Age of virtue to the present sorry state of morals, as Lactantius posits?[97] The divergent approaches relate to whether the author seeks to explain away the dubious sexual behavior of the Old Testament patriarchs (as does Methodius) or chastise contemporary Christians for their less than exemplary morals (as does Lactantius). The varying ideological functions of such arguments, not style, mark the difference.

Although ideology critique has received varying formulations since Marx's time[98]—most notably for my purposes here, by extending its sway beyond the level of economic stratification—two definitions are especially useful. From Anthony Giddens: ideology is "the mode in which forms of signification are incorporated within systems of domination so as to sanction their continuance."[99] From John B. Thompson: ideology expresses "the ways in which meaning serves, in particular circumstances, to establish and sustain relations of power which are systematically asymmetrical"; ideology is "meaning in the service of power."[100] Stressing power differentials and the role of discursive formations in the construction of the self, Giddens and Thompson eschew definitions that pit truth versus falsehood or imply that theorists themselves stand outside ideology.[101] Rejecting the association of ideology with "false consciousness," Fredric Jameson describes ideologies as "strategies of containment" that characteristically effect "structural limitation and ideological closure."[102] More recently, Michèle Barrett has argued that attending to "new social groups" (for example, women, people of color, and native residents of formerly colonialist countries) requires that notions of ideology based on economic class alone be discarded.[103] Barrett's claim links gender analysis with Louis Althusser's rejection of a simple economic determinism and his assignment of productive force to superstructural apparatuses such as law, education, and religion.[104]

Developing such Althusserian themes,[105] ideology critics informed by post-structuralist theory argue that "the subject" created by and under ideology is not a unitary consciousness, but is multiple and always under construction. This recognition, John Frow claims, leaves space for "the possible discontinuity between positions occupied within the economic, political, and symbolic orders,"[106] and acknowledges the likelihood of "uneven developments" among an individual's social, economic, educational, legal (and so on) statuses.[107] His point provides an important theoretical tool for an analysis of Christian women in late antiquity, who are prime candidates for "uneven development."

A post-structuralist version of ideology critique understands ideology's function as "fixing" representations of the self, as constituting "concrete individuals as subjects."[108] The "fixing" of the self operates through mechanisms such as stereotyping, claimed by Roland Barthes as ideology's dominant mode of operation—a claim well illustrated in early Christian writers' construction of "woman," as I illustrate below.[109] Moreover, ideology naturalizes and universalizes its subjects, ignoring the "historical sedimentation" that situates and individualizes them;[110] it implies that our society's values *have* no history, but are eternal and natural.[111] Humanly constructed situations are rationalized and legitimated as conforming to timeless truth. As Marx famously argued, ideology turns the consequences of society into the consequences of nature.[112]

Paradoxically, while ideology collapses history into "the natural," it nonetheless appeals to history in directing its subjects to emulate ideals of the past rather than to envision different futures. Traditional symbols and values are upheld in one arena—for example, gender—while other aspects of the social, economic, or political orders change. Closing the gap between the past and the present by privileging the past is thus one of the conservative operations of ideology.[113] Such tendencies are abundantly evident in the Church Fathers' exhortations to and chastisement of women, based on nostalgia for the ideals of a bygone era.

As Chapter 5 detailed, certain types of writing—myth and narrative—are especially adept at conveying these effects. Stories of the past told by the dominant classes "create a sense of belonging to a

community and to a history which transcends the experience of conflict, difference and division"; such stories, in John Thompson's
words, "justify the exercise of power by those who possess it" and
"serve to reconcile others to the fact that they do not."[114] It is, then,
no accident that patristic writers turn to biblical myths and historical
narratives in creating models of submission, "strategies of containment," for female audiences.[115]

The critic's task, then, is to show how "seemingly politically innocent objects, forms of subjectivity, actions, and events" are the effects
of power and authority, that is, the task is to denaturalize and rehis-
toricize what ideology has produced.[116] By an Althusserian symptomatic reading, the critic looks to the gaps and absences in the text,
reads what in effect is "illegible," and notes how the answers given
by a writer do not correspond to the questions posed.[117] As Pierre
Macherey describes this Althusserian-inspired form of ideology critique, the critic "should question the work as to what it does not and
cannot say," should note the "incoherence and incompleteness" that
seemingly bursts forth from the text, revealing "the active presence of
a conflict at its borders." In a literary work, he argues, "this ideological surge denotes the presence of a gap, a defect in the work, a com-
plexity which makes it *meaningful*."[118] In such ways the critic explores the use of symbolic forms in creating and sustaining relations
of domination.[119]

I have detailed numerous examples of stereotyping, universalizing,
and naturalizing of "woman" in patristic literature in my essays,
"The Lady Vanishes: Dilemmas of a Feminist Historian after the
'Linguistic Turn,'" and "Ideology, History, and the Construction of
'Woman' in Late Ancient Christianity";[120] here, I will briefly summa-
rize some points I there elaborated. These essays also illustrate the
inutility of historians' focus on such "natural objects" as "woman":
as detailed above, a distinctive contribution of Foucault to historical work was his "denaturalizing" and historicizing of such allegedly
"natural objects."

For Jerome, the stereotypic trait of "woman" is her weakness,
sometimes aligned with "softness of soul" or "fickle-mindedness"[121]
—yet he exploits the *topos* to produce a variety of ideological effects.
Sometimes he appeals to "female weakness" to deter women from
embarking on actions that would lure them toward irresistible pleasures—second marriage, for example, or a widow's public display of
her handsome male slaves.[122] The *topos* can also be deployed as a

shaming device for males, as when Jerome mocks men who, deficient in Aristotle and Cicero, dare to associate only with the uneducated and "weak women."[123] At other times, Jerome's appeal to female "weakness" serves to highlight, by contrast, the exemplary labors that a few token women undertook: Paula and Eustochium's ascetic renunciations are cases in point.[124] Here, even compliments occasion the denigration of women in general. John Chrysostom, for his part, warns men to eschew marriage by stereotyping women as wicked, false, insulting, garrulous, irrational, and given to drink—"all the vices dear to the sex."[125] To be sure, none of Jerome's or Chrysostom's *special* female friends, such as Paula or Olympias, shared these characteristics—but they were not, it seems, "woman."[126]

Other indications of ideology's work in naturalizing and universalizing "woman" are abundantly displayed in the writings of the Church Fathers. The varied uses of "nature" in patristic literature have often been remarked on,[127] many of which concern issues of sex and gender. Women's subjection to men is seen as "natural," that is, as instituted at creation by God's command,[128] although the alternative construction, that women were subjected to men only *after* the first sin, sits uncomfortably by its side in patristic writings.[129] The primary consistency in these appeals to "nature" lies in its use as a controlling device for sex- and gender-related behavior.

Nowhere is the universalizing tendency more obvious in patristic literature than in the amalgamation of all women with Eve. Scriptural verses such as 1 Timothy 2:11–15 blame Eve for the limitation on all women's activities and authority. Although numerous Church Fathers appeal to the identification of women with Eve as the justification for their submission to men and exclusion from the priesthood and public teaching offices,[130] perhaps none is so vociferous as Tertullian. Exhorting his female audience to clothe themselves in shabby "garments of penitence," Tertullian declaims:

> *You* are the Devil's gateway; *you* are the unsealer of that tree; *you* are the first foresaker of that divine law; *you* are the one who persuaded him hom the Devil was not brave enough to approach; *you* so lightly crushed the image of God, the man Adam; because of *your* punishment, that is, death, even the Son of God had to die. And you think to adorn yourself beyond your "tunics of skins" (Gen 3.21)?[131]

The universalizing message of the Christian master narrative thus conceals the subaltern status of many of its subjects. Stereotyping, naturalizing, universalizing—three common ideological mechanisms through which the Church Fathers constructed "woman."

A fourth device is the Fathers' "traditionalistic" appeal to a (largely mythical) past when women were allegedly chaste and submissive, in contrast to their present shocking behavior.[132] The Church Fathers fondly recall the "good old days" of Greece and Rome when women stayed at home, under strict control of their fathers and husbands. The distant past of Greece and Rome, however, little resembled the legal and social present,[133] in which women could retain their own property separate from their husband's, serve as guardians to their children, and initiate divorce.[134] The Fathers' appeals can be better understood if we contemplate their failure to change laws, or even general mores, pertaining to sexual activity and divorce: rhetorical exhortation was the major weapon they deployed to enforce their values among Christians.[135]

Macrina, Monica, and the "Social-Theological" Logic of the Text

I here borrow (and modify) Gabrielle Spiegel's notion of the "social logic of the text" to illuminate two late-fourth-century representations of women:[136] that of Gregory of Nyssa's sister Macrina in his *Life of Macrina* and *On the Soul and the Resurrection,* and that of Augustine's mother Monica in his *Confessions* and Cassiciacum dialogues. What is the "social (or here, 'socio-theological') logic" that attends the representations of these women as the pinnacles of Christian philosophy?

Macrina, Gregory confesses, stands as his teacher of wisdom,[137] although she had not (he makes clear) received even a literary, let alone a philosophical, education—pagan literature containing too many "undignified" tales about women. Her education consisted almost solely of Scripture study,[138] yet Gregory represents her as discoursing at length on theodicy, the human condition, the future life, and the soul.[139] In *On the Soul and the Resurrection,* Macrina is given an expanded platform—indeed, she "talks" for nearly seventy pages, instructing her brother on the Epicurean denial of providence, on atomistic theory, on humans as the microcosm of the universe, on the relation of the soul and body in the afterlife. She speaks of the love that draws us to the Good, evinces knowledge of Aristotelian logic, and alludes to astronomy and physics to make her case.[140] Her wisdom serves to shame less diligent Christians—particularly men.[141] In

Gregory's portrait, themes from Socrates' representation of his muse Diotima and the representation of "wisdom" as female in both Greek and Hebrew texts "hover over" his account.

Most important, Macrina serves as a tool with which Gregory can reflect on various troubling intellectual and theological problems of his day: Macrina is good to "think with."[142] Through Macrina, Gregory ponders the acceptability of a modified form of Origen's teaching that skirts the "dangerous" theological points that would shortly result in a posthumous condemnation of that third-century writer.[143] As a trope for Gregory, Macrina voices his own attempt to tame Origen into Christian respectability.[144] Rejecting the Origenist notion of the soul's "fall" into the body, Macrina nonetheless subtly preaches a nonphysical conception of hell, and changes Origen's equation of the body with the "coats of skins" that Adam and Eve received after the first sin (Gen. 3:21) into the "skins of irrationality" that trouble human life—sex, birth, old age.[145] Thus a first "Macrina-function" is to serve as spokesperson for Gregory's revised Origenist theology; through her, Gregory entertains Origenist themes without aligning himself too closely with "heresy." The socio-theological logic of the text, I posit, has less to do with the "real Macrina"—even as an encomium of Gregory's beloved, now-dead sister—than with an elaboration of theological points that troubled him and other theologians of his day.

Moreover, Macrina provides a living example of Gregory's teaching that in God's first creation of humans "in the image of God" (Gen. 1:26–27), there was no sexual division:[146] the "image" pertains to human rational capacities, not to bodies, which serve to differentiate the sexes.[147] As a virgin who rejected marriage, Macrina was en route to regaining that primal presexual condition in which the rational "image" remained pure.[148] Since as virgin and Christian philosopher Macrina has rejected sexual desire and proved the rationality of the "integral" mind, it does not surprise that Gregory doubts the propriety of naming her "woman."[149] She exemplifies the primal rational human who is "without sex."[150] Here, Macrina, exempt from the defects of femaleness, stands as moral and ascetic exemplar.

A second example of "woman as philosopher" is offered in Augustine's portrayal of his mother Monica in the *Confessions*[151] and some of his early treatises—but here, the representation serves somewhat different socio-theological functions than does Gregory's depiction of

Macrina. The *Confessions,* despite its extended focus on Augustine's childhood, is not a "family story" in any straightforward sense: his parents are progressively effaced.[152] Nonetheless, Monica proves indispensable to Augustine's message, since she offers (unlike Macrina) an exemplary paradigm of submissive matronhood,[153] and (like Macrina) stands as "faithful servant," God's "handmaid," not least in the rescue of her wayward son.[154] Yet Augustine borrows the *topos* of wisdom-as-woman to different effect than does Gregory.

In the Cassiciacum dialogues, Monica is depicted as participating in philosophical conversations on the country estate at which Augustine and his friends had gathered. She voices philosophical opinions and arrives independently at Cicero's definition of happiness.[155] Praising her astuteness, Augustine even claims that she beat him to the trenchant point he had reserved to clinch his argument.[156] As "philosopher," she, like Socrates, is fearless in facing discomfort and death.[157] She has found the Oneness and Beauty philosophers seek, not least among the manifestations of God's order in the world.[158] In their alleged "vision" at Ostia, Augustine represents Monica as expressing Plotinian notions of the soul's ascent; she becomes one with Beauty and "embraces Wisdom," the philosopher's goal.[159]

Yet Augustine's treatises make clear that Monica is uneducated; it remains doubtful whether she can read or write at all. This deficiency poses no theological or philosophical problem for Augustine's representation, however, for he claims that "the assurance that comes from theory"—men's province—"is one thing," while "that gained by native ability"—such as Monica's—is quite different.[160] Through various examples, Augustine discloses how throughout the ages even the uneducated have been able to reach wisdom.[161]

Here, I endorse Kim Power's suggestion that one function of Monica is to provide Augustine with an alternative model of piety to that of educated men. She illustrates a second route to wisdom, not that through study, which he and other elite men enjoy, but through a holiness that even simple, uneducated people—especially women— can embrace.[162] She represents, in effect, the great mass of untutored Christian laypeople, loyal sons and daughters of the Church: although, like them, Monica has not studied philosophy, she espouses truth and achieves the summit of the philosopher's quest.[163] Augustine assures her that if she steadfastly participates in the "sacred mysteries" (the Sacraments) and continues in virtue, this lower path will be good enough for her—and for God. She need not worry over problems of theodicy, the origin of evil, or the eternity of the world—points, Augustine implies, that can be reserved for educated males such as himself.[164] Monica's way, the way of the uneducated who nonetheless are faithful Christians, also leads to a heavenly home.

Although their representations differ, the socio-theological messages attending the depictions of Macrina and Monica both imply that lack of formal education poses no obstacle to the acquisition of Christian wisdom.[165] Gregory's portrayal of Macrina, however, harbors a more polemical edge: she is used to advance theological points within an inner-Christian debate over the appropriation of Origen's writings. Augustine's representation of his mother, by contrast, lauds the virtues of submissive matrons.

Have we then no "real" Macrina or Monica in these representations? We are reduced to this option only if we imagine that ancient treatises transparently "refer" to the events and people they depict. But if, with literary theorists, we abandon that view, we still have "lives" of Macrina and of Monica—but ones molded by literary representation. Moreover, their textual representations hint at "life outside the text," namely, (male) Christian writers' desire to stress that Christianity is open to all. Attending to the socio-theological logic of texts both allows room for considerations of linguistic representation and sometimes suggests the social forces at work in these constructions.[166]

Postcolonial Theory, the Roman Empire, and Early Christianity

The term "postcolonialism," Stephen Slemon comments, has variously been used, among other meanings, "as a way of ordering a critique of totalising forms of Western historicism; as a portmanteau term for a retooled notion of 'class'; as a subset of both postmodernism and post-structuralism . . . ; as the name for a condition of nativist longing in post-independence national groupings; . . . as an oppositional form of reading practice."[167] Just as colonialism manifested itself both in political relations and in signifying systems,[168] so "postcolonial" designates both the political critique of colonialism and a type of discourse theory ("critiques of the process of the production of knowledge about the Other")[169]—indeed, some theorists fear that "postcolonial" has come to signal little more than "marginality."[170] Yet the political aspect should stay linked to the signifying dimension,

Edward Said stresses, in that even though colonialism has largely ended as an imperialist practice, imperialism lingers on in the cultural sphere, and in "specific political, ideological, economic, and social practices."[171]

In the last two decades, debates within postcolonial studies and theory intensified around three points: (1) whether "postcolonial" can be used in a transhistorical sense (such as feminists sometime use "patriarchy") or should remain localized; (2) whether the colonized are assigned agency and an independent voice that is empowered to "talk back";[172] (3) whether postcolonial studies and theory constitute a subdivision of theories of post-structuralism and deconstruction.

On the first point, recent work emphasizes the "local" quality of the terms "colonial" and "post-colonial." As Anne McClintock understands it, places are postcolonial in different ways.[173] The distinctiveness of colonialism—and hence its "posts"—in India, various African countries, and elsewhere is underscored.[174] On the second issue, Gayatri Chakravorty Spivak, who earlier argued that the very position of being subaltern precluded having a voice, later modified her view.[175] Others, however, argue that the term "hegemony" (in which the conquered have some voice and power) is misleading if the commentator wishes to keep the dominance of the conquerors at the forefront.[176] As for the third issue, some celebrate postcolonial theory's alignment with postmodern thought, especially in their mutual refusal "to turn the Other into the Same,"[177] while others decry its "colonization" by "high" French theory.[178] (Gayatri Chakravorty Spivak appropriates Derrida;[179] Homi Bhabha favors Lacan.) Thus Kwame Anthony Appiah—a distinguished theorist of both "posts"—entitles an essay, "Is the 'Post-' in 'Postcolonial' the 'Post-' in 'Postmodern'?" concluding that the role the Third World plays in Euro-American postmodernist sensibility differs from the role postmodernism might play in the Third World itself.[180]

For scholars of late antiquity, still another question must be posed: is postcolonial theory, developed to explore colonial relations in modernity,[181] applicable to the premodern era? Several of its major themes, I suggest, helpfully illuminate ancient texts.[182] Despite the differing economic and governmental systems of capitalist Europe and late ancient Rome,[183] both concern empires. For both, territorial conquest economically and politically advantaged the metropole, but was often alleged by the conquerors to be for the benefit of those conquered.[184] Whether Rome's colonial rule wreaked comparable devastation to later manifestations of colonialism has been doubted. Edward Said, for example, cites Joseph Conrad's character Marlow in "Heart of Darkness," who contrasts Roman colonialization with that of modern empires: "their administration was merely a squeeze and nothing more."[185] Of course, to those on the ground at the time, the Roman invasion may have felt like something more vigorous than a squeeze.

Jane Webster, in "Roman Imperialism and the 'Post Imperial Age,'" selects four operations of postcolonial theory especially pertinent to the consideration of Roman colonialism: "decentring of Western categories of knowledge"; articulating active histories of the colonized, especially examining the subtle forms of their resistance; deconstructing the binary model of "the West" and "Others" by which the West has defined itself; and critiquing "the imperialism of representation," that is, examining "the relationship between power and knowledge in the production of the colonial Other."[186]

Breaking with a diffusionist, "top-down" model, and incorporating postcolonialist perspectives on the subtle ways that resistance and accommodation work together,[187] scholars studying the Romanization of the ancient Mediterranean have explored the means by which the Empire co-opted the subjugated into the ideology of the conquerors. (The favored term "Romanization" has been defined as "the processes of socio-cultural change resultant upon the integration of indigenous societies into the Roman Empire.")[188] Those who advocate a "dialectical" model that attends to the role of the indigenous peoples in the creation of the new culture sometimes prefer the term "acculturation," a concept that they assert allows a fuller role for the contributions of the conquered.[189] "Acculturation," these scholars claim, also counteracts the "excessively euro-centric" stress on Rome's "civilizing mission."[190] Nonetheless, "bottom-up" approaches remain elusive, given the nature of the remaining sources. Changes in cult, for example, could not have happened spontaneously, some scholars allege; there must have been a "top-down" movement from Rome to account for the similar patterns of change one finds in various provinces of the Roman Empire.[191]

The call for local specificity by postcolonial theorists is also championed by historians of late antiquity, who agree that Romanization was far more successful (from Rome's point of view) in some areas than in others.[192] For example, Greg Woolf argues that the Romans' conquest of Greece had different results and was differently justified than the Romans' move into Western territories. Since the Greeks, unlike the Western peoples subdued by Rome, enjoyed a higher standard of culture than their conquerors, Rome could not pretend to be "civilizing" them, but rather needed to allege that she was saving them from "decadence."[193] Moreover, Woolf argues, Romanization did not come in a "ready-made cultural package," but varied with time and place.[194]

Another debate among historians of antiquity concerns the types of evidence adduced for Romanization: to what extent should scholars look to "high culture" indicators? Some scholars argue that earlier studies gave too little attention to "ideational factors," and wish to call attention to "Roman cultural forms and values."[195] Clifford Ando's book, *Imperial Ideology and Provincial Loyalty in the Roman Empire,* explores in exhaustive detail the symbolic means by which Roman ideology was spread and appropriated. Ando stresses a "consensus" model: North Africans, for example, for the most part readily appropriated the culture and values of the Roman overlords.[196] This view suggests, as Peter Brunt has put it, that if "by culture and sentiment men were Romans, Romans they were."[197]

Others, such as P. W. M. Freeman, rejecting what he considers an overemphasis on factors such as language, art, and religion, argue that material culture needs to be taken more fully into account.[198] On this view, more attention should be paid to archeological finds, which, unaccountably, have not been thoroughly incorporated into many studies.[199] Brent Shaw concludes that scholars have focused on the consumption of urban elites, rather than on production; in particular, they have failed to attend to evidence pertaining to agrarian issues.[200]

How would the views of postcolonial theorists and ancient historians interested in Romanization play out in a specific study? Andrew Jacobs's *Remains of the Jews: The Holy Land and Christian Empire in Late Antiquity* examines late ancient Christian writings pertaining to Jews (especially to Jews in relation to what Christians called "the Holy Land") by such authors as Eusebius of Caesarea, Cyril of Jerusalem, Epiphanius of Salamis, Origen, Jerome, and various writers of travel and pilgrimage accounts. Most of these writers lived in the period when Christianity had achieved dominance within the Roman Empire. How Judaea, the home of "ethnic religious others," merged with the Christian "holy land" in such a way as to construct as well as to problematize Christian imperial identity ("a form of religious identification that is explicitly associated with the regimes and structures of the Roman Empire") is Jacobs's central question.[201]

Palestine in late antiquity, Jacobs argues, provides a rich site for analyzing asymmetrical relations of power via the lens of postcolonial criticism. There, representatives of "imperial Christianity" were able to cast the Jew into the role of the "colonial 'subaltern': that dominated object of fear, mistrust, and envy that, through disparate forms of intellectual construction, the Christian can transform into his or her own indispensable shadow." Through discourse about Jews of the Christian holy land, Christians elaborated a new mode of identity for themselves.[202]

Jacobs explains postcolonial theory's importance for his study: it first locates discourses of domination and power, and then uncovers how the colonized can find a voice even within these dominating structures. Postcolonial theory, he argues, is more advantageous than anthropological or sociological approaches in its double emphasis on the instability of the discourses involved and "the very real material and political consequences of those discourses . . . Materiality and instability have remained central components of postcolonial analyses."[203]

Jacobs also reconsiders debates among earlier scholars who studied the Christianization of Palestine with an eye to reconfiguring the relation between rhetoric and representation. As a practice of reading "against the grain" of cultural, political, and economic hegemony,[204] colonial discourse analysis refuses to separate rhetoric from reality. The "network of linguistic and material practices that we call discourse . . . is itself a site for the production of reality," Jacobs concludes. The "mechanics" by which the Jewish "other"—*and* Christian identity—were simultaneously constructed is the larger problem this book addresses.[205]

The above examples serve to illustrate how attending to various stripes of theory might illuminate ancient texts. By appropriating the "mental tools" made available by scholars whose disciplinary homes range across the humanities and social sciences, those who explore early Christian texts join the wider academy as contributors to, not just recipients of, a refurbished intellectual history.

Abbreviations and Frequently Cited Books

Abbreviations

The following abbreviations are used for editions of early Christian, Greek, and Latin sources:

CCL   *Corpus Christianorum,* Series Latina (Turnhout, 1953–)
CSEL   *Corpus Scriptorum Christianorum Latinorum* (Vienna, 1866–)
GCS   *Die Griechische Christliche Schriftsteller der ersten drei Jahrhunderte* (Leipzig, 1899–)
Jaeger *Gregorii Nyssensi Opera* (Berlin, 1921–)
PG   *Patrologia Graeca,* ed. J. P. Migne (Paris, 1857–1866)
PL   *Patrologia Latina,* ed. J. P. Migne (Paris, 1844–1865)
PLS   *Patrologia Latina Supplementum,* ed. Adalbert Hamman (Paris, 1958–)
SC   *Sources Chrétiennes* (Paris, 1943–)

Other common Latin abbreviations are *Ep.* = Letter, *Comm.* = Commentary, *Hom.* = Homily, *Serm.* = Sermon.

Frequently Cited Works

Frequently cited books are noted throughout by the abbreviations given in the list below. In many cases, subtitles in the endnotes are deleted. Original publication dates of books (when authors/editors have supplied them) are indicated in square brackets.

Althusser and Balibar, *Capital*

Althusser, Louis, and Etienne Balibar. *Reading Capital,* trans. Ben Brewster. London, 1979 [1968].

Anderson, *Tracks*

Anderson, Perry. *In the Tracks of Historical Materialism.* Chicago, 1983.

Ankersmit, *Representation*

Ankersmit, F. R. *Historical Representation.* Stanford, 2001.

Appleby, Hunt, and Jacob, *Telling the Truth*

Appleby, Joyce, Lynn Hunt, and Margaret Jacob. *Telling the Truth about History.* New York, 1994.

Attridge, Bennington, and Young, *Post-Structuralism*

Attridge, Derek, Geoff Bennington, and Robert Young, eds. *Post-Structuralism and the Question of History.* Cambridge, 1987.

Bannet, *Structuralism/ Dissent*

Bannet, Eve Tavor. *Structuralism and the Logic of Dissent: Barthes, Derrida, Foucault, Lacan.* Urbana, 1989.

Barthes, *Semiotic Challenge*

Barthes, Roland. *The Semiotic Challenge,* trans. Richard Howard. New York, 1988 [1985].

Benveniste, *Problems*

Benveniste, Emile. *Problems in General Linguistics,* trans. Mary Elizabeth Meek. Coral Gables, 1971 [1966].

Berkhofer, *Story*

Berkhofer, Robert E., Jr. *Beyond the Great Story: History as Text and Discourse.* Cambridge, Mass., 1995.

Bevir, *Logic*

Bevir, Mark. *The Logic of the History of Ideas.* Cambridge, 1999.

Bloch, *Craft*

Bloch, Marc. *The Historian's Craft,* trans. Peter Putnam. New York, 1953 [1949].

Boucher, *Texts*

Boucher, David. *Texts in Context: Revisionist Methods for Studying the History of Ideas.* Dordrecht, 1985.

Burke, *Perspectives*

Burke, Peter, ed. *New Perspectives on Historical Writing.* University Park, Pa., 1992 [1981].

Carrard, *Poetics*

Carrard, Philippe. *Poetics of the New History: French Historical Discourse from Braudel to Chartier.* Baltimore, 1992.

Chartier, *Edge*

Chartier, Roger. *On the Edge of the Cliff: History, Language, and Practices,* trans. Lydia G. Cochrane. Baltimore, 1997.

Collingwood, *Autobiography*

Collingwood, R. G. *An Autobiography.* Oxford, 1939.

Collingwood, *Idea*

Collingwood, R. G. *The Idea of History.* New York, 1957 [1946].

Croce, *History/Liberty* Croce, Benedetto. *History as the Story of Liberty,* trans. Sylvia Sprigge. New York, 1941 [1938].

Danto, *Analytical Philosophy* Danto, Arthur C. *Analytical Philosophy of History.* Cambridge, 1965.

Danto, *Narration* Danto, Arthur C. *Narration and Knowledge.* New York, 1985.

Davidson, *Foucault* Davidson, Arnold I., ed. *Foucault and His Interlocutors.* New York, 1997.

De Certeau, *Faiblesse* De Certeau, Michel. *La Faiblesse de croire,* ed. Luce Giard. Paris, 1987.

De Certeau, *Heterologies* De Certeau, Michel. *Heterologies: Discourse on the Other,* trans. Brian Massumi. Minneapolis, 1986.

De Certeau, *The Writing of History* De Certeau, Michel. *The Writing of History,* trans. Tom Conley. New York, 1988 [1975].

Derrida, *Grammatology* Derrida, Jacques. *Of Grammatology,* trans. Gayatri Chakravorty Spivak. Baltimore, 1976 [1967].

Domanska, *Encounters* Domanska, Ewa, ed. *Encounters: Philosophy of History after Postmodernism.* Charlottesville, 1998.

Dosse, *Structuralism* Dosse, François. *History of Structuralism. Volume I: The Rising Sign, 1945–1966. Volume II: The Sign Sets, 1967–Present,* both trans. Deborah Glassman. Minneapolis, 1997 [1991, 1992].

Dray, *Laws* Dray, William. *Laws and Explanation in History.* London, 1957.

Dray, *On History/Philosophers* Dray, William. *On History and Philosophers of History.* Leiden, 1989.

Dreyfus and Rabinow, *Beyond Structuralism* Dreyfus, Herbert L., and Paul Rabinow. *Michel Foucault: Beyond Structuralism and Hermeneutics.* 2d ed. Chicago, 1983 [1982].

Foucault, *Archaeology* Foucault, Michel. *The Archaeology of Knowledge,* trans. A. M. Sheridan Smith. New York, 1972 [1969].

Foucault, *Dits* Foucault, Michel. *Dits et écrits, 1954–1988,* ed. Daniel Defert and François Ewald. 4 vols. Paris, 1994.

Foucault, *Order* Foucault, Michel. *The Order of Things: An Archaeology of the Human Sciences.* New York, 1970 [1966].

Furet, *Workshop*   Furet, François. *In the Workshop of History*,
                                 trans. Jonathan Mandelbaum. Chicago, 1984
                                 [1982].

Gadamer, *Truth*   Gadamer, Hans-Georg. *Truth and Method*. 2d
                                 ed. New York, 1988 [1960].

Gardiner, *Theories of History* Gardiner, Patrick, ed. *Theories of History*.
                                 Glencoe, 1959.

Geertz, *Local Knowledge*   Geertz, Clifford. *Local Knowledge: Further
                                 Essays in Interpretive Anthropology*. New
                                 York, 1983.

Goldstein, *Knowing*   Goldstein, Leon J. *Historical Knowing*. Austin,
                                 1976.

Harlan, *Degradation*   Harlan, David. *The Degradation of American
                                 History*. Chicago, 1997.

Hobsbawm, *On History*   Hobsbawm, Eric. *On History*. New York, 1997.

Iggers, *Historiography*   Iggers, Georg G. *Historiography in the
                                 Twentieth Century: From Scientific Objectivity
                                 to the Postmodern Challenge*. Hanover, N.H.,
                                 1997 [1993].

Jakobson, *Six Lectures*   Jakobson, Roman. *Six Lectures on Sound and
                                 Meaning*, trans. John Mepham. Cambridge,
                                 Mass., 1978 [1976].

Jöckel, *"Nouvelle histoire"*   Jöckel, Sabine. *"Nouvelle histoire" und
                                 Literaturwissenschaft*, vol. I. Rheinfelden,
                                 1984.

Kaye and McClelland,   Kaye, Harvey J., and Keith McClelland, eds.
E. P. Thompson   *E. P. Thompson: Critical Perspectives*.
                                 Philadelphia, 1990.

Kellner, *Language*   Kellner, Hans. *Language and Historical
                                 Representation: Getting the Story Crooked*.
                                 Madison, 1989.

LaCapra, *Rethinking*   LaCapra, Dominick. *Rethinking Intellectual
                                 History: Texts, Contexts, Language*. Ithaca,
                                 1983.

LaCapra, *Soundings*   LaCapra, Dominick. *Soundings in Critical
                                 Theory*. Ithaca, 1989.

LaCapra and Kaplan,   LaCapra, Dominick, and Steven L. Kaplan, eds.
Intellectual History   *Modern European Intellectual History:
                                 Reappraisals and New Perspectives*. Ithaca,
                                 1982.

Langlois and Seignobos,   Langlois, Charles V., and Charles Seignobos.
Introduction   *Introduction to the Study of History*, trans.
                                 G. G. Berry. New York, 1925 [1898].

Lehmann and Richter, *Historical Terms*
Lehmann, Harmut, and Melvin Richter, eds. *The Meaning of Historical Terms and Concepts: New Studies on Begriffsgeschichte.* Washington, D.C., 1996.

Lévi-Strauss, *Conversations*
Lévi-Strauss, Claude/Didier Eribon. *Conversations with Claude Lévi-Strauss,* trans. Paula Wissing. Chicago, 1991 [1988].

Lévi-Strauss, *Structural Anthropology*
Lévi-Strauss, Claude. *Structural Anthropology,* trans. Claire Jacobson and Brooke Grundfest Schoepf. New York, 1963 [1958].

Lévi-Strauss, *Tristes Tropiques*
Lévi-Strauss, Claude. *Tristes Tropiques,* trans. John and Doreen Weightman. New York, 1974 [1955].

Macksey and Donato, *Controversy*
Macksey, Richard, and Eugenio Donato, eds. *The Structuralist Controversy: The Languages of Criticism and the Sciences of Man.* Baltimore, 1972 [1970].

Marrou, *Meaning*
Marrou, Henri-Irénée. *The Meaning of History,* trans. Robert J. Olsen [from 4th rev. French edition, 1959]. Baltimore, 1966.

McDonald, *Turn*
McDonald, Terrence J., ed. *The Historic Turn in the Human Sciences.* Ann Arbor, 1996.

Meyerhoff, *Philosophy of History*
Meyerhoff, Hans, ed. *The Philosophy of History of Our Time.* Garden City, 1959.

Momigliano, *Studies in Historiography*
Momigliano, Arnaldo. *Studies in Historiography.* New York, 1966.

Murphey, *Knowledge*
Murphey, Murray G. *Our Knowledge of the Historical Past.* Indianapolis, 1973.

Novick, *Dream*
Novick, Peter. *That Noble Dream: The "Objectivity Question" and the American Historical Profession.* Cambridge, 1988.

Putnam, *Realism*
Putnam, Hilary. *Realism with a Human Face,* ed. James Conant. Cambridge, Mass., 1990.

Putnam, *Reason*
Putnam, Hilary. *Reason, Truth, and History.* Cambridge, 1981.

Revel and Hunt, *Histories*
Revel, Jacques, and Lynn Hunt, eds. *Histories: French Constructions of the Past,* trans. Arthur Goldhammer et al. New York, 1995.

Ricoeur, *Contribution*
Ricoeur, Paul. *The Contribution of French Historiography to the Theory of History.* Oxford, 1980.

Ricoeur, *Time*

Ricoeur, Paul. *Time and Narrative,* trans. Kathleen McLaughlin and David Pellauer. 3 vols. Chicago, 1984 [1983], 1985 [1984], 1988 [1985].

Rüsen, *Studies in Metahistory*

Rüsen, Jörn. *Studies in Metahistory,* ed. Pieter Duvenage. Pretoria, 1993.

Saussure, *Cours*

Saussure, Ferdinand de. *Cours de linguistique générale,* ed. Tullio de Mauro. Paris, 1976.

Skinner, *Return*

Skinner, Quentin, ed. *The Return of Grand Theory in the Human Sciences.* Cambridge, 1985.

Veyne, *Writing History*

Veyne, Paul. *Writing History: Essay on Epistemology,* trans. Mina Moore-Rinvolucri. Middletown, 1984 [1971].

White, *Content*

White, Hayden. *The Content of the Form: Narrative Discourse and Historical Representation.* Baltimore, 1987.

White, *Metahistory*

White, Hayden. *Metahistory: The Historical Imagination in Nineteenth-Century Europe.* Baltimore, 1973.

White, *Tropics*

White, Hayden. *Tropics of Discourse: Essays in Cultural Criticism.* Baltimore, 1978.

Woodman, *Rhetoric*

Woodman, A. J. *Rhetoric in Classical Historiography: Four Studies.* London, 1988.

Young, *White Mythologies*

Young, Robert. *White Mythologies: Writing History and the West.* London, 1990.

Notes

Preface

1. Some readers will be disappointed that I do not treat psychoanalytic approaches to history. Although medievalists such as Dyan Elliott and Amy Hollywood have put psychoanalytic theory to good use in their work, the benefits to late ancient Christian studies have, to date, been less obvious— although Virginia Burrus's *The Sex Lives of Saints: An Erotics of Ancient Hagiography* (Philadelphia, 2003), may inspire more sophisticated work.
2. Some theorists argue that all written materials may be read as "texts" *or* as "documents"; the reader, not the material, provides the categorization.
3. The change of name is revealing. "Patristics" connotes a male- and church-oriented field of theological and philological study, usually undertaken by adherents of various Christian confessions; "late ancient Christian studies" signals the move to more inclusive approaches within social science and humanities disciplines.
4. Rey Chow, "The Interruption of Referentiality," *South Atlantic Quarterly* 101 (2002): 172. Chow here distinguishes "theory" from Frankfurt School critique, various forms of historicism, and sociological and anthropological theory. Chow suggests that the abandonment of referentiality problematizes the notion of agents' resistance (181–186).
5. Paul Strohm, "Introduction," *Theory and the Premodern Text* (Minneapolis, 2000), pp. xiii, xiv.
6. Gareth Stedman Jones, "From Historical Sociology to Theoretic History," *British Journal of Sociology* 27 (1976): 296.

Introduction

1. Novick, *Dream,* p. 628. Novick highlights splits of a social (more than of an intellectual) nature, and proclaims history's fragmentation, not its "demise."

2. Iggers, *Historiography,* chap. 10.
3. Appleby, Hunt, and Jacob, *Telling the Truth,* p. 237.
4. Keith Windschuttle, *The Killing of History: How Literary Critics and Social Theorists Are Murdering Our Past* (New York, 1997 [1996]).
5. Several reviewers suggest that Novick's gloom is unfounded. Allan Megill comments that the book itself does not take this "apocalyptic" tone ("AHR Forum: Fragmentation and the Future of Historiography," *American Historical Review* 96 [1991]: 693), while J. H. Hexter urges Novick to "cheer up" ("AHR Forum: Carl Becker, Professor Novick, and Me; or Cheer Up, Professor N.!" *American Historical Review* 96 [1991]: 680). Thomas L. Haskell asks readers to take Novick's "distress" "with a grain of salt" ("Objectivity Is Not Neutrality: Rhetoric vs. Practice in Peter Novick's *That Noble Dream,*" *History and Theory* 29 [1990]: 157).
6. Henry Ashby Turner Jr., "Symposium: History: As It Really Was?; Peter Novick and the 'Objectivity Question' in History," *Academic Questions* 8 (1995): 23. Turner's paper was presented at the 1994 convention of the National Association of Scholars.
7. Paul Strohm, "Introduction," *Theory and the Premodern Text* (Minneapolis, 2000), pp. xiii–xiv.
8. Megill, "AHR Forum: Fragmentation and the Future of Historiography," p. 695. On changes within English and philosophy since the mid-twentieth century, see M. H. Abrams, "The Transformation of English Studies: 1930–1995," and Hilary Putnam, "A Half Century of Philosophy, Viewed from Within," both in *American Academic Culture in Transformation,* ed. Thomas Bender and Carl E. Schorske (Princeton, 1997), pp. 123–149, 193–226.
9. Hayden White's *Metahistory,* published in 1973, was first translated into German in 1991. The book appears not to have been well known in German historians' circles in the late 1970s; in the collection of sixteen essays published as *Theorie und Erzählung in der Geschichte,* ed. Jürgen Kocka and Thomas Nipperdey (Munich, 1979), for example, I find only two references to White's work (pp. 96, 311). A few years later, White's work was discussed in Jörn Rüsen, "Geschichtsschreibung als Theorieproblem der Geschichtswissenschaft," in *Formen der Geschichtsschreibung,* ed. Reinhart Koselleck et al. (Munich, 1982), pp. 30–33, and in essays in Rüsen's *Studies in Metahistory.* Narrative theory (Arthur Danto) was familiar to Rüsen by the early 1980s (see his *Rekonstruktion der Vergangenheit: Grundzüge einer Historik II: Die Prinzipien der historischen Forschung* [Göttingen, 1986], p. 44). Two helpful assessments of Rüsen's work are provided by F. R. Ankersmit (review of *Rekonstruktion der Vergangenheit* in *History and Theory* 27 [1988]: 81–94) and Robert Anchor (review of *Lebendige Geschichte: Grundzüge einer Historik III: Formen und Funktionen des historischen Wissens* [Göttingen, 1989] in *History and Theory* 30 [1991]: 347–356). For history and hermeneutics, see Reinhart Koselleck

and Hans-Georg Gadamer, *Hermeneutik und Historik* (Heidelberg, 1987), pp. 9–36; Ute Daniel, "Quo vadis, Sozialgeschichte? Kleines Plädoyer für eine hermeneutische Wende," in *Sozialgeschichte, Alltagsgeschichte, Mikro-Historie,* ed. Winfried Schulze (Göttingen, 1994), pp. 54–64. Theory's late advent to German historical discussions is signaled by Wolfgang Hardtwig, "Alltagsgeschichte Heute," in *Sozialgeschichte, Alltagsgeschichte, Mikro-Historie,* pp. 19–20. In Rüsen's *Studies in Metahistory,* "theory" appears largely to mean "methodology"; although Rüsen claims Foucault as a major influence on German historiography ("Paradigm Shift and Theoretical Reflection in Western German Historical Studies," p. 177), French theory appears nowhere in the volume. I address the German contribution to *Alltagsgeschichte* and *Begriffsgeschichte* later in the book. For a sustained argument that both Foucault and Derrida took their primary material from Heidegger, see Luc Ferry and Alain Renaut, *French Philosophy of the Sixties* (trans., Amherst, 1990 [1985]), especially chaps. 3 and 4.

10. Classical correspondence theories of truth often assumed a metaphysical realist position, namely, that knowledge claims could be verified if a statement referring to the "real world" could be shown to be true (for example, "The belief that snow is white is true if and only if snow is white"). But problems arise: if it is a "fact" that snow is white, then we need to know what facts are, and we also need to know what it is for a belief to correspond to a fact—and these are issues that classical correspondence theories have not satisfactorily resolved. Although most philosophers have rejected the sort of realism that assumes a mind- or concept-independent way to test "reality," some (for example, Wilfrid Sellars) have argued that there can be a constructivist-realist position that holds that accuracy of reference "might not be a *criterion* for judging the truth of a claim but rather an *effect* of getting our claims right" (Terrence Tilley, *Inventing Catholic Tradition* [Maryknoll, N.Y., 2000], p. 160). The *construction* of the truth claim is different from its *assessment* as true. Here, the claim to truth seems to rest on the notion of the "acceptability" of the statement within a community of practitioners skilled in the particular subject; how we know our claims are right seems to rest only on our acknowledging that the claimant's skill lends her claim credence. Historians can object that even this reduced claim is problematic for their field since no "practical investigations" of the past can be made (except, of course, by the indirect means of consulting documents and other artifacts that remain in the present). And what would count as a "reliably produced claim" on which historians might agree can become more difficult for the distant past. For a recent discussion by a philosopher who concludes, "there can be no interesting correspondence theory," see Bernard Williams, *Truth and Truthfulnesss* (Princeton, 2002), pp. 64–65. I thank Terrence Tilley, Kenneth Surin, and Lewis Ayres for their assistance on this point.

11. Historian J. H. Hexter notes that for almost two decades after Carl Becker's

1931 presidential address to the American Historical Association, "relativism was perhaps the dominant way of thinking about history in the United States." Under the impact of the rise of Nazism, however, Becker's relativism gave way ("Carl Becker and Historical Relativism," in Hexter, *On Historians* [Cambridge, 1979], pp. 15, 39–40).

12. See, for example, Maurice Mandelbaum, *The Problem of Historical Knowledge* (New York, 1967 [1938]), pp. 20, 174, and Part II. Mandelbaum believes that historians in practice use a correspondence theory of truth and that they fall into relativism because they do not know how to answer the critics of this theory (185–186). But Mandelbaum expresses more optimism on this point than do the historians, perhaps because he believes that "it is a property of language to refer to non-linguistic entities" (186).

13. Kellner, "Conclusion," in idem, *Language*, pp. 332–333.

14. For the turn (and resistance) to "narrative," see Roger Chartier, "Zeit der Zweifel: Zum Verständnis gegenwärtiger Geschichtsschreibung," *Neue Runschau* 105 (1994): 13–18.

15. For resemblances between Foucault and analytical philosophy, especially Wittgenstein, see Arnold I. Davidson, "Foucault and the Analysis of Concepts," in his *The Emergence of Sexuality* (Cambridge, 2001), chap. 7.

16. For similarities and differences, see Paul Ricoeur, "Intellectual Autobiography," in *The Philosophy of Paul Ricoeur*, ed. Lewis Edwin Hahn (Chicago, 1995), pp. 40–41.

17. One notable exception is Michel Foucault, "La Philosophie analytique de la politique" [1978], in idem, *Dits*, III: 534–551, discussed in Arnold I. Davidson, "Structures and Strategies of Discourse: Remarks towards a History of Foucault's Philosophy of Language," in his *Foucault*, pp. 2–4. Foucault elsewhere notes the absence of specialized philosophy journals in France early in his career ("Structuralism and Post-Structuralism," *Telos* 16 [1983]: 211).

18. Peter Brooks, "Introduction," to Tzvetan Todorov, *Introduction to Poetics* (Minneapolis, 1981 [1968, 1973]), p. xvii.

19. See Leopold von Ranke's comment that the notion of a world spirit acting through time is "not adequate for historical research" ("The Pitfalls of a Philosophy of History" [1954], in *The Theory and Practice of History: Leopold von Ranke*, ed. Georg G. Iggers and Konrad von Moltke [trans., Indianapolis, 1973], p. 49). On French historians' fear of philosophy of history in the Spengler/Toynbee mode, see Roger Chartier, "Philosophie et histoire: Un dialogue," in *L'histoire et le métier d'historien en France 1945–1995*, ed. François Bédarida (Paris, 1995), p. 149; see p. 154 on Hegelian "philosophical history."

20. White, *Metahistory*, p. 135.

21. Reflecting on the "culture wars" that have surrounded the discipline of history, Paul Rabinow and William M. Sullivan posit that "[p]erhaps the deepest theme of the twentieth century . . . has been the shattering of the

triumphalist view of history bequeathed to us by the nineteenth" ("The Interpretive Turn: A Second Look," *Interpretive Social Science,* ed. Rabinow and Sullivan [Berkeley, 1987], p. 24). Whether *historians* consider the nineteenth-century understanding of history to have been "shattered" remains questionable.

22. See Antony Easthope, "Romancing the Stone: History-Writing and Rhetoric," *Social History* 18 (1993): 236–237.

1. Defending and Lamenting History

1. Novick, *Dream.* The phrase "noble dream" originates with Thomas Clarke Smith, whose essay, "The Writing of American History in America From 1884 to 1934," *American Historical Review* 40 (1935), was mocked by Charles Beard in "That Noble Dream," *American Historical Review* 41 (1935): 74–85.

2. Commentators note that American historians' dream of "objectivity" lacked Ranke's visionary overtone; see Martin Bunzl, *Real History* (London, 1997), p. 3; Iggers, *Historiography,* pp. 25–26. On Ranke's "idealistic" philosophy of history, see Jörn Rüsen, "Rhetoric and Aesthetics of History: Leopold von Ranke" [1990], in his *Studies in Metahistory,* chap. 9, especially p. 138.

3. Hayden V. White, "Translator's Introduction," in Carlo Antoni, *From History to Sociology* (trans., Detroit, 1959 [1940]), p. xv. On the displacement of Romantic by "scientific" historiography, see White, *Metahistory,* chap. 4; idem, "The Fictions of Factual Representation" [1976], in his *Tropics,* pp. 122–125; see also Hans Kellner, "Twenty Years After: A Note on *Metahistories* and Their Horizons," *Storia della Storiografia* 24 (1993): 113–114.

4. On nineteenth-century German historicism, see Georg G. Iggers, "Historicism: The History and Meaning of the Term," *Journal of the History of Ideas* 56 (1995): 129–152; F. R. Ankersmit, "The Dialectics of Narrativist Historism" [1995], in his *Representation,* pp. 123–148. The word "historism" echoes the German *historismus,* as in Friedrich Meinecke, *Die Entstehung des Historismus* (Munich, 1936). For varying uses of the word, see Georg G. Iggers, "Historismus im Meinungsstreit," in *Historismus in den Kulturwissenschaften,* ed. Otto G. Oexle et al. (Cologne, 1996), pp. 7–27. On Meinecke's influence, see Charles A. Beard and Alfred Vagts, "Currents of Thought in Historiography," *American Historical Review* 42 (1937): 466. A call to study historical investigation *before* the "historicist revolution" (for example, the history of laws and institutions) is made by J. G. A. Pocock, "The Origins of the Study of the Past," *Comparative Studies in Society and History* 4 (1962): 245.

5. Ranke's famous phrase, "wie es eigentlich gewesen," is found in the "Vorrede" to his *Geschichten der romanischen und germanischen Völker von*

1494 bis 1514 [3d ed.; Leipzig, 1885], p. vii. Hajo Holborn argued that the phrase derived from Thucydides (1.22) (*History and the Humanities* [Garden City, N.Y., 1972], pp. 90–91, cited in Anthony Grafton, *The Footnote* [Cambridge, Mass., 1997], p. 69); compare Wilhelm von Humboldt's claim that "the historian's task is to present what actually happened" ("On the Historian's Task" [1821; trans., 1967], in *The Theory and Practice of History: Leopold von Ranke,* ed. Georg G. Iggers and Konrad von Moltke [trans., Indianapolis, 1973], p. 5; German original ["Ueber die Aufgabe des Geschichtschreibers"] in von Humboldt, *Gesammelte Schriften* [Berlin, 1903], IV: 35–56 ["Die Aufgabe des Geschichtschreibers ist die Darstellung des Geschehenen . . . Wenn man die unbedeutendste Thatsache zu erzählen versucht, aber streng nur das sagen will, was sich wirklich zugetragen hat"]). Also see Arthur Danto's view that Ranke's phrase was not "an extraordinarily boastful claim" but a "humble disclaimer" that he did not aspire to judge the past or instruct the present for the benefit of the future (idem, *Analytical Philosophy,* pp. 131, 139); also see Felix Gilbert, *History: Politics or Culture? Reflections on Ranke and Burckhardt* (Princeton, 1990), pp. 19–20, 34–36; Hajo Holborn, "The History of Ideas," *American Historical Review* 73 (1968): 687. Henry Ashby Turner Jr. takes the phrase to be Ranke's declaration of history's independence from theology and philosophy ("Symposium History: As It Really Was?; Peter Novick and the 'Objectivity Question' in History," *Academic Questions* 8 [1995]: 17).

6. Leopold von Ranke, "On the Character of Historical Science" [manuscript of the 1830s], in *The Theory and Practice of History: Leopold von Ranke,* pp. 38, 44–45 (German original ["Idee der Universalhistorie"] ed. by Eberhard Kessel, *Historische Zeitschrift* 178 [1954]: 290–301). Thus prehistory is ruled out as "real" history; "history" as construed in India and China does not fare much better (46).

7. Leonard Krieger, *Ranke: The Meaning of History* (Chicago, 1977), pp. 22, 24, 28–29—despite Ranke's belief that God guided history.

8. Ibid., p. 3. For an early account of Ranke's turn from ancient to modern history, see Edward Gaylord Bourne, "Leopold von Ranke" [1895], in his *Essays in Historical Criticism* (New York, 1901), pp. 245–251. On Ranke's classical background, see Peter Gay, *Style in History* (New York 1974), pp. 70, 74. Arnaldo Momigliano comments, "Ranke may have started from Thucydides, but ultimately became himself the model of a new historiography: this really meant independence from classical models for modern history" ("The Place of Ancient Historiography in Modern Historiography," in his *Settimo contributo alla storia degli studi classici e del mondo antico* [Rome, 1984], p. 28).

9. Ranke muses on what he attempted in writing his *Englische Geschichte,* in his *Über die Epochen der neueren Geschichte,* ed. Hans Herzfeld (Schloss Laupheim, n.d.), p. 19, cited in Krieger, *Ranke,* p. 5; and his "Vorrede," *Geschichten der romanischen und germanischen Völker,* p. vii: "Strenge

Darstellung der Thatsache, wie bedingt und unschön sie auch sei, ist ohne Zweifel das oberste Gesetz."

10. Leopold von Ranke, Letter to Ferdinand Ranke (August 31, 1839), in *Neue Briefe*, ed. Berhard Hoeft and Hans Herzfeld (n.p., 1949), p. 268, cited and translated in Gay, *Style in History*, p. 70; Leopold von Ranke, "Preface to the History of the Popes," in *The Theory and Practice of History: Leopold von Ranke*, pp. 142–144. For his "joy" in historical detail, see Leopold von Ranke, "On the Relations of History and Philosophy" [a manuscript of the 1830s], in ibid., p. 30. In the archives, he hoped to find "a still unknown history of Europe" (from a letter of August 1827, cited in Bourne, "Leopold von Ranke," p. 251).

11. Arnaldo Momigliano's lifetime work was to demonstrate the antiquarian roots of modern historiography; he pushes back the latter's "birth" to before Ranke, thus challenging Ranke's pride of place. See especially Momigliano's "The Introduction of History as an Academic Subject and Its Implications" [1985], in his *Ottavo contributo alla storia degli studi classici e del mondo antico* (Rome, 1987), pp. 161–178. Momigliano, like Ranke, remained a historical objectivist; see his essay, "History in an Age of Ideologies," *American Scholar* 51 (1982): 495–505. For a helpful summary, see Mark Salber Phillips, "Reconsiderations on History and Antiquarianism: Arnaldo Momigliano and the Historiography of Eighteenth-Century Britain," *Journal of the History of Ideas* 57 (1996): 297, 300, 302, 315. Also see Peter Brown's moving tribute to Momigliano ("Arnaldo Dante Momigliano, 1908–1987") in *Proceedings of the British Academy* 74 (1988): 405–442; and others in *Rivista storica italiana* 100 (1988), a journal on whose editorial committee Momigliano long served. Brown notes that by the time Momigliano was twenty-six, he had published three monographs and 150 articles and reviews (409).

12. Grafton, *Footnote*, pp. 59–60, 64–65, 228–229. For a sharp critique of Ranke's alleged "objectivity" and "scientific methods," see M. I. Finley, "'How It Really Was'"[1984], in his *Ancient History* (London, 1985), chap. 4.

13. Georg G. Iggers, "The Image of Ranke in American and German Historical Thought," *History and Theory* 2 (1962): 20; Edward Gaylord Bourne, "Ranke and the Beginning of the Seminary Method in Teaching History," in his *Essays in Historical Criticism*, pp. 265–274, with citations from Ranke and his students on the success of the method.

14. Herbert Baxter Adams, "Seminary Libraries and University Extension," *Johns Hopkins University Studies in History and Political Science* 5 (1887): 445, cited in Cushing Strout, *The Pragmatic Revolt in American History: Carl Becker and Charles Beard* (New Haven, 1958), pp. 18–19.

15. Grafton, *Footnote*, pp. 224–227, with references to studies of the professional organization of history in nineteenth-century Germany. As Bonnie Smith notes, it also made for "a common brotherhood of professional prac-

titioners" over against female amateur historians (*The Gender of History: Men, Women, and Historical Practice* [Cambridge, Mass., 1998], pp. 110–111).

16. For a discussion of nineteenth-century anti-Rankean German historians, such as Karl Lamprecht, see Georg G. Iggers, *The German Conception of History* (revised ed.; Middletown, Conn., 1983 [1968]), pp. 197–200.

17. Friedrich Nietzsche, *Unzeitgemässe Betrachtungen. II: Von Nutzen und Nachtheil der Historie für das Leben* (Leipzig, 1874). For Foucault's appropriation and modification of Nietzsche's approach to history, see his "Nietzsche, Genealogy, History" [1971], trans. in idem, *Language, Counter-Memory, Practice,* ed. Donald F. Bouchard (Ithaca, 1977), pp. 139–164.

18. Friedrich Nietzsche, *Thoughts Out of Season. Part II: The Use and Abuse of History* (trans., Edinburgh, 1909), p. v.

19. See especially Friedrich Nietzsche, *The Birth of Tragedy* and *The Genealogy of Morals,* both in translation in *The Philosophy of Nietzsche* (New York, 1954); also see *Use and Abuse* 4, 6, 10 (pp. 32–33, 54, 99).

20. Nietzsche, *Use and Abuse* 4 (p. 33 [*"wandelnden Encyclopädien"*]).

21. Ibid., 1, 2, 3 (*"mumisiert"*), 4, 10 (pp. 16, 19, 27 30, 90–91, 95).

22. Ibid., 3 (p. 24). Workmen who dig out the data, however necessary this may be, are not to be confused with "great historians" (6 [55–56]).

23. Ibid., 10 (pp. 89–92).

24. Ibid., 6 (pp. 50–51). Don't draw the past down to your own level, he elsewhere warns (6 [54]).

25. Ibid., 6 (pp. 52, 54), citing lines from Schiller. Nietzsche also mocks the notion of general laws governing history (6 [53]).

26. Ibid., 10 (p. 95)—like placid cattle who know little and forget everything (Preface [1]).

27. Ibid., 10 (p. 95)—the *Unhistorische* and the *Überhistorische.* By "religion," Nietzsche did not mean Christianity as it existed in his day, denatured by its historical treatment (7 [59]).

28. See Nietzsche's pronouncements in *Thus Spake Zarathustra* 28 ("The Rabble"); *Ecce Homo* ("Why I Am a Destiny")—yet, as Steven E. Aschheim details, Nietzsche had a following among Socialists and members of the working classes (*The Nietzsche Legacy in Germany 1890–1990* [Berkeley, 1992], pp. 18–19).

29. Hayden White notes how several nineteenth- and early-twentieth-century novels and plays represent the protagonist as rejecting the "burden of history"; he cites Dorothea in George Eliot's *Middlemarch,* Hedda in Ibsen's *Hedda Gabler,* and Michael in Gide's *The Immoralist* ("The Burden of History" [1966], in his *Tropics,* pp. 32–35).

30. Wilhelm Dilthey, "Rede zum 70. Geburtstag," in his *Gesammelte Schriften* (Leipzig, 1921), V: 9. Presumably, Dilthey wished to do for history what Kant had done for epistemology: see his statement in his "Die Erkenntnis des universalhistorischen Zusammenhanges," in *Gesammelte Schriften* VII:

278. Doubting the link to Kant, and arguing for Dilthey as "the Bacon of the human sciences," is Antoni, *From History to Sociology,* pp. 18–19.

31. Wilhelm Dilthey, "On Understanding and Hermeneutics: Student Notes," in his *Selected Works. Volume IV: Hermeneutics and the Study of History,* ed. Rudolf A. Makkreel and Frithjof Rodi (Princeton, 1996), p. 233; idem, "Reminiscences on Historical Studies at the University of Berlin"; idem, "On Jacob Burckhardt's *The Civilization of the Renaissance in Italy*"; idem, "Friedrich Christoph Schlosser and the Problem of Universal History," all in idem, *Selected Works,* IV: 389, 271, 305, 313.

32. See Rudolf A. Makkreel and Frithjof Rodi, "Introduction," Dilthey, *Selected Works,* IV: 6, 17–19; Michael Ermarth, *Wilhelm Dilthey: The Critique of Historical Reason* (Chicago, 1978), p. 241. For Dilthey's rejection of historical positivism, see his "History and Science," in his *Selected Works,* IV: 261–269.

33. Part 4 of Book 2 of the *Einleitung in die Geisteswissenschaften* traces this development; and see Wilhelm Dilthey, "Entwürfe zur Kritik der historischen Vernunft," in his *Gesammelte Schriften,* VII: 232; Ermarth, *Wilhelm Dilthey,* pp. 310, 312. Dilthey resolutely opposed the introduction of God, the World Spirit, or other transcendent entities into the discussion of history; see Book 2 of his *Einleitung,* in his *Gesammelte Schriften,* I; trans., *Introduction to the Human Sciences* (Detroit, 1988), pp. 149–323.

34. See the nuanced discussion in Ermarth, *Wilhelm Dilthey,* chap. 5, esp. pp. 246–247.

35. Wilhelm Dilthey, "Ideen über eine beschreibende und zergliedernde Psychologie," in his *Gesammelte Schriften,* V: 144: "Die Natur erklären wir, das Seelenleben verstehen wir."

36. Ermarth, *Wilhelm Dilthey,* pp. 241, 256–267, 346, citation at 267. "*Verstehen,*" Dilthey wrote, "is what we call this process by which an inside is conferred on a complex of external sensory signs" ("The Rise of Hermeneutics," in his *Selected Works,* IV: 236). Compare this view to R. G. Collingwood's; see Chapter 6.

37. Wilhelm Dilthey, "Die Entstehung der Hermeneutik: Zusätze aus den Handschriften I," in his *Gesammelte Schriften,* V: 336, citing Humboldt (*Gesammelte Schriften,* IV: 47).

38. Ermarth, *Wilhelm Dilthey,* p. 252. This understanding of "interpretation" would receive modern dress in Hans-Georg Gadamer's *Truth and Method.*

39. Wilhelm Dilthey, *Gesammelte Schriften,* XIV/2: 724, cited in Ermarth, *Wilhelm Dilthey,* p. 243 (taken from Dilthey's *Preisschrift, Schleiermacher's Hermeneutical System in Relation to Earlier Protestant Hermeneutics*). Also see discussion in Ermarth, *Wilhelm Dilthey,* p. 347: hermeneutics should not be reserved for special texts such as the Bible, but should become "a general method for the human sciences." A "presentist" dimension attends Dilthey's theories: the historian, like everyone else, starts with "life," with "experience," although, to be sure, the historian must go beyond this

(Wilhelm Dilthey, "Studien zur Grundlegung der Geisteswissenschaften. Dritte Studie: Die Abgrenzung der Geisteswissenschaften," in his *Gesammelte Schriften*, VII: 313; and idem, "Die Erkenntnis des universalhistorischen Zusammenhanges," in ibid., p. 278). For critique, see Hans-Georg Gadamer, "The Problem of Historical Consciousness" [1963], in *Interpretive Social Science*, ed. Paul Rabinow and William M. Sullivan (Berkeley, 1979), pp. 124–125.

40. Wilhelm Dilthey, "Abhandlungen zur Geschichte des deutschen Idealismus," in his *Gesammelte Schriften*, IV: 528; see Ermarth, *Wilhelm Dilthey*, pp. 318–320.

41. Wilhelm Dilthey, "Plan der Fortsetzung zum Aufbau der geschichtlichen Welt in den Geisteswissenschaften," in his *Gesammelte Schriften*, VII: 216.

42. Dilthey, "Die Erkenntnis des universalhistorischen Zusammenhanges," in his *Gesammelte Schriften*, VII: 291: "Denn der Mensch ist ein Geschichtliches"; idem, "Das Wesen der Philosophie: Weltanschauungslehre," in his *Gesammelte Schriften*, V: 379, VIII: 199–201, discussed in Ermarth, *Wilhelm Dilthey*, p. 320.

43. Dilthey, "Abhandlungen zur Geschichte des deutschen Idealismus: Die drei Grundformen der Systeme in der ersten Hälfte des 19. Jahrhunderts," in his *Gesammelte Schriften*, IV: 529; see discussion of Gadamer's critique in Frank R. Ankersmit, "The Origins of Postmodernist Historiography," in *Historiography between Modernism and Postmodernism*, ed. Jerzy Topolski (Amsterdam, 1994), pp. 98–99.

44. George Burton Adams, "History and the Philosophy of History," *American Historical Review* 14 (1909): 236, cited in Strout, *The Pragmatic Revolt*, p. 20.

45. Benedetto Croce characterized Ranke as "a timid Conservative subservient to [the] Prussian Government," who used his editorship of the *Historisch-Politische Zeitschrift* as a means "to defend and propagate its antiquarian policies" (*History/Liberty*, p. 92). Croce mocked Ranke's explanation of the failure of Italian independence in the sixteenth century as due to the prevalence in the Italian peninsula of pederasty, syphilis, rhetorical education, effeminate modes of male dress, and the introduction of foreign manners (94, citing Ranke's *Geschichten der romanischen und germanischen Völker*, pp. 263–265). For Croce, Ranke is best remembered for his "neat and elegant style," his *"Lust zu fabulieren"* (99). For Ranke's influence on French historiography, see Chapter 4.

46. For Ranke, history provides the locus where God is witnessed, and historians stand as the "priests" who decipher its divinely guaranteed coherence; see Krieger, *Ranke*, chap. 2. Ranke writes that "the eternal dwells in the individual. This is the religious foundation on which our efforts rest. We believe that there is nothing without God, and nothing lives except through God" ("On the Character of Historical Science," p. 38).

47. Krieger, *Ranke*, pp. 354, 13. For Ranke's defense of his use of the phrase "the finger of God" in history, see Leopold von Ranke, "Erwiderung auf

Heinrich Leo's Angriff" [dated spring 1828], in his *Sämtliche Werke*, ed. Alfred Dove (Leipzig, 1890), LIII–LIV: 665–666; see also Gilbert, *History*, pp. 25, 27. Tracing "breaks" in Ranke's vision of universal meaning in history is Thomas A. Brady, "Ranke, Rom und die Reformation: Leopold von Rankes Entdeckung des Katholizismus," in *Jahrbuch des Historischen Kollegs 1999* (Munich, 1999), pp. 43–60.

48. Ernest Breisach, *Historiography: Ancient, Medieval, & Modern* (2d ed.; Chicago, 1994 [1983]), pp. 233–234. To judge the link between religious commitment and empirical investigation in Ranke's work, see selections from his writings translated in *The Theory and Practice of History: Leopold von Ranke*, especially pp. 29–50. Also see Dorothy Ross, "On the Misunderstanding of Ranke and the Origins of the Historical Profession in America," in *Leopold von Ranke and the Shaping of the Historical Discipline*, ed. Georg G. Iggers and James M. Powell (Syracuse, 1990), pp. 154–169.

49. Iggers, "The Image of Ranke," p. 18; idem, *The German Conception of History*, chap. 4; similarly, Strout, *The Pragmatic Revolt*, pp. 20–21.

50. Adams, "History and the Philosophy of History," p. 223, cited in Iggers, "The Image of Ranke," p. 22.

51. See William R. Keylor, *Academy and Community: The Foundation of the French Historical Profession* (Cambridge, Mass., 1975), p. 87.

52. Charles Beard characterizes Ranke as a conservative who simply wanted "peace" following the debilitating years of the French Revolution and its aftermath ("Written History as an Act of Faith," *American Historical Review* 39 [1934]: 221); Novick, *Dream*, pp. 157–158.

53. Beard and Vagts, "Currents of Thought in Historiography," pp. 464–465. The authors present to American readers Friedrich Meinecke's *Die Entstehung des Historismus*.

54. Novick, *Dream*, pp. 157–158.

55. See especially Foucault, "Nietzsche, Genealogy, History," pp. 139–164; and the interview with Foucault, "On the Genealogy of Ethics: An Overview of Work in Progress" [1983], in Dreyfus and Rabinow, *Beyond Structuralism*, especially pp. 237–248. In America, Hayden White's interest in German historiography is notable; see his essay, "Droysen's *Historik*: Historical Writing as a Bourgeois Science" [1980], in his *Content*, pp. 83–103. White argues that Droysen, in espousing "presentism," rejecting a Rankean version of "objectivity," and exploring ideology's "work," remains instructive today (83, 85–87).

56. For "the state of the field" in the early 1940s, see *Theory and Practice in Historical Study: A Report of the Committee on Historiography* (New York, n.d.), especially the essay by John Herman Randall Jr. and George Haines IV, "Controlling Assumptions in the Practice of American Historians," pp. 15–52. For the report's reception, see Novick, *Dream*, pp. 387–392.

57. Beard, "That Noble Dream," p. 76, countering Smith's assumptions (82–

84). Philosopher William H. Dray comments on Beard's list, "a very miscellaneous set of worries" (*Philosophy of History* [Englewood Cliffs, N.J., 1964], p. 22).

58. Beard, "That Noble Dream," p. 76; Ranke was not an impartial and disinterested historian (77–78).

59. Novick, *Dream,* pp. 1–2.

60. Peter Burke, "Overture: The New History, Its Past and Future," in his *Perspectives,* pp. 3–5.

61. Novick, *Dream,* p. 2.

62. Ibid., chap. 2, "The Professionalization Project." Novick cites statistics indicating that before 1927, few of the presidents of the American Historical Association held Ph.D.'s; before 1912, almost all were amateur historians (49). For history's entry as an academic discipline, see Arnaldo Momigliano, "Ancient History and the Antiquarian" [1950], in his *Studies in Historiography,* pp. 1–39.

63. Hayden White, "The Politics of Historical Interpretation: Discipline and De-sublimation" [1982], in his *Content,* p. 62. The construction of history as a discipline, he concludes, relied more on exclusions and proscriptions—on what historians *cannot* do—than on positive prescriptions of what they *should* do (68).

64. M. I. Finley, "'Progress' in Historiography," *Daedalus* 106 (1977): 137. My colleague Kalman Bland commented (conversation, Feb. 1, 2003) that perhaps "method" was understood to differ from "philosophical assumptions."

65. Novick, *Dream,* pp. 175–176.

66. George Macaulay Trevelyan, *Clio, A Muse and Other Essays* (new ed.; Freeport, N.Y., 1968 [1930]), p. 142.

67. White, *Metahistory,* p. 141.

68. Edward Hallett Carr, *What Is History?* (New York, 1962), p. 21. For Carr as historian, see Keith Jenkins, *On "What Is History?" From Carr and Elton to Rorty and White* (London, 1995), chap. 2.

69. Novick, *Dream,* chap. 1, pp. 538, 134–139. For an explanation of the significance of quantum mechanics for philosophy, see Hilary Putnam, "Realism with a Human Face," in his *Realism,* chap. 1. Putnam's rendition of Niels Bohr's version of the Copenhagen Interpretation: "every property of the system is considered to have meaning and existence only in relation to a particular measuring apparatus in a particular experimental situation" (4).

70. Raymond Aron, *Introduction to the Philosophy of History* (trans., London, 1961 [1948, 1938]), p. 288. This work, written between 1935–1937, was one of two theses Aron presented for his degree. See Robert Colquhoun, *Raymond Aron. Volume I: The Philosopher in History, 1905–1955* (London, 1986), chap. 6; summary, pp. 123–125, 129. Despite the attention the work received, Aron lost out on the "best thesis" prize in 1938 to Henri-Irénée Marrou's *Saint Augustin et la fin de la culture antique* (146).

71. Aron, *Introduction to the Philosophy of History,* p. 289. Since there is nothing that exists called "historical reality," the *historian* must create his object; this recognition Aron called "the dissolution of the object" (118: "la dissolution de l'objet" [French ed., 120]). Aron in this early work feared that relativism would lead to an "anarchy of values" (12, 291–294). See discussion in Colquhoun, *Raymond Aron,* I: 123–125, 129. Later Aron came to embrace relativism as a sign of philosophical progress, of the richness of life ("Relativism in History" [1950], in Meyerhoff, *Philosophy of History,* pp. 158–160).

72. Bloch, "Introduction," idem, *Craft,* p. 17. The French original on which the English translation was made *(Apologie pour l'histoire; ou Métier d'historien)* was based on materials left incomplete at the time of Bloch's death, and has now been given a critical edition by Etienne Bloch (Paris, 1993).

73. Carr, *What Is History?,* pp. 91–93, taking his model largely from physics. Henri-Irénée Marrou likewise comments on the "very naïve," indeed "elementary," view of science that nineteenth-century historians held (*Meaning,* p. 54); also see Beard, "Written History as an Act of Faith," pp. 222–225.

74. Claude Lévi-Strauss disavows the influence of modern artistic movements on the brand of structuralism *he* developed; unlike some of his structuralist colleagues, he took his cue from the natural sciences. See Lévi-Strauss, "A propos d'une Rétrospective" [1966], in his *Anthropologie structurale deux* (Paris, 1973), p. 327, commenting on a Picasso exhibit.

75. Novick, *Dream,* p. 134; compare Hannah Arendt, "The Concept of History," in her *Between Past and Future* (New York, 1961), p. 50. Cushing Strout notes Carl Becker's fascination with Joyce—although Becker's favorite novelist remained Henry James, and Becker's experiments with historical writing hardly resembled *Finnegan's Wake* (*The Pragmatic Revolt,* p. 79).

76. Hayden White, "The Burden of History" [1966], in his *Tropics,* pp. 43–44.

77. Novick, *Dream,* p. 15.

78. The phrase is from Jerzy Topolski, "Historians Look at Historical Truth," in *Epistemology and History,* ed. Anna Zeidler-Janiszewska (Amsterdam, 1996), p. 406. By "spontaneous," Topolski means that historians generally assume their epistemological positions without reflection or argument.

79. Berkhofer, *Story,* pp. 60, 63, 71.

80. So Appleby, Hunt, and Jacob, *Telling the Truth,* pp. 234, 256. Yet to concede that every historical statement must be qualified by the addition "from the so-and-so point of view" (argues philosopher of history William Dray) suggests that historians themselves admit that they deal in "mere appearances"—a view that, if taken seriously, would mean that "historians would have to give up all claim to tell us how the past really was"—a position that should embarrass a discipline "with any pretensions to epistemological respectability" ("Point of View in History" [1978] and "Introduction," both in his *On History/Philosophers,* pp. 65, 4).

81. G. R. Elton, *The Practice of History* (New York, 1967), p. v.

82. Berkhofer, *Story*, p. 29; Novick, *Dream*, pp. 52–53; compare Paul Ricoeur's formulation of the problem in *Time*, III: 143.

83. Roger Chartier, "Introduction," in his *Edge*, p. 9.

84. Roger Chartier, "On the Relation of Philosophy and History" [1987], in his *Cultural History: Between Practices and Representations* (trans., Ithaca, 1988), pp. 65–66. To be sure, theorists such as F. R. Ankersmit and Richard Rorty posit that epistemological dilemmas would disappear if scholars stopped asking "useless" questions pertaining to theories of knowledge and reference (F. R. Ankersmit, "Introduction," in his *Representation*, p. 21, and in the same volume, "The Linguistic Turn: Literary Theory and Historical Theory," pp. 66, 68, 74; "Danto on Representation, Identity, and Indiscernibles" [1998], pp. 237, 243; "Epilogue," p. 282 [Ankersmit advises historians to look rather to analytical philosophy, with its claim to "dissolve" philosophical problems ("The Linguistic Turn," pp. 63–64)]; Richard Rorty, "John Searle on Realism and Relativism" [1994], in his *Truth and Progress: Philosophical Papers, Volume 3* (Cambridge, 1998), p. 73; idem, "Afterword," in *Historians and Social Values*, ed. Joep Leerssen and Ann Rigney (Amsterdam, 2000), pp. 202, 198).

85. Berkhofer, *Story*, p. 14; Jenkins, *On "What Is History?"* p. 29. This discussion pertains only to texts, not to ruins and other material artifacts, which might give a different access to "the past."

86. Bloch, *Craft*, pp. 54–55, 57.

87. Michel de Certeau, "Histoire et mystique," *Revue de l'histoire de spiritualité* 48 (1972): 74.

88. Bunzl, *Real History*, p. 39; Berkhofer, *Story*, p. 63. The facts of history, as Carl Becker put it, consist only of mental images that historians make in order to comprehend what has "forever disappeared" ("Detachment and the Writing of History" [1910], in his *Detachment and the Writing of History: Essays and Letters of Carl L. Becker*, ed. Phil L. Snyder [Ithaca, 1958], p. 11).

89. Michel de Certeau, "History: Science and Fiction" [1983], in his *Heterologies*, p. 214.

90. Goldstein, *Knowing*, pp. xx–xxii, 73, 94, 144, 134, 136.

91. Gareth Stedman Jones, "From Historical Sociology to Theoretic History," *British Journal of Sociology* 27 (1976): 296.

92. Christopher Blake, "Can History Be Objective?" [1955], in Gardiner, *Theories of History*, p. 340.

93. Michael Oakeshott, *On History and Other Essays* (Totowa, 1983), pp. 33, 52, 80.

94. Michael Oakeshott, *Experience and Its Modes* (Cambridge, 1933; reprint 1966), pp. 112, 90, 93, 99.

95. Michael Oakeshott, "The Activity of being an Historian," in his *Historical Studies* (London, 1958), p. 17. Although Oakeshott's notion of "the

deadness" of the past" bears certain similarities to Michel de Certeau's, Oakeshott's scheme allows no "artificial respiration," no recalling of events from the dead, a process that he labels an "obscene necromancy" (18). Oakeshott adopts sexist metaphors reminiscent of von Ranke, but here, the dead past is a beloved "mistress of whom he [the historian] never tires and whom he never expects to talk sense" (19).

96. See Chapter 2 on Arthur Danto.

97. Keith Jenkins, "'After' History," *Rethinking History* 3 (1999): 8.

98. Elton, *The Practice of History*, p. 65; also see G. R. Elton, *Return to Essentials* (Cambridge, 1991), p. 9.

99. For another example, see Joyce Appleby, "Notes and Comment: One Good Turn Deserves Another: A Response to David Harlan," *American Historical Review* 94 (1989): 1328.

100. Novick, *Dream,* p. 98, reminds readers that charges of "presentism" were also leveled against Charles Beard's *An Economic Interpretation of the Constitution of the United States* (1913).

101. Benedetto Croce, *Theory & History of Historiography* (trans., London, 1921 [from 2nd Italian ed. of 1919]), p. 91: "The past does not live otherwise than in the present, resolved and transformed in the present"; see idem, *History/Liberty,* p. 19.

102. Carl L. Becker, "What Are Historical Facts?" [1955], in Meyerhoff, *Philosophy of History,* pp. 121, 125, 127, 133.

103. Frederick Jackson Turner's maxim: "Each age writes the history of the past anew with reference to the conditions uppermost in its own time"; see Frederick Jackson Turner, "The Significance of History," in *The Early Writings of Frederick Jackson Turner,* ed. Everett E. Edwards and Fulmer Mood (Madison, 1938), p. 52.

104. Aron, "Relativism in History," pp. 154, 157.

105. John Dewey, "Historical Judgments" [1938], in Meyerhoff, *Philosophy of History,* p. 168: "all history is necessarily written from the standpoint of the present." For a report of problems Dewey encountered regarding "objectivity" when he chaired a commission regarding charges against Trotsky, see Alan P. Spitzer, "John Dewey, the 'Trial' of Leon Trotsky, and the Search for Historical Truth," in idem, *Historical Truth and Lies about the Past* (Chapel Hill, 1996), pp. 13–34.

106. For example, Croce posited that all history has the character of "'contemporary history' because, however remote in time events recounted may seem to be, history in reality refers to present needs and present situations wherein those events vibrate" (*History/Liberty,* p. 19), while Turner wrote that "[e]ach age writes the history of the past anew with reference to the conditions uppermost in its own time" ("The Significance of History," p. 52). Their claims, however, even then were decried by their critics as not properly "historical" (Novick, *Dream,* pp. 92–98).

107. Bloch and Febvre's views on "the present" are discussed in Chapter 4.

108. Dominick LaCapra, "Intellectual History and Critical Theory," in his *Soundings*, p. 195.

109. Harlan, *Degradation*, pp. xxxii–xxxiii; contrast Richard Evans's view that post-structuralist history "demeans the dead" ("Truth Lost in Vain Views," *The Times Higher Education Supplement* [12 Sept. 1997]: 18), discussed in Robert Eaglestone and Susan Pitt, "Editorial: The Good of History: Ethics, Post-structuralism and the Representation of the Past," *Rethinking History* 2 (1998): 309.

110. Harlan, *Degradation*, p. 210. For a defense of presentism in the history of science, see David L. Hull, "In Defense of Presentism," *History and Theory* 18 (1987): 1–15.

111. Novick, *Dream*, p. 61, and chap. 3. Thomas L. Haskell, reviewing Novick's book, argues that Novick confuses "objectivity" with "neutrality" ("Objectivity Is Not Neutrality," *History and Theory* 29 [1990]: 131, 133–134, 136–139).

112. Novick, *Dream*, chap. 4. For Carl Becker's worries over America's political mood in 1932, see his "The Dilemma of Liberals in Our Time," in idem, *Detachment and the Writing of History*, pp. 188–213. Becker argues that "the really detached mind is a dead mind," in "Detachment and the Writing of History," in ibid., p. 24. Becker distances himself from Communism in "The Marxian Philosophy of History," in his *Everyman His Own Historian* (New York, 1935), pp. 113–131. Robert William Fogel calls Beard's and Becker's presidential addresses of the 1930s "the climax of disenchantment" with historical positivism ("'Scientific' History and Traditional History," in Fogel and G. R. Elton, *Which Road to the Past? Two Views of History* [New Haven, 1983], p. 13). Becker's presidential address in 1931, "Everyman His Own Historian," is reprinted in his *Everyman His Own Historian*, pp. 233–255.

113. Novick, *Dream*, pp. 172–173; Novick cites letters of recommendation by noted historians who assure prospective employers that the recommendees do not share the "distasteful qualities" associated with their "race." Also see Oscar Handlin's description of his rite of passage from Brooklyn to Harvard, where "the cordiality of older men" made him feel part of "a group of shared values and interests" (*Truth in History* [Cambridge, Mass., 1979], p. 3).

114. Novick, *Dream*, chap. 13, especially p. 461. The phrase "history from the bottom up" was first coined by the historian Frederick Jackson Turner in 1923 (442n.36).

115. Jewish historians, Novick posits, unlike many African American and feminist historians a few decades later, did not pursue research identified with their particular "constituency" and hence escaped charges of historical bias (*Dream*, p. 470n.1).

116. Arnaldo Momigliano, "A Hundred Years after Ranke" [1954], in his *Studies in Historiography*, p. 107. Momigliano has harsh words for Karl

Jaspers and Karl Löwith, religious interpreters, and the early *Annalistes* ("Historians in Contemporary Thought" [1961] and "An Unsolved Problem of Historical Forgery: The Scriptores Historiae Augustae" [1954], both in *Studies in Historiography,* pp. 224, 144). With good reason, Averil Cameron notes in the dedication of her edited volume, *History as Text: The Writing of Ancient History* (Chapel Hill, 1989), "in memory of Arnaldo/ who would not have liked it."

117. Novick emphasizes, as others do, that earlier in the century women had been active as historians, but in the postwar years, as home and motherhood became the norm for most women of the middle classes, their numbers in the historical profession declined dramatically, "rebounding" only from the late 1960s onward (*Dream,* pp. 366–367, 491–510).

118. Linda Gordon faults Novick's discussion of women historians as political activists rather than as scholars and intellectuals ("AHR Forum: Comments on *That Noble Dream,*" *American Historical Review* 96 [1991]: 687).

119. Joan Scott, "Women's History," in Burke, *Perspectives,* p. 58; also see Catriona Kelly, "History and Post-Modernism," *Past & Present* 133 (1991): 212 (feminist history sometimes advocates reading texts *out* of context, against the grain). Scott criticized Novick for not facing up to the divergent political interests that drove the question of objectivity. To fall back on a notion of "pluralism" that everyone can accept is, in Scott's view, a politically suspect ploy (discussion at AHA panel on Novick's book, reported by Dorothy Ross, "AHR Forum: Afterword," *American Historical Review* 96 [1991]: 707).

120. In another version of "how objectivity came under attack," social historians, by suggesting that there was no one national narrative, "dug a potentially fatal hole" into which, somewhat later, postmodernists fell. See Appleby, Hunt, and Jacob, *Telling the Truth,* p. 200. For an explication of how Kuhn backed away from "Gestalt switches" in his later work, see Hilary Putnam, "The Craving for Objectivity," in his *Realism,* p. 125.

121. Elton, *Return to Essentials,* pp. 67–68. Mocking studies on women and sexuality, Elton comments that "the facts of birth, copulation and death do not alter all that much through the ages" (117–118). For a critical discussion of Elton, see Jenkins, *On "What Is History?"* chap. 3. Elton's charge of "idleness" echoes the sentiments of an editorial in the *New York Times* in 1915, which raged against professors who "teach Socialism and shiftlessness"—and expect donors to fund the universities at which they teach (cited in Novick, *Dream,* pp. 64–65).

122. Handlin, *Truth in History,* p. viii.

123. Gertrude Himmelfarb, *The New History and the Old* (Cambridge, 1987), p. 88. Patrick Joyce suggests, to the contrary, that Elton and Himmelfarb discover "reds under the bed of postmodernism and poststructuralism"; see his "The End of Social History?: A Brief Reply to Eley and Nield" [1996], in *The Postmodern History Reader,* ed. Keith Jenkins (London, 1997), p. 346.

124. Gertrude Himmelfarb, "Postmodernist History and Flight from Fact," in idem, *On Looking into the Abyss* (New York, 1994), excerpted in *Historians on History,* ed. John Tosh (Harlow, 2000), p. 291, citing a line of T. S. Eliot on the artist; compare Ranke's claim that historians should "extinguish" themselves before the documents.

125. Reinhart Koselleck, *The Practice of Conceptual History* (trans., Stanford, 2002), p. 14.

126. Keith Jenkins, *Re-thinking History* (London, 1991), p. 17.

127. Hayden White, "Getting Out of History: Jameson's Redemption of Narrative" [1982], in his *Content,* p. 164.

128. Smith, *Gender of History,* pp. 1, 13, 9–10, 7, 39, 101. Despite their denigration as rank amateurs, women often wrote to support themselves and their families (162). Smith cites reviews of works that Charles Beard co-wrote with his historian wife, Mary Ritter Beard, in which reviewers assume that Charles was the sole author (85). Smith's discussion of the abuse and dismissal (including by modern authors and editors) accorded Athénais Michelet, wife and sometimes co-writer with her husband Jules, is especially revealing (87–101). If women were left out, however, the documents themselves, coded as "beautiful princesses," and archives, coded as "virgins" and "beautiful Italians," could stand in for "real" women (116, 119).

129. Joan Wallach Scott, "AHR Forum: History in Crisis? The Others' Side of the Story," *American Historical Review* 94 (1989): 690.

130. On cognitive relativism in relation to epistemological doubt in ancient Skepticism, see Chapter 2, note 55.

131. Thus J. Morgan Kousser, "The Revivalism of Narrative: A Response to Recent Criticisms of Quantitative History," *Social Science History* 8 (1984): 13; compare David Harlan's construal of the "objectivist" position in his "Reply to David Hollinger," *American Historical Review* 94 (1989): 625; and Clifford Geertz, "Anti Anti-Relativism," *American Anthropologist* 86 (1984): 265. On Hayden White's "relativism," see Wulf Kasteiner, "Hayden White's Critique of the Writing of History," *History and Theory* 32 (1993): 278–281, 294.

132. Harlan, *Degradation,* p. xxxi. The controversy over Paul de Man's anti-Semitic wartime journalism might stand as a good example. For Derrida's response to those who thought he had been too "soft" on de Man, see his "Biodegradables: Seven Diary Fragments," *Critical Inquiry* 15 (1989): 812–873; "what happened in 1940–42 in Brussels cannot, by definition, have anything to do with deconstruction" (825).

133. Tony Bennett, "Outside Literature," in *The Postmodern History Reader,* p. 221 (reprinted from Bennett's *Outside Literature* [London, 1990]).

134. Himmelfarb, "Postmodernist History and Flight from Fact," p. 290.

135. Hans Kellner, "The Deepest Respect for Reality," in his *Language,* p. 24.

136. White, "Translator's Introduction," in Antoni, *From History to Sociology,* p. xvii. As Antoni's book shows, it was within the field of German historiography and social theory that discussions of relativism surfaced early.

137. See discussion in Strout, *The Pragmatic Revolt,* pp. 158–161. Strout favors "pragmatic relativism" over "subjectivist-relativist-presentism" (9, 28).

138. Maurice Mandelbaum, *The Problem of Historical Knowledge* (New York, 1967 [1938]), pp. 36, 179–180. Mandelbaum assumes a correspondence theory of truth (albeit a sophisticated version): it is "a property of language to refer to non-linguistic entities" (185–186).

139. Richard Rorty, "Solidarity or Objectivity," in *Post-Analytic Philosophy,* ed. John Rajchman and Cornel West (New York, 1985), pp. 11, 14; compare Wittgenstein's claim (*Philosophical Investigations* 124) that philosophy "leaves everything as it is." Many analytic philosophers would deem Rorty's claims too "loose."

140. Richard Rorty, "Postmodernist Bourgeois Liberalism," *Journal of Philosophy* 80 (1983): 589. Rorty acknowledges that "relativism" is a self-refuting term (one's own position, too, is "relative"). Rorty suggests that the difficulties of "the Relativist" could be avoided by moving "everything over from epistemology and metaphysics to cultural politics" ("Hilary Putnam and the Relativist Menace" [1993], in his *Truth and Progress,* p. 57).

141. Rorty, "Solidarity or Objectivity," p. 6—a "negative" critique in that it does not advance any positive epistemological theory of its own. On Rorty's utility for historians, see Jenkins, *On "What Is History?"* chap. 4.

142. David A. Hollinger, "The Voice of Intellectual History in the Conversation of Mankind: A Note on Richard Rorty," in his *In the American Province: Studies in the History and Historiography of Ideas* (Bloomington, 1985), p. 171; Hollinger calls Rorty a "historian's philosopher" (167).

143. Lévi-Strauss, *Conversations,* p. 147. He went on to elaborate (165): "Cultural relativism confines itself to stating that a culture possesses no absolute criteria authorizing it to apply this distinction [namely, "higher" and "lower"] to the products of another culture"—although each culture may make such judgments about itself, he adds.

144. Novick, *Dream,* p. 144.

145. Geertz, "Anti Anti-Relativism," pp. 263, 275. The title connotes that Geertz does not consider himself "pro-relativist" (263–264); Christopher Lloyd suggests the term "localism" (*The Structures of History* [Oxford, 1993], p. 108).

146. Geertz, "Anti Anti-Relativism," pp. 265, 276. Also see the formulation of the point by historian David Harlan: "to assert that there are no *universal truths* is not to assert that there are no *particular* truths" ("Reply to David Hollinger," p. 625).

147. Geertz, "Anti Anti-Relativism," p. 264.

148. See discussion of Geertzian anthropology in Chapter 7.

149. De Certeau, "History: Science and Fiction," pp. 28–38.

150. Berkhofer, *Story,* p. 60.

151. Novick, *Dream,* pp. 567–568. Thus, for example, in a letter to the editor of the *New York Review of Books* (Dec. 16, 1982), Gordon S. Wood expresses his commitment to nineteenth-century epistemological positivism, which he

takes to mean "that the past 'out there' really existed and that [historians] can through the collection and ordering of evidence bring us closer to knowing the truth about that past 'as it really was,' even if the full and complete truth about the past will always remain beyond their grasp" (cited in Novick, *Dream,* 59).

152. See Nicholas B. Dirks, "Is Vice Versa? Historical Anthropologies and Anthropological Histories," in McDonald, *Turn,* p. 31.

153. Leopold von Ranke, Letter to Ferdinand Ranke, Nov. 11, 1836, in Leopold von Ranke, *Neue Briefe,* ed. Bernhard Hoeft and Hans Herzfeld (Hamburg, 1949), p. 230; Letter to Bettina von Arnim, Feb. 6, 1828, in Leopold von Ranke, *Briefwerk,* ed. Walter Fuchs (Hamburg, 1949), p. 139. See discussion in Smith, *Gender of History,* pp. 116, 119. For Benedetto Croce, history is not a "virgin" but a "noble matron," "mother of stern men trained in stern thought"; he faults Proust for treating her "as if she were a shameless hussy to provide exquisite titillations for . . . jaded nerves" ("Essay 29: Proust," in *My Philosophy,* p. 213). For Francis J. Couvares, writing in 1980, "cultural anthropology, 'thick description,' and semiotics" are the "new harlots" ("Telling a Story in Context; or, What's Wrong with Social History?" *Theory and Society* 9 [1980]: 675).

154. Lucien Febvre, "Vivre l'histoire," in his *Combats pour l'histoire* (2d ed.; Paris, 1965 [1953]). The image comes from a talk Febvre gave to young would-be historians at the Ecole Normal Supérieure in 1941. Historians' dominant metaphors and analogies themselves might well occasion an interesting study: W. B. Gallie *(Philosophy and the Historical Understanding)* appeals to cricket; Jack Hexter *(Doing History)* prefers baseball and cooking. Bonnie G. Smith comments: "By the mid-nineteenth century, what with the idea of searching out fairy princesses and assaulting the archives, the masculine identity of history was secure. If political power was for men, then so was professional history, its subject matter, methodology, and even its fantasies" ("Gender, Objectivity, and the Rise of Scientific Historiography," in *Objectivity and Its Other,* ed. Wolfgang Natter et al. [New York, 1995], pp. 56–57).

155. J. H. Hexter, *Doing History* (Bloomington, 1971), pp. 151–152.

156. Beverley Southgate, *History: What and Why?* (London, 1996), p. 87.

157. Carlo Ginzburg, "Preface," Lorenzo Valla, *La Donation de Constantin* (trans., Paris, 1993), p. xi: "une machine de guerre sceptique"; discussed in Roger Chartier, "History between Narrative and Knowledge" [1994], in his *Edge,* p. 26; see also Cushing Strout, "Border Crossings: History, Fiction, and *Dead Certainties," History and Fiction* 31 (1992): 153. Elsewhere, while faulting "theoreticians of historiography" who allegedly don't care about historians' work (Roland Barthes and Hayden White appear to be the chief culprits), Ginzburg acknowledges that historians have not reflected theoretically on their profession, thus contributing to the gap (*History, Rhetoric, and Proof* [Hanover, N.H., 1999], pp. 1, 38).

158. Himmelfarb reasons that if she and other modernist historians have "survived the 'death of God' and the 'death of man,' we will surely survive the 'death of history' . . . We will even survive the death of postmodernism" ("Postmodernist History and the Flight from Fact," p. 297).

159. Lawrence Stone, letter to *Harper's* 268 (June 1984): 4–5, cited in Novick, *Dream,* p. 610. Already in the 1970s, Himmelfarb was applauding Jacques Barzun's denunciations of psychohistory and quantification history in his *Clio and the Doctors* (New York, 1974); see Himmelfarb, "The 'New History,'" *Commentary* 59 (1975): 72–78.

160. Robert Eric Frykenberg, *History and Belief* (Grand Rapids, 1996), pp. 282, 279–280, 303. Frykenberg's particular target is Edward Said (289).

161. Iggers, "Historicism," p. 152.

162. Hexter, *On Historians,* p. 6.

163. Novick, *Dream,* p. 573.

164. Foucault, *Archaeology,* p. 14—especially at Foucault's emphasis on discontinuity and rupture.

165. Berkhofer, *Story,* p. 232. To be sure, more traditional historians can accuse their post-structuralist colleagues as behaving as if *they* were the ones "besieged": so Russell Jacoby, "AHR Forum: A New Intellectual History?" *American Historical Review* 97 (1992): 422. Here the "attackers" are (allegedly) contextualists.

166. Appleby, Hunt, and Jacob, *Telling the Truth,* pp. 206, 251. The authors admit that they had been instructed on the difference between postmodernism and post-structuralism (202n.4), but have nonetheless not corrected their nomenclature.

167. Jacques Derrida, "Positions: Interview with Jean-Louis Houdebine and Guy Scarpetta" [1971], in his *Positions* (trans., Chicago, 1981 [1972], pp. 56–60, citation at p. 57; he notes that probably his enclosing "history" in quotation marks led critics to think that he "rejects history" [60]). For a sympathetic discussion of the Enlightenment heritage of Derrida, see Christopher Norris, *Deconstruction and the "Unfinished Project of Modernity"* (New York, 2000), pp. 69–74. For Norris, Derrida (in a different version of Kant) seeks to establish the "condition-of-*im*possibility" (81).

168. Derrida, "Biodegradables," p. 821.

169. See Jacques Derrida, "Cogito and the History of Madness" [1964], in his *Writing and Difference* (trans., Chicago, 1978 [1967]), especially pp. 45–50.

170. Geoff Bennington, "Demanding History," in Attridge, Bennington, and Young, *Post-Structuralism,* p. 17.

171. Private letter of Joan Scott to Georg Iggers, Oct. 14, 1994, cited in Iggers, *Historiography,* p. 132.

172. Berkhofer, *Story,* p. 53.

173. F. R. Ankersmit, "Hayden White's Appeal to the Historians," *History and Theory* 37 (1998): 183.

174. Beverley Southgate, "History and Metahistory: Marwick versus White," *Journal of Contemporary History* 31 (1996): 212–213, citing Herbert Butterfield, *The Whig Interpretation of History* (Harmondsworth, 1973 [1931]), pp. 69, 70, 77, 25; and Edward Gibbon, *An Essay on the Study of Literature* (London, 1764), p. 107 ("If philosophers are not always historians, it were at least to be wished that all historians were philosophers").

175. Patrick Joyce, "History and Post-Modernism," *Past & Present* 133 (1991): 208.

176. Franklin Ankersmit, "The Use of Language in the Writing of History," in *Working with Language,* ed. Hywel Coleman (Berlin, 1989), pp. 57, 78. In his response to Peter Zagorin, Ankersmit similarly argues that "narrative substances" (that is, concepts such as "the Industrial Revolution" and "the Cold War") should be seen as *proposals for connecting things with words* ("Reply to Professor Zagorin," *History and Theory* 29 [1990]: 282, 280).

177. Ankersmit, "Reply to Professor Zagorin," p. 294; idem, "The Origins of Postmodernist Historiography," pp. 87–117.

2. Anglo-American Philosophy and the Historians

1. Hilary Putnam, "After Empiricism" [1985], in his *Realism*, p. 43.

2. Richard Rorty, "Introduction," in *The Linguistic Turn*, ed. Rorty (Chicago, 1967), p. 3.

3. Ludwig Wittgenstein, *Philosophical Investigations* 109 (#47e); also see Wittgenstein, *On Certainty* 31, 6e. As Michel de Certeau observed, Wittgenstein's philosophy stood as "a radical critique of the Philosopher as Expert" ("A Common Place: Ordinary Language," in his *The Practice of Everyday Life* [trans., Berkeley, 1984 (1980)], p. 9). Words, Wittgenstein argued, should be brought back "from their metaphysical to their everyday use" (*Philosophical Investigations,* Part I, 116).

4. Words were compared to tools in a toolbox: understanding a word entailed knowing its function and its use in various "language games." See Rorty, "Introduction," pp. 1–39; J. O. Urmson, "The History of Philosophical Analysis" [1962], in *Linguistic Turn*, pp. 294–301.

5. Louis O. Mink, "History and Fiction as Modes of Comprehension" [1970], in his *Historical Understanding,* ed. Brian Fay et al. (Ithaca, 1987), pp. 44, 55–56; Murphey, *Knowledge*, p. 67. For a good introduction, see William H. Dray, *Philosophy of History* (Englewood Cliffs, N.J., 1964). Although Collingwood's *The Idea of History* was published posthumously in 1946, it was based on lectures given in the 1930s; see the "Editor's Preface," Collingwood, *Idea*, pp. v–vi.

6. Dray, *Laws*, p. 4; Dray notes that Karl Popper and Carl Hempel sought "to forestall the conclusion that history may operate successfully with procedures and criteria of its own." Others countered, if history does not have a

separate terminology or a special form of explanation, how could it count as a distinctive field? (Murphey, *Knowledge,* pp. 2, 6; also see Morton White, "Historical Explanation," *Mind* n.s. 52 [1943]: 212–229).

7. Meyerhoff, *Philosophy of History,* p. 161; Isaiah Berlin, "Historical Inevitability" [1954], in ibid., pp. 267–269; F. R. Ankersmit, "Hayden White's Appeal to the Historians" [1998], in his *Representation,* p. 251; also see Quentin Skinner, "The Limits of Historical Explanations," *Philosophy* 41 (1966): 202.

8. Karl Popper, *The Logic of Scientific Discovery* (London, 1959 [1935]), p. 59. It is only the "generalizing sciences," not history, that form laws. See Karl Popper, *The Open Society and Its Enemies. Volume II: The High Tide of Prophecy* (5th ed. revised; Princeton, 1966 [1945]), pp. 262, 264; discussion in Malachi Haim Hacohen, *Karl Popper—The Formative Years, 1902–1945* (Cambridge, 2000), p. 488; Dray, *Laws,* pp. 1–2; and Louis O. Mink, "Philosophy and Theory of History," in *International Handbook of Historical Studies,* ed. Georg G. Iggers and Harold T. Parker (Westport, Conn., 1979), p. 19. I thank my colleague Malachi Hacohen for his assistance with Popper.

9. The notion that history entails "prediction" was one that Popper originally shared with Eastern European and Soviet colleagues, even though they later became the objects of his attack (Karl L. Popper, *The Poverty of Historicism* [Boston, 1957 (1945)], p. 3). This book was developed from papers Popper gave from 1935 onward; see discussion in Hacohen, *Karl Popper,* pp. 353–355.

10. For science as a "system of hypotheses," see Popper, *The Logic of Scientific Discovery,* pp. 316–317; for the unpredictability of the growth of knowledge and hence of humanity's future course, p. 279n.2, added to the English edition. For Popper's notion of prediction, see Hacohen, *Karl Popper,* pp. 377–378, 380.

11. Popper, *The Poverty of Historicism,* pp. 161, xx, 143.

12. Ibid., p. 3; Hacohen, *Karl Popper,* pp. 355–357, 488; Michael Stanford, *An Introduction to the Philosophy of History* (Malden, 1998), p. 155; Georg G. Iggers, "Historicism: The History and Meaning of the Term," *Journal of the History of Ideas* 56 (1995): 136–137. Popper's use of the term "historicism" has confused readers ever since.

13. Popper, *The Logic of Scientific Discovery,* p. 16 (a formulation added to the book's 1959 edition).

14. See Hacohen, *Karl Popper,* p. 487. For Popper, universal laws came to seem rare even in natural science, which, like the social sciences, explained more by "trendlike regularities" than by "universal laws"; in both naturalistic and social sciences, theories were probabilistic, not causal (488, 491).

15. Ibid., pp. 492, 487.

16. See Dray, "Introduction," in his *On History/Philosophers,* p. 1. Popper hints that Hempel "lifted" his idea of causal explanation in history, but

changed the meaning so that an explanation could be called "historical" if it conformed to a sociological term or theory (*The Open Society*, p. 144n.1).

17. Carl G. Hempel, "The Function of General Laws in History," *Journal of Philosophy* 39 (1942): 48. See Danto, *Analytical Philosophy*, pp. 203–210, for discussion of Hempel's assumptions.

18. Hempel, "The Function of General Laws," pp. 35, 40, 47.

19. Ibid., p. 44. Hempel aims at R. G. Collingwood. As Arthur Danto notes, "Verstehen" does not enable us to get into other historical periods insofar as they *are* other ("Historical Understanding: The Problem of Other Periods," in his *Narration*, pp. 286, 291, 293). On the translation of Dilthey's "Verstehen" into Collingwood's "empathy," see Michael Bentley, *Modern Historiography* (London, 1999), p. 87.

20. Hempel, "The Function of General Laws," pp. 35, 38–39, 42; Dray, *Laws*, p. 5. See Alan Donagan, "Explanation in History" [1957], in Gardiner, *Theories of History*, p. 431.

21. The phrase is from Murphey, *Knowledge*, p. 67.

22. Donagan, "Explanation in History," p. 439; idem, "Historical Explanation: The Popper-Hempel Theory Reconsidered," *History and Theory* 4 (1964): 13. Also see Dray, *Laws*, pp. 45, 47; Maurice Mandelbaum, *The Problem of Historical Knowledge* (New York, 1967 [1938]), pp. 187–188.

23. Louis O. Mink, "The Autonomy of Historical Understanding" [1966], in his *Historical Understanding*, pp. 77–79. As Mink puts it (77), historians, unlike scientists, cannot simply note each other's results; they have to read the books themselves and be convinced by the arguments contained therein.

24. Goldstein, *Knowing*, pp. 184–185.

25. Donagan, "Historical Explanation," p. 25; also see Murphey, *Knowledge*, p. 205.

26. W. B. Gallie, "Explanations in History and the Genetic Sciences" [1955], in Gardiner, *Theories of History*, p. 395.

27. Goldstein, *Knowing*, pp. xxiii, 184; also see Murphey, *Knowledge*, p. 84.

28. Richard Rorty, "Afterword," in *Historians and Social Values*, ed. Joep Leerssen and Ann Rigney (Amsterdam, 2000), p. 200.

29. Mink, "The Autonomy of Historical Understanding," p. 74. Mink alludes to Virgil's role as Dante's guide in the *Inferno* and *Purgatorio*.

30. Yet Morton White's writings of the late 1940s shows that this reconstruction had not yet won the day ("Toward an Analytic Philosophy of History," in *Philosophic Thought in France and the United States*, ed. Marvin Farber [2d ed.; Albany, 1968 (1950)], p. 710).

31. Patrick Gardiner, *The Nature of Historical Explanation* (London, 1952), pp. 40–42, 61, 15–16.

32. W. H. Walsh, *An Introduction to the Philosophy of History* (3d revised ed.; London, 1967 [1951]), pp. 59, 61–62; see Walsh's defense of colligation in "The Practical and the Historical Past," in *Politics and Experience*, ed. Preston King and B. C. Parekh (Cambridge, 1968), p. 11.

33. W. H. Walsh, "'Meaning' in History," in Gardiner, *Theories of History,* p. 297.
34. Danto, *Analytical Philosophy,* p. 67.
35. Dray, *Laws,* p. 19.
36. This description of Dray is in Danto, *Analytical Philosophy,* pp. 213–215; compare Dray, *Laws,* pp. 78–79, 167.
37. William Dray, "'Explaining What' in History," in Gardiner, *Theories of History,* pp. 403–408; Dray, *Laws,* pp. 55–56.
38. Arthur C. Danto, "Responses and Replies," in *Danto and His Critics,* ed. Mark Rollins (Oxford, 1993), p. 195.
39. Danto, *Analytical Philosophy,* pp. 95 (overlooking the fact that, in physics, experiments are repeatable?), 111.
40. Nonetheless, Danto writes that historians do not "peer through a screen of documents" in order to catch sight of "a landscape of past events"; rather, they try "to test, or support, or check up on some *account* of past events by peering at 'history-as-record'" (ibid., pp. 100–101).
41. Ibid., pp. 89, 114, and chap. 6. Danto argues that to see something as "evidence" (as historians customarily do) is already to be looking through it to something beyond, an "actuality" (89, 91).
42. For Danto's own later approximation to a correspondence theory of verification, see Arthur C. Danto, "Historical Language and Historical Reality," in his *Narration,* pp. 318, 319; idem, "Interview," in Domanska, *Encounters,* pp. 175–176.
43. Danto, *Analytical Philosophy,* p. 113.
44. Ibid., pp. 115, 142, 169, 183. It is only later events that give significance to earlier ones (11); Hegel's owl of Minerva takes flight only at dusk (284). Danto elaborates these points in chaps. 13 and 15 of *Narration.* For a similar argument, see Walsh, "The Practical and the Historical Past," p. 12.
45. Arthur C. Danto, "Narration and Knowledge," in his *Narration,* pp. 345–347. As Hans Kellner puts it, "the 'reality of the past' is exactly what is invisible to contemporary witnesses, who live in a world of illusion that the historian represents almost as a sentimental reminder of their blindness" ("'As Real As It Gets': Ricoeur and Narrativity" [1990], in *Meanings in Texts and Actions: Questioning Paul Ricoeur,* ed. David E. Klemm and William Schweiker [Charlottesville, 1993], pp. 60–61). Gary Shapiro adds that in this respect, Danto is a "self-acknowledged Hegelian who holds that our present knowledge alters and completes the meaning of the past" ("Art and Its Doubles: Danto, Foucault, and Their Simulacra," in *Danto and His Critics,* p. 130.)
46. Danto, *Analytical Philosophy,* p. 158. Danto gives another such example in his interview with Ewa Domanska (*Encounters,* p. 177): "The Thirty Years War began in 1618"—in 1618, no one would have known that the war would last for thirty years, or even that it was a war.
47. Hayden White, "Interview," in Domanska, *Encounters,* p. 20.

48. Jerzy Topolski, "Historians Look at Historical Truth," in *Epistemology and History,* ed. Anna Zeidler-Janiszewska (Amsterdam, 1996), pp. 408, 410.

49. F. R. Ankersmit, "The Dilemma of Contemporary Anglo-Saxon Philosophy of History," *History and Theory* 25 (1986): 17. For Danto's later interest in the topic, see his "Historical Language and Historical Reality," pp. 312–313.

50. Arthur C. Danto, "The Decline and Fall of the Analytical Philosophy of History," in *A New Philosophy of History,* ed. Frank Ankersmit and Hans Kellner (Chicago, 1995), p. 70.

51. Goldstein, *Knowing,* p. 22. See also Ankersmit, "The Dilemma of Contemporary Anglo-Saxon Philosophy of History," p. 17, critiqued by A. P. Fell, "'Epistemological' and 'Narrativist' Philosophies of History," in *Objectivity, Method and Point of View,* ed. W. J. van der Dussen and Lionel Rubinoff (Leiden, 1991), pp. 72–86.

52. Dray, *On History/Philosophers* pp. 4, 64–65.

53. Mandelbaum, *The Problem of Historical Knowledge,* p. 186.

54. Danto, *Narration,* pp. 318–319.

55. These debates resonate with those over "harder" or "softer" versions of ancient Skepticism; see, for the "softer" interpretation, Michael Frede, "The Sceptic's Two Kinds of Assent and the Question of the Possibility of Knowledge," in *Philosophy in History: Essays on the Historiography of Philosophy,* ed. Richard Rorty et al. (Cambridge, 1984), especially pp. 276, 255–256, 265–266; for the "harder" interpretation, M. F. Burnyeat, "The Sceptic in His Time and Place," in ibid., especially pp. 232–232, 241, 244. For Skepticism's effect on eighteenth-century historiography, see Arnaldo Momigliano, "Ancient History and the Antiquarian" [1950], in his *Studies in Historiography,* pp. 1–39.

56. For Danto's view that narrative is the essential form of historical writing, see Chapter 5.

57. J. G. A. Pocock, "'History and Theory,'" *Comparative Studies in Society and History* 4 (1962): 526.

58. Ibid., p. 529; Pocock quotes the words of Cushing Strout (in "Causation and the American Civil War: II," *History and Theory* 1.2 [1961]: 185), "narration is a form of explanation, which aims not at logical rigour of implication but at dramatic comprehensibility, appropriate to the untidy, passionate and value-charged activi[t]ies of men." Pocock discusses the failure of the Popper-Hempel model to explain "historical explanation" (527–529). In this early essay, Pocock proposes a turn to "the historical investigation of the historian's language" (534–535), soon to be his hallmark.

59. Novick, *Dream,* p. 399.

60. As Nancy Partner admits, historians have failed to offer "a very effective linguistically based counteroffensive . . . to defend the coherence and integrity of historical knowledge" ("Hayden White: The Form of the Content," *History and Theory* 37 [1998]: 171).

61. For Peirce as a Kantian, not a pragmatist, see Richard Rorty, "Pragmatism, Relativism, and Irrationalism" [1980], in his *Consequences of Pragmatism* (Minneapolis, 1982), pp. 160–161.

62. Hilary Putnam, "Two Philosophical Perspectives," in his *Reason,* p. 49; idem, "Realism and Reason," in his *Meaning and the Moral Sciences* (London, 1978), pp. 124–126; idem, "Realism with a Human Face" [1988], in his *Realism,* pp. 27–29. Chris Lorenz ("Historical Knowledge and Historical Reality: A Plea for 'Internal Realism,'" *History and Theory* 33 [1994]: 308) presumably has the "old version" of Putnam in mind when he writes that "internal realism" presupposes that "reality exists independently of our knowledge thereof" and that "scientific statements—including our theories—refer to this independently existing reality."

63. Hilary Putnam, "Brains in a Vat," in his *Reason,* p. 15.

64. Putnam, "Two Philosophical Perspectives," p. 74; idem, "Realism with a Human Face," p. 28 (Realism is thus an "impossible" position).

65. Hilary Putnam, "A Defense of Internal Realism," in his *Realism,* p. 41.

66. Hilary Putnam, "Preface," in his *Reason,* p. xi. In the view of Christopher Norris, internal realism "amounts to little more than a relativism that dare not speak its name" (*Deconstruction and the "Unfinished Project of Modernity"* [New York, 2000], p. 200).

67. Putnam, "Two Philosophical Perspectives," pp. 49–50 (Putnam's emphasis). Putnam here argues that Kant was, in effect, the first internal realist because he denied that we can know "things-in-themselves," only "things-for-us" (60–62).

68. Ibid., p. 55 (Putnam's emphasis).

69. Hilary Putnam, "Fact and Value," in his *Reason,* p. 134.

70. Hilary Putnam, "Values, Facts and Cognition," in his *Reason,* pp. 201, 203.

71. Putnam, "Two Philosophical Perspectives," p. 55; idem, "Meaning and Knowledge: Lecture II," in his *Meaning and the Moral Sciences,* p. 30. This lecture is an expanded version of Putnam's "What Is 'Realism'?" *Proceedings of the Aristotelian Society* (1975–76): 177–194. See also idem, "Realism with a Human Face," p. 21, acknowledging a debt to Dewey.

72. And this despite Putnam's one-line dismissal of pragmatism's description of truth as "not acceptable" because of "other historic applications" (which are left unsaid) ("Two Philosophical Perspectives," p. 50).

73. Hilary Putnam, "A Problem about Reference," in his *Reason,* pp. 38–39. Putnam, however, rejects Rorty's brand of relativism.

74. Hilary Putnam, "Reason and History," in his *Reason,* pp. 162, 167. Despite his admiration for Dewey, Putnam admits that Dewey's "objective relativism" cannot handle the case of the Nazis, in which a choice must be made between good and evil, *tout court* (168).

75. Putnam, "Two Philosophical Perspectives," pp. 52, 67; idem, "Two Conceptions of Rationality," in his *Reason,* p. 107.

76. John Dewey, "Historical Judgments" [1938], in Meyerhoff, *Philosophy of History*, pp. 165–166, 169.

77. Richard Rorty, *Philosophy and the Mirror of Nature* (Princeton, 1979), p. 298.

78. Richard Rorty, "Introduction," in his *Consequences of Pragmatism*, p. xxvi; idem, "Solidarity or Objectivity?" [1984], in *Post-Analytic Philosophy*, ed. John Rajchman and Cornel West (New York, 1985), p. 7.

79. Rorty, *Philosophy and the Mirror of Nature*, pp. 281, 293. Rorty's discussion (281–298) is framed by his account of Putnam's move from metaphysical realism to internal realism.

80. Rorty, "Dewey's Metaphysics" [1977], in his *Consequences of Pragmatism*, p. 82. Rorty's view appears to be one interpretation of Wittgenstein's famous claim (*Philosophical Investigations* 124) that philosophy "leaves everything as it is." The debate also resonates with those over ancient Skepticism; see note 55 above. For an overview of Rorty's concerns, see John Trimbur and Mara Holt, "Richard Rorty: Philosophy without Foundations," in *The Philosophy of Discourse*, ed. Chip Sills and George H. Jensen (Portsmouth, N.H., 1992), pp. 70–94.

81. Danto, "Historical Language and Historical Reality," pp. 307, 320, 331.

82. Rorty retorts that analytical philosophy is another variant of Kantianism, albeit with representation displaced from the realm of the mental to that of the linguistic (*Philosophy and the Mirror of Nature*, p. 8).

83. Appleby, Hunt, and Jacob, *Telling the Truth*, pp. 247–251, 259, 261; Harlan, *Degradation*, p. 98; Martin Bunzl, *Real History* (London, 1997), pp. 106–107, 15, also faulting these authors' loose appeal to pragmatism.

84. Lorenz, "Historical Knowledge and Historical Reality," p. 326, calls for a translation of "internal realism" from the philosophy of science to history.

85. James T. Kloppenberg, "Deconstruction and Hermeneutic Strategies for Intellectual History: The Recent Work of Dominick LaCapra and David Hollinger," *Intellectual History Newsletter* 9 (1987): 7. Kloppenberg continues: Derrida's approach is useful *only* "to puncture the claims of structuralism and semiotics" (9), and concludes that "history must be studied as something other than a text to be deconstructed" (13).

86. James T. Kloppenberg, "Objectivity and Historicism," *American Historical Review* 94 (1989): 1018–1019, 1026, 1029, 1030, 1029. Rorty characterizes Dewey not as a pragmatist, but as "a post-modernist before his time" ("Postmodernist Bourgeois Liberalism," *Journal of Philosophy* 80 [1983]: 588).

87. Gertrude Himmelfarb, *The New History and the Old* (Cambridge, Mass., 1987).

88. As does Bunzl, *Real History*, pp. 20–21, 73. Historian David D. Roberts agrees, arguing that historians can claim only (but at least) "weak" justification for their theses (*Nothing but History* [Berkeley, 1995], pp. 287–288, 300, 301, 309). Similarly, Geoffrey Elton proposes that history "aims at ex-

planations which approximate to an unverifiable truth"—but does not explain how a historian would recognize that his or her explanations "approximate" a truth if that truth is not ascertainable and verifiable ("Two Kinds of History," in Robert William Fogel and Elton, *Which Road to the Past?* [New Haven, 1983], pp. 101–103, and n. 20). For early arguments over epistemological skepticism, see Cicero's *Academia* (repeating arguments developed by Greek philosophers), Augustine's *Contra Academicos,* and essays listed in note 55 above.

89. So Thomas L. Haskell, "Farewell to Fallibilism: Robert Berkhofer's *Beyond the Great Story* and the Allure of the Postmodern," *History and Theory* 37 (1998): 352, 353, 357, arguing that postmodernists, not historians, are obsessed with a desire for certainty.

3. Language and Structures

1. Dosse, *Structuralism,* I: 392–393; II: 39–41, 45, 48, 405; for Foucault's opposition, II: 240, 242. "The speaking subject" (assumed by analytical philosophy) was a primary center of attack for French theorists/philosophers. For an early intervention, see Emile Benveniste, "Analytical Philosophy and Language" [1963], in his *Problems,* pp. 231–238. On structuralists' indifference to Anglo-American philosophy, see Thomas Pavel, with Linda Jordan, *The Feud of Language: A History of Structuralist Thought* (Oxford, 1989 [1988]), chap. 6. (Pavel argues that what the French called "Anglo-Saxon philosophy" was "an amalgam of the philosophies of science and language practiced between the two wars in Austria, Germany, Czechoslovakia, Poland, Scandinavia, England and the United States" [130].) Also see Edward Said, "*Abecedarium culturae:* Structuralism, Absence, Writing," *TriQuarterly* 20 (1971): 57–58. For American ignorance of structuralism until the 1966 conference on structuralism at Johns Hopkins University, see Macksey and Donato, *Controversy,* the conference volume.

2. On the structuralist breaking up and redistribution of the subject, see Gilles Deleuze, "How Do We Recognize Structuralism?" [1967], in Charles J. Stivale, *The Two-Fold Thought of Deleuze and Guattari* (New York, 1998), p. 280. Colin Gordon comments that despite the "anti-humanist" sentiment of structuralism, it roundly advanced the "human sciences" ("Afterword," in Michel Foucault, *Power/Knowledge,* ed. Gordon [New York, 1980], p. 230).

3. For example, structural analysis need not proceed diachronically (Claude Lévi-Strauss, *From Honey to Ashes* [trans., New York, 1973 (1966)], pp. 354–355). For Marshall Sahlins's assessment of structural anthropology as "anti-historical," see his *Historical Metaphors and Mythical Realities* (Ann Arbor, 1981), pp. 3, 6; for Sahlins's earlier view, see his "On the Delphic Writings of Claude Lévi-Strauss," *Scientific American* 214 (1966): 132, 134, reviewing Lévi-Strauss's *Structural Anthropology.*

4. Dosse, *Structuralism*, I: xxiv, xix.

5. Ibid., I: 159, 191, 382–383, 387, 390–391; II: 47, 450; "experience" and "consciousness" were to be set aside (I: 293). On the political, social, and intellectual circumstances of the "counter-structuralists," see Bannet, *Structuralism/Dissent*, pp. 229, 231–232, 237, 240.

6. Michel Foucault, "Structuralism and Post-Structuralism," trans. in *Telos* 16 (1983): 196, 198. Recasting the notion of the subject was central (205).

7. Roland Barthes, *Roland Barthes* (trans., New York, 1977 [1975]), p. 117. Jean-Michel Rabaté assigns to Barthes the founding moment of theory in writing (Barthes's *Writing Degree Zero* of 1953); see Rabaté's *The Future of Theory* (Oxford, 2002), pp. 72, 76–77.

8. Dosse, *Structuralism*, I: 356; Claude Lévi-Strauss, *La Pensée Sauvage* (Paris, 1962), p. 326, cited and discussed in Jonathan Culler, *In Pursuit of Signs* (Ithaca, 1981), p. 33; Foucault, "Structuralism and Post-Structuralism," p. 205. Surrealism seems the more apt comparison within art history: for Lacan and Surrealist painting, see Jacques Lacan, "Of Structure as an Inmixing of an Otherness Prerequisite to Any Subject Whatsoever," in Macksey and Donato, *Controversy*, p. 197; for Lévi-Strauss and Surrealism, see Lévi-Strauss, *Conversations*, pp. 34–35; he denies a connection between structuralism and Cubism, while acknowledging that Jakobson thought there was one (173).

9. Dosse, *Structuralism*, I: 91, 114, 118, 204, 373.

10. Michel Foucault," La Scène de la philosophie" [1978], in his *Dits*, III: 590.

11. Roland Barthes, "The Structuralist Activity" [1963], in his *Critical Essays* (trans., Evanston, 1972 [1964]), p. 214; compare Claude Lévi-Strauss, *The Savage Mind* (trans., Chicago, 1966 [1961]), p. 250: to constitute the object of inquiry, researchers must first decompose and then recompose the human sciences on a different plane. See Jean-Marie Benoist, *The Structural Revolution* (London, 1978 [1975]), chap. 1.

12. Dosse, *Structuralism*, I: 180, 187, 212, 292; II: 219, 409–410. Also see Claude Lévi-Strauss, "Culture et langage" in *Entretiens avec Claude Lévi-Strauss*, ed. Georges Charbonnier (Paris, 1961), p. 181; trans., "Culture and Language," in *Conversations with Claude Lévi-Strauss*, ed. G. Charbonnier (London, 1969), p. 153 (anthropology has the same work of observation, description, classification, and interpretation as does zoology and botany). Note Lévi-Strauss's checklist of what "structure" would have to include in order to qualify as a science (system, prediction, and so forth), in "Structure sociale," *Bulletin de psychologie* 7 (1953): 359–360.

13. Dosse, *Structuralism*, I: 386, 23, and Michael Lane, "Introduction," to *Structuralism: A Reader* (London, 1970), pp. 16–17: synchronic and "anticausal" explanation stood against traditional historical assumptions. For the structuralist rejection of the study of origins, see André Burguière, "History and Structure" [1971], trans. and excerpted in Revel and Hunt, *Histories*, p. 232.

14. Lévi-Strauss, *The Savage Mind,* pp. 254, 262. For a discussion of Lévi-Strauss's attack on "pseudo-evolutionary" history, see Marc Gaborian, "Structural Anthropology and History" [1963], in *Structuralism: A Reader,* pp. 156–169. On Lévi-Strauss's anti-historicist bent, see Susan Sontag, "The Anthropologist as Hero" [1963], in her *Against Interpretation* (New York, 1967), who finds his attack on Sartre unconvincing (pp. 79–81).

15. Algirdas Julien Greimas, *Sémantique structurale,* p. 31, cited and discussed in Dosse, *Structuralism,* I: 212.

16. Jacques Lacan, "L'Amour et le signifiant," in *Le Séminaire de Jacques Lacan, Livre XX, Encore, 1972–1973,* ed. Jacques-Alain Miller (Paris, 1975), p. 45. Lacan posits that the signifier does not need a sign for a subject, since a signifier can serve as the subject for another signifier. Thus the saying that "where there is smoke, there is fire," is emended to "where there is smoke, there is smoke." This elimination of the referent stands against history (48). Also see Lacan's mockery of historians in "The Function and Field of Speech and Language in Psychoanalysis" [1956] in his *Ecrits: A Selection* (trans., New York, 1977 [1966]), pp. 51–52: history is as little good for understanding the recent past as it is for predicting tomorrow; historians do a bit of retouching to permit "predictions about what happened yesterday."

17. Lacan, "Of Structure as an Inmixing of an Otherness," p. 199.

18. Louis Althusser, *Lire de Capital* (Paris, 1967), II: 94: a *"chute";* Althusser here critiques Gramsci's understanding of Marxism. Althusser sharply distinguished the earlier "humanist" (and Hegelian) Marx from the later "scientific" Marx, whose program he endorsed: see Dosse, *Structuralism,* I: 301–303; Young, *White Mythologies,* pp. 48–64.

19. Foucault argues that early forms of structuralism were not hostile to history in "Return to History" [1972], in idem, *Aesthetics, Method, and Epistemology,* ed. James D. Faubion (trans., New York, 1994), pp. 419–432. Claude Lévi-Strauss renders his appreciation to Foucault while admitting that the latter took "some liberties with chronology" (Lévi-Strauss, *Conversations,* p. 72).

20. Barthes, "The Structuralist Activity," pp. 213–214. These characteristics are distinctive to Marxist histories; see Chapter 4.

21. Lane, "Introduction," pp. 13–14; Dosse, *Structuralism,* I: xxii, 200. For the Saussurean model's spread, see A. J. Greimas, "L'Actualité du Saussurisme," *Le Français moderne* 24 (1956): 191–203. Greimas notes the irony that social anthropologists, literary theorists, and musicologists made use of Saussurean linguistics, whereas French scholars of historical linguistics/philology either ignored or rejected the development (191, 201–203).

22. Jacques Derrida, "Interview," in *Dialogues with Contemporary Philosophers,* ed. Richard Kearny (Manchester, 1984), p. 123; see Dosse, *Structuralism,* I: 388; II: 286–287. Maurice Merleau-Ponty's *Signes* (Paris, 1960) introduced philosophers to modern linguistics; see Dosse, *Structuralism,* I:

38, 40. A good example is provided by Jacques Lacan: "What the psycho-analytic experience discovers in the unconscious is the whole structure of language" ("The Agency of the Letter in the Unconscious or Reason since Freud," in his *Ecrits,* p. 147, from a lecture on May 9, 1957). He wrote, "It is the world of words that creates the world of things" ("The Function and Field of Speech and Language," in ibid., p. 65 [the Rome Congress speech of 1953 in which Lacan moved to "de-biologize" psychoanalysis]), and re-ferred to his psychoanalytic work as an "exegesis" (50). Also see Emile Benveniste, "Remarks on the Function of Language in Freudian Theory" [1956], in his *Problems,* pp. 65–75.

23. Ernst Cassirer, "Structuralism in Modern Linguistics," *Word* 1 (1945): 99, cited in Culler, *In Pursuit of Signs,* p. 24.

24. On Saussure as "the precursor of modern structuralism . . . except for the term," see Emile Benveniste, "'Structure' in Linguistics" [1962], in his *Problems,* pp. 79–80. In his own lifetime, Saussure was better known as a scholar of Indo-European comparative linguistics; see Wlad Godzich, "The Semiotics of Semiotics," *Australian Journal of Cultural Studies* 2 (1984): 13–17. The novelty of Saussure's work is contested by Pavel, *The Feud of Language,* pp. 21, 23–25.

25. Emile Benveniste, "Recent Trends in General Linguistics" [1954], in his *Problems,* p. 4. This characterization applies only to the situation of the "ordinary language-user," for whom diachrony does not exist; see Derek Attridge, "Language as History/History as Language: Saussure and the Ro-mance of Etymology," in Attridge, Bennington, and Young, *Post-Structuralism,* p. 184, who notes that Saussure gives more space in the *Cours* to diachrony than to synchrony. For pre-Saussurean linguistics, see Roman Jakobson, "Lecture I," *Six Lectures,* pp. 1–21.

26. Ferdinand de Saussure, "Notes inédites de F. Saussure," *Cahiers Ferdinand de Saussure* 13 (1954), #20 (p. 68); idem, *Cours,* pp. 439–440n.129. The *Cours* was reconstructed by editors from students' lecture notes; see David Holdcroft, *Saussure* (Cambridge, 1991), pp. 13–16; Roy Harris, *Saussure and His Interpreters* (New York, 2001), chaps. 2 and 3.

27. Saussure, *Cours,* pp. 97, 98, 100–102; idem, "Notes inédites," #11, 20 (pp. 60, 69); see Rulon S. Wells, "De Saussure's System of Linguistics" [1947], in *Structuralism: A Reader,* pp. 85–123.

28. Saussure, *Cours,* pp. 100, 182. Saussure made two exceptions regarding the "arbitrariness" of the sign: onomatopoeia and interjections/exclamations (101–102). That Saussure generalized too rapidly from the purely differen-tial character of phonemes to the whole of the linguistic system is acknowl-edged by Roman Jakobson, "Lecture III," in his *Six Lectures,* p. 64; also see his critique in "Quest for the Essence of Language," *Diogenes* 51 (1965): 35–36. For discussion of "arbitrariness," see Jonathan Culler, *Saussure* (London, 1985 [1976]), pp. 19–29.

29. Saussure, *Cours*, pp. 182–183; see Roy Harris, *Reading Saussure* (London, 1987), pp. 132, 219.

30. Saussure, "Notes inédites," #14 (p. 63); idem, *Cours*, pp. 144, 168–169. See Jacques Derrida, "Semiology and Grammatology: Interview with Julia Kristeva" [1968], in his *Positions* (trans., Chicago, 1982 [1972]), p. 26, and discussion in Culler, *Saussure*, p. 124. Also see Derrida, *Grammatology*, pp. 70, 23, 62—yet even within *differance*, there is always a "trace" (46, 62, 73).

31. Saussure, *Cours*, pp. 157, 30.

32. Harris, *Reading Saussure*, p. 31; idem, *Saussure and His Interpreters*, pp. 177, 181, 212.

33. Saussure, *Cours*, pp. 25, 31, 100–101.

34. Emile Benveniste, "Nature du signe linguistique," *Acta linguistica* 1 (1939): 23–29.

35. Ibid., pp. 24, 28, discussing Saussure, *Cours*, p. 100. That Saussure's examples were not always consistent with this "first principle" of arbitrariness is stressed by Harris, *Reading Saussure*, pp. 64–65; compare Jakobson, "Lecture VI," in his *Six Lectures*, pp. 110–111, and Saussure, *Cours*, p. 100.

36. Benveniste, "Nature du signe linguistique," p. 26. For Benveniste's influence on Ricoeur's theory of discourse, see Ricoeur, "Intellectual Autobiography," in *The Philosophy of Paul Ricoeur*, ed. Lewis Edwin Hahn (Chicago, 1995), p. 24.

37. Harris, *Saussure and His Interpreters*, p. 4; Emile Benveniste, "Saussure after Half a Century" [1963], in his *Problems*, pp. 38–39.

38. Harris, *Saussure and His Interpreters*, registers indignation at the alleged misuse of Saussure by later theorists (chaps. 8 and 10); also see Raymond Tallis, *Not Saussure: A Critique of Post-Saussurean Literary Theory* [2d ed.; New York, 1995]); Pavel, with Jordan, *The Feud of Language*, pp. vii, 54, 70. Michel Foucault proclaims Merleau-Ponty's importance in bringing Saussure's work to the attention of a larger public apart from linguists ("Structuralism and Post-Structuralism," p. 198).

39. Saussure, *Cours*, pp. 19, 21, 33; idem, "Notes inédites," #11, p. 60: to understand (as did the American linguist W. D. Whitney) that language is a human institution, Saussure acknowledged, "changed the axis of linguistics." Jakobson stresses Saussure's debt to Whitney in his "Quest for the Essence of Language," pp. 24–25. See discussion in Holdcroft, *Saussure*, p. 5.

40. Saussure, *Cours*, pp. 33, 35; Harris, *Reading Saussure*, p. 20; compare Saussure, *Cours*, pp. 45, 101 (an example: the Chinese who prostrates himself nine times in saluting the emperor). In America, Charles Sanders Peirce had already elaborated a semiotics in which the whole universe, including "man," was said to be "perfused with signs if it is not composed entirely of signs"; his views, however, had little influence on the development of the discipline. Charles Sanders Peirce, *Collected Papers* (Cambridge, Mass.,

1931–1958), V: 448; compare VII: 570, cited and discussed in Culler, *The Pursuit of Signs*, pp. 23–25. Paul Ricoeur appropriates Peirce in order to "get outside of" the text; see his "What Is a Text? Explanation and Understanding" [1970], in his *Hermeneutics and the Human Sciences*, ed. John B. Thompson (Cambridge, 1981), p. 163.

41. Roland Barthes, "Saussure, the Sign, Democracy" [1973], in his *Semiotic Challenge*, pp. 152, 154.

42. See especially Roland Barthes, "Science versus Literature," *Times Literary Supplement*, September 28, 1967, p. 897; idem, *Elements of Semiology* (trans., New York, 1973 [1964]), pp. 9–11; idem, "To Write: An Intransitive Verb?" in Macksey and Donato, *Controversy*, p. 136. For Saussure, "language is no more than a particular case of the Theory of Signs" ("Notes inédites," #16 [p. 64]). On this divergence, see Annette Lavers, *Roland Barthes: Structuralism and After* (Cambridge, 1982), pp. 5–6. Jonathan Culler argues that Barthes consciously decided (*contra* Saussure) that semiology was a branch of "a comprehensive linguistics," and chose the name "semiology" for his field when he was elected to a chair at the Collège de France; see Culler, *Roland Barthes* (New York, 1983), pp. 73, 71. Roy Harris attributes Barthes's reversal to his borrowing from the Danish semiologist Louis Hjelmslev (*Saussure and His Interpreters*, pp. 133–135). For Barthes's later approach to semiology, see his "Introduction: The Semiological Adventure" [1974], in his *Semiotic Challenge*.

43. Harris, *Saussure and His Interpreters*, p. 210: Barthes reaches a "quasi-Marxist conclusion," Harris scoffs. In Chapter 5, I detail Barthes's discussion of ideology and myth, and in Chapter 7, his views on texts and readers.

44. Saussure, "Notes inédites," #14 (p. 63); idem, *Cours*, pp. 168–169; and discussion in Culler, *Saussure*, p. 124. See Antony Easthope, "Romancing the Stone: History-Writing and Rhetoric," *Social History* 18 (1993): 236–237.

45. See, for example, Said, "*Abecedarium culturae*," pp. 49–50.

46. Predictably, reactions varied: some, such as Marc Bloch, rued historians' ignorance of linguistics (*Craft*, pp. 68–69); others, such as Emmanuel Le Roy Ladurie, mocked the "linguistic turn," claiming that he had spent "less time looking at words than looking at the things the words stand for" ("History That Stands Still" [1970; 1978], in his *The Mind and Method of the Historian*, [trans., Chicago, 1981 (1978)], pp. 3–4); he had his "work cut out for him learning to count," he proclaimed, "never mind learning to read as well!"

47. Said, "*Abecedarium culturae*," p. 48.

48. Claude Lévi-Strauss, "Preface" (to Jakobson, *Six Lectures*), pp. xi–xiii; also see his tribute to Saussure in "De L'Art comme système de signes," in Lévi-Strauss/Charbonnier, *Entretiens*, p. 131. For background, see Dosse, *Structuralism*, I: 21–23. Commentators note that mathematics might have provided a better formulation for the kinship system: see Richard Macksey and

Eugenio Donato, "The Space Between—1971," in Macksey and Donato, *Controversy,* p. xi.

49. Culler's assessment, *In Pursuit of Signs,* p. 28.

50. Claude Lévi-Strauss, *The Scope of Anthropology* (trans., London, 1967 [1960]), pp. 16–17. Despite this tribute to Saussure, it was Jakobson's emphases, especially on phonemes as "purely differential and contentless signs," that more directly influenced Lévi-Strauss: see Lévi-Strauss, "Preface" (to Jakobson, *Six Lectures*), p. xxi.

51. Claude Lévi-Strauss, "Postscript to Chapter XV," in his *Structural Anthropology,* p. 328.

52. Lévi-Strauss, *Conversations,* pp. 112–113; and see his tribute to Franz Boas for claiming, as early as 1911, that "laws of language function on an unconscious level, beyond the control of speaking subjects" (39).

53. Claude Lévi-Strauss, *The Raw and the Cooked* (trans., New York, 1969 [1964]), p. 11; see p. 12 (he does not aim to show "how men think in myths, but how myths operate in men's minds without their being aware of the fact"); see also idem, "Preface" (to Jakobson, *Six Lectures*), p. xix.

54. Claude Lévi-Strauss, *The Naked Man* (trans., New York, 1981 [1971]), pp. 38, 624, 679; see p. 675 ("Mythic thought operates essentially through a process of transformation"); idem, "Preface" (to Jakobson, *Six Lectures*), pp. xiii, xxi; idem, *The Origin of Table Manners* (trans., New York, 1978 [1968]), pp. 230, 227–228, 200.

55. Claude Lévi-Strauss, *The Elementary Forms of Kinship* (revised ed.; trans., Boston, 1969 [1949; 1967]), pp. 492–493. In a later essay, Lévi-Strauss posits that kinship and marriage rules had remained "unintelligible" until they were understood as a kind of language, and as operating by the laws of exchange ("Language and the Analysis of Social Laws" [1951], in his *Structural Anthropology,* pp. 60–61). Also see his comment that anthropologists had behaved like amateur botanists, picking up miscellaneous specimens and having no idea how to order them ("Social Structure" [1953], in ibid., p. 315).

56. Lévi-Strauss, *The Elementary Forms of Kinship,* p. 496; he further explains that woman stands *both* as "a sign and a value," and hypothesizes that this fact "explains why the relation between the sexes have preserved that affective richness, ardour and mystery which doubtless permeated the entire universe of human communications." Two years later, he clarified his meaning: "words do not speak, while women do; as producers of signs, women can never be reduced to the status of symbols or tokens" ("Language and the Analysis of Social Laws" [1951], p. 61). In a later interview, he expressed regret that women had "misunderstood" his notion of women as signs; he had "taken pains to state that all human societies look upon their women as values as much as signs." He continued, "Women are not signs, but in the societies in question marriage rules are rules of exchange" (Lévi-Strauss, *Conversations,* pp. 105–106).

57. Claude Lévi-Strauss, "Linguistics and Anthropology" [1953], in his *Structural Anthropology*, p. 79. Later in life, Lévi-Strauss revealed that it was Roman Jakobson who encouraged him to write this work (Lévi-Strauss, *Conversations,* p. 43). In 1953, Lévi-Strauss confided that anthropologists might well be filled with "melancholy" and "envy" at the success linguistics had achieved—presumably in comparison with anthropology's second-place status (68). But by the late 1960s and early 1970s, structuralism had triumphed across a range of disciplines (Dosse, *Structuralism,* II: chaps. 13–14).

58. Lévi-Strauss, *The Elementary Forms of Kinship,* p. xxvi.

59. See Dosse, *Structuralism,* I: 12, 22; for Lévi-Strauss's exile from France and his time in New York, see Lévi-Strauss, *Conversations,* chap. 3.

60. Lévi-Strauss, "Preface" (to Jakobson, *Six Lectures*), pp. xi, xiv; Lévi-Strauss heard these lectures decades earlier. Likewise, he compared the "revolutionary character" of Marcel Mauss's *Essay on the Gift* to the advances brought to linguistics by Troubetzkoy and Jakobson (Claude Lévi-Strauss, "Introduction à l'oeuvre de Marcel Mauss," in Mauss, *Sociologie et anthropologie* [Paris, 1950], pp. xxxii–xxxiii, xxxv).

61. See Claude Lévi-Strauss, "Réponses à quelques questions," *Esprit* 11 (1963): 640: studying the myths of a society can be compared to attempting to make a "grammar" for a little-known language.

62. Lévi-Strauss, "Preface" (to Jakobson, *Six Lectures*), pp. xi–xii; Dosse, *Structuralism,* I: 19; compare Lacan's "de-medicalizing" and "de-biologizing" of psychoanalysis (101–102, 105, 110). Eugenio Donato argues that linguistics provided Lévi-Strauss with "the notion of discontinuity" ("The Two Languages of Criticism," in Macksey and Donato, *Controversy,* p. 93). His own teachers, Lévi-Strauss wryly notes, were more apt to favor Bergson than Saussure (*Tristes tropiques,* p. 55).

63. Lévi-Strauss, "Preface" (to Jakobson, *Six Lectures*), p. xviii.

64. Lévi-Strauss, *Elementary Forms of Kinship,* p. 479. Throughout his life's work, Lévi-Strauss continued to stress the similarity between the structures of linguistics and those of kinship systems ("Structural Analysis in Linguistics and Anthropology" [1945], in his *Structural Anthropology,* pp. 32, 46).

65. Lévi-Strauss, "Structural Analysis," pp. 29, 31. This essay predates the publication of *Elementary Forms of Kinship.*

66. Lévi-Strauss, *The Scope of Anthropology,* p. 31.

67. French edition of the four volumes published by Librairie Plon, 1964–1971; English translations by John and Doreen Weightman published by Harper and Row, 1969–1981.

68. Lévi-Strauss recalls the aridity and "metaphysical tendencies" of phenomenology and existentialism; they provided metaphysics with "alibis." He emerged from years of this training, he confesses, with beliefs just as unsophisticated as those he had held at age fifteen (*Tristes tropiques,* pp. 52, 58). Even as a student, Bergsonian philosophy, he thought, overemphasized "appearance," "immediate awareness" (Lévi-Strauss, *Conversations,* p. 8).

69. See discussion in Marc Gaborian, "Anthropologie structurale et histoire," *Esprit* 322 (1963): 580–581.

70. Claude Lévi-Strauss, "Rousseau, Father of Anthropology," *UNESCO Courier* 16 (1963): 11, citing Rousseau, *Essay on the Origin of Languages* VIII. Elsewhere, Lévi-Strauss proclaimed Rousseau to be *"un intime,"* despite his mistaken political theory: "Interview (with Jean-Marie Benoist): Claude Lévi-Strauss Reconsiders: From Rousseau to Burke," *Encounter* 53 (1979): 22. Later, he admitted that he had "stretched" the comparison a bit—but after all, he was asked to help celebrate the 250th anniversary of Rousseau's birth (Lévi-Strauss, *Conversations*, pp. 168–169).

71. Claude Lévi-Strauss, *Race and History* (Paris, 1952), p. 45.

72. Lévi-Strauss, *The Scope of Anthropology*, p. 11.

73. Lévi-Strauss, "Introduction: History and Anthropology" [1949], in his *Structural Anthropology*, pp. 1–28.

74. Lévi-Strauss, "History and Dialectic" [1961], reprinted as chap. 9 of idem, *The Savage Mind*, is a sharp critique of Sartre's historicism and humanism. Dan Sperber favors translating *La Pensée sauvage* as "untamed thinking"— something that all humans share for certain kinds of thinking: see his "Claude Lévi-Strauss," in *Structuralism and Since,* ed. John Sturrock (Oxford, 1979), pp. 26–27.

75. Lévi-Strauss, "Introduction: History and Anthropology," pp. 14–16. My colleague Orin Starn notes that most anthropologists would find Lévi-Strauss's critique odd, since Malinowski and Mead might rather be faulted for not having "any history at all, suspending their natives instead in a timeless ethnographic present" (private communication, Feb. 23, 2003).

76. Lévi-Strauss, "Introduction: History and Anthropology," pp. 17–18, 25.

77. Lévi-Strauss, *The Scope of Anthropology,* p. 25; compare François Furet, "Les Intellectuels français et le structuralisme," *Preuves* 192 (1967): 8. See James Boon's comment that Lévi-Strauss did not "ignore" history as is often charged, but denied its status as a "privileged form of consciousness" ("Claude Lévi-Strauss," in Skinner, *Return*, pp. 169–170).

78. Lévi-Strauss, *From Honey to Ashes*, pp. 474–475; valid investigations of structural anthropology must recognize "the powerful inanity of events."

79. Lévi-Strauss, *The Origin of Table Manners*, pp. 230, 227–228.

80. Lévi-Strauss, *The Naked Man*, pp. 38, 607.

81. Lévi-Strauss, *The Raw and the Cooked*, p. 16.

82. Lévi-Strauss, *The Naked Man*, pp. 606–607.

83. Lévi-Strauss, "Introduction: History and Anthropology," p. 19; idem, *The Scope of Anthropology*, p. 28. On the introduction of psychoanalysis into France two decades earlier and its effect, see idem, *Tristes tropiques*, p. 55.

84. Lévi-Strauss, "Introduction: History and Anthropology," pp. 21, 25, 22, 24. Franz Boas is faulted for his timidity in not venturing beyond the conscious thought of individuals (20–21); see also Lévi-Strauss's appreciation for Febvre's work in Lévi-Strauss, *Conversations*, pp. 120–121.

85. Claude Lévi-Strauss, "Structuralisme et critique littéraire" [1965], in his *Anthropologie structurale deux* (Paris, 1973), pp. 324–325.

86. Lévi-Strauss, *Conversations,* pp. 120, 102, 125, 124. He continued: "primitive" (unlike "hot") societies wish to remain in a primordial state (125). For his discussion of societies "without history," see "Cultural Discontinuity and Economic and Social Development" [1963], in Claude Lévi-Strauss, *Structural Anthropology. Volume II* [trans., New York, 1976 (1973)], pp. 321–322.

87. Furet, "Les Intellectuels français et le structuralisme," pp. 5, 9, 12.

88. Lévi-Strauss, *The Scope of Anthropology,* p. 52.

89. Claude Lévi-Strauss, "Les Trois Humanismes" [1956], in his *Anthropologie structurale deux,* pp. 319–322.

90. Lévi-Strauss, "Interview: Claude Lévi-Strauss Reconsiders," pp. 23–24. A central concern in Lévi-Strauss's attack on humanistic history is his desire to eliminate "illusions of subjectivity." See discussion in Gaborian, "Anthropologie structurale et histoire," pp. 592, 593. Gaborian notes that Lévi-Strauss's hint that there could be "diachronic structures" that define rhythms of transformation (and hence could constitute a form of historical analysis) remained only a project for the future (591).

91. Lévi-Strauss, "Interview: Claude Lévi-Strauss Reconsiders," pp. 24, 26. Discriminating between human and nonhuman living species is one form of "original sin," he proclaimed (24).

92. For a critique of Sartre on similar grounds, see Michel Foucault, "L'Homme est-il mort?" interview [1966], and idem, "Foucault répond à Sartre," interview [1968], both in idem, *Dits,* I: 541, 789–795. For a not-too-convincing attempt to find similarities between Sartre and Lévi-Strauss, see David Michael Levin, "On Lévi-Strauss and Existentialism," *American Scholar* 38 (1968): 69–82.

93. Lévi-Strauss, "History and Dialectic," p. 249; see Lawrence Rosen, "Language, History, and the Logic of Inquiry in Lévi-Strauss and Sartre," *History and Theory* 10 (1971): 269–294. That Lévi-Strauss's structuralism was "a response to the rupture of the long-established tradition of Eurocentricity" is a thesis of Masao Miyoshi, "Ivory Tower in Escrow," *boundary 2* 27 (2000): 40.

94. Lévi-Strauss, "History and Dialectic," p. 248.

95. Raymond Aron asks whether the ethnologist himself participates in "barbarism" when he defines these peoples as "savages" in contrast to his own civilization. If the "civilized" are those who do not deny humanity to any members of the human species, then the actual "barbarians" he studies, who *do* deny that humanity to others, are still "barbarians," not the morally superior people that Lévi-Strauss makes them out to be. If we adopt this sort of cultural relativism, on what grounds can the ethnologist (and others of the "civilized") condemn racists? See Aron, "Le Paradoxe du même et de l'autre," in *Echanges et communications: Mélanges offerts à Claude Lévi-*

Strauss, ed. Jean Pouillon et Pierre Maranda (The Hague, 1970), II: 943, 944.

96. Lévi-Strauss, "History and Dialectic," p. 251. For Raymond Aron's challenge to Lévi-Strauss's critique of Sartre, see Aron, "Le Paradoxe," pp. 949, 952, 950. Aron broke with Sartre over political issues in 1947: Sartre emerged as more anti-de Gaulle and pro-Marxist (and Aron more "centrist"), despite their earlier friendship and co-editorship of *Les Temps modernes.* See the discussion in Robert Colquhoun, *Raymond Aron* (London, 1986), I: chap. 15.

97. Lévi-Strauss, "History and Dialectic," pp. 253–254 (emphasis in the original), 254, 255.

98. Lévi-Strauss, *Conversations,* pp. 117, 120.

99. Lévi-Strauss, "History and Dialectic," p. 249.

100. Lévi-Strauss, "Language and the Analysis of Social Laws," p. 117.

101. Lévi-Strauss, "History and Dialectic," pp. 253–254.

102. Ibid., pp. 261, 256, 263. Earlier (1955) in his *Tristes tropiques,* Lévi-Strauss was willing to consider anthropology "a form of history" (p. 58); see also his "Interview: Claude Lévi-Strauss Reconsiders," p. 20: "History gives me the feeling of extending the ethnographic experience."

103. Rosen, "Language, History and the Logic of Inquiry in Lévi-Strauss and Sartre," p. 285.

104. Lévi-Strauss, "Interview: Claude Lévi-Strauss Reconsiders," p. 21.

105. Lévi-Strauss, *The Naked Man,* pp. 629, 645, 638, 687, 640.

106. Lévi-Strauss, "History and Dialectic," pp. 257–258.

107. Ibid., p. 260. The different significances of events under different historical "codes" is reminiscent of Braudel.

108. Paul Ricoeur, "Structure et herméneutique," *Esprit* 31 (1963): 596–627.

109. Derrida, *Grammatology,* pp. 101–140.

110. Anderson, *Tracks,* pp. 32–55.

111. Pierre Macherey, *A Theory of Literary Production* (trans., London, 1978 [1966]), passim, especially chap. 20.

112. Dosse, *Structuralism,* I: 317.

113. Especially important among the latter would be Gilles Deleuze and Félix Guatteri's *Anti-Oedipus,* in part an attack on Foucault and Lacan. See Dosse, *Structuralism,* II: 210–211, for its significance in this context.

114. Ricoeur, "Intellectual Autobiography," p. 28; see idem, "The Question of the Subject: The Challenge of Semiology," in his *The Conflict of Hermeneutics,* p. 250.

115. Paul Ricoeur, "Structure, Word, Event" [1968 (1967)], in his *The Conflict of Interpretations,* ed. Don Ihde (trans., Evanston, 1974 [1969]), pp. 85, 83–84, 87; idem, "Intellectual Autobiography," in *The Philosophy of Paul Ricoeur,* pp. 19, 22–24; idem, "The Hermeneutical Function of Distanciation" [1975], in his *Hermeneutics and the Human Sciences,* p. 140.

116. Ricoeur, "Structure, Word, Event," pp. 80, 90.

117. Paul Ricoeur, "The Model of the Text: Meaningful Action Considered as a Text," *Social Research* 38 (1971): 557–561, 536; idem, *Interpretation Theory* (Fort Worth, 1976), pp. 87–88. Ricoeur looked forward to reflective philosophy's incorporation of corrections and lessons from psychoanalysis and semiology ("The Question of the Subject," pp. 265–266).

118. Ricoeur, "Intellectual Autobiography," p. 19.

119. Ricoeur, *Interpretation Theory*, p. 86.

120. Ricoeur, "Structure et herméneutique," p. 606. For Ricoeur's work on narrative, see Chapter 5.

121. Ricoeur, "Structure et herméneutique," p. 607; compare 617: "structuralist thought remains a thought which does not think itself."

122. Ibid., pp. 607, 609, 614, 617, 607–613, 618, cf. 619.

123. Lévi-Strauss, "Réponses," p. 633; similarly, idem, *The Raw and the Cooked*, pp. 10–11.

124. Lévi-Strauss, "Réponses," pp. 631–632, 636.

125. Ibid., pp. 648–649.

126. Lévi-Strauss, *The Raw and the Cooked*, p. 1; idem, *From Honey to Ashes*, p. 473; idem, *The Naked Man*, pp. 321, 639.

127. Lévi-Strauss, *From Honey to Ashes*, p. 474; idem, *The Origin of Table Manners*, p. 507; idem, *The Naked Man*, p. 639.

128. Derrida, *Grammatology*, pp. 44, 45.

129. Ibid., pp. 46, 52, 55. As Geoffrey Bennington explains the concept, Derrida derives his view of "archi-writing" from his demonstration that speech and writing share common characteristics—"repetition, absence, risk of loss, death"—and thus must relate to a common root; and if "writing" means that "*every* signifier refers only to other signifiers, then 'writing' will name properly the functioning of language in general" ("Derridabase," in Bennington and Jacques Derrida, *Jacques Derrida* [trans., Chicago 1993 (1991)], pp. 49–50, 60–61).

130. Derrida applauds Roland Barthes's move to lodge semiology within linguistics; in doing so, he was carrying out "the profoundest intention of the *Cours*" (*Grammatology*, p. 51).

131. Jacques Derrida, "Structure, Sign, and Play in the Discourse of the Human Sciences," in Macksey and Donato, *Controversy*, pp. 251, 262–263.

132. Derrida, *Grammatology*, p. 102.

133. Lévi-Strauss, "The Writing Lesson," in his *Tristes tropiques*, pp. 294–304. The meeting with the hostile group was arranged at Lévi-Strauss's request. That Lévi-Strauss himself, as well as the chieftain and his peoples, here received protection by the ruse of the chieftain's pretended reading is not as clearly acknowledged as it might be.

134. Ibid., pp. 298–299, 300.

135. Lévi-Strauss, "'Primitifs' et 'civilisés,'" in Lévi-Strauss/Charbonnier, *Entretiens*, pp. 28–33. He admits that some societies that have writing still have slavery ("Les Niveaux d'authenticité," in ibid., p. 51).

136. Lévi-Strauss, *Tristes tropiques*, pp. 283, 287, 288, 290, 293. Already in 1966, Derrida had criticized Lévi-Strauss's "ethic of archaic and natural innocence" ("Structure, Sign, and Play," p. 264).

137. See, for example, Lévi-Strauss's words at the end of his inaugural lecture at the Collège de France, *The Scope of Anthropology*, that he can never repay his debt to these peoples, and wants always to be "their pupil, their witness" (p. 53), as well as his passionate decrial of racism in the pamphlet he prepared for UNESCO, *Race and History*. James Boon claims that "*Tristes tropiques* stands in the great Ruskinesque tradition of transvaluing decay" ("Claude Lévi-Strauss," in Skinner, *Return*, p. 162).

138. Derrida, *Grammatology*, pp. 117, 118, 135; Derrida caustically questions what Marx and Freud, Lévi-Strauss's alleged masters, would have made of this alleged "goodness and sweetness" (118). Also see François Furet, "French Intellectuals: From Marxism to Structuralism" [1967], in his *Workshop*, p. 31.

139. Derrida, *Grammatology*, pp. 135, 114, 139, 120; Lévi-Strauss's exaltation of the primitives' "ethic of the living word" rests on a delusion (139). To be sure, as an anthropologist working with preliterate subjects, Lévi-Strauss might well privilege speech over writing.

140. Ibid., pp. 110, 139–140. In his critique, Derrida also assumes that meaning is created by "difference."

141. A point to which I return in exploring Clifford Geertz's textual analogy for anthropological practice; see Chapter 7.

142. Anderson, *Tracks*, pp. 43, 44–45.

143. Ibid., pp. 48–49.

144. Macherey, *A Theory of Literary Production*, pp. 100–101, 155; also see the translator's preface, p. viii.

145. Ibid., pp. 48–49, 141–144.

146. Ibid., pp. 153, 101.

147. Ibid., pp. 7 (emphasis in original), 154, 155.

148. Ibid., p. 41.

149. Ibid., pp. 78, 149, 151.

150. Ibid., pp. 150, 154.

151. Dosse, *Structuralism*, II: 409, 451, 195, 410–411.

4. The Territory of the Historian

1. I borrow the title from Emmanuel Le Roy Ladurie, *The Territory of the Historian* (trans., Hassocks, 1979 [1973]).

2. For an overview of the development of *Annales*, see Peter Burke, *The French Historical Revolution: The "Annales" School, 1929–89* (Cambridge, 1990), summary, p. 2; Emmanuel Le Roy Ladurie, "History in France," in *Ideas from France*, ed. Lisa Appignanesi (London, 1985), pp. 43–47; A[ndré] Burguière, "Annales (Ecole des)," in *Dictionnaire des*

sciences historiques, ed. Burguière (Paris, 1986), pp. 46–52; François Furet, "Beyond the *Annales*," *Journal of Modern History* 55 (1983): 391–392; Iggers, *Historiography,* chap. 5. Sabine Jöckel notes the belated reception (post–World War II) of *Annales* historiography by German historians (*"Nouvelle histoire,"* I: 8–9).

3. Jacques Revel, "Introduction," in Revel and Hunt, *Histories,* pp. 5–6; H. Stuart Hughes, *The Obstructed Path: French Social Thought in the Years of Desperation, 1930–1960* (New York, 1966), p. 24. For Febvre's views on the defeat of 1870 and subsequent historiography, see Alice Gerard, "A l'Origine du combat des Annales: Positivisme historique et système universitaire," in *Au Berceau des Annales: Le Milieu strasbourgeois,* ed. Charles-Olivier Carbonell and Georges Livet (Toulouse, 1983), p. 88.

4. Revel, "Introduction," pp. 3–6; William R. Keylor, *Academy and Community: The Foundation of the French Historical Profession* (Cambridge, Mass., 1975), chap. 2 ("History's Role in the Regeneration of the Fatherland"); on French historians' "[l]argely inaccurate understanding" of Ranke's historical method, see ibid., p. 8.

5. Keylor, *Academy and Community,* p. 87.

6. Langlois and Seignobos, *Introduction.* See Paul Ricoeur, *Contribution,* p. 8; Maurice Aymard, "The *Annales* and French Historiography (1929–72)," *Journal of European Economic History* 1 (1972): 494; Jacques Le Goff, "History as a Science: The Historian's Craft," in his *History and Memory* (trans., New York, 1992 [1977]), p. 198. For a more favorable view, see Michael Bentley, *Modern Historiography* (London, 1999), p. 104.

7. Langlois and Seignobos, *Introduction,* pp. 214, 302; Keylor, *Academy and Community,* chap. 4.

8. Langlois and Seignobos, *Introduction,* pp. 2, 298, 316.

9. Ibid., pp. 153, 171, 303, 319.

10. Ibid., pp. 300, 314, 321.

11. Marrou's comments on historical "positivism" are scathing (*Meaning,* pp. 10, 54); Langlois and Seignobos try to turn the historian into a "factory-worker intent upon the transformation of raw material" (56, 63). Anthony Grafton characterizes Langlois and Seignobois's *Introduction* as "a late nineteenth-century manual of historical writing, so old-fashioned that parts of it now look strangely modern" (*The Footnote* [Cambridge, Mass., 1997], p. 26); for examples, see Langlois and Seignobos, *Introduction,* pp. 171, 166, 216.

12. Hughes, *The Obstructed Path,* pp. 25–28; Martin Siegel, "Henri Berr et la *Revue du Synthèse Historique,*" in *Au Berceau des Annales,* pp. 205–218; Keylor, *Academy and Community,* chap. 8.

13. François Simiand, "Historical Method and Social Science" [1903], *Review* 9 (1985): 186, 210–211. Simiand thought most histories written in the late nineteenth century should simply go out of business (175). Nonetheless, Simiand's program for reform via the social sciences did not escape positivism.

14. Hughes, *The Obstructed Path*, p. 62, notes the lack of philosophical interest on the part of Bloch and Febvre, and the "curiously provincial" stance of French historians (62–63); also see Geoff Eley, "Is All the World a Text? From Social History to the History of Society Two Decades Later," in McDonald, *Turn*, p. 204; and François Furet, *Workshop*, p. 1, on French historians' having "little taste for epistemology or for the history of its own history."

15. See Lucien Febvre's witty attack on Spengler and Toynbee, "Deux Philosophies opportunistes de l'historie: De Spengler à Toynbee" [1936], in his *Combats pour l'histoire* (2d ed.; Paris, 1965 [1953]), pp. 119–143; also see citations from Febvre in Georges Livet, "Lucien Febvre et Strasbourg," in *Au Berceau des Annales*, p. 51.

16. Furet, "Beyond the *Annales*," p. 408. Eric Hobsbawm, however, declares that young British historians at Cambridge in the 1930s were instructed to read *Annales* ("British History and the *Annales*" [1978], in his *On History*, p. 179).

17. Jacques Le Goff, "L'Histoire nouvelle," in *La Nouvelle Histoire*, ed. Le Goff (Paris, 1988 [1978]), p. 53; idem, "Une science dans l'enfance" (prologue to the 1978 edition), in *La Nouvelle Histoire*, p. 34. Likewise, only Veyne took an interest in the narrative preferences of Anglo-American philosophy of history; see Ricoeur, *Contribution*, p. 4.

18. Burguière, "Annales," pp. 48–51 (although the *Annalistes* did have new methods of description and analysis).

19. Marc Bloch and Lucien Febvre, "La Vie scientifique: sur les routes de l'entr'aide," *Annales d'histoire économique et sociale* (9) 1937: 75–76.

20. Jöckel, "*Nouvelle histoire*," I: 62–63; Immanuel Wallerstein, "*Annales* as Resistance" [1978], excerpted in Revel and Hunt, *Histories*, pp. 368, 369.

21. Cited in Ricoeur, *Contribution*, p. 9 (no reference given for quotation).

22. Lucien Febvre, "A New Kind of History" [1949], in idem, *A New Kind of History: From the Writings of Febvre*, ed. Peter Burke (London, 1973), p. 41, trans. from Febvre's *Combats pour l'histoire*. Also see Aymard, "The *Annales*," pp. 496–497.

23. Bloch, *Craft*, pp. 45, 47. Bloch insisted that the documents "speak only when properly questioned" (64). Bloch began the book in 1941, three years before his murder by German forces.

24. Jacques Le Goff, "The Historical Mentality," in his *History and Memory*, p. 130; Furet, *Workshop*, pp. 20–21; Burguière, "Annales," p. 51.

25. Colin Lucas, "Introduction," *Constructing the Past*, ed. Jacques Le Goff and Pierre Nora (Cambridge, 1985), pp. 2–3. This volume translates ten essays from *Faire de l'histoire* (Paris, 1974). For the status of the early *Annalistes* in the French historical profession, see Hughes, *The Obstructed Path* and Burke, *The French Historical Revolution*. These professors eventually themselves became "the establishment"; a special section (VI) of the Ecole pratique des hautes études was created as a base for *Annales*-type

historiography, separate from the traditional home for historical studies in section IV.

26. Bentley, *Modern Historiography,* p. 112. André Burguière, "Annales," p. 48, remarks that in the early days of the journal, some thought it Marxist because of its emphasis on economic and social structures. Yet *Annales* seemed bourgeois to others; see Michel de Certeau, "The Historiographical Operation" [1974], in his *The Writing of History,* p. 67.

27. Fernand Braudel, "History and the Social Sciences: The *Longue Durée*" [1958], excerpted in Revel and Hunt, *Histories,* p. 119.

28. Le Goff, "L'Histoire nouvelle," p. 40.

29. Emmanuel Le Roy Ladurie, "The 'Event' and the 'Long Term' in Social History: The Case of the Chouan Uprising" [1972], in his *The Territory of the Historian,* p. 111. This essay argues for linking "long term" and "single event" history (119). In his inaugural lecture at the Collège de France on November 30, 1973, Le Roy Ladurie attacked the recent "rehabilitation *à la Seignobos*" of "event-history" ("History That Stands Still," in his *The Mind and Method of the Historian* [trans., Chicago, 1981], p. 2; essays in this volume are taken from *Le Territoire de l'historien,* vol. 2 [Paris, 1978]).

30. Structuralism and post-structuralism agreed that "the imagined sovereign bourgeois ego is a product of ideology" (Nicholas B. Dirks, "Is Vice Versa? Historical Anthropologies and Anthropological Histories," in McDonald, *Turn,* p. 25).

31. Bloch, "History, Men, and Time," in his *Craft,* p. 26 ("Le bon historien, lui, resemble à l'ogre de la légende. Là où il flaire la chair humaine, il sait que là est son gibier"). Some of Bloch's historiographical emphases strike a modern or even postmodern note: a rejection of the quest for "origins," in which "lurks the . . . danger of confusing ancestry with explanation"; an insistence that history can deal only with the "tracks" of the past; a refusal of monocausal explanation; the utility to the historian of "unintentional evidence" (29–32, 54–55, 193, 89).

32. Fernand Braudel attributes the phrase *l'histoire évémentielle* to François Simiand ("History and the Social Sciences: The *Longue Durée,*" p. 118). A standard quip was that *Annales* history was the history of society "with politics left out." See Georg G. Iggers, "Introduction: The Transformation of Historical Studies in Historical Perspective," in *International Handbook of Historical Studies,* ed. Iggers and Harold T. Parker (Westport, Conn., 1979), p. 10.

33. Ricoeur, *Contribution,* pp. 9–11.

34. Braudel, "History and the Social Sciences," p. 120: "It was only yesterday that they proved the saviors of our profession." Braudel also names Marx, the first "to construct true social models, on the basis of a historical *longue durée*" (141–142).

35. Jacques Rancière, *The Names of History: On the Poetics of Knowledge* (Minneapolis, 1994 [1992]), pp. 11–12.

36. Ricoeur, *Contribution,* chap. 4, emphasizing that economic history did not remain dominant. When serial history was applied to such topics as the study of death, religion, sex, and so forth, it merged with intellectual history (27–32).

37. Michel Vovelle, "Serial History or Case Studies: A Real or False Dilemma in the History of Mentalities?" [1985], in his *Ideologies and Mentalities* (trans., Chicago, 1990), p. 235, citing the work of François Furet.

38. Lucas, Introduction," p. 10.

39. Le Roy Ladurie, "History That Stands Still," p. 27.

40. Robert Darnton, "Conclusion," *The Great Cat Massacre and Other Episodes in French Cultural History* (New York, 1984), pp. 257–258; similarly, see discussion in Pierre Bourdieu, Roger Chartier, and Robert Darnton, "Dialogue à propos de l'histoire culturelle," *Actes de la recherche en sciences sociales* 59 (1985): 87–88. For a contrast with Febvre and Bloch, see Robert Mandrou, "Histoire sociale et histoire des mentalités," *La Nouvelle Critique* 49 (1972): 41, 44.

41. Lynn Hunt, "French History in the Last Twenty Years: The Rise and Fall of the *Annales* Paradigm," *Journal of Contemporary History* 21 (1986): 213–214. Michel Vovelle argues that serial history remains indispensable, even as the newer "case study" approach gains favor ("Serial History or Case Studies?" pp. 243–244). Vovelle summarizes critiques by Carlo Ginzburg and Roger Chartier: serial history erases sudden change, masks conflict and eliminates difference, and emphasizes normalization and the diffusion of cultural models, rather than the mechanisms of literary production (238).

42. Ricoeur, *Contribution,* p. 43; Jöckel, *"Nouvelle histoire,"* I: 61–62. Lawrence Stone's "History and the Social Sciences in the Twentieth Century," summarizes contributions of the "New History," in *The Future of History,* ed. Charles F. Delzell (Nashville, 1977), pp. 20–23. Benedetto Croce characterizes Ranke's books as "history devoid of a historical problem" (*History/Liberty,* pp. 99, 93, 96). Croce elsewhere blames the "legacy of Descartes" for the lack of historical understanding among the French: "Essay 29: Proust: An Example of Decadent Historical Methods," in his *My Philosophy and Other Essays* (trans., London, 1949), p. 213.

43. Furet, *Workshop,* pp. 7, 9, 12.

44. Ibid., pp. 6, 56; Revel, "Introduction," p. 9; Burguière, "Annales," p. 51. Paul Ricoeur wrote that he learned from Bloch that "[t]the document was not a document before the historian came to ask it a question" ("Objectivity and Subjectivity," in his *History and Truth* [Evanston, 1965 (1955, 1964)], p. 23).

45. See Stone, "History and the Social Sciences in the Twentieth Century," pp. 20–22; Jöckel, *"Nouvelle histoire,"* I: 107–139, for an informative discussion of *"mentalité,"* stressing influences from anthropology (especially Lévy-Bruhl) and the relation of *"mentalité"* to "ideology." For "history of mentalities," see Robert Mandrou, "L'histoire des mentalités," *Encyclo-*

paedia universalis VII (1968): 436–438; for an earlier account, see Georges Duby, "Histoire des mentalités," in *L'Histoire et ses methodes. Encyclopédie de la Pléiade* 11, ed. Charles Samaran (Paris, 1961), pp. 937–966, at 965.

46. Lucas, "Introduction," p. 4.

47. Revel, "Introduction," pp. 9–10: a goal proposed years earlier on a Durkheimian sociological model, but stalled by World War I and its aftermath. Immanuel Wallerstein argues that *Annales'* interdisciplinary success in the period between 1945 and 1967 lay in its strategic position in the Cold War era: it resisted *both* "Anglo-Saxon intellectual hegemony" *and* "sclerotic official Marxism" ("Beyond *Annales?" Radical History Review* 49 [1991]: 9).

48. Iggers, *Historiography,* p. 53.

49. Fernand Braudel, "Introduction," in Traian Stoianovich, *French Historical Method: The* Annales *Paradigm* (Ithaca, 1976), pp. 11–12; see also Furet, "Beyond the *Annales,"* p. 392.

50. See Bentley, *Modern Historiography,* pp. 106, 108–110; Jöckel, *"Nouvelle histoire,"* I: 51–53; Burguière, "Annales," p. 49; also see Iggers, *Historiography,* p. 52. For the growth of the study of geography in France, see Numa Broc, "Les Seductions de la nouvelle géographie," in *Au Berceau des Annales,* pp. 247–263.

51. Régine Robin, *Histoire et linguistique* (Paris, 1973), pp. 64–66.

52. Bloch, *Craft,* p. 53. That his admonition was later heeded is shown in such works as *The "Annales" School and Archaeology,* ed. John Bintliff (Leicester, 1991).

53. Emmanuel Le Roy Ladurie, "Writing the History of the Climate" [1959], in his *The Territory of the Historian,* p. 285.

54. Braudel, "Débats et combats: Histoire et sciences sociales: La longue durée," *Annales E.S.C.* 13 (1958): 752–753.

55. Paul Ricoeur charged that "interdisciplinarity" allowed the *Annalistes* to overlook the central role of time in historiography. Does history even remain history in this "marriage of convenience," he asks? (*Time* I: 108–110).

56. For the recent turn to politics within an *Annales* framework, see Burguière, "Annales," p. 51.

57. Ricoeur, *Contribution,* pp. 47–51. Yet Furet inveighs against historians imagining themselves as anthropologists ("Beyond the *Annales,"* p. 402).

58. Ricoeur, *Contribution,* p. 47. Jacques Revel credits changes in French political sentiment in the 1960s with shaking confidence in the older history ("Mentalités," in *Dictionnaire des sciences historiques,* p. 454).

59. Ricoeur, *Contribution,* p. 62. Ricoeur worries (65) that stressing the "absence" of the past might lead to a new "neo-Kantian idealism" in which "[a]ncient Egypt is simply the product of Egyptology." Is this not, he asks, "to make the dead die twice over by denying their ever having once existed?"

60. See discussion in Stoianovich, *French Historiographical Method,* pp. 112–113, 134–135, 170, noting that Braudel in turn faulted Marxists for clinging to a "congealed" social model that needed loosening up (152).
61. Duby, "Histoire des mentalités," p. 965.
62. Hans Kellner, "Interview," in Domanska, *Encounters,* p. 48; see discussion in Stuart Clark, "The *Annales* Historians," in Skinner, *Return,* pp. 181–182.
63. For helpful discussions of the "stages" of mentalités history, see Revel, "Mentalités," pp. 450–456; Jacques Le Goff, "Mentalities: A History of Ambiguities," in his *Constructing the Past,* pp. 170–172.
64. Vovelle, "History of Mentalities," p. 155.
65. Michel Vovelle, "Introduction: Ideologies and Mentalities—A Necessary Clarification," in his *Ideologies and Mentalities,* p. 12.
66. Le Goff, "Mentalities," pp. 166, 176.
67. See Iggers, *Historiography,* p. 58. Febvre headed a committee charged to produce the *Encyclopédie française* in the 1930s; Volume 1 was entitled *L'outillage mental.* See Peter Burke, "Introduction," *Lucien Febvre, A New Kind of History,* p. xiii; idem, *The French Historical Revolution,* pp. 26, 29. Febvre's essay, "History and Psychology," from the *Encyclopédie française,* vol. 3, is especially important for this discussion; see translation in Febvre, *A New Kind of History,* pp. 1–11. Robert Darnton argues that the *outillage mentale* made culture "too inert," detracting from its status as an activity of appropriating signs and symbols ("Dialogue à propos de l'histoire culturelle," p. 88).
68. Lucien Febvre, *Le Problème de l'incroyance au XVIe siècle: la religion de Rabelais* (Paris, 1962 [1943]).
69. Lucien Febvre, "La Sensibilité et l'histoire: Comment reconstituer la vie affective d'autrefois?" *Annales d'histoire sociale* 3 (1941): 5, 7–8, 18, 13–16. André Burguière posits that Febvre's view of *mentalité* history focused on "historical psychology," whereas Bloch retained a more Durkheimian position ("L'anthropologie historique," in *L'histoire et le métier d'historien en France 1945–1995,* ed. François Bédarida [Paris, 1995], pp. 174–176).
70. Le Goff, "Mentalities," pp. 166–180, quotation at 176. "The history of mentalities is to the history of ideas as the history of material culture is to economic history," Le Goff claimed (169); also see Jöckel, *"Nouvelle histoire,"* I: 138.
71. Robert Darnton, "The History of *Mentalités:* Recent Writings on Revolution, Criminality, and Death in France," in *Structure, Consciousness, and History,* ed. Richard Harvey Brown and Stanford M. Lyman (Cambridge, 1978), p. 112.
72. Michel Vovelle, "History of Mentalities, History of Resistances, or the Prisons of the *Longue Durée*" [1980], in his *Ideologies and Mentalities,* p. 156; Le Goff, "Mentalities," p. 169.
73. Le Goff, "Mentalities," pp. 174–175.

74. See Dosse, *Structuralism,* II: 227–233, 266.

75. Claude Lévi-Strauss, interview on "Les Lundis de l'histoire," France-Culture, January 25, 1971, cited in Dosse, *Structuralism,* II: 227.

76. See Claude Langlois and André Vauchez, "L'histoire religieuse," in *L'histoire et le métier d'historien en France,* pp. 317–318.

77. Furet, "Beyond the *Annales,*" pp. 404–405; idem, "Introduction," *Workshop,* pp. 15–17. Furet also critiques the reliance on literary evidence; the materials are "inevitably subjective, untypical, and ambiguous" ("From Narrative History to Problem-oriented History" [1975], in ibid., 64–65). Aymard comments that the *Annalistes* made the period from the eleventh to the eighteenth centuries their special territory ("The *Annales* and French Historiography," p. 510).

78. Hughes, *The Obstructed Path,* pp. 62–63; also see Furet, "Introduction," *Workshop,* p. 1, on French historians' lack of "taste for epistemology or for the history of its own history." German historian Jörn Rüsen criticizes *Annales* historiography for its lack of "theory," by which he appears to mean lack of "scientific method" ("What Is Theory in History?" [1990] and "Paradigm Shift and Theoretical Reflection in Western German Historical Studies" [1986], both in his *Studies in Metahistory,* pp. 32–33, 175).

79. Furet, "Beyond the *Annales,*" p. 408: an historian can work on "new" topics, such as peasants or daily life, and still employ "old" approaches.

80. Ricoeur, *Contribution,* p. 4.

81. Le Goff, "L'Histoire nouvelle," p. 53 for Aron.

82. Raymond Aron, "The Philosophy of History," in *Philosophic Thought in France and the United States,* ed. Marvin Farber (Albany, 1968 [1950]), pp. 307–308; Marrou, *Meaning,* pp. 20–22 on the importance of Dilthey, and chap. 7, "Explanation and Its Limitations."

83. Aron, "The Philosophy of History," pp. 303–305, 312, 315, 309, 319. Aron paraphrases Marx's dictum (from the *Eighteenth Brumaire of Louis Napoleon*) that men, born into a situation they did not choose, make their history, by repositioning it in a phenomenological framework (312).

84. Marrou, *Meaning,* pp. 245, 23, 246.

85. Ibid., pp. 56 (of Langlois and Seignobos's text), 63–68, 81–82; also see Ricoeur, *Contribution,* pp. 4, 12, 17–20.

86. Marrou, *Meaning,* p. 45, cf. 56.

87. Veyne, *Writing History,* pp. 286, 214, 223. Thus Thomas Aquinas could not have known how to recognize social classes, paternalism, conspicuous consumption, and so forth (214).

88. Ricoeur, *Contribution,* pp. 1–2, 34. The animus against event history eliminated "the narrative dimension" from French history-writing (34). For Veyne's views on narrative, see Chapter 5.

89. Veyne, *Writing History,* p. 26. For a more recent critique of *Annalistes'* failure to register the literary dimensions of history, see Rancière, *The Names of History.*

90. Veyne, *Writing History*, pp. 59, 12, 7.
91. Ibid., pp. 5 (referring to the work of Gérard Genette), 87–88, 90, 93, 14.
92. Ibid., pp. 87–88. "Explanation" is simply the meaning that the historian gives to the account (90).
93. Ibid., p. 91.
94. See Stoianovich, *French Historiographical Method*, p. 219.
95. Veyne, *Writing History*, pp. 13, 17–18, 11. Despite his critique of historiography, Veyne claims "truth" for the historians' enterprise, a point criticized by Michel de Certeau ("Une Epistémologie de transition: Paul Veyne," *Annales ESC* 27 [1972]: 1319–1321), who also faults Veyne for failing to attend to actual historiographical practice (1319, 1322, 1327).
96. Veyne, *Writing History*, pp. 48, 83, 81, 17 (the words are ascribed to George Leigh Mallory who set out to climb Mount Everest in 1924).
97. Iggers, *Historiography*, chap. 9; Carrard, *Poetics*, p. 34; Revel, "Introduction," p. 41; Roger Chartier, "Four Questions for Hayden White" [1993], in his *Edge*, p. 28.
98. De Certeau, "Une Epistémologie de transition," p. 1327; compare pp. 1319, 1323, 1325; see discussion in Roger Chartier, "Michel de Certeau: History, or Knowledge of the Other" [1987], in his *Edge*, pp. 41–42; and idem, "Four Questions for Hayden White," pp. 28–29. De Certeau also critiques Veyne's implication that language assumes a certain transparency to its referent ("Une Epistémologie," p. 1321).
99. Paul Veyne, "Foucault Revolutionizes History" [1978], in Davidson, *Foucault*, p. 147. Veyne argued that Marxist historians believe in "natural objects" (such as "the relation of production"), which Foucault aimed to destabilize (180–181).
100. Ibid., pp. 152–155, 146, 167, 159, 160, 182.
101. Ibid., pp. 147, 172, 151, 153–155, 157. "Man" is likewise a false object (175).
102. Ibid., pp. 181, 177, 158, 164. Thus phenomenology, a philosophy of the *cogito*, is faulted for describing things on the basis of consciousness (179–180).
103. Ibid., p. 181.
104. Dosse, *Structuralism*, II: 114, 116, 227. Dosse reports that Maoist protesters shouted, "Althusser is useless!" (II: 119).
105. Ibid., II: 117, and chap. 34; in linguistics, semiotics, poetics, literary history, and psychoanalysis, history was recuperated.
106. Ibid., II: 372–373.
107. It is significant that *Annales* 19 (1964) dedicated a section to Lévi-Strauss's work, especially *The Savage Mind*. Roland Barthes, introducing the issue, notes that despite *Annalistes'* wish to discuss "this important book," it was mostly philosophers who responded to the invitation to offer an essay ("Les Sciences humaines et l'oeuvre de Lévi-Strauss," *Annales E.S.C.* 19 [1964]: 1085, 1089).

108. Michel Vovelle, "The Event in the History of Mentalities," in his *Ideologies and Mentalities,* p. 229. Ann Rigney comments that historians' current interest in trauma reflects concerns with the unintelligibility of events (*Imperfect Histories: The Elusive Past and the Legacy of Romantic Historicism* [Ithaca, 2001], p. 66).

109. See André Burguière's "Histoire et structure," the introduction to the issue of *Annales* that sought to link the two (*Annales* 26 [1971]: i–vii, trans. as "History and Structure," excerpted in Revel and Hunt, *Histories*). Burguière summons up Foucault, Braudel, and Le Roy Ladurie as examples of historians who accommodate "structure." See also Marshall Sahlins, *Historical Metaphors and Mythical Realities* (Ann Arbor, 1981), pp. 7–8, 72.

110. Burguière, "History and Structure," pp. 235, 238.

111. Dosse, *Structuralism,* II: 54–56. Tzvetan Todorov, lecturing to the international symposium on "The Languages of Criticism and the Sciences of Man" at Johns Hopkins University in 1966, felt obliged to introduce Bakhtin to his audience: "a great Soviet literary critic" ("Language and Literature," in Macksey and Donato, *Controversy,* p. 128).

112. For discussion of Foucault as historian (or not), see Chapter 6.

113. Dosse, *Structuralism,* I: 143; II, chaps. 22–23. Roland Barthes for example, classified Foucault's early work, *Madness and Civilization,* as a "structural history" ("Taking Sides" [1961], in his *Critical Essays,* pp. 163–170, especially 166).

114. For a convenient summary of historiographical changes, see William M. Reddy, *Money and Liberty in Modern Europe* (Cambridge, 1987), pp. 4–8. For an early example of an historian's attention to the language and assumptions of workers, see idem, "The Textile Trade and the Language of the Crowd at Rouen, 1752–1871," *Past & Present* 74 (1977): 62–89.

115. François Furet, *Interpreting the French Revolution* (trans., Cambridge, 1981 [1978]), pp. 48, 49. As Furet pointedly later remarked, "All Marxist interpretations of the French Revolution postdate Marx" (*Marx and the French Revolution* [trans., Chicago, 1988 (1986)], p. 3).

116. William H. Sewell Jr., *A Rhetoric of Bourgeois Revolution: The Abbé Sieyes and "What is the Third Estate?"* (Durham, 1994), p. 204.

117. Ibid., p. 36. Sewell faults Furet and Keith Baker (in *Inventing the French Revolution*) for either construing "the social" too narrowly or collapsing it into "the intellectual" (30).

118. As was favored by some second-generation *Annalistes,* such as Fernand Braudel. For microhistory, see Giovanni Levi, "On Microhistory," in Burke, *Perspectives,* p. 106; Edward Muir, "Introduction: Observing Trifles," in *Microhistory and the Lost Peoples of Europe,* ed. Muir and Guido Ruggiero (trans., Baltimore, 1991), p. vii; Roger Chartier, "Intellectual History or Sociocultural History? The French Trajectories," in LaCapra and Kaplan, *Intellectual History,* pp. 29–30. Braudel, however, drafting *La Meditérranée* in a German prison camp, thought that the short view of "events"

could lead a historian to despair: see J. H. Hexter, "Fernand Braudel and the Monde Braudellien . . ."[1972], in Hexter, *On Historians* (Cambridge, 1979), p. 104. For Braudel's later critique of microhistory, see Hans Medick, "Mikro-Historie," in *Sozialgeschichte, Alltagsgeschichte, Mikro-Historie,* ed. Winfried Schulze (Göttingen, 1994), p. 40.

119. Jacques Revel, "Microanalysis and the Construction of the Social" [1996], in Revel and Hunt, *Histories,* pp. 494–497, appealing to the ideas of historian Eduardo Grendi. The anti-functionalist character of microanalysis was strongly influenced by Clifford Geertz, Revel notes (499–500).

120. Carlo Ginzburg and Carlo Poni, "The Name and the Game: Unequal Exchange and the Historiographic Marketplace" [1979], in *Microhistory and the Lost Peoples of Europe,* pp. 3, 8 (microhistory can thus be defined as *scienza del vissuto*); Thomas Kuehn, "Reading Microhistory: The Example of *Giovanni and Lusanna,*" *Journal of Modern History* 61 (1989): 515.

121. Natalie Zemon Davis, "The Reasons of Misrule" [1971], in her *Society and Culture in Early Modern France* (Stanford, 1975), p. 122.

122. Peter Burke, "Overture," in his *Perspectives,* p. 16.

123. Ginzburg and Poni, "The Name and the Game," p. 7.

124. Gene Brucker, *Giovanni and Lusanna: Love and Marriage in Renaissance Florence* (Berkeley, 1986).

125. Emmanuel Le Roy Ladurie, *Montaillou: The Promised Land of Error* (trans., New York 1978 [1975]); Carlo Ginzburg, *The Cheese and the Worms: The Cosmos of a Sixteenth-Century Miller* (trans., Baltimore, 1980 [1976]).

126. Judith Brown, *Immodest Acts: The Life of a Lesbian Nun in Renaissance Italy* (New York, 1986).

127. Natalie Zemon Davis, *The Return of Martin Guerre* (Cambridge, Mass., 1983).

128. Giovanni Levi, *Inheriting Power: The Story of an Exorcist* (trans., Chicago, 1988 [1985]). Although Levi focuses on a particular priest of Santena (Italy) at the turn to the eighteenth century, he also includes considerable data on (for example) land prices and ownership that expand this "small story" with considerations of economic history.

129. Emmanuel Le Roy Ladurie, *Carnival in Romans* (trans., New York, 1980 [1979]).

130. Darnton, *The Great Cat Massacre,* often cited as an example of microhistory, although Darnton aligns himself with the history of *mentalités* and cultural history (pp. 258–259). Darnton identifies himself as a cultural historian in "Dialogue à propos de l'histoire culturelle," p. 87.

131. Levi, "On Microhistory," pp. 103, 105–106. Peter Burke alleges that in celebrating the "little people," microhistorians (and their readers) may forget where power in a society is located and how it operates ("Overture," p. 32).

132. See note 125.

133. For this relation, see Medick, "Mikro-Historie," p. 40. For an overview of

currents in twentieth-century German historiography, see Rüsen, "Paradigm Shift," pp. 161–186.

134. See Norbert Elias, "Zum Begriff des Alltags," in *Materialien zur Soziologie des Alltags,* ed. Kurt Hammerich and Michael Klein (Opladen, 1978), p. 26, for a list of these and what they "oppose."

135. Wolfgang Hardtwig, "Alltagsgeschichte heute," in *Sozialgeschichte, Alltagsgeschichte, Mikro-Historie,* pp. 21–24. For *Alltagsgeschichte* as a German protest against excessive industrialization, the anonymity of state and economic organization (and so forth), see Wolfgang Hardtwig, *Geschichtskultur und Wissenschaft* (Munich, 1990), p. 53.

136. Hardtwig, "Alltagsgeschichte heute," pp. 24–26.

137. So Eduardo Grendi, "Sei Storie Württemberghesi," *Quaderni Storici* 63 (1986): 979, of David Sabean's *Power in the Blood.*

138. So Robert Finlay of Natalie Zemon Davis's *The Return of Martin Guerre,* in *"AHR* Forum: *The Return of Martin Guerre:* The Refashioning of Martin Guerre," *American Historical Review* 93 (1988): 571.

139. Kuehn, "Reading Microhistory," pp. 515, 533; Anthony Molho, "Review" (of Gene Bruckner's *Giovanni and Lusanna*), *Renaissance Quarterly* 40 (1987): 99. Leonard Boyle's critique of Le Roy Ladurie's *Montaillou,* on the other hand, argues that the author "loses" the very people whose stories he narrates; the "potted personal histories" the author presents do not treat the characters "as persons but as puppets who are jerked about to document a gamut of preconceived headings" ("Montaillou Revisited: Mentalité and Methodology," in *Pathways to Medieval Peasants,* ed. J. A. Raftis [Toronto, 1981], p. 127).

140. See especially Jörn Rüsen, "Historical Enlightenment in the Light of Postmodernism: History in the Age of the 'New Unintelligibility'" [1989], in his *Studies in Metahistory,* pp. 229–230 (of *Montaillou* and *The Cheese and the Worms*). Rüsen's own predilections are revealed in his borrowing of Habermas's title *(Die Neue Unübersichtlichkeit).*

141. Peter Burke, *History and Social Theory* (Ithaca, 1992), pp. 41–42. Or, Burke asks, are we dealing with (in Carlo Poni's phrase) "the exceptional normal," an exceptional case that reveals social mechanisms failing to work?

142. For example, regarding the sources for *Montaillou,* the records are incomplete; witnesses spoke in the vernacular, but their testimony was recorded in Latin, but later translated back into vernacular for them to give their assent, and so forth. See Boyle, "Montaillou Revisited," pp. 120–122.

143. See Kuehn, "Reading Microhistory," p. 515 for a critique. Kuehn faults historians for failing to appreciate the problems of using legal documents for their narrative work; he offers suggestions (515, 534). Berkhofer, *Story,* p. 151, faults both Ginzburg and Le Roy Ladurie for suppressing "the Inquisitorial power structure that produced and preserved the words . . ." Keith Luria notes Carlo Ginzburg's assumption, when writing *Night Bat-*

tles, that "because the *benandati*'s beliefs in no way corresponded to the inquisitors' that the judges are likely to have recorded the testimony accurately" ("The Paradoxical Ginzburg," *Radical History Review* 35 [1986]: 82).

144. Especially for his book *Dead Certainties (Unwarranted Speculations)* (New York, 1991).

145. Simon Schama, "The Monte Lupo Story," *London Review of Books* (Sept. 18–1 Oct., 1980): 23, reviewing Carlo Cipolla's *Faith, Reason, and the Plague.*

146. Renato Rosaldo, "From the Door of His Tent: The Fieldworker and the Inquisition," in *Writing Culture,* ed. James Clifford and George E. Marcus (Berkeley, 1986), pp. 77–97.

147. Ibid., pp. 79–80, 81, 82.

148. Ibid., pp. 79, 82, 83, 87. The *Annales* paradigm leads the historian to believe that "his subjects resemble him because of demonstrable structural continuities over a long timespan *(longue durée)*" (82).

149. Ibid., pp. 86, 87, 84.

150. Muir, "Introduction: Observing Trifles," p. xii; Iggers, *Historiography,* p. 109.

151. See Ginzburg, "Clues: Roots of an Evidential Paradigm," in his *Clues, Myths, and the Historical Method* (trans., Baltimore, 1989 [1986]), pp. 96–125, 200–214.

152. Muir, "Introduction: Observing Trifles," p. viii. The approach is allegedly borrowed from C. S. Peirce's notion of "abduction," basically defined as "hypothesis" (xviii). For Peirce, Thought is Abduction (= working hypotheses), from which we proceed to act, absorb, experience, and make adjustments or conclusions (I thank Gail Hamner for this explanation).

153. Lynn Hunt, "Postscript," in Domanska, *Encounters,* p. 273, mentioning *Montaillou, The Cheese and the Worms,* and *The Return of Martin Guerre.*

154. Ginzburg, in "Carlo Ginzburg: An Interview," pp. 100–101, 110.

155. Harvey J. Kaye, "E. P. Thompson, the British Marxist Historical Tradition and the Contemporary Crisis," in Kaye and McClelland, *E. P. Thompson,* pp. 244–245.

156. See discussion in Kate Soper, "Socialist Humanism," in Kaye and McClelland, *E. P. Thompson,* pp. 213–215, discussing Thompson in particular.

157. Dirks, "Is Vice Versa?" p. 32.

158. Christopher Hill, *The Century of Revolution 1603–1714* (New York, 1966 [1961]); idem, *The World Turned Upside Down* (London, 1975 [1972]). Hill's explicit statements on the subject are in his essay "Marxism and History," *Modern Quarterly* 3 (1948), excerpted in *Historians on History,* ed. John Tosh (Harlow, 2000), especially pp. 84–86, 89; Hill credits Marxist historiography with the recognition of the social origins of human thought (that is, ideology), the "new relativism," the use of documentary records, and the priority given to "economic facts" (85–86).

159. Raphael Samuel, "People's History," in *People's History and Socialist Theory*, ed. Samuel (London, 1981), excerpted in *Historians on History*, p. 114. Samuel reminds readers that "people's history" can also serve Right-wing purposes, citing Peter Laslett's *The World We Have Lost* as an example (112).

160. Of special interest to historians of antiquity is G. E. M. de Ste. Croix's, *The Class Struggle in the Ancient Greek World from the Archaic Age to the Arab Conquests* [2d corrected printing; London, 1983 (1981)]. De Ste. Croix faults most ancient historians and classicists for their failure to attend to Marxist theory—and blasts fellow Leftist historians for obscuring (in his view) the Marxian concepts of class and class struggle. Although de Ste. Croix announces his Marxist orientation at every step, he fails to critique historiography's epistemological foundations (19–20, 43, 59–65). On the connection between very low productivity of the ancient world, assumptions of leisure for some, and the extraction of surplus labor from others, see p. 39. Marxist analysis helps explain (not just describe) the disintegration of the Roman world (453, 497; for Christianity's role, 495, 420).

161. William H. Sewell Jr., "How Classes are Made: Critical Reflections on E. P. Thompson's Theory of Working-class Formation," in Kaye and McClelland, *E. P. Thompson*, p. 51. Given this acclamation, it is curious that the work was not translated into French until 1988: see Jacques Revel, "Microanalysis and the Construction of the Social" [1996], excerpted in Revel and Hunt, *Histories*, p. 498. Although Marxist zeal fuels Thompson's book, only eleven references to Marx are noted in the index.

162. See Kaye, "E. P. Thompson," pp. 268–269.

163. E. P. Thompson, *The Making of the English Working Class* (New York, 1964), p. 12. A standard critique has been that the working class was not entirely in place by the period that Thompson's book ends (*ca.* 1830): see Geoff Eley, "Edward Thompson, Social History and Political Culture," in Kaye and McClelland, *E. P. Thompson*, especially pp. 22–25.

164. Thompson, *The Making of the English Working Class*, pp. 340, 342, 346, 348, 369. One assumes that the title of Chapter 11, "The Transforming Power of the Cross," drips with sarcasm. In his preface, apologizing to Scottish readers for not including more on Scottish laboring class movements, he writes, "Calvinism was not the same thing as Methodism, although it is difficult to say which, in the early 19th century, was worse" (13). As Dominick LaCapra notes, it is hard to square Thompson's working-class identification with his antipathy for Methodism: many of the workers were Methodist, but Thompson makes it difficult to see what appeal Methodism could have held for them ("Intellectual History and Critical Theory," in his *Soundings*, pp. 197–198).

165. Keith McClelland, "Introduction," in Kaye and McClelland, *E. P. Thompson*, p. 3.

166. See Thompson's discussion in the "Foreword" to his *The Poverty of Theory*

& Other Essays (New York, 1978), p. i. ("Theory" here denotes Althusserianism.) Thompson attributes his suspension to the views he had expressed as editor of the journal *The Reasoner* ("reasoning" was out of favor with the Party's leaders, he later claimed; see Anderson, *Tracks*, p. 71).

167. See Soper, "Socialist Humanism," p. 205.

168. Thompson, "The Poverty of Theory, or an Orrery of Errors," in Thompson, *The Poverty of Theory*, p. 141. Thompson failed to recognize that Althusser's (and other French theorists') Marxism owed more to Mao than to Stalin.

169. Young, *White Mythologies*, pp. 48–53.

170. Ibid., pp. 50–51; see Louis Althusser, "On the Young Marx" [1960], in his *For Marx* (trans., London, 1990 [1965]), pp. 51–86; and idem, chap. 5 ("Marxism Is Not a Historicism"), in his *Capital*. His Marxism was to be "purged of its Hegelian paternity and of all contamination by bourgeois humanism" (François Furet, "Les Intellectuels français et le structuralisme," *Preuves* 192 [1967]: 11). For Althusser's assessment of Marx's "going back to Hegel in order to rid himself of Hegel," see his "Elements of Self-Criticism" [1974], in his *Essays in Self-Criticism* (London, 1976), p. 133. David Bromwich argues that Althusser's anti-humanism in the 1950s was a disciplinary weapon against the socialist humanism of Eastern European political thinkers ("Literature and Theory" [1986], in his *A Choice of Inheritance* [Cambridge, 1989], p. 279).

171. Althusser, "Elements of Self-Criticism," pp. 111, 156–157. For a brief discussion of Althusser's philosophical interests, discovery of the early Marx manuscripts, and the theory of "epistemological break," see Perry Anderson, *Considerations on Western Marxism* (London, 1976), pp. 50–58, 70–72.

172. Althusser, "Elements of Self-Criticism," pp. 151, 153.

173. Young, *White Mythologies*, p. 51: thus the critique of existentialism. Althusser borrows "epistemological break" from Bachelard (see Althusser, "Elements of Self-Criticism," p. 114). Thus Althusser complemented histories in a new mode, such as Foucault's *Madness and Civilization* and *The Birth of the Clinic*, while he critiqued historical approaches that relied on totalizing narratives and appeals to "human experience" (*Capital*, p. 103).

174. Soper, "Socialist Humanism," pp. 206, 213, 215. Yet Althusser defends his early essays: they championed Marxist theory and "the proletarian class struggle" against what Althusser calls "the most threatening forms of bourgeois ideology—humanism, historicism, pragmatism, evolutionism, philosophical idealism, etc." ("Elements of Self-Criticism," p. 146). For Althusser's later admission that his early separation of science and ideology was misguided, see Susan James, "Louis Althusser," in Skinner, *Return*, pp. 155–156. For the potential and the failure of Althusser's theories for historians, see Pierre Vilar, "Marxist History, a History in the Making: Towards a Dialogue with Althusser," *New Left Review* 80 (1973): 65–106.

Vilar posits that the message of Marxism is "[t]o think everything historically" (105).

175. Thompson, "The Poverty of Theory," pp. 12–13; also see Soper, "Socialist
Humanism," p. 206; E. P. Thompson, "Socialist Humanism, an Epistle to
the Philistines," *New Reasoner* 1 (1957), cited in Soper, "Socialist Humanism," p. 208, no page number given for citation. For example, in *The
Making of the English Working Class,* Thompson claims that "class"
should not be thought of as a "structure," but with reference to "real people" (9, 11). For other critique of "structures," see E. P. Thompson, "History and Anthropology" [1976] in his *Making History: Writings on History
and Culture* (New York, 1994), pp. 211–217.

176. Thompson, "The Poverty of Theory," pp. 3, 5, 13, 98, 174, 183, 46. Writing in 1986, Thompson declares that he is "less and less interested in Marxism as a Theoretical System" ("Agenda for a Radical History" [1986], in his
Persons & Polemics [London, 1994], p. 362).

177. Thompson, "History and Anthropology," p. 222.

178. E. P. Thompson, "The Peculiarities of the English" [1965], in idem, *The
Poverty of Theory*, pp. 279, 286.

179. Thompson, "The Poverty of Theory," p. 4

180. Thompson, "Agenda for a Radical History," p. 363. This talk was given in
1985 at a panel held at the New School for Social Research, in which Eric
Hobsbawm, Christopher Hill, Perry Anderson, and Thompson partici-
pated. The contributions of the other panelists are printed in *Radical History Review* 36 (1986).

181. Sewell, "How Classes Are Made," pp. 59–60. A different critique, inspired
by post-structuralist literary theory, faults Thompson for treating his narrative "as if it were a neutral medium, rather than a culturally constructed
form selected from a range of possible modes" (Renato Rosaldo, "Celebrating Thompson's Heroes: Social Analysis in History and Anthropology,"
in Kaye and McClelland, *E. P. Thompson,* p. 115). Rosaldo notes that
Thompson seemed rather unreflectively to have chosen the aesthetic form
of the melodrama for his literary medium, and asked how a history of the
radical tradition by an "anti-melodramatic" writer such as Foucault, who
makes traditions strange rather than familiar, would look (115–117, 120).
Hayden White notes that Thompson, despite his claim to be producing a
history based on "reality" rather than inspired by "method," utilizes the
very literary tropes (for example, metaphor, metonymy, irony) that White
later was to signal in *Metahistory* ("Introduction: Tropology, Discourse,
and the Modes of Human Consciousness," in his *Tropics,* pp. 15–19).

182. Antony Easthope, *British Post-Structuralism Since 1968* (London, 1988)
pp. 97–98, 104, 105.

183. Perry Anderson, *Arguments within English Marxism* (London, 1980),
pp. 28, 82–83, 28, 85, 80, chap. 4. There is not, Anderson concluded, the
"slightest justification" for Thompson's representation of Althusser as a

Stalinist (112). Anderson comments elsewhere that England was probably superior in its production of Marxist historians, though the culture as a whole lacked notable Marxist influence: a case of "uneven development" (*Considerations on Western Marxism*, p. 102).

184. Anderson, *Tracks*, pp. 32–55. After critiquing the structuralist elements of Althusser's form of Marxism (37–39), Anderson faults structuralism and post-structuralism for their "exorbitation of language," "attenuation of truth," and "randomization of history" (40–49).

185. Paul Q. Hirst, "The Necessity of Theory," *Economy and Society* 8 (1979): 429; Thompson's assumption of a unitary experience of a self and a universal human subject had earlier been demolished by French theorists (430); see also Easthope, *British Post-Structuralism*, p. 98.

186. Hirst, "The Necessity of Theory," pp. 430, 432. Antony Easthope summarizes the debate: "To Thompson's assumption of an intelligible totality in the real must correspond a knowing subject with access to that unified intelligibility. However, experience depends upon discourse . . . and discourse offers no transparency through which 'definite statements about observables' may be able to pass unchanged like rays of light through a window pane" (*British Post-Structuralism*, p. 102).

187. Robert Gray, "History, Marxism and Theory," in Kaye and McClelland, *E. P. Thompson*, pp. 176–77.

188. Joan W. Scott, "The Evidence of Experience," *Critical Inquiry* 17 (1991): 784–786; also see Easthope, *British Post-Structuralism*, p. 101, who faults Thompson's "phallocentric assumption" of an "essence of woman." Critics agree that Thompson's work needs revision regarding gender (McClelland, "Introduction"; Gray, "History, Marxism and Theory"; Kaye, "E. P. Thompson, the British Marxist Historical Tradition and the Contemporary Crisis"; Catherine Hall, "The Tale of Samuel and Jemima: Gender and Working-class Culture in Nineteenth-century England," all in Kaye and McClelland, *E. P. Thompson*, pp. 4, 178, 258, 99). LaCapra suggests that the book really concerns "the unmaking" of the English working class—"at least as a revolutionary 'subject' in history"; "an unexamined narrative subtext jars with his ostensible plot" ("Intellectual History and Critical Theory," p. 198n.8).

189. Thompson, "The Poverty of Theory," pp. 8–9, 28.

190. Hobsbawm, "British History and the *Annales*," p. 183; idem, "What Do Historians Owe to Karl Marx?" [1969], in his *On History*, p. 144.

191. See Eric Hobsbawm's essays, "Has History Made Progress?," "What Can History Tell Us about Contemporary Society?," "What Do Historians Owe to Karl Marx?," "Marx and History" [1984], all in his *On History*, references at pp. 65, 31, 152, 153, 159, 165.

192. Hobsbawm, "What Do Historians Owe to Karl Marx?," pp. 149, 155.

193. Eric Hobsbawm, "The New Threat to History," *New York Review* (Dec. 15, 1993): 62–64, citation at 63.

194. Eric Hobsbawm, "Preface," in *On History,* p. viii.
195. Eric Hobsbawm, "Postmodernism in the Forest" [1990], in his *On History,* pp. 197, 288n.8, 195.
196. Eric Hobsbawm, "Identity History Is Not Enough" [1994], in his *On History,* p. 271.
197. Ibid.
198. Namely, that if all views are equal, Holocaust deniers will arise everywhere and we will have to fight World War II all over again (Harlan, *Degradation,* p. xxxi).
199. Hobsbawm, "Identity History Is Not Enough," pp. 271–272.
200. See Gabrielle M. Spiegel, "History and Post-Modernism," *Past & Present* 135 (1992): 198–200, for a discussion of "mediation."

5. Narrative and History

1. Berkhofer, *Story,* pp. 36–38; Ernst Breisach, *Historiography* (2d ed; Chicago, 1994), pp. 333–335.
2. As, for example, in Henri Pirenne, "What Are Historians Trying to Do?" [1931], in Meyerhoff, *Philosophy of History,* p. 94. For a scathing critique of the discovery of rhetoric by ignorant "new ideologists," see Arnaldo Momigliano, "History in an Age of Ideologies," *American Scholar* 51 (1982): 495–496.
3. F. R. Ankersmit, "The Dilemma of Contemporary Anglo-Saxon Philosophy of History," *History and Theory* 25 (1986): 16.
4. W. B. Gallie, *Philosophy and the Historical Understanding* (New York, 1964); Danto, *Analytical Philosophy;* for Mink, see various essays listed in notes 15–17.
5. W. B. Gallie, "Explanations in History and the Genetic Sciences" [1955], in Gardiner, *Theories of History,* p. 395; Gallie, *Philosophy and the Historical Understanding,* pp. 72, 105, 95, 107. For a critique of the identification of "description" with "explanation," see White, *Metahistory,* pp. 142–143, 167, 186.
6. Gallie, *Philosophy and the Historical Understanding,* p. 107—but history's stories are based on evidence (105).
7. Gallie conceives all history as "a narrative of events" (ibid., p. 69); see Chapter 4 for the *Annalistes'* critique.
8. J. H. Hexter, "The Rhetoric of History" [1968], in his *Doing History* (Bloomington, 1971), p. 38.
9. For historical "rupture," see the discussion of Foucault in Chapter 6.
10. Danto, *Analytical Philosophy,* pp. 111, 11. Danto here touches on the question whether narratives are "in" reality or does the historian construct them. See Breisach, *Historiography,* pp. 333–335; F. R. Ankersmit, "The Dialectics of Narrativist Historism" [1995], in his *Representation,* pp. 135–136. For a variety of views, see David Carr, "Narrative and the Real

World," *History and Theory* 15 (1986): 117–131; idem, "Getting the Story Straight: Narrative and Historical Knowledge," in *Historiography between Modernism and Postmodernism,* ed. Jerzy Topolski (Amsterdam, 1994), pp. 19–33; T. Carlos Jacques, "The Primacy of Narrative in Historical Understanding," *Clio* 19 (1990): 197–214; Noël Carroll, "Interpretation, History, Narrative" [1990], in *History and Theory,* ed. Brian Fay et al. (Malden, 1998), pp. 40, 47; Dray, *On History/Philosophers,* pp. 134–135, 151, 160, 163; White, *Metahistory,* pp. 6–7; idem, "Historical Pluralism," *Critical Inquiry* 12 (1986): 487; Bevir, *Logic,* p. 306; Andrew P. Norman, "Telling It Like It Was: Historical Narratives on Their Own Terms," *History and Theory* 30 [1991]: 119–135 (those who assume that narrative is "there" in lived experience are named "plot-reifiers" [133]). For an early expression of narrative as embedded "in" experience, see Stephen Crites, "The Narrative Quality of Experience," *Journal of the American Academy of Religion* 39 (1971): 291–311.

11. Danto, *Analytical Philosophy,* pp. 122, 141, 201, 233–235, 242–243, 251, 253, 255. For Danto's continuing interest in "narrative sentences," see his "Narration and Knowledge," in his *Narration,* p. 347. See Hayden White's pointed comment: "narrative is not a large sentence" ("Interview," in Domanska, *Encounters,* p. 20). On historical explanation and narrative, see Murphey, *Knowledge,* pp. 85, 123.

12. Danto, *Analytical Philosophy,* pp. 44, 140.

13. Emmanuel Le Roy Ladurie, "The 'Event' and the 'Long Term' in Social History: The Case of the Chouan Uprising" [1972], in idem, *The Territory of the Historian* (trans., Hassocks, 1979 [1973]), p. 111. Analytic philosophers of history are faulted for the "simplicity" of their approach by Reinhart Koselleck, *The Practice of Conceptual History* (trans., Stanford, 2002), p. 116.

14. Ricoeur, *Contribution,* p. 45, presumably referring to certain forms of *Annales* historiography. See below for Ricoeur's reading of Braudel's *The Mediterranean* as "narrative."

15. Louis O. Mink, "Narrative Form as a Cognitive Instrument" [1978], in his *Historical Understanding,* ed. Brian Fay et al. (Ithaca, 1987), pp. 197, 199, 202.

16. Louis O. Mink, "On the Writing and Rewriting of History," in his *Historical Understanding,* p. 91.

17. Louis O. Mink, "Everyman His or Her Own Annalist" [1981], in *On Narrative,* ed. W. J. T. Mitchell (Chicago, 1981), p. 239; idem, "Narrative Form as a Cognitive Instrument," pp. 199, 201–202. For Mink's work in relation to subsequent theory, see Brian Fay et al., "Introduction," in Mink, *Historical Understanding,* p. 25.

18. Chris Lorenz, "Historical Knowledge and Historical Reality: A Plea for 'Internal Realism,'" *History and Theory* 33 (1994): 327: narrativism as "a move from the swamps of positivism to the quicksands of postmodernism."

Lorenz overlooks the fact that "narrativism" flourished long before "postmodernism" became a household word.

19. Hexter, "The Rhetoric of History," p. 71.

20. Novick, *Dream*, p. 623.

21. J. Morgan Kousser, "The Revivalism of Narrative: A Response to Recent Criticisms of Quantitative History," *Social Science History* 8 (1984): 137, 140, critiquing Lawrence Stone and other "revivalists."

22. So Goldstein, *Knowing*, pp. 148, 141–142; also see 150–179; compare Alun Munslow, *Deconstructing History* (London, 1997), pp. 164, 5; and Arthur Marwick's "Two Approaches to Historical Study: The Metaphysical (Including 'Postmodernism') and the Historical," *Journal of Contemporary History* 30 (1995): 9, 19, 21, 29.

23. See Ann Rigney, *The Rhetoric of Historical Representation* (Cambridge, 1990), pp. 65, 91; idem, *Imperfect Histories* (Ithaca, 2001), pp. 64, 100 ("the flip side of selection is exclusion").

24. Goldstein, *Knowing*, pp. 132, 176, and 182: the cognitive function of history is "the task of explaining historical evidence by means of a hypothetical reconstruction of the human past." Also see Maurice Mandelbaum, "A Note on History as Narrative," *History and Theory* 6 (1967): 413–419; and discussion in William H. Dray, "Narrative and Historical Realism," in his *On History/Philosophers*, p. 131; Marwick, "Two Approaches to Historical Study," p. 29. Richard Vann contrasts Hayden White's views with Leon Goldstein's advocacy of history as an "epistemological" discipline: for the latter, historians discover "what happened," then "all that remained was the unproblematic process of 'writing up.' If nobody, even in England, could write that way today," Vann concludes, "we have Hayden White to thank" ("The Reception of Hayden White," *History and Theory* 37 [1998]: 161). Some philosophers even challenged historians—once again—to attempt to uncover the "laws" underlying historical interpretation (Murphey, *Knowledge*, pp. 123–124).

25. Carrard, *Poetics*, pp. 34–35; Berkhofer, *Story*, p. 27; Peter Burke, "Overture," in his *Perspectives*, pp. 3–4.

26. Bloch, *Craft*, p. 13.

27. François Furet, "Beyond the *Annales*," *Journal of Modern History* 55 (1983): 397, 409.

28. Fernand Braudel, "History and the Social Sciences: The *Longue Durée*" [1958], in Revel and Hunt, *Histories*, p. 121.

29. Jacques Le Goff, "Préface à la nouvelle édition," in *La Nouvelle Histoire*, ed. Le Goff (2d ed.; Paris, 1988 [1978]), pp. 12, 15, 16, 17 (despite his praise for Lawrence Stone).

30. Ibid., pp. 14, 15; Febvre's "*combats pour l'histoire*," it appeared, had not entirely won the day.

31. Carrard, *Poetics*, p. 72. Carrard mentions Le Roy Ladurie's *Montaillou* (37–38), Davis's *The Return of Martin Guerre*, and Ginzburg's *The Cheese*

and the Worms (68—although these latter read like "case studies" of a narrative sort, he adds). Carrard quips that the table of contents for *Montaillou* strongly resembles that of Evans-Pritchard's *The Nuer* (37–39). Peter Burke, *The French Historical Revolution: The "Annales" School, 1929–1989* (Cambridge, 1990), p. 89, links this "return to narrative" within *Annales* with a "return to politics."

32. So Jonathan Culler, "Foreword," in Gérard Genette, *Narrative Discourse* (trans., Ithaca, 1980 [1972]), p. 8.

33. Tzvetan Todorov, *Introduction to Poetics* (trans., Minneapolis, 1981 [1968, 1973], p. 7.

34. See Genette's *Narrative Discourse.*

35. Ricoeur, *Time,* I: 78; II: 3, 158 (history is "true narrative" as distinguished from fiction); also see III: 142: "recourse to documents does indicate a dividing line between history and fiction. Unlike novels, historians' constructions do aim at being *reconstructions* of the past." For a post-structuralist critique of Ricoeur on "intention," see Hans Kellner, "'As Real As It Gets': Ricoeur and Narrativity" [1990], in *Meanings in Texts and Actions: Questioning Paul Ricoeur,* ed. David E. Klemm and William Schweiker (Charlottesville, 1993), p. 60.

36. Ricoeur, *Time,* I: 95–96; Ankersmit, "The Dilemma of Contemporary Anglo-Saxon Philosophy of History," p. 22.

37. For Hayden White, Ricoeur's work constitutes "a metaphysics of narrativity"; see White, "The Question of Narrative in Contemporary Historical Theory" [1984], in his *Content,* p. 49. For Ricoeur's assessment of hermeneutics' relation to phenomenology and existentialism, see his "Intellectual Autobiography," in *The Philosophy of Paul Ricoeur,* ed. Lewis Edwin Hahn (Chicago, 1995), pp. 11–12, 34–36.

38. Paul Ricoeur, "Dialogue" [1981 interview], in *Dialogues with Contemporary Continental Thinkers,* ed. Richard Kearny (Manchester, 1984), p. 17. Yet Ricoeur rejects Anglophone philosophers' reduction of history to a species of "story" ("Intellectual Autobiography," pp. 45–46).

39. Ricoeur, *Time,* I: 91; see Hans Kellner, "Narrativity in History: Post-Structuralism and Since," *History and Theory* 26 (1987): 29.

40. Ricoeur, "Dialogue," p. 20.

41. Kellner, "'As Real As It Gets,'" p. 53; among other things, gone are the gaps (65). Kellner elsewhere comments that Ricoeur fears that a loss of narrative in history diminishes "the human power of communication" ("Narrativity in History," p. 28).

42. Ricoeur, *Time,* I: 154, 178, 142, 148, 111, 115.

43. Ricoeur, "Intellectual Autobiography," pp. 30–31.

44. Ricoeur, *Time,* I: 149–152 (discussing Gallie's *Philosophy and the Historical Understanding*).

45. Ibid., p. 125 (121–131 explicate Dray's position, which Ricoeur finds congenial, but modifies).

46. Ibid., p. 156.

47. Ibid., pp. 82, 174. Fernand Braudel, *The Mediterranean and the Mediterranean World in the Age of Philip II* (Paris, 1949; 2d ed., 1966; English trans., New York, 1972–1973); see Jacques Revel, "Introduction," in Revel and Hunt, *Histories*, pp. 17–18, 20, 23, 29–30.

48. Ricoeur, *Time*, I: 209–225, 177, 66; II: 157. See Stuart Clark, "The *Annales* Historians," in Skinner, *Return*, p. 185, on Braudel's use of the language of agency when speaking of mountains, the sea, and so forth. Hans Kellner notes Ricoeur's reliance on "quasis" to carry his argument ("'As Real As It Gets,'" pp. 54–55, 59). Earlier, Braudel referred to the *longue durée* as a "cumbersome personnage" ("Débats et combats: Histoire et sciences sociales: La longue durée," *Annales E.S.C.* 13 [1958]: 733). G. R. Elton's appraisal of *La Mediterranée* is more caustic: the book "offers some splendid understanding of the circumstances which contributed to the shaping of policy and action; the only things missing are policy and action" (*The Practice of History* [New York, 1967], pp. 132–133).

49. Ricoeur, *Time*, I: 75.

50. Ibid., pp. 175–176.

51. As does Kellner, "Narrativity in History," pp. 25–26, 28.

52. J. Hillis Miller, "But Are Things As We Think They Are?" *Times Literary Supplement* (9–15 Oct. 1987): 1104–1105.

53. Veyne, *Writing History*. Chapters 12 and 13 critique historians' overreliance on social science.

54. Ibid., pp. 46, 11, x.

55. Ibid., pp. 87–88, 33, cf. 39.

56. Ibid., pp. 17–18. "[D]eceptive continuities" also arise when scholars employ general concepts such as "religion" (134). Veyne's comment that historians know only one aspect of one period and something different from the sources of another suggests that he was already familiar with Foucault's notion of *epistemes*.

57. Ibid., pp. 87, 93 ("to explain more is to narrate better"; the "historian explains plots" [88]; "explanation" is simply the meaning that the historian gives to the account [90]). Ricoeur (*Contribution*, pp. 39, 44–45) comments that Veyne's identification of "explaining" with "showing the development of the plot and making it comprehensible" [*Writing History*, p. 112 French] fails to account for "how history can remain a narrative when it ceases to be eventful."

58. Veyne, *Writing History*, pp. 93, 289. For Michel de Certeau's critique of Veyne's failure to acknowledge his own "place" of enunciation and to attend to historical practice, see his "Une Epistémologie de transition: Paul Veyne," *Annales ESC* 27 (1972): 1312, 1323, 1327.

59. Paul Veyne, "Foucault Revolutionizes History" [1978], in Davidson, *Foucault*, p. 181.

60. Régine Robin, "Introduction," *Discours et archives* (Liège, 1994), pp. 15, 11.

61. See Giovanni Levi, "On Microhistory," in Burke, *Perspectives,* pp. 105–106; Peter Burke, "History of Events and the Revival of Narrative," in ibid., pp. 233–235; C. Vann Woodward, "A Short History of American History," *New York Times Book Review* (8 Aug. 1982): 14, and discussion in Novick, *Dream,* p. 622. J. Morgan Kousser rejects the notion that lay-people should understand historical writing: "The Revivalism of Narrative," pp. 141–142. Kousser strangely equates Lawrence Stone's call for a "revival of narrative" with Hayden White's program (135–136). Also see F. R. Ankersmit, "Historical Representation," *History and Theory* 27 (1988): 226–227.

62. See the list in Lawrence Stone, "The Revival of Narrative: Reflections on a New Old History," *Past & Present* 85 (1979): 15.

63. Ibid., pp. 3–24.

64. Ibid., pp. 3, 19, 5, 9, 12. The rhetoric of an early article by Stone is unpacked by Antony Easthope, "Romancing the Stone: History-Writing and Rhetoric," *Social History* 18 (1993): 235–249.

65. Note Hans Kellner's point that although *Annalistes* claimed "quantitative objectivity," they freely used allegory in the terms they chose, such as *mentalité, longue durée,* and *outillage mental* ("Triangular Anxieties: The Present State of European Intellectual History," in LaCapra and Kaplan, *Intellectual History,* pp. 131–132).

66. Carrard, *Poetics,* pp. 68, 37, 74, 86–87; see also Novick, *Dream,* p. 622; Stone, "The Revival of Narrative," pp. 3–24. Eric Hobsbawm claims, "there is very little narrative history among the works Stone cites or refers to" ("The Revival of Narrative: Some Comments," *Past & Present* 86 [1980]: 4). Gertrude Himmelfarb complains that the books with which Stone illustrates "the revival of narrative" narrate only a single event, such as Le Roy Ladurie's *Montaillou,* and hence are not truly narrative (*The New History and the Old,* pp. 96–97).

67. Kellner, "Narrativity in History," p. 29.

68. Burke, "History of Events and the Revival of Narrative," pp. 235, 237, 240.

69. Levi, "On Microhistory," pp. 106, 107, 109.

70. Natalie Zemon Davis, "Les Conteurs de Montaillou," *Annales E.S.C.* 34 (1979): 70. For Ginzburg's *The Cheese and the Worms* as a detective story, see Dominick LaCapra, "*The Cheese and the Worms:* The Cosmos of a Twentieth-Century Historian," in his *History & Criticism* (Ithaca, 1985), p. 53. For Ginzburg's exploration of clues and the "evidential paradigm," see his "Clues: Roots of an Evidential Paradigm," in his *Clues, Myths, and the Historical Method* (trans., Baltimore, 1989 [1986]), pp. 96–125, 200–214. Also see Edward Muir, "Introduction," *Microhistory and the Lost Peoples of Europe,* ed. Muir and Guido Ruggiero (trans., Baltimore, 1991), p. viii.

71. See the stories encapsulated in Gene Brucker, *Giovanni and Lusanna: Love and Marriage in Renaissance Florence;* Emmanuel Le Roy Ladurie, *Mont-*

aillou: The Promised Land of Error; Carlo Ginzburg, The Cheese and the Worms: The Cosmos of a Sixteenth-Century Miller; Giovanni Levi, Inheriting Power: The Story of an Exorcist; Emmanuel Le Roy Ladurie, Carnival in Romans; Robert Darnton, The Great Cat Massacre and Other Episodes in French Cultural History (although Darnton would likely reject being called a "microhistorian"); Judith Brown, Immodest Acts: The Life of a Lesbian Nun in Renaissance Italy; Natalie Zemon Davis, The Return of Martin Guerre. Ginzburg reports that he once thought of becoming a novelist; see "Carlo Ginzburg: An Interview," with Keith Luria and Romulo Gandolfo, Radical History Review 35 (1986): 90, 103.

72. For Carlo Ginzburg and Carlo Poni's argument for a history "saturated with anthropology," see their essay, "The Name and the Game: Unequal Exchange and the Historiographic Marketplace," in Microhistory and the Lost Peoples of Europe, p. 4.

73. Levi, Inheriting Power, pp. 29–30.

74. Ginzburg and Poni, "The Name and the Game," pp. 4–5.

75. Carl Ginzburg, "The Inquisitor as Anthropologist," in his Clues, pp. 156, 159. Ginzburg appeals to anthropology to argue that extreme skepticism is an inappropriate stance for historians (164). He mourns that historians cannot produce "tangible evidence" such as anthropologists have (164).

76. LaCapra, "The Cheese and the Worms," pp. 62–63. LaCapra, who claims subversive messages for high culture (65), notes with irony that social historians such as Ginzburg who work on the "lowly" claim high status in the profession: "a bizarre and vicious paradox whereby a vicarious relation to the past serves as a pretext for contemporary pretensions to dominance" (69); similarly, idem, "Culture and Ideology: From Geertz to Marx" [1988], in his Soundings, p. 148.

77. Ginzburg, in "Carlo Ginzburg: An Interview," p. 100.

78. Natalie Zemon Davis, "On the Lame: AHR Forum: The Return of Martin Guerre," American Historical Review 93 (1988): 596, 597.

79. Stressing the inventiveness of the people whose tales these are, Davis shows how "[t]urning a terrible action into a story is a way to distance oneself from it, at worst a form of self-deception, at best a way to pardon the self" (Natalie Zemon Davis, Fiction in the Archives: Pardon Tales and Their Tellers in Sixteenth-Century France [Stanford, 1987], p. 47).

80. Ibid., p. 3.

81. Note Roland Barthes's argument that there is no neutral system of reading (Roland Barthes, "History or Literature?" in his On Racine [trans., New York, 1983 (1964; 1960)], pp. 171–172). For a brief account of Barthes's battle with Raymond Picard, traditional Racine scholar at the Sorbonne, see Dosse, Structuralism, I: 223–224.

82. Roland Barthes, "The Discourse of History" [1967], trans. in Comparative Criticism: A Yearbook, ed. E. S. Shaffer (Cambridge, 1981), III: 7–20. On the critique of history through novels, see Linda Orr, "The Revenge of Literature: A History of History," New Literary History 18 (1986): 19.

83. Roland Barthes, *Writing Degree Zero* (trans., New York, 1968 [1953]), p. 29; idem, "Introduction to the Structural Analysis of Narratives" [1966], in his *Semiotic Challenge,* p. 134. Even if, with Momigliano, the development of history as a discipline is pushed back earlier than the nineteenth century, the novel is there, too.

84. Barthes, "The Discourse of History," p. 18.

85. Kellner, "The Deepest Respect for Reality," in his *Language,* p. 21.

86. Hans Kellner, "Interview," in Domanska, *Encounters,* pp. 55–56. Kellner marks the turning point with Barthes's *S/Z.*

87. Barthes, "The Discourse of History," pp. 10–11, no reference given for citation.

88. Ibid., pp. 16–17. See Richard T. Vann, "Turning Linguistic: History and Theory and *History and Theory,* 1960–1975," in *A New Philosophy of History,* ed. Frank Ankersmit and Hans Kellner (Chicago, 1995), pp. 57–58.

89. Barthes, "The Discourse of History," p. 18; idem, "To Write: An Intransitive Verb?", in Macksey and Donato, *Controversy,* p. 144.

90. Roland Barthes, "L'Effet de Réel," *Communications* 11 (1968): 84–89; trans. "The Reality Effect," in his *The Rustle of Language* (New York, 1986 [1984]), pp. 141–148. Compare Barthes's "effect of the real" in literary writing with Michel de Certeau's "effect of the gaze" in the production of mystical experience: see de Certeau, "The Gaze of Nicholas of Cusa," *Diacritics* 17 (1987): 27.

91. Barthes, *Writing Degree Zero,* pp. 67–68.

92. Barthes, "L'Effet de Réel," pp. 84–85, 88, 86, 89. Barthes also elaborates "the reality effect" in a discussion of Balzac's novella *Sarrasine,* in "Masculin, féminine, neutre," in *Echanges et communications: Mélanges offerts à Claude Lévi-Strauss,* ed. Jean Pouillon and Pierre Maranda (The Hague, 1970), II: 893–907. Another "effect of the real" has been analyzed by Joel Fineman: the use of the anecdote in the writing of New Historicists ("The History of the Anecdote: Fiction and Fiction," in *The New Historicism,* ed. H. Aram Veeser [New York, 1989], pp. 61–62). For a critique of the anecdote in New Historicism (especially in Greenblatt's work), see Lynn Hunt, "History as Gesture; or, The Scandal of History," in *Consequences of Theory,* ed. Jonathan Arac and Barbara Johnson (Baltimore, 1991), pp. 91–107, citation at 97. Dominick LaCapra warns against historians' use of "stories" that "take the form of ingratiating anecdote that void historiography of a critical impetus and induce premature 'anecdotage'" ("Criticism Today," in his *Soundings,* p. 25).

93. Hayden White, "The Question of Narrative in Contemporary Historical Theory" [1984], in his *Content,* pp. 36–37.

94. For the changing fate of the concept of "ideology" in the writings of Marx and Engels, see Etienne Balibar, "The Vacillation of Ideology," in *Marxism and the Interpretation of Culture,* ed. Cary Nelson and Lawrence Grossberg (Urbana, 1988), pp. 159–209. For a brief description of Althusser's no-

tion of ideology, see Perry Anderson, *Considerations on Western Marxism* (London, 1976), pp. 84–85.

95. Roland Barthes, "Introduction: The Semiological Adventure" [1974], in his *Semiotic Challenge*, p. 5. Roy Harris attributes this alleged reversal to Barthes's borrowing from the Danish semiologist L. T. Hjelmslev (*Saussure and His Interpreters* [New York, 2001], pp. 133–135). A study linking linguistics and ideology is Michel Pêcheux, *Language, Semantics and Ideology* (trans., New York, 1982 [1975]).

96. Roland Barthes, "Myth Today," in his *Mythologies* (trans., New York, 1972 [1957], pp. 112, 129, 151. In his preface to the 1970 edition of the book (reprinted in ibid., p. 9), Barthes comments that he had a double theoretical frame in mind: an ideological critique of mass-culture language, and "a first attempt to analyse semiologically the mechanics of this language." He had just read Saussure, Barthes recalls, and wanted to account for "the mystification which transforms petit-bourgeois culture into a universal nature." Barthes admits that both ideology critique and semiological analysis have become more sophisticated in the decades since.

97. Ibid., pp. 116, 130, 142.

98. Barthes, "Introduction: The Semiological Adventure," pp. 5, 8; Roland Barthes, *Roland Barthes* (trans., New York, 1977 [1975]), p. 104. Barthes understood Brecht's *Verfremdungseffekt* as a form of ideology critique.

99. Arnaldo Momigliano, "The Rhetoric of History and the History of Rhetoric: On Hayden White's Tropes," in *Comparative Criticism,* ed. E. S. Shaffer, III: 261.

100. Natalie Zemon Davis, in *Fiction in the Archives,* highlights how "remission stories succeeded in creating a sense of the real" (p. 47), and demonstrate that the ability to invent "was widely distributed throughout society" (111).

101. John B. Thompson, *Ideology and Modern Culture* (Stanford, 1990), pp. 61–62; idem, *Studies in the Theory of Ideology* (Berkeley, 1984), p. 11. Contemporary theologians, philosophers, and feminists tend to view narrative more positively, stressing its role in creating "community": from the standpoint of ideology critique, that "community" is precisely founded on exclusion.

102. For a summary of the claims, see Keith Jenkins, *On "What Is History"?: From Carr and Elton to Rorty and White* (London, 1995), pp. 146–147.

103. Hayden White, "The Burden of History" [1966], in his *Tropics,* p. 43.

104. White, *Metahistory,* pp. x–xi. Elsewhere, White argues that history is a "craftlike discipline," "governed by convention and custom rather than by methodology and theory," and utilizes ordinary language ("Response to Arthur Marwick," *Journal of Contemporary History* 30 [1995]: 243).

105. White, *Metahistory,* pp. xii, 37–38, 42. The debates thus were over what form of "realism" a historian's work might take (432). Hans Kellner, a sympathetic reader of White, points out that the first section of the book,

"the formal description of the poetics of the historical text," was based on sources already considered out-of-date by literary critics and theorists; the book was nonetheless "received as an unconventional and perhaps dangerous manifesto" ("Twenty Years After: A Note on *Metahistories* and Their Horizons," *Storia della Storiografia* 24 [1993]: 110).

106. White, *Metahistory,* p. 427.

107. Elsewhere, White labels the "formist" option "ideographic" ("Interpretation in History" [1971–1972], in his *Content,* p. 70).

108. White, *Metahistory,* see summary pp. 426–427. Fredric Jameson comments that "the ultimate possibilities are so staggering as to suggest that something in the machinery has gone haywire" ("Figural Relativism, or The Poetics of Historiography," *Diacritics* 6 [1976]: 5).

109. White, *Metahistory,* pp. 3n.4, ix, 7–9. Thus in Romance, the hero is liberated from the world of experience and good triumphs over evil, while the opposite holds for Satire. Comedy and Tragedy stand between these extremes: in Comedy, disagreements are reconciled, while in Tragedy, although the hero falls, there is no threat of total diremption.

110. Ibid., pp. 13, 30–31, 431.

111. Ibid., p. 38.

112. Ibid., pp. xi, 142.

113. White, "Interpretation in History," pp. 69–71.

114. Kellner, "Narrativity in History," p. 24; this is the "mythic" aspect of narrativity, stressed by Roland Barthes and a prominent theme in poststructuralist analysis (3–4, 8–9).

115. White, "The Question of Narrative in Contemporary Historical Theory," pp. 31–33.

116. Dominick LaCapra, "A Poetics of Historiography: Hayden White's *Tropics of Discourse*" [1978], in his *Rethinking,* p. 72.

117. Dominick LaCapra, "Intellectual History and Critical Theory," in his *Soundings,* p. 202.

118. White had acknowledged his debt to structuralists Roman Jakobson and Claude Lévi-Strauss (*Metahistory,* pp. 31–32n.13, 38, ix). For White's alleged obscuring of the research process, see, for example, Jörn Rüsen's essays, "Rhetoric and Aesthetics of History: Leopold von Ranke" [1990]; "New Directions in Historical Studies" [1988]; "Historical Narration: Foundations, Types, Reasons" [1987], all in his *Studies in Metahistory,* pp. 137, 217, 6.

119. Hans Kellner, "A Bedrock of Order: Hayden White's Linguistic Humanism," *History and Theory* 19 (1980): 20.

120. Ibid., pp. 18, 29, referring to *Metahistory,* p. 38.

121. Kellner, "A Bedrock of Order," pp. 20–21, 17. Roger Chartier asks how White's emphasis on the "freedom" of the historian can square with his "post-Saussurean linguistics" ("Four Questions to Hayden White" [1993], in his *Edge,* p. 32). Chartier faults White for neglecting the procedures

proper to history, such as "gathering a documentary corpus, verifying information and testing hypotheses, and constructing an interpretation" (37, 35).

122. Kellner, "A Bedrock of Order," pp. 12, 13.

123. For relativism/nihilism, see Eugene O. Golob, "The Irony of Nihilism," in *Metahistory: Six Critiques. History and Theory,* Beiheft 19 (1980), pp. 56, 64–65. Novick comments that only a few American historians who worked in European intellectual history engaged with White's work (*Dream,* pp. 601, 605, 599). David Harlan sees White as a religious thinker, as "a theorist of redemption in an age of simulacra" (*Degradation,* p. 125).

124. Stone, "The Revival of Narrative," p. 3n.3.

125. Chartier, "Four Questions for Hayden White," pp. 28–29. Harlan (*Degradation,* chap. 5) shows the derivative character of White's "props," borrowed from Northrop Frye, Stephen Pepper, Kenneth Burke, and others, but "derivativeness" cannot account for the French neglect.

126. Philip Pomper, "Tropologies and Cycles in Intellectual History," in *Metahistory: Six Critiques,* pp. 34–37; John S. Nelson, "Tropal History and the Social Sciences: Reflections on Struever's Remarks," in *Metahistory: Six Critiques,* pp. 98–100.

127. Nancy S. Struever, "Topics in History," in *Metahistory: Six Critiques,* pp. 66–79 passim, especially 43–44 (citing *Metahistory,* p. 5); compare 75 (White's "powerful tropes" are depicted as "manipulating raw and resistant historical data").

128. Golob, "The Irony of Nihilism," pp. 56, 58–59; compare Ankersmit, "The Dilemma of Contemporary Anglo-Saxon Philosophy of History," pp. 19, 1. Elsewhere, Ankersmit calls White's *Metahistory* "the most revolutionary book in philosophy of history over the past twenty-five years" ("Historiography and Postmodernism," *History and Theory* 28 [1989]: 143).

129. Struever, "Topics in History," pp. 67, 77, 79.

130. Jameson, "Figural Relativism," pp. 9, 6: the book warrants the charge of "idealist." Jameson hints that White should have looked to the newer structural histories rather than the older "realistic" historiography. Also see Pomper, "Tropologies," 32, 37; Nelson, "Tropal History," pp. 92, 94; Maurice Mandelbaum, "The Presuppositions of *Metahistory*," in *Metahistory: Six Critiques,* pp. 39–42.

131. F. W. Ankersmit, "Hayden White's Appeal to the Historians," *History and Theory* 37 (1998): 187.

132. Kellner, "A Bedrock of Order," p. 16.

133. Kellner, "Twenty Years After," p. 116.

134. Ibid., p. 115. For Hayden White's rather hostile approach to the "Absurdist" critics (Foucault, Barthes, and Derrida) in an early essay, see his "The Absurdist Moment in Contemporary Literary Theory" [1973], in his *Tropics,* pp. 261–282, reference at 262.

135. White, "Interview," pp. 15, 25; tropology provides "a theory of swerve" (20).

136. Ibid., pp. 19–20, 27; White also describes himself as a "formalist" in "The Politics of Historical Representation," in his *Content,* p. 76.

137. White, "Interview," pp. 25–26, 29–30, 32–34.

138. Paul Ricoeur fears that White's scheme erases the boundaries between fiction and history, and that his focus on rhetoric obscures "intentionality" (*Time,* III: 154). See also Noël Carroll's critique, "Interpretation, History, and Narrative," pp. 44, 47, 52).

139. White, "Response to Arthur Marwick," pp. 239–240. Thus White writes: "The relation between facts and events is always open to negotiation and reconceptualization, not because the events change with time, but because we change our ways of conceptualizing them. And if this is true for events, it is even more true of facts. We not only change our ideas of what the facts are of a given matter but our notions of what a fact might be, how facts are constructed, and what criteria should be used to assess the adequacy of a given array of facts to the events of which they purport to be descriptive." See White's comments on the "double representation" the historian must elaborate—that is, of the object of interest as well as of his/her thought about the object ("An Old Question Raised Again: Is Historiography Art or Science? [Response to Iggers]," *Rethinking History* 4 [2000]: 392, 396–397).

140. Hayden White, "Droysen's *Historik:* Historical Writing as a Bourgeois Science" [1980], in his *Content,* p. 102. For White's misleading language, see Georg G. Iggers, "Historiography between Scholarship and Poetry: Reflections on Hayden White's Approach to Historiography," *Rethinking History* 4 (2000): 383–384.

141. White, "Interview," pp. 26, 16 (although Carlo Ginzburg accused White of subjectivism, White rejoins that Ginzburg himself frequently manipulates his material for aesthetic effect).

142. Kellner, "A Bedrock of Order," p. 28; Hayden White, "Rhetoric and History," in *Theories of History,* ed. White and Frank E. Manuel (Los Angeles, 1978), p. 3.

143. White, "Rhetoric and History," pp. 4, 5–7; idem, "The Politics of Historical Interpretation: Discipline and De-sublimation" [1982], in his *Content,* p. 124.

144. As Hans Kellner notes, some degree of "ideological skepticism" is now a common mark of historical writings. Historians apparently found this aspect of White's work easier to appropriate than his "linguistic skepticism" ("A Bedrock of Order," p. 12).

145. F. R. Ankersmit, *History and Tropology: The Rise and Fall of Metaphor* (Berkeley, 1994), p. 13; Hayden White, "The Fictions of Factual Representation," in *The Literature of Fact,* ed. Angus Fletcher (New York, 1976), pp. 21–44, references at 34–35. Hans Kellner notes that the notion of "tropes" appears perhaps once in *The Content of the Form* ("Interview," in Domanska, *Encounters,* p. 56). For changes in White's thought, see Wulf Kansteiner, "Hayden White's Critique of the Writing of History," *History*

and Theory 32 (1993): 273–295. Even in *Metahistory* (for example, pp. 27–28), there is some discussion of ideology in relation to forms of emplotment.

146. Hayden White, "Method and Ideology in Intellectual History: The Case of Henry Adams," in LaCapra and Kaplan, *Intellectual History,* p. 288.

147. Hayden White, "Preface," to his *Content,* p. ix; Vann, "The Reception of Hayden White," pp. 157–158.

148. White, "Rhetoric and History," p. 24; idem, "The Politics of Historical Interpretation," p. 82.

149. Hayden White, "Storytelling: Historical and Ideological," in *Centuries' Ends, Narrative Means,* ed. Robert Newman (Stanford, 1996), p. 59.

150. White, "The Value of Narrativity in the Representation of Reality" [1980], in his *Content,* p. 24; idem, "The Historical Text as Literary Artifact," in *The Writing of History,* ed. R. H. Canary and H. Kozicki (Madison, 1978), pp. 48–49, 61. In Hans Kellner's phrase, "Narrative exists to make continuous what is discontinuous" ("Boundaries of the Text: History as Passage," in his *Language,* p. 55).

151. White adopts Althusser, "Ideology," p. 162; White, *Content,* p. x. See also Michel de Certeau's critique of narrative historiography: "History: Science and Fiction" [1983], in his *Heterologies,* p. 219.

152. White, "The Value of Narrativity in the Representation of Reality," pp. 14, 21, 10. As White remarks, the sequence of real events does not come to an end; narrative does (23). White recognizes that not all historians (for example, Braudel) employ narrative (2).

153. White, "Preface," in his *Content,* p. xi; idem, "The Question of Narrative in Contemporary Historical Theory" [1984], in ibid., p. 27.

154. White, "The Historical Text as Literary Artifact," p. 61. Historical narrative, White posits, lends to real events the "kinds of meaning found otherwise only in myth and literature" ("The Question of Narrative in Contemporary Historical Theory," p. 45).

155. White, "The Value of Narrativity in the Representation of Reality," p. 13; idem, "Preface," in his *Content,* p. x.

156. White, "The Question of Narrative in Contemporary Historical Theory," p. 35. White thinks that Ricoeur, whose work he describes as "a metaphysics of narrativity," presents the "strongest claim for the adequacy of narrative to realize the aims of historical studies made by any recent theorist of historiography" (49, 54).

157. White, "The Politics of Historical Interpretation," pp. 71–72. On Droysen and ideology, see White, "Droysen's *Historik,*" p. 86, 98. In contrast, French historians Charles Langlois and Charles Seignobos earlier advised budding historians that there was nothing to be gained from reading Droysen's *Grundriss der Historik* (*Introduction,* p. 5).

158. Hayden White, "Getting Out of History: Jameson's Redemption of Narrative" [1982], in his *Content,* p. 167.

159. Jenkins, *On "What Is History"?* p. 138. See White's discussion of Hegel in

"The Question of Narrative in Contemporary Historical Theory," pp. 29–30.

160. See Carrard's discussion of Hayden White and Sande Cohen in *Poetics,* pp. 76–77.

161. Thompson, *Ideology and Modern Culture,* pp. 61–62; idem, *Studies in the Theory of Ideology,* p. 11.

162. Sande Cohen, *Historical Culture* (Berkeley, 1986), p. 16.

163. Mink, "Everyman His or Her Own Annalist," p. 234.

164. William H. Dray, "Narrative and Historical Realism," in his *On History/ Philosophy,* p. 157.

165. Barbara Herrnstein Smith, "Narrative Versions, Narrative Theories," in *On Narrative,* p. 231.

166. Jean-François Lyotard, *The Post-Modern Condition* (trans., Minneapolis, 1984 [1979]), p. 60.

167. Kellner, "Narrativity in History," p. 29.

168. Joan Wallach Scott, "Comment: Agendas for Radical History," *Radical History Review* 36 (1986): 43.

169. Kellner, "Narrativity in History," p. 13.

6. The New Intellectual History

1. For the dominance of social history in America during the 1960s and 1970s, see Robert Darnton, "Intellectual and Cultural History," in *The Past Before Us,* ed. Michael Kamen (Ithaca, 1980), pp. 331–335. For developments in Germany, see Jörn Rüsen, "Paradigm Shift and Theoretical Reflection in Western German Historical Studies" [1986], in his *Studies in Metahistory,* pp. 171, 173. Women historians' attempts to teach social history by exploiting such everyday documents as train schedules, laundry lists, architectural designs, and cookbooks—the joy of recent social historians—were mocked by male colleagues (Bonnie G. Smith, *The Gender of History: Men, Women, and Historical Practice* [Cambridge, Mass., 1998], pp. 115, 207–208).

2. Darnton, "Intellectual and Cultural History," p. 327. For changed understandings of "intellectual history," see Roger Chartier, "Intellectuelle (histoire)," in *Dictionnaire des sciences historiques,* ed. André Burguière (Paris, 1986), pp. 372–374. In 1977, Paul K. Conkin could still declare, "I know of no new approaches to intellectual history" ("Intellectual History: Past, Present, and Future," in *The Future of History,* ed. Charles F. Delzell [Nashville, 1977], pp. 120–121).

3. Geoff Eley, "Is All the World a Text? From Social History to the History of Society Two Decades Later," in McDonald, *Turn,* pp. 193–197, 204, 213, 225. Eley's essay is an important contribution to recent changes in historiography. The major "casualty" of these developments, he writes elsewhere, "has been the traditional notion of social totality in its various Marxist and non-Marxist forms" (Geoff Eley, "Between Social History and Cultural

Studies: Interdisciplinarity and the Practice of the Historian at the End of the Twentieth Century," in *Historians and Social Values*, ed. Joep Leerssen and Ann Rigney [Amsterdam, 2000], p. 106).

4. G. R. Elton, *Return to Essentials* (Cambridge, 1991), pp. 12, 60. Elton faults Hayden White and his followers who have no experience in trying to write history, especially "history beyond the narrow confines of the history of ideas" (34, 52).

5. Arthur O. Lovejoy, "The Historiography of Ideas" [1938], in his *Essays in the History of Ideas* (Baltimore, 1948), p. 8; idem, *The Great Chain of Being: A Study of the History of an Idea* (reprint ed.; New York, 1960 [1936]), pp. 3, 15. Donald R. Kelley argues that Lovejoy's "unit-ideas" nonetheless attempted to preserve "the intellectual hegemony of philosophy" ("On the Margins of Begriffsgeschichte," in Lehmann and Richter, *Historical Terms*, pp. 35–36).

6. Lovejoy, *The Great Chain of Being*, pp. 7, 10, 11.

7. Ibid., pp. 20, 15–16, 17–19. For the later adoption of Lovejoy's themes, see John C. Greene, "Objectives and Methods in Intellectual History," *Mississippi Valley Historical Review* 44 (1957–1958): 59, 68.

8. Lovejoy, "The Historiography of Ideas," pp. 3, 10; idem, "Reflections on the History of Ideas" [1940], in *The History of Ideas*, ed. Donald R. Kelley (Rochester, 1990), p. 7.

9. Lovejoy, "Reflections on the History of Ideas," p. 18. Lovejoy aimed to show how "the Platonistic scheme of the universe" was turned "upside down" once the postulate of the "complete rational intelligibility of the world" was abandoned: both "the original complete and immutable Chain of Being" and God were assimilated to the realm of "Becoming" (*The Great Chain of Being*, pp. 325–326, 329).

10. The elitist quality of "history of ideas" is defended by Paul Conkin: verbal culture is distinctive to humans ("Intellectual History," pp. 112, 114, 123–126).

11. John Dewey, "Historical Judgments" [1938], in Meyerhoff, *Philosophy of History*, pp. 165–166; "all history is necessarily written from the standpoint of the present" (166, 168). Lovejoy responded in "Present Standpoints and Past History" [1939], excerpted in Meyerhoff, *Philosophy of History*, pp. 173–187, arguing that historical questions need not be directed to the present (179).

12. William H. Dray, *Philosophy of History* (Englewood Cliffs, 1964), pp. 35–39. For Dray on "values," see L[eon] Pompa, "Value and History," in *Objectivity, Method and Point of View*, ed. W. J. van der Dussen and Lionel Rubinoff (Leiden, 1991), pp. 112–132. Recent disputes over presentism here find an earlier analogue.

13. Maurice Mandelbaum, "The History of Ideas, Intellectual History, and the History of Philosophy," in *History and Theory*, Beiheft 5: *The Historiography of the History of Ideas* ('S-Gravenhage, 1965), pp. 37–38 ("[t]hey

almost seem to have continuous life-histories of their own"), 54. Mandelbaum argues that although ideas do not necessarily "continue," they sometimes "recur" after falling into abeyance (38–39). Here the theme of historical discontinuity, later to be prominent, receives recognition.

14. Leo Spitzer, "Geistesgeschichte vs. History of Ideas as Applied to Hitlerism" [1944], in *The History of Ideas,* pp. 39, 40, 42, 43.

15. John Dunn, "The Identity of the History of Ideas," *Philosophy* 43 (1968): 85, 86–87. Dunn spots a problem soon to receive much discussion: context (98).

16. Bernard Williams, *Truth and Truthfulness* (Princeton, 2002), p. 237.

17. T. M. Knox, "Editor's Preface," to Collingwood, *Idea,* pp. v, xxi.

18. Collingwood, *Autobiography,* pp. 79, 99, 114, 115, 133, 127–128.

19. Ibid., pp. 31, 33, 55, 74, 122–125, 109. For Collingwood's "detective" work on Hadrian's Wall, attempting to locate the purpose and thought embodied in its structure, see G. S. Couse, "Collingwood's Detective Image of the Historian and the Study of Hadrian's Wall," *History and Theory,* Beiheft 29: *Reassessing Collingwood* (1990): 57–77.

20. Collingwood, *Idea,* p. 204, a point that Collingwood shares with Croce.

21. Ibid., pp. 228, 132–133, 233, 249–250.

22. Croce, *History/Liberty,* pp. 173, 270; idem, *History: Its Theory and Practice* (trans., New York, 1921 [2d Italian ed. (1919) of Croce's four-volume *Philosophy of the Spirit*]), pp. 173, 178; on presentism (11).

23. Collingwood, *Idea,* pp. 199, 221, 115. Collingwood appears to adopt Hegel's claim that although history is the history of rationality, history in its cunning can use the passions to achieve its purposes (116).

24. Ibid., pp. 218, 222, 305. For the later influence of this notion, see Greene, "Objectives and Methods in Intellectual History," p. 67.

25. Collingwood, *Idea,* pp. 213, 214–215, 204, 228, 283, 304.

26. Although Collingwood's fellow-sympathizer Croce refers to Marxist historiography as "anti-intellectual and stupefying," a "stupidifying 'virus'" (*History,* p. 202), Collingwood's autobiography suggests that he was more attuned to the Left by the end of his life. For a sympathetic reading of Collingwood on this point, see William Dray, "R. G. Collingwood and the Understanding of Actions in History" [1978], in his *Perspectives on History* (London, 1980), pp. 9–26. Henri-Irénée Marrou, otherwise sympathetic to Collingwood, argues that since the past is really "past," there can be no "harmonic resonance" between historians and the objects of their studies (*Meaning,* pp. 45, 248).

27. Collingwood, *Autobiography,* pp. 106, 141, 113–114.

28. Collingwood, *Idea,* p. 248; only the *historian's* contemplation of "evidence" makes it "evidence" (246–247).

29. Collingwood, *Autobiography,* p. 65. Collingwood compares his colleagues to girls who think that "this year's hats are the only ones that could ever have been worn by a sane woman."

30. For example, that we "study history in order to see more clearly into the situation in which we are called upon to act," and "to attain self-knowledge" (Collingwood, *Autobiography*, p. 114; idem, *Idea*, p. 315).

31. Collingwood, *Autobiography*, pp. 159–167.

32. Stefan Collini, "What Is Intellectual History . . . ?" and Quentin Skinner, "What Is Intellectual History . . . ?," both in *What Is History Today . . . ?*, ed. Juliet Gardiner (Houndsmills, 1988), pp. 106–108, 110. For charges: Richard J. Evans, *In Defence of History* (London, 1997), p. 206; David A. Hollinger, "Historians and the Discourse of Intellectuals" [1979], in his *In the American Province: Studies in the History and Historiography of Ideas* (Bloomington, 1985), pp. 138, 133.

33. For an early (1971) call to link intellectual history to concerns of politics, economics, and social forces, see Felix Gilbert, "Intellectual History," *Daedalus* 100 (1971): 80–97, especially p. 94, who provides a good review of older currents in intellectual history. For critiques leveled against Mark Bevir's notion of "the logic of the history of ideas" as neglecting politics and power, see commentators' remarks in "Roundtable: "The Logic of the History of Ideas," *Rethinking History* 4 (2000): 308, 311; Bevir admits that he tried to divert history of ideas from a Foucauldian emphasis on sociology and power ("Philosophy, Rhetoric, and Power: A Response to Critics," in ibid., 341).

34. Darnton, "Intellectual and Cultural History," p. 337; anthropologists' notion of "culture" is more coherent than historians' (347). Roger Chartier questioned Darnton's (and other historians') appropriation of Geertzian anthropological models when in fact they were dealing with texts ("Dialogue à propos de l'histoire culturelle," *Actes de la recherche en sciences sociales* 59 [1985]: 92); see Chapter 7. For an early spotting of some now-dominant trends, see Leonard Krieger, "The Autonomy of Intellectual History" [1973], in *The History of Ideas*, pp. 109–110.

35. Despite the "textualist turn," Donald Kelley alleges, many historians of ideas still appear to be "working 'behind the back' of language" ("On the Margins of Begriffsgeschichte," pp. 38–39).

36. For example, Evans, *In Defence of History*, p. 74.

37. Ibid., pp. 85, 86.

38. This suspicion seems to lie behind William Bouwsma's critique in his review of *Modern European Intellectual History* that the authors identify themselves with the interests of the European intellectual community, thus isolating themselves from other kinds of historians (*History and Theory* 23 [1984]: 232–234). Also see Russell Jacoby, "A New Intellectual History?" *American Historical Review* 97 (1992): 420, reviewing (negatively) Sande Cohen, *Historical Culture* (Berkeley, 1986).

39. Evans, *In Defence of History*, pp. 139, 111, 182.

40. Ibid., p. 160. When Nancy Partner asserts that academic historians have nothing to gain and everything to lose "by dismantling their special visible

code of evidence-grounded reasoning," she speaks to the interests of social, political, and economic historians ("Historicity in an Age of Reality-Fictions," in *A New Philosophy of History,* ed. Frank Ankersmit and Hans Kellner [Chicago, 1995], p. 22).

41. On intellectual history in Germany, see Hajo Holborn, "The History of Ideas," *American Historical Review* 73 (1968): 688–690.

42. Hans-Georg Gadamer, "On the Scope and Function of Hermeneutical Reflection" [English trans., 1970], in his *Philosophical Hermeneutics,* ed. David E. Linge (Berkeley, 1976), p. 28; Michael Pickering, "History as Horizon: Gadamer, Tradition and Critique," *Rethinking History* 3 (1999): 179.

43. Gadamer, *Truth,* p. 246. David Boucher explains: as linguistic beings, "we belong to a forestructure of meanings in terms of which and by means of which we encounter the thought of the past" (*Texts,* p. 27). For another discussion of Heidegger, see Gadamer, "The Problem of Historical Consciousness" [trans., 1963], in *Interpretive Social Science,* ed. Paul Rabinow and William M. Sullivan (Berkeley, 1979), pp. 128–135, 152–153. Gadamer adopted from Heidegger the view that "human reality is determined by its linguisticality *(Sprachlichkeit)*" (Martin Jay, "Should Intellectual History Take a Linguistic Turn? Reflections on the Habermas-Gadamer Debate," in *Intellectual History,* pp. 91, 95, 95).

44. Gadamer, *Truth,* pp. 239–240, 247, 266.

45. David E. Linge, "Introduction," in Hans-Georg Gadamer, *Philosophical Hermeneutics,* pp. xiv–xv. Similarly, William Outhwaite, "Hans-Georg Gadamer," in Skinner, *Return,* p. 26, citing Gadamer's *Truth and Method,* p. 245.

46. Gadamer, "The Problem of Historical Consciousness," pp. 145, 155–156, 158.

47. Linge, "Introduction," p. xv. F. R. Ankersmit argues that Gadamer's importance lies in his shifting the center of discussion from the "experience" of historical agents to the "historicity of experience and of the language in which it is expressed." Text and language thus interrupt "the preverbal experience that we have of reality" ("The Postmodernist 'Privatization' of the Past" [1996], in his *Representation,* p. 162). Ankersmit does not, however, comment on experience.

48. Gadamer, *Truth,* pp. 271, 268. Gadamer here obliquely disputes the common understanding of Collingwood's claim that the historian can enter the minds of past historical agents; see Michael Stanford, *An Introduction to the Philosophy of History* (Malden, 1998), pp. 198–199. Yet Gadamer appropriates Collingwood's notion that texts put questions to the interpreter, as well as vice versa; see Iain Wright, "History, Hermeneutics, Deconstruction," in *Criticism and Critical Theory,* ed. Jeremy Hawthorn (London, 1984), p. 95, citing Gadamer, *Truth and Method,* p. 333. Gadamer here refers to the section "Question and Answer" in Collingwood's *Autobiography.*

49. Gadamer, *Truth,* pp. 268–273, 337. Gadamer acknowledges his debt to Husserl for this term and its use, namely, "to characterize the way in which thought is tied to its finite determination (217, 269); Linge, "Introduction," pp. xxi, xxviii; Gadamer, *Truth* p. 340.

50. So expressed by Hans Robert Jauss, "Literary History as a Challenge to Literary Theory" [1970], in his *Toward an Aesthetic of Reception* (trans., Minneapolis, 1982), pp. 29–30.

51. Hans-Georg Gadamer, "Rhetoric, Hermeneutics, and the Critique of Ideology: Metacritical Comments on *Truth and Method*" [1967], in *The Hermeneutics Reader,* ed. Kurt Mueller-Vollmer (New York, 1985), p. 282.

52. For critique, see especially Jürgen Habermas, "A Review of Gadamer's *Truth and Method*" [1967], and idem, "The Hermeneutic Claim to Universality" [1970], both in *The Hermeneutic Tradition From Ast to Ricoeur,* ed. Gayle L. Ormiston and Alan D. Schrift (Albany, 1990), especially pp. 235–241, 245–272. Also see Pickering, "History as Horizon," in ibid., pp. 190–191. For Gadamer's tendency to ignore power relations, see Robert C. Holub, *Reception Theory* (London, 1984), pp. 44–45. Gadamer replied that Habermas and others had misunderstood his appeals to "tradition" and "authority," labeling him a conservative ("Reply to My Critics" [1971], in *The Hermeneutic Tradition,* pp. 273–297; idem, "Rhetoric, Hermeneutics, and the Critique of Ideology," pp. 274–292). For a helpful explication of the Gadamer–Habermas debate, see Paul Ricoeur, "Hermeneutics and the Critique of Ideology" [1973], trans. in *The Hermeneutic Tradition,* especially pp. 298–321. Ricoeur wished to overcome Gadamer's opposition between "distanciation" that alienates and "belonging" ("The Hermeneutical Function of Distanciation" [1975], in *Hermeneutics and the Human Sciences,* ed. John B. Thompson [Cambridge, 1981], p. 131); also see Domenico Jervolino, "Gadamer and Ricoeur on the Hermeneutics of Praxis," in *Paul Ricoeur: The Hermeneutics of Action,* ed. Richard Kearney (London, 1996), pp. 63–79. Gadamer's relevance for literary criticism, despite his overestimation of "the classical," is signaled by Jauss, "Literary History," pp. 22, 29–32.

53. For comments on the background and development of *Begriffsgeschichte,* with its double roots in social history and sociolinguistics, see Reinhart Koselleck, "Einleitung," in *Historische Semantik und Begriffsgeschichte,* ed. Koselleck (Stuttgart, 1979), pp. 9–10.

54. Reinhart Koselleck, "A Response to Comments on the *Geschichtliche Grundbegriffe,*" in Lehmann and Richter, *Historical Terms,* p. 62; also see Keith Tribe, "Translator's Introduction," to Reinhart Koselleck, *Futures Past: On the Semantics of Historical Time* (trans., Cambridge, Mass., 1985 [1979]), p. xv. Hence the importance of Gadamer for the project, Tribe notes (viii, xiii).

55. Reinhart Koselleck, "Begriffsgeschichte and Social History" [1972], in his *Futures Past,* p. 80. Jörn Rüsen argues that what makes historical concepts

specifically "historical" is the explicit or implicit chronological quality that the concept expresses (*Rekonstruktion der Vergangenheit: Grundzüge einer Historik II: Die Prinzipien der historischen Forschung* [Göttingen, 1986], pp. 80–81).

56. Koselleck, "Begriffsgeschichte and Social History," pp. 73, 77; idem, "A Response to Comments," pp. 67–68.

57. Melvin Richter, "Appreciating a Contemporary Classic: The *Geschichtliche Grundbegriffe* and Future Scholarship," in Lehmann and Richter, *Historical Terms,* p. 7.

58. Reinhart Koselleck, "Richtlinien für das Lexikon politisch-sozialer Begriffe der Neuzeit," *Archiv für Begriffsgeschichte* 11 (1967): 81, cited in translation in Tribe, "Translator's Introduction," in Koselleck, *Futures Past,* p. xi.

59. Reinhart Koselleck, "'Space of Experience' and 'Horizon of Expectation'" [1976], in his *Futures Past,* p. 268. Geoff Eley, on the other hand, comments that modern German historiography "has not been distinguished by its methodological and theoretical radicalism during the last three decades" ("Is All the World a Text?" p. 200). See Koselleck's collection of essays, *The Practice of Conceptual History* (trans., Stanford, 2002), which provides helpful examples of *Begriffsgeschichte* and advocates a more theoretically sophisticated history.

60. Kelley, "On the Margins of Begriffsgeschichte," p. 39.

61. Gabriel Motzkin, "On Koselleck's Intuition of Time in History," in Lehmann and Richter, *Historical Terms,* p. 41.

62. J. G. A. Pocock, "Concepts and Discourses: A Difference in Culture?" in Lehmann and Richter, *Historical Terms,* pp. 47–48.

63. Ibid., p. 47: Pocock forthrightly admits his own deficiency on this point.

64. For the critique of Pocock's approach, see Chapter 7.

65. For discussion of "symptomatic reading" that looks for silences, the "invisible," the lacunae in texts, see Althusser and Balibar, *Capital,* pp. 27–28, 86, 88, 143, 193; also see Bannet, *Structuralism/Dissent,* p. 5, and Rosemary Hennessy, *Materialist Feminism and the Politics of Discourse* (New York, 1993), pp. xvii, 93. For a symptomatic reading of Saussure's *Cours,* see Derek Attridge, "Language as History/History as Language: Saussure and the Romance of Etymology," in Attridge, Bennington, and Young, *Post-Structuralism,* p. 196.

66. "I have never been a Freudian, I have never been a Marxist and I have never been a structuralist": Michel Foucault, "Structuralism and Post-Structuralism," trans. in *Telos* 16 (1983): 198, in the context of noting his association with Georges Canguilhem. Also see his disclaimer in "Foreword to the English Edition," *Order,* p. xiv. For Derrida on Foucault, history, and structuralism, see Jacques Derrida, "Cogito and the History of Madness" [1964], in his *Writing and Difference* (Chicago, 1978 [1967]), p. 44.

67. See Allan Megill, "The Reception of Foucault by Historians," *Journal of*

the History of Ideas 48 (1987): 126–127, 133. Megill reports that after a brief notice of Foucault's *History of Madness* in *Annales* in 1962, there was no other reference to Foucault's work in *Annales* throughout the rest of the 1960s; between 1970–1981, however, Foucault was cited in thirty-six articles (130).

68. Hayden White, "Foucault Decoded: Notes from Underground" [1973], in his *Tropics,* p. 234.

69. Michel Foucault, in a speech at the University of Vermont (Oct. 27, 1982), cited by Megill, "The Reception of Foucault by Historians," p. 117.

70. White considers the title ironic, for Foucault did not believe that "the world of things *has* an order" ("Foucault Decoded," p. 232). White characterizes the work as "a kind of post-Nietzschean 'Phänomenologie des Geistes,' which is to say that it is an account of the development of human consciousness with both the 'Phänomen' and the 'Geist' left out" (233). The book sold "like hotcakes" upon its publication in 1966 (twenty thousand copies in just four months: so Megill, "The Reception of Foucault," p. 122, citing various notices and reviews; Dosse, *Structuralism,* I: 330, cites a figure of fifteen thousand copies in six months). Michel de Certeau claims that the book sold out its first printing after one month ("The Black Sun of Language: Foucault" [1969], in his *Heterologies,* p. 171). Dosse reports that Foucault originally intended to subtitle the book *An Archaeology of Structuralism* (*Structuralism,* I: 331).

71. Peter Gay calls Foucault's books on punishment and madness "empirical catastrophes" ("'Do Your Own Thing'," in *Historians and Social Values,* p. 33). Thomas Pavel, however, notes the pointlessness of blaming Foucault for "empirical ineptness" if his topic is "a discourse on the conditions of possibility of historical concepts" (Pavel with Linda Jordan, *The Feud of Language: A History of Structuralist Thought* [Oxford, 1989 (1988)], p. 93).

72. Foucault's description of his project in *Archaeology,* p. 205.

73. Young, *White Mythologies,* p. 69.

74. Michel Foucault, in *France-Culture,* July 10, 1969, cited in Dosse, *Structuralism,* I: 340. Dosse here signals Foucault's nominalism, his approach to words as physical entities, like things.

75. Cited without reference in Megill, "The Reception of Foucault by Historians," p. 119. *Madness and Civilization* bears as its subtitle, *A History of Insanity in the Age of Reason.* Similarly, in his late book, *The Use of Pleasure,* Foucault claimed that he was writing a history of thought, not of behavior or of representations (*History of Sexuality, Volume 2: The Use of Pleasure* [trans., New York, 1985 (1984)], p. 10).

76. Michel Foucault, interview in *Le Monde,* May 3, 1969, cited in Dosse, *Structuralism,* II: 237; Foucault, *Archaeology,* p. 136. Foucault praises Marc Bloch's attempt to show how notions of time differed in the rural areas on which he worked ("La Scène de la philosophie," interview [1978], in

idem, *Dits*, III: 580). David Hollinger concluded of Foucault, "Nothing nettles him more than to be mistaken for a writer of intellectual histories, and nothing in his theoretical writing is more obscure and unpersuasive than his efforts to explain why this characterization of his *Order of Things*, for example, is a mistake ("Historians and the Discourse of Intellectuals," p. 149).

77. Foucault, "Structuralism and Post-Structuralism," p. 203.

78. Although the critique of Foucault's historical work was faulted here, too: see Luc Ferry and Alain Renaut, *French Philosophy of the Sixties: An Essay on Antihumanism* (trans., Amherst, 1990 [1985]), pp. 92–96.

79. Michel Foucault, "Power and Sex: An Interview with Michel Foucault," trans. in *Telos* 32 (1977): 153, 157; idem, "Truth and Power" [1977], in idem, *Power/Knowledge: Selected Interviews and Other Writings, 1972–1977*, ed. Colin Gordon (trans., New York, 1980), p. 118. Unlike some ideology critics, Foucault does not claim that he possesses "truth" and is unmasking falsity. See the succinct analysis in Michael J. Shapiro, *The Politics of Representation* (Madison, 1988), p. 19. In an interview conducted in May 1984, Foucault added "individual behavior" to his themes of truth and power ("Le Retour de la morale," *Les Nouvelles Littéraires* [28 juin–5 juillet 1984; taken from an interview on May 29, 1984]: 38).

80. Foucault, *Archaeology*, pp. 5, 8–9, 131, 137–139, 143–144, 169, 203–204; idem, "*Les Mots et les choses*" (interview [1966]), in idem, *Dits*, I: 498; Dreyfus and Rabinow, *Beyond Structuralism*, p. 17. For Foucault's attack on exegetical approaches that attempt to recover authorial intention, see his "On Ways of Writing History" [1967], in idem, *Aesthetics, Method, and Epistemology*, ed. James D. Faubion (trans., New York, 1994), pp. 286–287. For an early presentation of Derrida and Foucault as intellectual historians to Anglophone audiences, see E. M. Henning, "Archaeology, Deconstruction, and Intellectual History," in LaCapra and Kaplan, *Intellectual History*, pp. 153–196.

81. Michel Foucault, "The Discourse on Language" [1971], trans. in his *Archaeology*, p. 220.

82. Régine Robin and Jacques Guilhaumou, "Introduction," in Guilhaumou, Denise Maldidier, and Robin, *Discours et archive: expérimentations en analyse du discours* (Liège, 1994), pp. 11–12; Régine Robin, *Histoire et linguistique* (Paris, 1973), p. 79.

83. Robin and Guilhaumou, "Introduction," in *Discours et archive*, pp. 11–13; Guilhaumou and Denise Maldidier, "Courte critique pour une longue histoire" [1979], in ibid., pp. 82–83. *Annalistes* during this period ignored issues of textualization; only in the early 1980s did some historians of *mentalités* concern themselves with questions of language. Robin, an early proponent of discourse analysis, claims that she felt like "a voice crying in the wilderness" until the late 1970s, so slow was the historians' guild to attend to questions of language ("Introduction," p. 15).

84. Foucault, "On the Ways of Writing History," p. 282; history had been the object of a "curious sacralization" (280). Foucault claims that by "archaeology" he designated a "desynchronisation between ideas about madness and the constitution of madness as an object" ("Structuralism and Post-Structuralism," p. 203).

85. Foucault, *Archaeology*, pp. 137–138, 143–144, 139–140.

86. On the relation of these points to Foucault's structuralist framework, see Gilles Deleuze, "Un Nouvel Archiviste," *Critique* 274 (1970): 204. Foucault himself denied that he was advancing a structuralist history (*Archaeology*, pp. 15–16, 204); he claims (200–201) that he never once used the word "structuralist" in *The Order of Things*.

87. Foucault, *Order*, pp. 47–49.

88. White, "Foucault Decoded," p. 38. Foucault discusses "representing" in *Order*, chap. 3. Foucault claims he and others saw Nietzsche as a way out of phenomenology (as later thinkers saw him as a way out of Marxism) ("Structuralism and Post-Structuralism," p. 199). For the prime importance of Nietzsche for Foucault, see Ferry and Renaut, *French Philosophy of the Sixties*, chap. 3.

89. Emphasized in Paul Veyne's path-breaking essay, "Foucault révolutionne l'histoire," in his *Comment on écrit l'histoire* (2d ed.; Paris, 1978), pp. 215, 218, 227; English trans. in Davidson, *Foucault*, pp. 146–182.

90. Foucault, *Archaeology*, pp. 209, 210, 138.

91. Foucault, "Preface," *Order* pp. xxiii, 386; idem, "L'Homme est-il mort?" [1966], in idem, *Dits* I: 540–541: only in the nineteenth century was a notion of human subjectivity developed, a short-lived phenomenon soon called into question by Freud's notion of the unconscious and Darwin's linking of human and simian life, among other developments. See Lynn Hunt's review of James Miller's book, *The Passion of Michel Foucault* (New York, 1993), noting Miller's attention to Foucault's new emphasis on "self" and "subject" ("The Revenge of the Subject/The Return of Experience," *Salmagundi* 97 [1993]: 45–53). Also see Jacques Derrida on "the name of man" ("Structure, Sign, and Play in the Discourse of the Human Sciences," in Macksey and Donato, *Controversy*, pp. 264–265).

92. Foucault, "The Subject, Knowledge, and the 'History of Truth,'" trans. in his *Remarks on Marx: Conversations with Duccio Trombadori* (trans., New York, 1991 [1981; interview from 1978]), pp. 56, 58; Foucault denies that they (with the exception of Lévi-Strauss) were structuralists.

93. Michel Foucault, "Interview," "France-Culture," rebroadcast June 1984, cited in Dosse, *Structuralism*, I: 334.

94. Foucault, *Order*, p. 386; idem, *Archaeology*, p. 211 (his humanist critics should not imagine that "man's" longevity will be greater than God's); see Dosse, *Structuralism*, I: 331. Dominick LaCapra comments that the theme of the "death of God" has not been sufficiently explored in studies on Foucault (*History and Reading: Tocqueville, Foucault, French Studies* [Toronto, 2000], p. 147n.16).

95. Foucault, *Archaeology*, p. 14.

96. Dosse, *Structuralism*, I: 335–336.

97. Foucault's essay, "What Is An Author?" is discussed in Chapter 7.

98. Michel Foucault, discussion following "Qu'est-ce qu'un auteur?" [1969], in idem, *Dits*, I: 789–821, cited and discussed in Roger Chartier, "The Chimera of the Origin: Archaeology of Knowledge, Cultural History, and the French Revolution" [1994], in his *Edge*, p. 68.

99. Michel de Foucault, "Adorno, Horkheimer, and Marcuse: Who Is a 'Negator of History'?" [1978 interview], trans. in idem, *Remarks on Marx*, pp. 122–123. For Derrida's agreement, albeit within a Heideggerian framework, see his "The Original Discussion of 'Différance'" [1968], in *Derrida and Différance*, ed. David Wood and Robert Bernasconi (Evanston, 1988), pp. 85–86. For Luc Ferry and Alain Renaut, all that is "intelligible" in Derrida's work is taken from Heidegger; the only difference lies in the style of writing (*French Philosophy of the Sixties*, chap. 4, especially pp. 123–124, 146).

100. Foucault, *Archaeology*, pp. 12, 203.

101. Hayden White, "Foucault's Discourse: The Historiography of Anti-Humanism" [1979], in his *Content*, p. 105.

102. See Foucault's response to his critics in *Archaeology*, p. 200.

103. Ibid., pp. 11, 172–173, 210.

104. Foucault, *Order*, pp. 50–51; idem, *Archaeology*, pp. 5, 8–9, 11–14, 142, 169–171. Marx also is credited with decentering "man" as the topic of history, emphasizing instead relations of production and class struggle (12–13); see *Beyond Structuralism*, p. 106; White, "Foucault Decoded," p. 27. Gilles Deleuze declares that in *The Archaeology of Knowledge*, the theory of "breaks" is the essential element in the system ("Un Nouvel Archiviste," p. 209). See Megill, "The Reception of Foucault by Historians," p. 130, arguing that with *Discipline and Punish*, Foucault abandoned the notion of "radical historical discontinuity," a move "less threatening to generic historians"; also see Mark Philip, "Michel Foucault," in Skinner, *Return*, p. 78, citing Foucault's essay, "Nietzsche, Genealogy, History" [1971], in *Language, Counter-Memory, Practice*, ed. Donald F. Bouchard (trans., Ithaca, 1977), pp. 153–154.

105. Foucault, *Archaeology*, pp. 139, 152, 169.

106. Foucault, "Nietzsche, Genealogy, History," p. 162. For "discontinuity" in Foucault's earlier writings, see Bannet, *Structuralism/Dissent*, p. 95; de Certeau, "The Black Sun of Language," p. 176.

107. Michel Foucault, "The Order of Discourse" (Foucault's Inaugural Lecture at the Collège de France, December 2, 1970 [1971]), trans. in his *Archaeology*, p. 231; see also idem, "Return to History" [1972], in idem, *Aesthetics, Method, and Epistemology*, pp. 429, 431.

108. See Foucault's testimony to Bachelard and Canguilhem in *Archaeology* (p. 4); see also Michel Foucault, "La Vie: l'experience et la science," *Revue de métaphysique et de morale* 90 (1985): 3–14; idem, "La Scène de la

philosophie," interview [1978], in idem, *Dits*, III: 583. Foucault found important Canguilhem's way of conceptualizing "life" ("La Vie," p. 12), and elsewhere testifies to Canguilhem's influence ("The Subject, Knowledge, and the 'History of Truth,'" p. 68). See Arnold I. Davidson, "Introductory Remarks to Pierre Hadot," in his *Foucault*, p. 201. Foucault faults *Annales* in never, until about 1970, discussing historians of science such as Canguilhem and Bachelard; *Annales* stuck resolutely to social history ("Le Style de l'histoire," interview [1984], in idem, *Dits*, IV: 655). For Canguilhem's report on Foucault's thesis *(Folie et déraison)*, see Didier Eribon, *Michel Foucault* (2d ed.; Paris, 1991 [1989]), pp. 358–361. Canguilhem himself proposes that Foucault moved from an early interest in science to an interest in power ("On *Histoire de la folie* as an Event," in Davidson, *Foucault*, p. 28). Also see Young, *White Mythologies*, pp. 69–70; Dosse, *Structuralism*, I: 333. For the use of the concept "epistemological breaks" by various French theorists, see Louis Althusser, "A Letter to the Translator," in Althusser and Balibar, *Capital*, pp. 323–324.

109. Foucault, *Archaeology*, p. 4. See Foucault's remark, "Knowledge is not made for understanding; it is made for cutting" ("Nietzsche, Genealogy, History," p. 154). Also see Jeffrey Weeks, "Uses and Abuses of Michel Foucault," *Ideas from France: The Legacy of French Theory*, ed. Lisa Appignanesi (London, 1985), p. 22.

110. White, "Foucault Decoded," p. 50. See Chapter 4 for a critique of micro-history's penchant for nostalgia and "familiarizing" past peoples and cultures.

111. Bannet, *Structuralism /Dissent*, p. 178.

112. So Dosse, *Structuralism*, I: 336.

113. See François Furet's comments on how Barthes and Foucault, following Lévi-Strauss, attempted an "ethnology" of contemporary society ("French Intellectuals," p. 225).

114. David Bromwich, "Literature and Theory" [1986], in idem, *A Choice of Inheritance* (Cambridge, Mass., 1989), p. 278.

115. Foucault, *Archaeology*, p. 179, commenting on his book, *Madness and Civilization*; see Weeks, "Uses and Abuses of Michel Foucault," p. 22. For Geoff Eley, "deconstructing the social" means historicizing the category "society"—a notion that owes much to Foucault ("Between Social History and Cultural Studies," p. 107).

116. Veyne, *Comment on écrit l'histoire*, pp. 167–171.

117. Chartier, "The Chimera of the Origin," pp. 69–70.

118. White, "Foucault Decoded," p. 32. Foucault's project resonates with founding *Annaliste* Lucien Febvre's study of Rabelais.

119. Foucault, *Order*, p. xxii—less a history than an "archaeology," Foucault here proclaims; idem, *Archaeology*, pp. 191–192. See de Certeau, "The Black Sun of Language," p. 173. Hayden White reads Foucault's *epistemes* as a theory of tropes ("Foucault's Discourse," p. 116).

120. Foucault, *Order,* pp. xxi, 168.

121. Henning, "Archaeology, Deconstruction, and Intellectual History," p. 158; Foucault maintains continuity within each epoch and discontinuity between them, thus overlooking the differences *within* epochs and the continuities *between* them (179–183).

122. Dosse, *Structuralism,* II: 234–239, appealing to Foucault, *Archaeology,* pp. 103, 138, 207—yet in this book, Foucault discounted a structuralist approach, claiming that although the latter was appropriate to the analysis of language *(langue),* mythologies, dreams, poems and works of literature, and film, it was less appropriate to the "scientific discourse" he was investigating (*Archaeology,* p. 201). Foucault described structuralism as the search for logical structures wherever they could occur ("Interview" [1968], in idem, *Dits,* I: 653). He later alleged that given "theory's" popularity in France, many found *Madness and Civilization* to be *too* historical ("The Subject, Knowledge, and the 'History of Truth,'" pp. 76–77). Foucault pinpointed his "shift" to the years 1975–1976 ("Le Retour de la morale," p. 37). For Althusser's praise for these structuralist-inspired "great works," see Althusser and Balibar, *Capital,* p. 103; and for a scathing denunciation of Althusser's praise, see Pierre Vilar, "Marxist History, a History in the Making: Towards a Dialogue with Althusser," *New Left Review* 80 (1973): 85–86. The move "away" is discussed in Dreyfus and Rabinow, *Beyond Structuralism,* pp. xxiv–xxv; Dosse, *Structuralism,* II: chap. 22.

123. Dreyfus and Rabinow, *Beyond Structuralism,* pp. 102–103; Foucault, *Archaeology,* pp. 117, 131, 162, 164, 207. Joan W. Scott uses the word "discourse" in this Foucauldian sense ("A Reply to Criticism," *International Labor and Working-Class History* 32 [1987]: 40). That Foucault also linked knowledge to practices in *Madness and Civilization* and *The Birth of the Clinic* is emphasized by Arnold I. Davidson in "On Epistemology and Archeology: From Canguilhem to Foucault," in his *The Emergence of Sexuality* (Cambridge, 2001), p. 204.

124. Dreyfus and Rabinow, *Beyond Structuralism,* pp. 103, 106, 105, 108–109.

125. Foucault, "Nietzsche, Genealogy, History," p. 142.

126. Foucault, *Archaeology,* pp. 162, 164; emphasized by Chartier in "The Chimera of the Origin," especially pp. 58–60, 69.

127. Foucault, "The Order of Discourse," pp. 233–234.

128. See Young, *White Mythologies,* pp. 70, 81, citing Foucault, "Truth and Power," p. 117. For the varied ways interpreters have construed "genealogy," see Jan Goldstein, "Introduction," *Foucault and the Writing of History,* ed. Goldstein (Oxford, 1994), p. 14. For genealogy as linking power and knowledge, see Davidson, "On Epistemology and Archeology," pp. 203–204; and Dreyfus and Rabinow, *Beyond Structuralism,* pp. xxv, 112, 114.

129. Foucault, "Nietzsche, Genealogy, History," p. 152.

130. Davidson, "On Epistemology and Archeology," referring to Foucault, "Ré-

ponse à une question," in idem, *Dits,* I: 680; Foucault, "La Volonté de savoir," in idem, *Dits,* II: 241.

131. Foucault, "Nietzsche, Genealogy, History," p. 148; idem, *Discipline and Punish: The Birth of the Prison* (New York, 1979 [1975]), p. 25. For a critique of genealogy in the name of tradition, see Alasdair MacIntyre, *Three Rival Versions of Moral Enquiry* (Notre Dame, 1990), chaps. 2 and 9.

132. See Steven Best and Douglas Kellner, *Postmodern Theory* (New York, 1991), pp. 56, 66, 69; Mark Poster, "Foucault, Post-Structuralism, and the Mode of Interpretation" [1984], in *The Aims of Representation,* ed. Murray Krieger (New York, 1987), especially pp. 126, 127, although Poster claims that Foucault, of all the post-structuralists, is most concerned with issues of historical materialism (107), and argues that for Foucault, once the mode of production changed to a mode of information, linguistic theory, rather than traditional Marxist emphases, dominated (114).

133. Veyne, *Comment on écrit l'histoire,* pp. 204, 226, 230, 240, 214.

134. Foucault, *Order,* p. 262. After *Order,* Foucault learned a different Marxism through Althusser's work: see Dosse, *Structuralism,* I: 341. Foucault testifies that currents from the Frankfurt School never found an intellectual home in France ("Structuralism and Post-Structuralism," p. 200); for Foucault's critique of "the subject" in critical theory, see his "Adorno, Horkheimer, and Marcuse," pp. 119–120, 124–125. Colin Gordon quips: "the trouble with Foucault's work was that its originality was in inverse proportion to its utility for Marxism" ("Afterword," in Foucault, *Power/Knowledge,* p. 232).

135. Michel Foucault, *The History of Sexuality. Volume 1: An Introduction* (trans., New York, 1978), pp. 151–152.

136. See, for example, the citations from Foucault's one-page text of 1976, "Le Discours ne doit pas être pris comme . . ." [1976], in idem, *Dits,* III: 123–124, discussed in Arnold I. Davidson, "Structures and Strategies of Discourse: Remarks towards a History of Foucault's Philosophy of Language," in his *Foucault,* pp. 4–5.

137. Dosse, *Structuralism,* II: 243, 245 (on the reception of *Archaeology:* "Foucault never articulated the discursive level with the articulated whole of social formation"). Discursive practice, Foucault wrote, had not to do with "a thinking, knowing, speaking subject" (*Archaeology,* p. 55).

138. Dosse mentions several late essays of Foucault ("Subjectivity and Truth," "Hermeneutics of the Subject," and "Governing the Self and Others") that inspired his last volumes, the *History of Sexuality.* Dosse links Foucault's return of interest in "the subject" to his retreat to a Zen monastery in Japan where he undertook spiritual exercises, and to his recognition that he had AIDS (*Structuralism,* II: 343). On this later period of Foucault's life, see Eribon, *Michel Foucault,* chaps. 8–9. For a discussion of Foucault's retrieval of the "self" in his later writings, see Arnold I. Davidson, "Ethics as Ascetics: Foucault, the History of Ethics, and Ancient Thought," in *Foucault*

and the Writing of History, pp. 63–80. Gilles Deleuze worries that "an analogue of the 'constituting subject'" may have reappeared in the *History of Sexuality* volumes ("Desire and Pleasure," in *Foucault,* pp. 184–185). Ferry and Renaut argue that Foucault in his later work retracted many of his earlier arguments (*French Philosophy of the Sixties,* pp. 97, 107–118). For critique from ancient historians, see especially David Cohen and Richard Saller, "Foucault on Sexuality in Greco-Roman Antiquity," in *Foucault and the Writing of History,* pp. 35–59. That Foucault's "subject" was male has been pointedly noted by Amy Richlin, "Zeus and Metis: Foucault, Feminism, Classics," *Helios* 18 (1991): 160–180; see Elizabeth A. Clark, "Foucault, the Fathers, and Sex," *Journal of the American Academy of Religion* 56 (1989): 619–641.

139. Foucault, "Structuralism and Post-Structuralism," p. 204; idem, "Truth and Power"[1977], in idem, *Power/Knowledge,* pp. 131; Gordon, "Afterward," in ibid., pp. 239, 242. Such especially was the power of *askêsis* as a "technique of the self," Foucault came to think in his late works.

140. Michel Foucault, *L'Herméneutique du sujet,* ed. Frédéric Gros (Paris, 2001); see Gros's discussion of the circumstances of the lectures, pp. 489–526. Eribon highlights the role Paul Veyne played in orienting Foucault toward ancient history (*Michel Foucault,* pp. 345, 347).

141. Arnold I. Davidson, "Introductory Remarks to Pierre Hadot," in his *Foucault,* pp. 200–201.

142. For de Certeau, "ideas" cannot be separated from "production," that is, "labor" ("Making History: Problems of Method and Problems of Meaning" [1970], in his *The Writing of History,* p. 29). André Burguière comments that a central significance of de Certeau's work was to annul the difference between production and cultural consumption ("[Intellectuelle] histoire," p. 376). Jacques Revel claims that all de Certeau's work can be classified as a project of "topography" ("Michel de Certeau historien: l'institution et son contraire," in Luce Girard, Hervé Martin, and Jacques Revel, *Histoire, mystique at politique: Michel de Certeau* [Grenoble, 1991], p. 111).

143. See Michel de Certeau, "The Inversion of What Can Be Thought: Religious History in the Seventeenth Century" [1969], in his *The Writing of History,* p. 137.

144. De Certeau, "Histoire et mystique," *Revue de l'histoire de la spiritualité* 48 (1972): 74–75. This essay was reprinted in Michel de Certeau, *L'Absent de l'histoire* (Tours, 1973), pp. 153–167, and is excerpted in English translation in Revel and Hunt, *Histories,* pp. 437–447.

145. De Certeau, "History: Science and Fiction" [1983], in his *Heterologies,* p. 214.

146. Michel de Certeau, *The Possession at Loudun* (trans., Chicago, 1996 [1970]), pp. 7–8.

147. De Certeau, "Making History," p. 22. Elsewhere, de Certeau explains what

he means by the "historical": "the analysis which considers its materials as effects of symptoms (economic, social, political, ideological, etc.) and which aims at elucidating the temporal operations (causality, intersection, inversion, coalescence, etc.) which were able to produce such effects" ("The Freudian Novel: History and Literature" [1981], in his *Heterologies*, p. 21).

148. Michel de Certeau, "Introduction: Writings and Histories," in his *The Writing of History*, p. 5.

149. De Certeau, "History: Science and Fiction" [1983], in his *Heterologies*, p. 214; yet for history, the past remains "the other," while for psychoanalysis, the past is recognized *in* the present (idem, "Psychoanalysis and Its History" [1978], in ibid., p. 4. Jacques Revel notes the "timidity" of *mentalités* historians in warming to de Certeau's psychoanalytically inspired history ("Mentalités," in *Dictionnaire des sciences historiques*, p. 456).

150. De Certeau, "Making History," p. 36; similarly, 46–47; idem, "The Historiographical Operation" [1974], in his *The Writing of History*, pp. 78–79.

151. De Certeau, "Histoire et mystique," p. 73; idem, "Making History," p. 46; idem, *The Mystic Fable. Volume I: The Sixteenth and Seventeenth Centuries* (trans., Chicago, 1992 [1982]), pp. 4–5; idem, "The Historiographical Operation," p. 100.

152. De Certeau, *The Mystic Fable*, p. 81; idem, "Autorités chrétiennes et structures sociales" [1969–1970], in his *Faiblesse de Croire* (Paris, 1987), p. 113 (it is Jesus' death that *permits* the Christian community); idem, "Lacan: An Ethics of Speech" [1982], in his *Heterologies*, p. 60; idem, "De Corps à l'écriture, un transit chrétien," in his *Faiblesse*, p. 303 (like Jews deprived of their country, Christian believers are handed over to the road "with texts for baggage"); idem, "La Rupture instauratice" [1971], in ibid., p. 212 (by the Son's effacement of himself in death, he not only bears witness to the Father, but also "'gives place' to the faithful community which he makes possible").

153. Michel de Certeau, "Cultures et spiritualités" [1966], in his *Faiblesse*, p. 41.

154. Michel de Certeau, "The Fiction of History: The Writing of *Moses and Monotheism*," in his *The Writing of History*, p. 323; idem, "The Freudian Novel," p. 31.

155. De Certeau and other historians of his stripe thus presumably are exempt from the critique that Rey Chow makes of post-structuralism's inability to deal with the "other" except by an act of temporal displacement; for de Certeau, history *means* permanent temporal displacement. See Chow, "The Interruption of Referentiality," *South Atlantic Quarterly* 101 (2002): 182–183.

156. De Certeau, "Histoire et mystique," p. 73, referring to Derrida's *On Grammatology*.

157. Michel de Certeau, "Montaigne's 'Of Cannibals': The Savage 'I'" [1981], in his *Heterologies*, p. 78.

158. De Certeau, *The Possession at Loudun*, chap. 12, especially p. 181.

159. Michel de Certeau, "Ethno-graphy: Speech, or the Space of the Other: Jean de Léry," in his *The Writing of History,* p. 215.
160. De Certeau, "Making History," p. 35.
161. Ibid., p. 43. Like the *Annalistes,* de Certeau advocates that historians borrow tools from sociology, economics, and other disciplines ("The Historiographical Operation," p. 80, taking the phrase "borrowed tools" from Pierre Vilar).
162. De Certeau, "Making History," pp. 35–36.
163. Michel de Certeau, "Micro-techniques and Panoptic Discourse: A Quid Pro Quo" [1982], in his *Heterologies,* p. 192.
164. De Certeau, "The Black Sun of Language," p. 176; idem, "The Historiographical Operation," p. 80.
165. De Certeau, "Histoire et mystique," p. 72.
166. De Certeau, "The Historiographical Operation," pp. 78, 80–81, 83.
167. Ibid., p. 79. See Hervé Martin, "Michel de Certeau et l'institution historique," in Giard, Martin, and Revel, *Histoire, mystique et politique,* pp. 60, 75.
168. Michel de Certeau, "Mystic Speech" [1976], in his *Heterologies,* p. 84.
169. De Certeau, "Histoire et mystique," p. 71, a recognition that prompted further reflection on the writing of history. Roger Chartier marks a central question in de Certeau's work on mystics: "how to explain the words and the actions of a spirituality that remained outside ecclesiastical institutions and that challenged the clergy's exclusive appropriation of the sacred" ("Michel de Certeau: History, or Knowledge of the Other" [1987], in his *Edge,* p. 40).
170. De Certeau, *The Mystic Fable,* I: 108, 113, 140–141.
171. De Certeau, "Historie et mystique," p. 80; idem, "The Fiction of History," p. 346: what if those silenced traditions have *not* said all that they know?
172. Michel de Certeau, "Mystique et psychanalyse," in *Michel de Certeau,* ed. Luce Giard (Paris, 1987), p. 187; idem, "Histoire et mystique," p. 69. My colleague Kenneth Surin comments that the above represents de Certeau's rendition of the Lacanian Real, the absent cause of History (private communication of February 17, 2003).
173. De Certeau, "Making History," pp. 20, 21, 30, 41, 43; idem, "Introduction: Writings and Histories," p. 11; idem, "The Historiographical Operation," p. 58; also see Philippe Carrard, "History as a Kind of Writing: Michel de Certeau and the Poetics of Historiography," *South Atlantic Quarterly* 100 (2001): 469.
174. De Certeau, "The Historiographical Operation," p. 95. On "split discourse," see Carrard, "History as a Kind of Writing," p. 469. De Certeau attempted explicitly to display this split structure in *The Possession at Loudun.*
175. De Certeau, "The Historiographical Operation," pp. 60–61. Religious studies scholars will be interested in de Certeau's reflections on American

religious studies conventions in "Lieux de transit," *Esprit* 41 (1973): 607–625. He criticizes modern scientific biblical criticism for omitting the institutional body of the Church ("La Misère de la théologie" [1973], in his *Faiblesse*, p. 257).

176. De Certeau, "The Historiographical Operation," p. 64. For "death" in Foucault's own discourse, see de Certeau, "The Black Sun of Language," pp. 182–183.

177. De Certeau, "The Historiographical Operation," pp. 62–63.

178. De Certeau, "History: Science and Fiction," pp. 217–18. For de Certeau's utility for feminist scholars, see Claire Colebrook, "Certeau and Foucault: Tactics and Strategic Essentialism," *South Atlantic Quarterly* 100 (2001): 543–574.

179. De Certeau, "History: Science and Fiction," pp. 203, 206. See discussion in Torbjörn Wandel, "Michel de Certeau's Place in History," *Rethinking History* 4 (2000): 59, 65. For de Certeau, the Church's present weakness is signaled by its ceasing to be a "place of production" ("Du Corps à l'écriture, un transit chrétien" [1974], in his *Faiblesse*, p. 273).

180. Luce Giard, "Cherchant Dieu," in *Faiblesse*, p. vii: Giard reports that of Marx's writings, de Certeau favored the *Eighteenth Brumaire of Louis Napoleon;* he also studied Gramsci and Althusser.

181. De Certeau, "The Historiographical Operation," p. 67; he defines ideology as the denial of specificity of place (69). For de Certeau's assimilation of ideology critique as useful in unmasking "misrecognition," see Martin, "Michel de Certeau," pp. 61–62.

182. De Certeau, "History: Science and Fiction," p. 207; idem, "The Historiographical Operation," p. 96.

183. De Certeau, "Making History," pp. 35, 42–43, 41; also see Carrard, "History as a Kind of Writing," p. 469, and Chartier, "L'Histoire ou le savoir de l'autre," pp. 161–162.

184. De Certeau, "Histoire et mystique," p. 79. Carrard notes that de Certeau "curiously" never discussed the work of Hayden White, which might have seemed like a target for his critique ("History as a Kind of Writing," p. 469).

185. De Certeau, "Historie et mystique," p. 79.

186. Roger Chartier, "Michel de Certeau," in his *Edge*, p. 45, discussing "The Historiographical Operation": if the process of changing documents into the historical text counts as a "scientific" operation, then perhaps history can be classified as one.

187. De Certeau, "The Black Sun of Language," "Micro-techniques and Panoptic Discourse," and his tribute to Foucault after the latter's death, "The Laugh of Michel Foucault," all in his *Heterologies*, pp. 171–184, 185–192, 193–198. Martin notes that historians probably disliked de Certeau's structuralism as much as they did Foucault's, but de Certeau's "impeccable eru-

dition" saved him from the reproaches they directed at Foucault ("Michel de Certeau," pp. 94–95).

188. De Certeau, "Micro-techniques and Panoptic Discourse," pp. 189, 190–191.

189. De Certeau, "La Rupture instauratice," p. 200.

190. De Certeau, "The Black Sun of Language," p. 178.

191. Carrard, "History as a Kind of Writing," pp. 476–477, citing de Certeau, *L'Invention du quotidien*, pp. 71–72. See Michel de Certeau, "Foucault and Bourdieu," in his *The Practice of Everyday Life* (trans., Berkeley, 1984 [1980]), pp. 47–48; de Certeau, "The Black Sun of Language," p. 178, suggesting, as had earlier philosophers, that historians' conclusions are not "detachable" from their research.

192. De Certeau, "Micro-techniques and Panoptic Discourse," p. 188; idem, "Foucault and Bourdieu," p. 48. For similar critiques of Foucault, see Wlad Godzich, "Foreword: The Further Possibility of Knowledge," in de Certeau, *Heterologies*, pp. xiii–xiv; and Catherine Driscoll, "The Moving Ground: Locating Everyday Life," *South Atlantic Quarterly* 100 (2001): 389–390, for a summary.

193. Giard, "Cherchant Dieu," p. viii.

194. Godzich, "Foreword," p. xiii.

195. Chartier, "The World as Representation" [1989], excerpted in Revel and Hunt, *Histories*, p. 550; Chartier, "From Court Festivity to City Spectators" [1994], in his *Forms and Meanings* (Philadelphia, 1995), pp. 43–82.

196. Chartier, "The World as Representation," pp. 550, 555, 551, citing as an example H. R. Jauss, *Literaturgeschichte als Provokation* (Frankfurt, 1970), pp. 144–207.

197. Chartier, "The World as Representation," p. 551.

198. Ibid., p. 546; compare Chartier, "History between Narrative and Knowledge" [1994], in his *Edge*, p. 19.

199. Chartier, "The World as Representation," pp. 549, 552.

200. Roger Chartier, "Intellectual History or Sociocultural History? The French Trajectories," in LaCapra and Kaplan, *Intellectual History*, pp. 16–17. Elsewhere, Chartier adds that the new intellectual history, unlike hermeneutics, recognizes that "the categories which engender experiences and interpretations are historical, discontinuous, and differentiated" ("Popular Appropriations: The Readers and Their Books" [1993], in his *Forms and Meanings*, p. 89).

201. Chartier, "Intellectual History," p. 23. Chartier rues that some *Annalistes* became so statistically oriented that they overlooked (for example) the Italian microhistorians (29–31; 33–39 for a larger critique of statistics); idem, "Introduction," in his *Edge*, p. 2; also see his critique of *mentalité* history above.

202. For de Certeau, see Chartier's essay, "Michel de Certeau: History, or the

Knowledge of the Other" [1987]; for Marin, see Chartier, "The Powers and Limits of Representation" [1994], both in his *Edge*. Chartier interprets Foucault as insistent not to conflate "practices" of a material nature with "discourse" (which Chartier understands as "language") ("The Chimera of the Origin," pp. 60–61).

203. "Popular culture is a category of the learned," Chartier writes ("Popular Appropriations," p. 83).

204. Chartier, "Intellectual History," pp. 33–39, quotation at p. 39.

205. Roger Chartier, "Introduction," in his *Forms and Meanings*, p. 4.

206. Such is Chartier's criticism of Robert Darnton's "The Great Cat Massacre": "a real text with a status of its own stands between the observer and the oral or festive supposed 'text'" ("Texts, Symbols, and Frenchness: Historical Uses of Symbolic Anthropology," *Journal of Modern History* 57 [1985]: 685; it remains "a massacre in writing" [692]). For a critique of Emmanuel Le Roy Ladurie's *Montaillou*, see Carrard, *Poetics*, p. 131; Berkhofer, *Story*, p. 151, faults Carlo Ginzburg's *The Cheese and the Worms* on the same grounds.

207. For example, Roger Chartier, "Writing the Practices," *French Historical Studies* 21 (1998): 258; idem, "The Chimera of the Origin," p. 69, writing of Foucault but agreeing with the position; idem, "Discourses and Practices: On the Origins of the French Revolution" [1992], in his *Edge* p. 74.

208. Chartier, "Writing the Practices," p. 262; idem, "The Chimera of the Origin," p. 69. Chartier particularly favors Pierre Bourdieu's work on "practices" ("Writing the Practices," p. 263); also see Chartier, "Discourses and Practices," p. 77.

209. Chartier, "Introduction," in his *Edge*, p. 7; idem, "Discourses and Practices," p. 77. See Keith Baker, *Inventing the French Revolution* (Cambridge, 1990), and idem, "A Foucauldian French Revolution?" in *Foucault and the Writing of History*, pp. 187–205.

210. Chartier, "History between Narrative and Knowledge," p. 20.

211. Chartier, "Popular Appropriations," p. 96.

212. Chartier, "History between Narrative and Knowledge," p. 18; idem, "Introduction," in his *Edge*, p. 8; idem, "Popular Appropriations," p. 95. As William H. Sewell Jr. remarks, most Americans deem the "linguistic turn" "a French import" ("Language and Practice in Cultural History: Backing Away from the Edge of the Cliff," *French Historical Studies* 21 [1998]: 243). This view has been particularly critiqued by Jonathan Dewald, "Roger Chartier and the Fate of Cultural History," *French Historical Studies* 21 (1998): 224–226, 233–234. Dewald (with good reason) questions Chartier's interpretation of Foucault's distinction between "discourse" and "practice" (229–231).

213. Dominick LaCapra, "Introduction," in his *Rethinking*, pp. 18–19.

214. Dominick LaCapra, "Rethinking Intellectual History and Reading Texts" [1980], in LaCapra and Kaplan, *Intellectual History*, pp. 82–83, 68.

215. Dominick LaCapra, "*The Cheese and the Worms:* The Cosmos of a Twentieth-Century Historian," in his *History & Criticism* (Ithaca, 1985), p. 65. Critiquing Geertz, LaCapra argues for a clearer differentiation among concepts of "culture"; high or elite culture (to be distinguished from "hegemonic culture"), he argues, may contain within itself "critical or contestatory tendencies" ("Culture and Ideology: From Geertz to Marx" [1988], in his *Soundings,* p. 137).

216. Dominick LaCapra, "Introduction," in his *Soundings,* p. 3.

217. Dominick LaCapra, "Intellectual History and Critical Theory," in his *Soundings,* p. 205.

218. Ibid., p. 196. LaCapra acknowledges that social scientific history should be recognized for some "spectacular" achievements; historical narrative, however, has remained close to the conventional forms of the traditional novel (197).

219. Dominick LaCapra, "History, Language, and Reading: Waiting for Crillon," *American Historical Review* 100 (1995): 803, 804.

220. Ibid., p. 804.

221. LaCapra, "Rethinking Intellectual History," p. 79.

222. LaCapra, "Criticism Today" [1987], in his *Soundings,* pp. 16–17. On LaCapra's particular interest in Derrida, see John H. Zammito, "Are We being Theoretical Yet? The New Historicism, the New Philosophy of History, and 'Practicing Historians,'" *Journal of Modern History* 65 (1993): 807–808.

223. Dominick LaCapra, "Rhetoric and History," in idem, *History & Criticism,* pp. 19–20, 38. His comment resonates with Roland Barthes's: "Our knowing *how to read* can be determined, verified at its inaugural stage, but it very quickly becomes a knowledge without basis, without rules, without degrees, and without end" ("On Reading" [1976], in idem, *The Rustle of Language* [trans., New York, 1986 (1984)], p. 35).

224. See, for example, Collini, "What Is Intellectual History . . .?" p. 105. Jacques Le Goff opts for a somewhat different interpretation, declaring that every document is a "text," that there is never a "pure" document, one that is "purely objective" (*History and Memory* [trans., New York, 1992 (1977)], p. 112). Le Goff cites Nicole Loraux's work on Thucydides' history, which (in Le Goff's summary of her argument) is "not a document in the modern sense of the word, but rather a text, . . . a discourse situated within the realm of rhetoric."

225. LaCapra, "Rethinking Intellectual History and Reading Texts," pp. 52–53, alluding to Heidegger's notion of the "worklike."

226. Dominick LaCapra, "On Grubbing in My Personal Archives: An Historical Exposé of Sorts (or How I Learned to Stop Worrying and Love Transference)," *boundary* 2 13 (1985): 45, 59.

227. Dominick LaCapra, "Is Everyone a *Mentalité* Case? Transference and the 'Culture' Concept" [1984], in his *History & Criticism,* p. 92.

228. LaCapra, "History, Language, and Reading," pp. 804, 807, 808.

229. LaCapra, "Introduction," in his *Soundings* p. 7.

230. LaCapra, "History, Language, and Reading," pp. 805, 808.

231. Ibid., pp. 805, 812, 813.

232. James T. Kloppenberg, "Deconstruction and Hermeneutic Strategies for Intellectual History: The Recent Work of Dominick LaCapra and David Hollinger," *Intellectual History Newsletter* 9 (1987): 13. See LaCapra's response on the question of referentiality, "Of Lumpers and Readers," *Intellectual History Newletter* 10 (1988): 5. Kloppenberg unwittingly reveals his notion of theoretical criticism when he asks, citing Wilhelm Dilthey, what "discoveries" LaCapra has made (3). The appropriate response seems to be that of Richard Rorty: "One can always make English departments look silly by asking them what they have contributed to knowledge lately. But humanists can make biology or mathematics departments look bad by asking what they have done lately for human freedom" ("John Searle on Realism and Relativism" [1994], in his *Truth and Progress: Philosophical Papers, Volume 3* [Cambridge, 1998], p. 81n.21).

233. LaCapra, "History, Language, and Reading," pp. 813–814; compare 822, where LaCapra concedes that Derrida's attempts to situate reference and reality are not always successful.

234. LaCapra, "Criticism Today," p. 19. Elsewhere, LaCapra notes that Derrida has increasingly "insisted upon the role of discursive and institutional practices"; "deconstruction is not simply a hermeneutic but a political practice" ("Up Against the Ear of the Other: Marx after Derrida," in his *Soundings,* p. 157).

235. LaCapra, "History, Language, and Reading," pp. 814, 816.

7. *Texts and Contexts*

1. Hayden White, "The Context in the Text: Method and Ideology in Intellectual History" [1982], in his *Content,* p. 186; for context "in" text, pp. 212–213. Some philosophers might argue that "text and context" is a nonproblem (or a problem that should in Wittgensteinian fashion be dissolved) in that both context and text are constructions we make for our own purposes. Although most historians presumably would not reject the notion that what serves as a text in one account might serve as a context in another—hence acknowledging that there is nothing "essentially" delimiting to the terms—their debates center more on "what counts as which" in particular circumstances. Moreover, although historians tend to imagine "contexts" as something existing apart from written remains, one could rejoin that those extratextual contexts are nonetheless largely *constructed* from textual remains.

2. John Mowitt, *Text: The Genealogy of an Antidisciplinary Object* (Durham, 1992), p. 94.

3. Claims such as E. P. Thompson's, that "history is a discipline of context and

of process" ("History and Anthropology," in his *Making History* [New York, 1994], p. 211), and Reinhart Koselleck's, that historians, unlike theologians and philologists, use texts as "witnesses" to a nontextual reality ("Historik und Hermeneutik," in Koselleck and Hans-Georg Gadamer, *Hermeneutik und Historik* [Heidelberg, 1987], pp. 25–26—adding that this reality is constituted only by verbal means; nonetheless, the writing of history should be distinguished from a philologically oriented hermeneutic; reading Hitler's *Mein Kampf* before and after Auschwitz exemplifies the difference that "context" makes [26–27]).

4. On history's changing conversation partners, see Geoff Eley, "Is All the World a Text? From Social History to the History of Society Two Decades Later," in McDonald, *Turn*, p. 199.

5. See Mowitt: "The notion of the text attempts to embody the fact that both the reading and the read are marked by a set of precise institutional *constraints* that unsettle the cognitive sovereignty of both the author and the critic" (*Text*, pp. 94–95).

6. Gérard Genette, *Palimpsests: Literature in the Second Degree* (trans., Lincoln, Neb., 1997 [1982]), p. 1.

7. Ibid., pp. 7, 394, 398–400.

8. Roland Barthes, "The Death of the Author" [1968] and "From Work to Text" [1971], both in his *Image, Music, Text,* (trans., New York, 1977) pp. 146, 159–160 (on the etymology of text as "tissue").

9. Barthes, "From Work to Text," pp. 159–160. On texts as networks of referrals to other texts, see Jacques Derrida, "Semiology and Grammatology: Interview with Julia Kristeva" [1968], in his *Positions* (trans., Chicago, 1981 [1972]), p. 33. For an accessible discussion of Derrida, see David Hoy, "Jacques Derrida," in Skinner, *Return*, pp. 41–64.

10. Kristeva borrows the notion (in which "speech" is used metaphorically) from M. M. Bakhtin, *The Dialogic Imagination,* ed. Michael Holquist (trans., Austin, 1981 [1975]), especially pp. xix, 291–294; and Mowitt, *Text,* chap. 4. This notion should not enclose us in a "prison house of language" (Fredric Jameson's famous critique of "hermetic" reading practices [*The Prison-House of Language: A Critical Account of Structuralism and Russian Formalism* (Princeton, 1974)]), but open up language to the other; also see Geoffrey Bennington, "Derridabase," in Bennington and Jacques Derrida, *Jacques Derrida* (trans., Chicago, 1993 [1991]), p. 248; Bannet, *Structuralism/Logic,* pp. 212–213. Barthes extended the notion of "text" to "read" fashion as a semiotic system (Roland Barthes, *The Fashion System* [trans., New York, 1983 (1967)]).

11. Derrida, *Grammatology,* pp. 158–159. Supplements, for Derrida, both "add to" and "substitute for."

12. Jacques Derrida, "The Attending Discourse" [1969], in his *Dissemination* (Chicago, 1981 [1972]), p. 328. "Pretext" in the sense of something standing "before" the text.

13. Derrida, "Living On: Border Lines," in *Deconstruction and Criticism,* ed.

Harold Bloom et al. (New York, 1979), p. 84. Dominick LaCapra interprets Derrida's notion of "text" as "relational networks of 'instituted traces'" ("Of Lumpers and Readers," *Intellectual History Newsletter* 10 [1988]: 5); see discussion below of Derrida on "text." For other definitions/discussions: Jacques Derrida, "Ellipsis" [1967], in idem, *Writing and Difference* (trans., Chicago, 1978 [1967]), p. 294; idem, *Grammatology*, p. 102; also see Spivak, "Translator's Preface," *Grammatology*, p. xii.

14. See Martin Donougho, "The Derridean Turn," in *The Philosophy of Discourse*, ed. Chip Sills and George H. Jensen (Portsmouth, N.H., 1992), p. 83.

15. See Jacques Derrida, "Finis," in Derrida, *Aporias* (trans., Stanford, 1993 [1993]), pp. 12–21; idem, "Qual Quelle: Valéry's Sources," in his *Margins of Philosophy* (trans., Chicago, 1982 [1972]), p. 305. Wlad Godzich argues that Paul de Man was the best thinker of aporias (*The Culture of Literacy* [Cambridge, 1994], p. 173). Godzich notes that the group associated with *Tel Quel* used the language of "production" to suggest, in a Marxist vein, the "work" a text does, thus moving beyond structuralism's injunction to synchronic description, whereas for Derrida, "production" is itself a text that "brings forth the Other" (183–184). Jean-Michel Rabaté comments that the *Tel Quelians* read Saussure through Derrida, Marx through Althusser, and Freud through Lacan (*The Future of Theory* [Oxford, 2002], p. 107).

16. Roland Barthes, "The Theory of the Text" [1973], in *Untying the Text*, ed. Robert Young (Boston, 1981), pp. 36–37, crediting Kristeva; see Mowitt, *Text*, p. 7.

17. Mowitt, *Text*, pp. 94–95. In John Sturrock's phrase, "The Text is a sort of verbal carnival, in which language is manifestly out on parole from its humdrum daily tasks . . . A Text comes, in fact, from consorting with the signifiers and letting the signifieds take care of themselves; it is the poetry of prose" ("Roland Barthes," in *Structuralism and Since*, ed. Sturrock [Oxford, 1979] p. 69). Paul Ricoeur resisted these post-structuralist moves and appealed to Dilthey's "understanding" ("What Is a Text? Explanation and Understanding," in idem, *Hermeneutics and the Human Sciences*, ed. John B. Thompson [Cambridge, 1981], pp. 148–164).

18. See Robert Young, "Post-Structuralism: An Introduction," in *Untying the Text*, p. 8; Godzich, *The Culture of Literacy*, p. 181 (textuality as "the space of an operativity"); for a Marxist critique, see Fredric Jameson, "The Ideology of the Text" [1975/76], in his *The Ideologies of Theory: Essays 1971–1986* (Minneapolis, 1988), I: 17–71.

19. Barthes, "From Work to Text" [1971], pp. 157, 160; idem, "The Death of the Author," p. 146; also see idem, "Introduction: The Semiological Adventure"[1974], in his *Semiotic Challenge*, p. 7; Mowitt, *Text*, pp. 88, 99.

20. Barthes, "From Work to Text," pp. 160, 163.

21. Barthes, "The Death of the Author," p. 148. "Although entirely derived from books," Barthes writes, "these codes, by a swivel characteristic of

bourgeois ideology, which turns culture into nature, appear to establish reality, 'Life'" (Barthes, *S/Z* [trans., New York, 1974 (1970)], p. 206); discussed in Jonathan Culler, *Roland Barthes* (New York, 1983), pp. 84–85. Here, Barthes's structuralist understanding of the subject intersects with his notion of "the effect of the real" and of ideology. Barthes became fascinated by the structure of the Japanese language that "turns the subject, precisely, into a great envelope empty of speech, and not that dense kernel which is supposed to direct our sentences" (*The Empire of Signs* [trans., New York, 1982 (1970)], p. 7).

22. Barthes, *S/Z*, pp. 5–6, 10; idem, "The Death of the Author," p. 147; idem, "On Reading" [1976], in his *The Rustle of Language,* p. 42; see discussion in Culler, *Roland Barthes,* pp. 81–85. "Deciphering" a text, rather than "disentangling" it, is presumably the task of an older hermeneutics that Barthes rejects.

23. Barthes, "The Death of the Author," pp. 147–148.

24. Roland Barthes, *Criticism and Truth* (trans., London, 1987 [1966]), pp. 36–59, 85.

25. Ibid., pp. 86, 33.

26. Michel Foucault, "What Is an Author?" [1969], in *Textual Strategies,* ed. Josué V. Harari (Ithaca, 1979), pp. 141–160.

27. Roland Barthes, "Writing Reading" [1970], in his *The Rustle of Language,* p. 30.

28. Foucault, "What Is an Author?" pp. 148–150. Foucault notes that in the Middle Ages, a scientific (but not a literary) text needed to provide the name of its author in order for its truth value to be recognized; in the seventeenth and eighteenth centuries, however, a reversal took place, such that scientific discourses could remain anonymously authored if their contents seemed true to other scientists, but literary texts were accepted only when their authors announced themselves.

29. Foucault's "chronology" could be questioned: the school curriculum for some centuries prior to Jerome had enshrined a canon of "most significant authors" in the minds of young males of a certain class.

30. Foucault, "What Is an Author?" pp. 150–151.

31. Ibid., p. 160. In our culture, by contrast, the "author-function" serves as a "system of constraint" to limit meaning, to exclude its proliferation. This view affords a sharp contrast to the traditional characterization of the author as (in Foucault's words) "the genial creator of a work in which he deposits, with infinite wealth and generosity, an inexhaustible world of significations" (159). Foucault here labels the modern author-function as "a principle of thrift." For "strategies of containment" as an approach to ideology, see Fredric Jameson, *The Political Unconscious* (Ithaca, 1981), pp. 52–53.

32. Derrida, *Grammatology,* p. 158: "il n'y a pas de hors-texte"; Derrida, "Outwork," in his *Dissemination,* p. 36.

33. Jacques Derrida, "Afterword: Toward an Ethic of Discussion" [1988], in

his *Limited Inc* (trans., Evanston, 1988), p. 137; nor is it a book in a library, Derrida adds (150). Similarly, Jacques Derrida, "Interview," in *Dialogues with Contemporary Continental Thinkers,* ed. Richard Kearney (Manchester, 1984), p. 123.

34. Derrida, "Living On: *Border Lines,*" p. 84.
35. Bennington, "Derridabase," p. 83.
36. Derrida, "Interview," in *Dialogues with Contemporary Continental Thinkers,* pp. 123–124, 125, 126.
37. Paul Ricoeur, "The Hermeneutical Function of Distanciation" [1975], in his *Hermeneutics and the Human Sciences,* p. 133. For a discussion of human action as a text in Ricoeur, see David Pellauer, "The Significance of the Text in Paul Ricoeur's Hermeneutical Theory," in *Studies in the Philosophy of Paul Ricoeur,* ed. Charles E. Reagan (Athens, Ohio, 1979), pp. 108–110.
38. Paul Ricoeur, *Interpretation Theory* (Forth Worth, 1976), pp. 14–19.
39. Paul Ricoeur, "The Model of the Text: Meaningful Action Considered as a Text," *Social Research* 38 (1971): 540–546.
40. Gadamer, *Truth,* p. 336. Historians should rather concentrate on the ideas that the author "unquestionably accepted" from his or her environment (337), that is, on ideology.
41. For Gadamer, the quest for "origins" characterized the Romantic school of hermeneutics (*Truth,* p. 244); see David E. Linge, "Editor's Introduction," in Hans-Georg Gadamer, *Philosophical Hermeneutics* (Berkeley, 1976), p. xxi.
42. Linge, "Editor's Introduction," p. xxiv.
43. Gadamer, *Truth,* pp. 299, 331–333.
44. Hans-Georg Gadamer, "Hermeneutics and Logocentrism" [1987], in *Dialogue and Deconstruction: The Gadamer-Derrida Encounter,* ed. Diane P. Michelfelder and Richard E. Palmer (Albany, 1989), pp. 117–118.
45. Fred R. Dallmayr, "Hermeneutics and Deconstruction: Gadamer and Derrida in Dialogue" [1987], in *Dialogue and Deconstruction,* p. 77.
46. Hans-Georg Gadamer, "Reply to My Critics" [1971], in *The Hermeneutic Tradition from Ast to Ricoeur,* ed. Gayle L. Ormiston and Alan D. Schrift (Albany, 1990), p. 277.
47. Jacques Derrida, "Three Questions to Hans-Georg Gadamer" [1984], trans. in *Dialogue and Deconstruction,* p. 53.
48. Hans-Georg Gadamer, "Text and Interpretation" [1984], trans. in *Dialogue and Deconstruction,* pp. 32, 40, 42, 43, 44.
49. Hans-Georg Gadamer, "Rhetoric, Hermeneutics, and the Critique of Ideology: Metacritical Comments on *Truth and Method*" [1967], trans. in *The Hermeneutics Reader,* ed. Kurt Mueller-Vollmer (New York, 1985), p. 278.
50. Derrida, "Three Questions," pp. 53–54. On the phenomenological background of Gadamer, see Linge, "Editor's Introduction," p. xlii; see also Richard Kearney, "Introduction," in *Dialogues with Contemporary Continental Philosophers,* pp. 3–4.
51. Gadamer, *Truth,* p. 414 (my emphasis). Elsewhere, responding to Reinhart

Koselleck's discussion of "History and Hermeneutics," Gadamer praised Koselleck for arguing that historians should attend to Heidegger's discussion of *Dasein* ("Historik und Sprache—eine Antwort," in Koselleck and Gadamer, *Hermeneutik und Historik*, p. 29; see Linge, "Editor's Introduction," p. xlvii). Paul Ricoeur, whose approach is closer to Gadamer than to Derrida, criticizes Derrida's prying apart of speech and writing and his (alleged) advocacy of the "absolute text" (*Interpretation Theory*, pp. 26, 30, 36–37).

52. Derrida, "Interview," in *Dialogues with Contemporary Continental Philosophers*, p. 109.

53. Mueller-Vollmer, "Introduction: Language, Mind, and Artifact," in *The Hermeneutics Reader*, p. 39; Koselleck, "Historik und Hermeneutik," p. 21.

54. Derrida, "Interview," in *Dialogues with Contemporary Continental Philosophers*, pp. 115–116. Writing for Derrida is thus more "subversive" than speech.

55. Derrida, "Three Questions," pp. 53–54.

56. Dallmayr, "Hermeneutics and Deconstruction," pp. 84, 76; and see Derrida, "Interpreting Signatures (Nietzsche/Heidegger): Two Questions" [1986], in *Dialogue and Deconstruction*.

57. Some distinguish contextualists, who look to *linguistic* contexts, from conventionalists, who explore the *social conventions* that produce linguistic meaning: see Bevir, *Logic*, p. 32. For a discussion of contexualism as a methodology, see Berkhofer, *Story*, pp. 31–36.

58. Quentin Skinner, "What Is Intellectual History . . .?" in *What Is History Today. . . .?* ed. Juliet Gardiner (Houndsmills, 1988), pp. 110–111, borrowing from Heidegger and Wittgenstein. Skinner is labeled a "conventionalist" by Mark Bevir et al., in "Roundtable: The Logic of the History of Ideas," *Rethinking History* 4 (2000): 302, 322.

59. Quentin Skinner, "Meaning and Understanding in the History of Ideas," *History and Theory* 8 (1969): 50–52, 29; idem, "Motives, Intentions and the Interpretation of Texts," *New Literary History* 3 (1972): 407; idem, *Liberty before Liberalism* (Cambridge, 1998), pp. 117, 112; idem, *Reason and Rhetoric in the Philosophy of Hobbes* (Cambridge, 1996), p. 15.

60. Quentin Skinner, "Rhetoric and Conceptual Change," *Finnish Yearbook of Political Thought* 3 (1999): 61–62; idem, "Meaning and Understanding," pp. 10–11, 17. Skinner critiques an older "history of ideas."

61. For a brief discussion of Skinner's appropriation of Austin and Wittgenstein, see James Tully, "The Pen Is a Mighty Sword: Quentin Skinner's Analysis of Politics" [1983], in *Meaning and Context: Quentin Skinner and His Critics*, ed. Tully (Cambridge, 1988), p. 8, and Skinner, "A Reply to My Critics," in the same volume, pp. 260–261. For the influence of the British idealist tradition (especially Oakeshott and Collingwood), as well as Austin and Wittgenstein, see Boucher, *Texts*, pp. 3, 30, 93, 261.

62. Quentin Skinner, "From Hume's Intentions to Deconstruction and Back,"

Journal of Political Philosophy 4 (1996): 148, 151; idem, "Meaning and Understanding," pp. 45–46; also see Skinner's references to Austin's *How To Do Things with Words* in "'Social Meaning' and the Explanation of Social Action" [1972], in *Meaning and Context,* p. 83.

63. Quentin Skinner, "Hermeneutics and the Role of History," *New Literary History* 7 (1975): 215. Skinner differentiates his position from the "strong" version of contextualism (namely, that contexts themselves "serve to yield what the text must mean") in his early essay, "Meaning and Understanding," p. 45.

64. Skinner, "Meaning and Understanding," pp. 43, 48, 49; idem, "'Social Meaning,'" p. 95; idem, *The Foundations of Modern Political Thought* (Cambridge, 1978), I: xi, xiii; idem, "Rhetoric and Conceptual Change," p. 67.

65. Skinner, "From Hume's Intentions," pp. 153–154 (thus scholars need not endorse the truth claims of propositions); idem, "A Reply to My Critics," pp. 256–257.

66. Skinner, "Hermeneutics and the Role of History," p. 212; see Boucher, *Texts,* chap. 5; Quentin Skinner, "Some Problems in the Analysis of Political Thought and Action," *Political Theory* 2 (1974): 283, 284, adopting J. L. Austin's notion of the "illocutionary" aspect of speech, cited in Peter L. Janssen, "Political Thought as Traditionary Action: The Critical Response to Skinner and Pocock," *History and Theory* 24 (1985): 131. For a description, see Nancy S. Struever, "Historical Discourse," in *Handbook of Discourse Analysis. Volume I: Disciplines of Discourse,* ed. Teun A. Van Dijk (London, 1985), p. 251. Skinner rejects approaches based on the scholar's "empathy" with an author/text; "intentions" must be "publicly legible" ("A Reply to My Critics," p. 279); idem, "Motives," pp. 402–404, quotation at 404. Boucher (*Texts,* p. 151) notes that Skinner's view on this point differs from Pocock's, for whom language stands first.

67. Skinner, "From Hume's Intentions," p. 147; "meaning" is polysemic (p. 150). See Skinner, "Meaning and Understanding," pp. 22–23; idem, "A Reply to My Critics," pp. 269–272 (Skinner here agrees that complex texts always carry more meaning than the author "intended"). Skinner, in his later writing, would doubtless rebut Mark Bevir's charge that he tries to derive hermeneutic meaning from linguistic meaning: see Bevir, *Logic,* pp. 42, 45–48.

68. For his inspiration in Wittgenstein ("Words are also deeds"), see Skinner, *Reason and Rhetoric in the Philosophy of Hobbes,* pp. 7–8, citing Wittgenstein, *Philosophical Investigations,* para. 546, p. 146e; see Bevir, *Logic,* p. 44.

69. Skinner, "A Reply to My Critics," p. 281. Skinner rejects Gadamer's view of our limited horizon and "fore-expectation" as unduly constraining the quest for intentionality ("Introduction: The Return of Grand Theory," in his *Return,* p. 7; idem, "A Reply to My Critics," pp. 272, 276; idem, "The

Idea of Negative Liberty: Philosophical and Historical Perspectives," in *Philosophy in History,* ed. Richard Rorty et al. [Cambridge, 1984], p. 202).

70. See Pocock's "The Origins of Study of the Past," *Comparative Studies in Society and History* 4 (1962): 204–246, in which he argues for the centrality of legal studies in early modernity to the development of historicism and historiography in a modern sense.

71. Pocock, "The Concept of a Language and the *métier d'historien,*" in *The Languages of Political Theory in Early-Modern Europe,* ed. Anthony Pagden (Cambridge, 1987), p. 20.

72. J. G. A. Pocock, "Languages and Their Implications: The Transformation of the Study of Political Thought," in his *Politics, Language and Time* (New York, 1971), pp. 5–6, 11–12.

73. J. G. A. Pocock, *Barbarism and Religion* (Cambridge, 1999), II: 9: Pocock notes that the notion of "contexts" was one not developed until the eighteenth century. He does not rule out other kinds of contexts: idem, "A New Bark Up an Old Tree," *Intellectual History Newsletter* 8 (1986): 7; idem, "Texts as Events: Reflections on the History of Political Thought," in *Politics of Discourse,* ed. Kevin Sharpe and Steven N. Zwicker (Berkeley, 1987), p. 25; idem, "The Concept of a Language," p. 21. Since language does not mirror social reality, the historian (working like an archeologist) should explore how language does, or does not, reveal the context of its formation (idem, "Texts as Events," p. 25; idem, "Languages and Their Implications," p. 38; idem, "The Concept of a Language," p. 23; idem, *Barbarism and Religion,* II: 16).

74. Pocock, "Texts as Events," pp. 21–22, 23, 29.

75. Ibid., p. 27; idem, "The Concept of a Language," p. 22—especially Burke's notion of "languages" as having rhetorics and grammars.

76. Pocock, "The Concept of a Language," pp. 29, 37 (on the distinction between *langue* and *parole*).

77. Kuhn on "paradigms" and their shifts; Pocock develops the notion of "paradigmatic languages" ("Languages and Their Implications," pp. 13–15). Boucher (*Texts,* pp. 178–181, 262) argues that Pocock appears to harbor a correspondence theory of truth and a notion of the past "as it really was," views that sit poorly with his theories on language.

78. Pocock, "Languages and Their Implications," p. 6.

79. Ibid., pp. 23–24, with the caveat that authors cannot convey messages that the linguistic resources of their time render impossible.

80. Pocock, "Texts as Events," pp. 24–25.

81. Ibid., p. 31.

82. Bevir, *Logic,* pp. 310, 314.

83. Bevir, "Roundtable," pp. 298, 341.

84. Bevir, *Logic,* pp. 38–42, 45–46 (Skinner in his later work rejects Bevir's assumption). Bevir cites the example of Mrs. Malaprop in Richard Sheridan's play, *The Rivals:* to get the joke, the audience must be able to (and does) fig-

ure out that when she *says* "a nice derangement of epitaphs," she *means* "a nice arrangement of epithets." Having a language presupposes linguistic conventions, but accepting this presupposition (indebted to Wittgenstein and Peter Strawson) differs from claiming that convention determines the "meaning" of a particular statement (pp. 45–48, citing Strawson's essay, "Intention and Convention in Speech-Acts," *Philosophical Review* 73 [1974]: 439–460).

85. Bevir, *Logic,* pp. 37, 48, 50–51. In his "Roundtable" discussion, however, Bevir allows that readers, too, contribute to the constitution of hermeneutic meaning (298).

86. Bevir, *Logic,* pp. 42, 45–49, 32, 48–50; 34–35 for further critique of Pocock. Others might argue that the use of linguistic conventions is necessary to say unconventional things. Skinner in his later work denies that he constructs a theory of "meaning." As an example of words used conventionally to challenge commonplace assumptions/meanings, Bevir differentiates Machiavelli's statement that "princes must learn when not to be virtuous" from Mrs. Malaprop's case, in which words *themselves* are used unconventionally (50).

87. Ibid., pp. 41, 51.

88. Dominick LaCapra, "Reading Exemplars: *Wittgenstein's Vienna* and *Wittgenstein's Tractatus*" [1979], in La Capra and Kaplan, *Intellectual History,* p. 85; idem, "Writing the History of Criticism Now?" in his *History & Criticism* (Ithaca, 1985), p. 105; idem, "Intellectual History and Defining the Present as 'Postmodern,'" in *Innovation/Renovation,* ed. Ihab Hassan and Sally Hassan (Madison, 1983), pp. 53, 55.

89. Dominick LaCapra, "Intellectual History and Critical Theory," in his *Soundings,* pp. 191, 203; idem, "Of Lumpers and Readers," p. 5 ("context" cannot be taken simply as "explanatory"). LaCapra faults New Historicists and formalists for their approach to "context" ("Intellectual History and Critical Theory," pp. 192–193).

90. LaCapra, "Intellectual History and Critical Theory," p. 203.

91. LaCapra, "AHR Forum: Intellectual History and Its Ways," *American Historical Review* 97 (1992): 430; idem, "Reading Exemplars," p. 91; idem, "Intellectual History and Defining the Present as 'Postmodern,'" p. 55.

92. LaCapra, "Intellectual History and Critical Theory," p. 205; idem, "Intellectual History and Its Ways," p. 430.

93. So Michael Ermarth, "Mindful Matters: The Empire's New Codes and the Plight of Modern European Intellectual History," *Journal of Modern History* 57 (1987): 516.

94. Dominick LaCapra, "Rethinking Intellectual History and Reading Texts" [1980], in LaCapra and Kaplan, *Intellectual History,* pp. 51–52; idem, "Culture and Ideology: From Geertz to Marx" [1988], in his *Soundings,* p. 144; idem, "Intellectual History and Defining the Present as 'Postmodern,'" pp. 55, 53. Similarly, Anthony Pagden, "Rethinking the Linguis-

tic Turn: Current Anxieties in Intellectual History," *Journal of the History of Ideas* 49 (1988): 520–521.

95. LaCapra, "Rethinking Intellectual History and Reading Texts," pp. 57–58; see the critiques of Joseph V. Femia, "An Historicist Critique of 'Revisionist' Methods of Studying the History of Ideas," and John Keane, "More Theses on the Philosophy of History," both in *Meaning and Context,* pp. 157–169, 206–211.

96. LaCapra, "Rethinking Intellectual History and Reading Texts," pp. 51–52.

97. LaCapra, "Intellectual History and Critical Theory," p. 199; see above for Pocock's interest in the "unthought." LaCapra reveals his Derridean-oriented approach in this comment: speech-act theory presumably does not count as "theory" for LaCapra.

98. LaCapra, "Intellectual History and Critical Theory," pp. 200–201. See Tony Bennett: texts are "kept alive only at the price of being always other than 'just themselves'"; moreover, if texts exist only through reading formations, then there must be, in effect, different texts for different readers ("Texts in History: The Determinations of Readings and Their Texts," in Attridge, Bennington, and Young, *Post-Structuralism,* pp. 69–71, 76). Bennett here critiques Marxist literary theorists who argue that the interpreter must return the text to its "conditions of origin"; for Bennett, discursive processes *are* "social and material processes produced within specifiable institutional conditions" (75).

99. Harlan, *Degradation,* pp. 15, 22. Harlan notes that contextualists take speech rather than writing as the model (chap. 1); also see Harlan, "AHR Forum: Intellectual History and the Return of Literature," *American Historical Review* 94 (1989): 593, 586–587.

100. Harlan, "AHR Forum: Intellectual History," pp. 595–596.

101. Ibid., p. 595; compare Hans Kellner's views on the role of narrativity in contextualization ("Conclusion," in his *Language,* p. 332).

102. Harlan, "AHR Forum: Intellectual History," pp. 586–587, 600, 587–588, 600–602; Harlan hints that Gadamer's approach might be construed as "Catholic." Replying to Harlan, David A. Hollinger defends contextualism in "AHR Forum: The Return of the Prodigal: The Persistence of Historical Knowing," *American Historical Review* 94 (1989): 618.

103. Derrida, "Signature Event Context" [1971; trans., 1977], in his *Limited Inc* (Evanston, 1988), pp. 1–23.

104. Derrida, "Limited Inc a b c" [trans., 1977], in his *Limited Inc,* pp. 29–110.

105. Derrida, "Signature Event Context," pp. 2–3, 15, 18—yet "no meaning can be determined out of context" (idem, "Living On," pp. 76, 81).

106. Derrida, "Signature Event Context," p. 9.

107. Derrida, "Afterword: Toward an Ethic of Discussion," pp. 131–132, 136.

108. See discussion in Hoy, "Jacques Derrida," pp. 56–57: an aspect of Derrida's debate with Foucault on social practices in relation to texts (59–60).

109. Derrida, "Afterword: Toward an Ethic of Discussion," p. 136. Ann Rigney

suggests how the notion is useful to historians: the *hors-texte* consists of "all those phenomena that have escaped representation"; Rigney links the notion to discussions of the "sublime" (*Imperfect Histories* [Ithaca, 2001], pp. 101, 103, 115, 119).

110. Jacques Derrida, "Biodegradables: Seven Diary Fragments," *Critical Inquiry* 15 (1989): 841, 821.

111. LaCapra, "Of Lumpers and Readers," p. 5; idem, "Criticism Today," in his *Soundings*, p. 19. Rabaté notes that Derrida here signals "the aporetic impossibility of deciding exactly where 'text' would end and 'world' would begin" (*The Future of Theory*, p. 107).

112. "J'ai oublié mon parapluie"; see Jacques Derrida, *Spurs: Nietzsche's Styles/ Eperons: Les Styles de Nietzsche* (trans., Chicago, 1979 [1978]), pp. 122–139. On "undecidables" in relation to Gödel's theorem, see Donougho, "The Derridean Turn," p. 68.

113. Derrida, "Limited Inc a b c," p. 63.

114. Derrida, "Afterword: Toward an Ethic of Discussion," pp. 148–149.

115. For a careful explication of "undecidability" in Derrida that critiques the use of the term by Paul de Man and J. Hillis Miller, see Jeffrey T. Nealon, "The Discipline of Deconstruction," *PMLA* 107 (1992): 1271–1272.

116. A point made by Hoy, "Jacques Derrida," p. 56.

117. Derrida, "Signature, Event, Context," p. 3. Derrida also uses the word "writing" to denote a larger field: "all that gives rise to inscription in general" (*Grammatology*, p. 9). Commentator E. M. Henning notes, "'Writing' consequently becomes a name for that inevitably shifting and uncertain process whereby all forms of symbolism are established and institutionalized" ("Archaeology, Deconstruction, and Intellectual History," in LaCapra and Kaplan, *Intellectual History*, p. 190).

118. Derrida, "Signature Event Context," pp. 3, 7–8 (as Plato condemned in the *Phaedrus*).

119. Ibid., pp. 13–15, cf. 18: on Austin's assumptions, "conscious intention would have to be totally present and immediately transparent to itself and to others, since it is a determining center [*foyer*] of context." It should be noted that not all speech-act theorists would ascribe such importance to authorial intention.

120. Derrida, "Limited Inc a b c," p. 37.

121. Derrida, "Signature Event Context," pp. 17–18. Derrida concedes that there are different kinds of iterability; an actor repeating words in a play and someone's recitation of a poem stand as examples. Ann Rigney sees the "essence of textuality" as lying in "reproducibility," in a text's "apparent 'refusal' to be expendable" (*Imperfect Histories*, p. 126).

122. Derrida, "Afterword: Toward an Ethic of Discussion," p. 119; idem, "Limited Inc a b c," p. 62. I thank Kenneth Surin for helpful explication.

123. Bennington, *Derridabase*, pp. 84–86, 90–91. The point is that a reader could easily imagine numerous contexts for such a sentence. Bennington

discusses Derrida in "Afterword," p. 131; see also Boucher's critique of contextualism (*Texts,* pp. 255, 266–271).

124. The various attempts to decide the meaning of the Nag Hammadi texts on the basis of some presumed context provide a salient example.

125. Essays especially influential in the humanities are: Clifford Geertz, "Deep Play: Notes on the Balinese Cockfight" [1972]; idem, "Religion as a Cultural System" [1966]; idem, "Ethos, World View and the Analysis of Sacred Symbols" [1957], all in his *The Interpretation of Cultures* (New York, 1973), pp. 412–453, 87–125, 126–141.

126. Clifford Geertz, *Negara: The Theatre-State in Nineteenth-Century Bali* (Princeton, 1980), p. 135. Similarly, idem, "Thick Description: Toward an Interpretive Theory of Culture," in his *The Interpretation of Cultures,* pp. 5, 10, 14; idem, "Deep Play," pp. 448–449, 452; Clifford Geertz, "Introduction," in his *Local Knowledge,* pp. 3, 5; idem, "Blurred Genres: The Refiguration of Social Thought" [1980], in his *Local Knowledge,* pp. 21, 23, 30, 31–32. Geertz's assertion resonates with the project of D. F. McKenzie, scholar of bibliography studies, who likewise enlarges the meaning of "text" to include symbolic systems such as maps and musical scores; see discussion of McKenzie's *Bibliography and the Social Sciences* in Roger Chartier, "Texts, Forms, and Interpretations" [1991], in his *Edge,* pp. 81–89.

127. Benedict Anderson, "Djojo on the Corner," *London Review of Books* (24 August 1995): 20. Anderson calls *The Religion of Java* "an astonishingly Edenic text," with no bibliography, almost no footnotes or references to other anthropologists of importance, or to "the vast corpus of Dutch-colonial Javanological studies" (19–20). Anderson's essay, ostensibly a review of Geertz's *After the Fact,* provides a stimulating introduction to changes in twentieth-century anthropology and its relation to colonialism, global capitalism, and theory.

128. It is ironic that Geertz's work has been received more enthusiastically in disciplines *other* than anthropology (William H. Sewell Jr., "Geertz, Cultural Systems, and History," *Representations* 59 [1977]: 36), although his influence in anthropology was considerable. Benedict Anderson places his influence: between 1960 and the mid-1980s, Geertz was "after Lévi-Strauss, the most widely-known and influential anthropologist around" ("Djojo on the Corner," p. 19).

129. See Fred Ingilis, *Clifford Geertz: Culture, Custom and Ethics* (Cambridge, 2000), pp. 112, 128; Geertz, "Thick Description," pp. 6, 16, 26. Geertz appropriates the term from philosopher Gilbert Ryle.

130. Geertz, "Deep Play," p. 452.

131. Geertz, "Thick Description," p. 10; idem, "Blurred Genres," p. 31; idem, "Introduction," in his *Local Knowledge,* p. 10; idem, "The Uses of Diversity" [1986], in his *Available Light* (Princeton, 2000), p. 84.

132. Clifford Geertz, "'From the Native's Point of View': On the Nature of An-

thropological Understanding" [1974], in *Meaning in Anthropology*, ed. Keith H. Basso and Henry A. Selby (Albuquerque, 1976), p. 235.

133. George E. Marcus, "Afterword: Ethnographic Writing and Anthropological Careers," in *Writing Culture: The Poetics and Politics of Ethnography*, ed. James Clifford and George E. Marcus (Berkeley, 1986), pp. 262–263. See Clifford Geertz, "Being There: Anthropology and the Scene of Writing," in idem, *Works and Lives: The Anthropologist as Author* (Stanford, 1988), pp. 7–8, for anthropology as a "literary" discipline.

134. For Geertz as "anti-structuralist," see James Boon, "Introduction to the English Edition," *Between Belief and Transgression: Structuralist Essays in Religion, History, and Myth*, ed. Michel Izard and Pierre Smith (trans., Chicago, 1982 [1979]), p. viii.

135. Geertz, "Introduction," in his *Local Knowledge*, p. 12; idem, "Anti Anti-Relativism," *American Anthropologist* 86 (1984): 268; idem, "Art as a Cultural System" [1976], in his *Local Knowledge*, p. 120; idem, "Blurred Genres, p. 53.

136. Geertz, "Deep Play," p. 449n.38.

137. Geertz, "Thick Description," p. 26; similarly, idem, "The Way We Think Now: Toward an Ethnography of Modern Thought" [1982], in his *Local Knowledge*, p. 150.

138. Clifford Geertz, "The World in a Text: How to Read 'Tristes Tropiques'" [1987], in his *Works and Lives*, p. 27.

139. William Roseberry, "Balinese Cockfights and the Seduction of Anthropology," in his *Anthropologies and Histories* (New Brunswick, 1989), p. 20.

140. Clifford Geertz, "The Cerebral Savage: On the Work of Claude Lévi-Strauss"[1967], in his *The Interpretation of Cultures*, pp. 345–359.

141. Geertz, "The World in a Text," pp. 25–48.

142. Geertz, "The Cerebral Savage," pp. 346–347, 352, 356, 351, 356.

143. Geertz, "The Uses of Diversity," p. 75; he prefers Richard Rorty's "messy populism," but now he praises Lévi-Strauss's attack on the UNESCO-brand of multiculturalism that obscures the gaps and asymmetries in cultures (78). For Geertz's affinity with pragmatism, see James A. Boon, *Other Tribes, Other Scribes* (Cambridge, 1982), p. 141.

144. Geertz, "The World in a Text," pp. 27, 26; idem, "Being There," p. 4.

145. Geertz, "The World in a Text," pp. 40–44, noting (41) James A. Boon, *From Symbolism to Structuralism: Lévi-Strauss in a Literary Tradition* (New York, 1972), which Boon states (p. 230) is "a dialectic between Symbolist poetics and structural mythologies."

146. Geertz, "Blurred Genres," p. 23; idem, "Deep Play," pp. 443, 450; idem, "Being Here: Whose Life Is It Anyway?" in his *Works and Lives*, p. 141.

147. Geertz, "Deep Play," pp. 446, 450; idem, "Preface," in his *Works and Lives*, p. vi; idem, "The Way We Think Now," p. 153. Inglis stresses Burke's importance, and the influence of R. P. Blackmur and F. R. Leavis (*Clifford Geertz*, pp. 48–53, 126–127, 108).

148. Stephen Greenblatt, "The Touch of the Real," *Representations* 59 (1997): 14, 19–20; see Geertz, "The World in a Text," p. 46. Greenblatt's title is suggestive: the New Historicist would like to conjure up a "real" (as opposed to "imagined") world, but must remember that in historical work, all that remains are "traces"; hence, "the touch" (21–22). Also see Sherry B. Ortner's tribute to Geertz's wide-ranging influence, "Introduction: The Fate of 'Culture': Geertz and Beyond," *Representations* 59 (1997): 1. Catherine Gallagher and Stephen Greenblatt claim that Geertz's view of culture as a text greatly expanded "the range of objects available to be read and interpreted" (*Practicing New Historicism* [Chicago, 2000], pp. 9, 16).

149. James Clifford, "On Ethnographic Authority," *Representations* 1 (1983): 130–132.

150. Ibid., p. 137. As Stephen Greenblatt notes, if everything is textual, then "it makes all the difference what kind of text you are talking about ("The Touch of the Real," p. 16). While Geertz concedes that "easy realism" will from now on be both less "easy" and "less persuasive," he offers no helpful answer to the philosophical problem of representation; rather, he counsels anthropologists to "get used to it" ("Being Here," pp. 135, 137, 138; idem, "Thick Description," p. 19n.3).

151. George E. Marcus and Dick Cushman, "Ethnographies as Texts," *Annual Review of Anthropology* 11 (1982): 43.

152. See Geertz's commendation of speech-act theorist J. L. Austin, in "The Way We Think Now," p. 153; Marcus and Cushman, "Ethnographies as Texts," p. 43.

153. Geertz, "Thick Description," p. 24.

154. Clifford Geertz, *A Life of Learning* (New York, 1999), p. 15. Renato I. Rosaldo Jr. reminds readers that Geertz did not think that the world was, literally, a "text"; rather, he wished to explore the textual analogy's productiveness ("A Note on Geertz as a Cultural Essayist," *Representations* 59 [1997]: 31).

155. Geertz, "Thick Description," p. 9.

156. Geertz, "Introduction," in his *Local Knowledge,* p. 12; idem, "Thick Description," p. 17.

157. Geertz, "Thick Description," p. 18; how a thing *is* can be judged by "how it *acts*" (Inglis, *Clifford Geertz,* p. 168).

158. Ronald G. Walters, "Signs of the Times: Clifford Geertz and the Historians," *Social Research* 47 (1980): 547. Hence, I suspect, Geertz's special appeal to New Historicists.

159. Stressed by Ortner ("Introduction," p. 6); Sewell ("Geertz, Cultural Systems, and History," p. 39). Borrowing Ricoeur's notion of the "inscription of action," Geertz claims that the ethnographer "'inscribes' social discourse" ("Thick Description," p. 19). I thank Orin Starn for pointing out that Geertz's emphasis on the public accessibility of symbols is also a reaction against the assumption of cognitive anthropology that anthropologists could "get inside" the informant's head.

160. Geertz, "Preface," in his *Available Light,* pp. xi–xii; a view attributed to Husserl as well as the late Wittgenstein in idem, "Thick Description," p. 12.

161. Geertz, "Art as a Cultural System," p. 119; idem, *After the Fact: Two Countries, Four Decades, One Anthropologist* (Cambridge, Mass., 1995), p. 127.

162. Inglis, *Clifford Geertz,* p. 127; for Geertz's appropriation of Wittgenstein, pp. 46–48.

163. Clifford Geertz, "Found in Translation: On the Social History of the Moral Imagination" [1977], in his *Local Knowledge,* p. 48. Thus theories are aligned with structuralist "metaphysics" (idem, "The Cerebral Savage," p. 347).

164. Geertz, "Art as a Cultural System," pp. 118–119.

165. Clifford Geertz, "Local Knowledge: Fact and Law in Comparative Perspectives," in his *Local Knowledge,* p. 167.

166. George E. Marcus, "Imagining the Whole: Ethnography's Contemporary Efforts to Situate Itself," *Critique of Anthropology* 9 (1989): 15 (the author rejects this allegation, at least for himself and James Clifford); see Marcus and Cushman, "Ethnographies as Texts," pp. 25, 29–33, 64.

167. See, *inter alia,* Roseberry, "Balinese Cockfights"; Dan Sperber, "L'Interpretation en anthropologie," *L'Homme* 21 (1981): 69–92; Vincent Crapanzano, "Hermes' Dilemma: The Masking of Subversion in Ethnographic Description," in *Writing Culture,* pp. 51–76; Edward W. Said, "Representing the Colonized: Anthropology's Interlocutors," *Critical Inquiry* 15 (1989): 205–225; Richard G. Fox, "Introduction: Working in the Present," in *Recapturing Anthropology,* ed. Fox (Santa Fe, 1991), chap. 1; Aletta Biersack, "Local Knowledge, Local History: Geertz and Beyond," in *The New Cultural History,* ed. Lynn Hunt (Berkeley, 1989), pp. 72–96; George E. Marcus and Michael M. J. Fischer, *Anthropology as Cultural Critique* (2d ed.; Chicago, 1999 [1986]), pp. 86, 114–115; Marshall Sahlins, "Goodbye to *Tristes Tropes:* Ethnography in the Context of Modern World History," *Journal of Modern World History* 65 (1993): 25; Michael Agar, "Text and Fieldwork: Exploring the Excluded Middle," *Journal of Contemporary Ethnography* 19 (1990): 73–88; Roger Keesing, "Anthropology as Interpretive Quest," *Current Anthropology* 28 (1987): 161–176.

168. Pierre Bourdieu, in "Dialogue à propos de l'histoire culturelle," *Actes de la recherche en sciences sociales* 59 (1985): 92.

169. Graham Watson, "Rewriting Culture," in *Recapturing Anthropology,* pp. 80–81.

170. James Clifford, "Introduction: Partial Truths," in *Writing Culture,* pp. 2, 4, 14. Clifford urges anthropologists to reflect on their activity of *writing* texts, not "reading" culture as a "text."

171. David Chioni Moore, "Anthropology Is Dead, Long Live Anthro(a)pology: Poststructuralism, Literary Studies, and Anthropology's 'Nervous Present,'" *Journal of Anthropological Research* 50 (1994): 345–365, references

at 347, 346, 348, 358, 354–355. Orin Starn reports that, in 2002, anthropologists seem less "nervous" than they were when Moore wrote his essay, and have perhaps adopted a form of "soft objectivism" (private conversation, April 29, 2002).

172. See, for example, Thompson, "History and Anthropology," p. 201.

173. The following features of anthropology she finds especially helpful for historians: "close observation of living processes of social interaction; interesting ways of interpreting symbolic behavior; suggestions about how the parts of a social system fit together; and material from cultures very different from those which historians are used to studying." The analysis of materials pertaining to religion, to "small-scale interactions," and to "mechanisms of exchange," she claims, are among the aspects of anthropological work that can most profit the writing of history (Natalie Zemon Davis, "Anthropology and History in the 1980s," *Journal of Interdisciplinary History* 12 [1981]: 267, 269–270).

174. Paul Rabinow, "Representations Are Social Facts: Modernity and Post-Modernity in Anthropology," in *Writing Culture,* pp. 241–242.

175. William H. Sewell Jr., *Work and Revolution in France: The Language of Labor from the Old Regime to 1848* (Cambridge, 1980), pp. 5–12, citation at 12.

176. See Chapter 4. Sewell nonetheless makes clear that he wishes to integrate the literary with social history approaches.

177. Geertz, "The Cerebral Savage," p. 355.

178. Clifford Geertz, "The State of the Art" (= "History and Anthropology" [1990]), in his *Available Light,* pp. 118–119. Geertz alludes, *inter alia,* to works by Natalie Zemon Davis, Gene Brucker, Robert Darnton, Giovanni Levi, Carlo Ginzburg, and by himself, an interesting self-identification with historians.

179. Geertz, "The State of the Art" (= "History and Anthropology"), p. 120.

180. Geertz, *A Life of Learning,* pp. 14, 120–121. Geertz attributes the saying to L. P. Hartley. For the dilemma of anthropology, a discipline with an allochronic discourse, yet within which fieldwork is carried out "coevally, on the basis of shared intersubjective Time and intersocial contemporaneity," see Johannes Fabian, *Time and the Other: How Anthropology Makes Its Object* (New York, 1983), pp. 31, 143, 148, 153–154.

181. Geertz, "The State of the Art" (= "History and Anthropology"), pp. 121, 128. As noted above, despite his claim, Geertz's critics thought that he fell short at this task. Elsewhere, he likewise aligns anthropology with history as disciplines in which Foucault's "author-function" remain (idem, "Being There," p. 7).

182. Walters, "Signs of the Times," pp. 541, 543, 553. Also see William H. Sewell Jr.'s defense of Geertz, which necessitates taking a nontraditional, more synchronic, approach to what counts as history ("Geertz, Cultural Systems, and History," pp. 37, 40–42, 46).

183. Lynn Hunt, "History beyond Social Theory," in *The States of "Theory,"* ed. David Carroll (New York, 1990), pp. 109, 100, 106. "Aestheticization" can serve conservative political ends; Hunt urges readers to take a lesson from Fredric Jameson, explicitly mentioning *The Political Unconscious.* She alleges that Geertz amalgamates contexts with "texts" (100–101, 108). Hunt notes that her own book on the French Revolution was critiqued for her shift from causal to textual modes of analysis (104).

184. Hunt, "History beyond Social Theory," pp. 97–99, 101, 105, 102.

185. Giovanni Levi, "On Microhistory," in Burke, *Perspectives,* pp. 275–276; the "hermeneutic circle" is here called "vicious" (276).

186. LaCapra, "Culture and Ideology," p. 133 (commenting on Geertz's essay, "Ideology as Cultural System").

187. Ibid., pp. 135, 152–153. On Geertz's work as involving a "redemptive" reading," see LaCapra, "History, Language, Reading," pp. 819–820.

188. LaCapra, "Culture and Ideology," p. 152.

189. Dominick LaCapra, "Chartier, Darnton, and the Great Symbol Massacre" [1988], in his *Soundings,* p. 73.

190. Roger Chartier, "History between Narrative and Knowledge" [1994], in his *Edge,* p. 20. Chartier here appears to agree with Pierre Bourdieu, who criticized ethnologists for describing rituals as if they were writings, a fault he blames on structuralism; see Pierre Bourdieu and Chartier, "La Lecture: une pratique culturelle. Débat entre Pierre Bourdieu et Roger Chartier," in *Pratiques de la lecture,* ed. Chartier (Paris, 1993 [1985]), pp. 268–269. By "discourse," Chartier (unlike Foucault) means "language." Chartier appears here to reject the post-structuralist critique of "experience" such as offered by Joan W. Scott, "The Evidence of Experience," *Critical Inquiry* 17 (1991): 773–797.

191. Roger Chartier, "The World as Representation" [1989], in Revel and Hunt, *Histories,* p. 550.

192. Chartier, "History between Narrative and Knowledge," p. 21.

193. Robert Darnton, "Workers Revolt: The Great Cat Massacre of the Rue Saint-Séverin," in his *The Great Cat Massacre and Other Episodes in French Cultural History* (New York, 1984), pp. 75–104, 270–272.

194. I here omit critiques by historians such as Harold Mah, who focuses on Darnton's neglect of the political dimensions of the tale, which the latter represents as a "story of liberation" rather than that of a failed revolt from which the workers learned "obedience" ("Suppressing the Text: The Metaphysics of Ethnographic History in Darnton's Great Cat Massacre," *History Workshop* 31 [1991]: 2–3, 11, 15–16). For Mah as for other critics, Geertz's ethnography lends an apolitical tone to history-writing produced under its influence.

195. Giovanni Levi, "I pericoli del geertzismo," *Quaderni Storici* 58 (1985): 269–77, especially 275–276; 270, 273 for critique of "hermeneutic" assumptions. Levi notes that although Geertz borrows some theoretical props

from Paul Ricoeur (for example, the "inscription" of action as discourse), for Ricoeur, discourse always emerges from a situation of speech between persons present to each other (272–273). How, Levi asks, do Geertz and Darnton connect "texts" and the world (272)?

196. Roger Chartier, "Text, Symbols, Frenchness," *Journal of Modern History* 57 (1985): 682–695, reviewing Darnton's *The Great Cat Massacre.* Chartier's essay is reprinted in his collection, *Cultural History: Between Practices and Representations* (trans., Ithaca, 1988), pp. 95–111. For Darnton's response, see Robert Darnton, "The Symbolic Element in History," *Journal of Modern History* 58 (1986): 218–234.

197. Chartier, "Texts, Symbols, Frenchness," p. 683 (citing Darnton, *The Great Cat Massacre,* p. 258).

198. Ibid., pp. 683–684, citing Geertz, "Religion as a Cultural System," p. 89: culture as "an historically transmitted pattern of meanings embodied in symbols, a system of inherited conceptions expressed in symbolic form by means of which men communicate, perpetuate and develop their knowledge about and attitudes towards life."

199. Chartier, "Texts, Symbols, Frenchness," pp. 684, 688–690.

200. Ibid., pp. 684, 685, 687, 690, 694. Chartier suggests the "genre" to which the "Cat Massacre" text belongs: "the time-honored tradition of texts that purport to reveal to the public the secrets and the practices, true or supposed, of particular professional, ethnic, or religious communities" (691). In "historicizing" the document, Chartier provides a "thicker" description than Darnton himself does. Chartier doubts that it is "legitimate to consider as 'texts' actions carried out or tales told" (685).

201. Ibid., pp. 685, 690, 692.

202. Ibid., p. 694. This critique is not well registered by James Fernandez, "Historians Tell Tales: Of Cartesian Cats and Gallic Cockfights," *Journal of Modern History* 60 (1988): 115–117, 123.

203. Darnton, "The Symbolic Element in History," pp. 218–234.

204. Ibid., p. 219, citing Michael Herzfeld, "An Indigenous Theory of Meaning and Its Elicitation in Performative Context," *Semiotica* 34 (1981): 130.

205. Darnton, "The Symbolic Element in History" pp. 230, 234, 227–230, 228. Thus the journeymen "staged a virtuous performance: polysemic symbolism compounded by polymorphic ritualism."

206. Ibid., pp. 218, 222, 232, 234.

8. History, Theory, and Premodern Texts

1. The study of early Christian authors' varying appeals to "continuity" and "discontinuity" of the tradition shows how ideologically fraught they are.

2. For example, the numerous studies by Georges Dumézil on Indo-European, Roman, and Etruscan religion, and by Jean-Pierre Vernant on Greek myth, tragedy, and religion. If Michel Foucault is correct in his observation that,

for French intellectuals, structuralism provided an escape from Marxism (and earlier, from phenomenology), the absence of Marxist affiliation among patristic scholars may provide one clue to the bypassing of structuralism ("Structuralism and Post-Structuralism," trans. in *Telos* 16 ([1983]: 196, 198). For Lévi-Strauss's tribute to Dumézil, see his "Réponse" to Dumézil's speech upon the latter's election to the Académie française in *Discours de reception de M. Georges Dumézil à l'Académie française* (Paris, 1979), pp. 45–76. Foucault preferred Dumézil's treatment of myth to Lévi-Strauss's ("Ronde table: La Vérité et les formes juridiques" [1974], in idem, *Dits,* II: 635–636). It was a Francophone scholar (Daniel Patte) who helped to introduce stucturalist exegesis to Anglophone biblical scholars (see his *What Is Structural Exegesis?* [Philadelphia, 1976]).

3. See Louis O. Mink, "Philosophy and Theory of History," in *International Handbook of Historical Studies,* ed. Georg G. Iggers and Harold T. Parker (Westport, Conn., 1979), pp. 18–19.

4. Averil Cameron, "Eusebius' *Vita Constantini* and the Construction of Constantine," in *Portraits: Biographical Representations in the Greek and Latin Literature of the Roman Empire,* ed. M. J. Edwards and Simon Swain (Oxford, 1997), p. 145.

5. R. A. Markus, "Evolving Disciplinary Contexts for the Study of Augustine, 1950–2000: Some Personal Reflections," *Augustinian Studies* 32 (2001): 189–190. All in the field are deeply grateful that Markus did not abandon his investigations of other late ancient texts upon his novice-master's advice.

6. Peter Brown, "The World of Late Antiquity Revisited," *Symbolae Osloenses* 72 (1997): 10, 21.

7. See, for example, Jacques Derrida, "Circumfession," in Geoffrey Bennington and Derrida, *Jacques Derrida* (trans., Chicago, 1993 [1991]), pp. 3–315; Fredric Jameson, "On the Sexual Production of Western Subjectivity; or, Saint Augustine as a Social Democrat," in *Gaze and Voice as Love Objects,* ed. Renata Salecl and Slavoj Žižek (Durham, 1996), pp. 154–178; Jean-François Lyotard, *The Confession of Augustine* (trans., Stanford, 2000 [1998]).

8. Russell Jacoby, "A New Intellectual History?" *American Historical Review* 97(1992): 419, 424.

9. A critique of Joan Scott's *Gender and the Politics of History* (New York, 1988) by historian Claudia Koonz, "Post Scripts," *Women's Review of Books* 6 (1989): 19. See also Scott's *Only Paradoxes to Offer: French Feminists and the Rights of Man* (Cambridge, Mass., 1996).

10. Cushing Strout, "Border Crossings: History, Fiction, and *Dead Certainties,*" *History and Fiction* 31 (1992): 156–158.

11. See Dominick LaCapra, "AHR Forum: Intellectual History and Its Ways," *American Historical Review* 97 (1992): 430–431.

12. Geoff Eley, "Is All the World a Text? From Social History to the History of Society Two Decades Later," in McDonald, *Turn,* p. 208.

13. Gabrielle M. Spiegel, "History, Historicism, and the Social Logic of the Text in the Middle Ages," *Speculum* 65 (1990): 59–86, now excerpted in her *The Past as Text: The Theory and Practice of Medieval Historiography* (Baltimore, 1997), pp. 3–28. I cite the original.

14. Spiegel, "History, Historicism," pp. 59, 68, 60, 77. Spiegel deems New Historicists especially guilty of this "absorption" (77).

15. Ibid., pp. 77, 64, 68–71, 74–75, 85, 84 (citing Carroll Smith-Rosenberg, "The Body Politic," in *Coming to Terms: Feminism/Theory/Politics,* ed. Elizabeth Weed [New York, 1989]).

16. Gabrielle Spiegel, "History and Post-Modernism," *Past & Present* 135 (1992): 208.

17. Spiegel, "History, Historicism," pp. 77–78 (on the "social environment of the text"), 62.

18. Ibid., pp. 72, 82, 83.

19. Isabel V. Hull also notes how "mid-level theory" often proves most helpful for the historian ("Feminist and Gender History through the Literary Looking Glass: German Historiography in Postmodern Times," *Central European History* 22 [1989]: 286).

20. See Spiegel, "History, Historicism," p. 64; for a different view on text/context, see Dominick LaCapra, "Rethinking Intellectual History and Reading Texts," in LaCapra and Kaplan, *Intellectual History,* pp. 53–57. Joan Scott, "A Statistical Representation of Work: *La Statistique de l'industrie à Paris, 1847–1848*" [1986], in her *Gender and the Politics of History,* pp. 113–138, argues against separating statistical reports from other kinds of historical texts; imagining that "numbers are purer" "denies the inherently political aspects of representation" (114–115).

21. Spiegel, "History, Historicism," p. 78–83. Spiegel discusses the Anonymous of Bethune's *Historie des ducs de Normandie et des rois d'Angleterre* and the vernacular *Pseudo-Turpin Chronicle.* The allusion is to Fredric Jameson, *The Political Unconscious.*

22. Spiegel, "History, Historicism," pp. 68–71.

23. See, for example, the critiques by Patrick Joyce and Catriona Kelly, "History and Post-Modernism," *Past & Present* 133 (1991): 206–207, 208, 210–212.

24. Alun Munslow, *Deconstructing History* (London, 1997), pp. 90–91.

25. Gabrielle Spiegel, "Orations of the Dead/Silences of the Living: The Sociology of the Linguistic Turn," in her *The Past as Text,* pp. 29–43, especially p. 43.

26. Gabrielle Spiegel, "Introduction," in her *The Past as Text,* pp. xvii, xix; idem, "Towards a Theory of the Middle Ground" [1995], in ibid., p. 52.

27. Spiegel, "Introduction," p. xxi.

28. Spiegel, "Towards a Theory of the Middle Ground," p. 51.

29. Spiegel, "History, Historicism," pp. 64–66.

30. See discussion of LaCapra in Chapters 6 and 7.

31. Spiegel, "History, Historicism," p. 76.

32. Spiegel, "Orations of the Dead," pp. 43, 34.

33. Spiegel, "Towards a Theory of the Middle Ground," p. 56.

34. See, among others, G. W. Bowersock, *Fiction as History* (Berkeley, 1994), p. 12; T. J. Luce, *The Greek Historians* (London, 1997), p. 4; various essays in *History as Text: The Writing of Ancient History,* ed. Averil Cameron (Chapel Hill, 1989); and especially Woodman, *Rhetoric.*

35. M. I. Finley, *The Use and Abuse of History* (New York, 1975), pp. 71–72, citing E. R. Dodds, *The Greeks and the Irrational* (Berkeley, 1964 [1951]), pp. viii–ix; compare Jacques Le Goff: "Greco-Roman antiquity did not have a genuine sense of history" (*History and Memory* [trans., New York, 1992 (1977)], p. 159). E. H. Carr comments that historians of antiquity can enjoy the illusion of having all (but still a manageable number of) facts at their disposal only because there *are* so few. Historians of modernity, Carr alleged, would be deemed shockingly incompetent if they knew as little about their subjects as do historians of antiquity (Edward Hallett Carr, *What Is History?* [New York, 1962], pp. 11–13).

36. Finley, *Use and Abuse,* pp. 72, 74. See Arnaldo Momigliano's comments on the early modern teaching of history: ancient history was taught as a commentary on the ancient historians; since Livy, Tacitus, Suetonius, and others had already written Roman history, "[t]here was no reason why it should be written again" ("Ancient History and the Antiquarian" [1950], in his *Studies in Historiography,* pp. 6–7).

37. M. I. Finley, "'Progress' in Historiography," and "Epilogue," both in his *Ancient History* (London, 1985), pp. 6, 104, 105; Finley (6) mocks Fergus Millar's claim that he had not contaminated his evidence "with conceptions drawn from wider sociological studies" (Millar, *The Emperor in the Roman World* [Ithaca, 1977], pp. xii–xiii).

38. See Marc Bloch: most saints' *Vitae* "can teach us nothing concrete about those pious personages whose careers they pretend to describe." Rather, we can find in them things "the writer had not the least intention of revealing," for example, "the way of life or thought peculiar to the epoch in which they were written" (*Craft,* p. 63).

39. A. J. Woodman, "From Hannibal to Hitler: The Literature of War," *University of Leeds Review* 26 (1983): 111; Finley, *Use and Abuse,* p. 31.

40. Collingwood, *Idea,* p. 27; discussed in Finley, *Use and Abuse,* p. 31.

41. For example, contemporary historians would insist on meticulous handling of sources and the accurate rendition of quotations—concerns not particularly important for ancient historians.

42. Woodman, "From Hannibal to Hitler," p. 120. In *Rhetoric,* Woodman argues against K. J. Dover's view that ancients and moderns share the same view of historiography (202). See also Momigliano's *Studies in Historiography,* chaps. 1 and 11, for a charting of some historiographical "breaks."

43. Luce, *Greek Historians,* p. 4.

44. T. P. Wiseman, "Lying Historians: Seven Types of Mendacity," in *Lies and Fiction in the Ancient World*, ed. Christopher Gill and T. P. Wiseman (Austin, 1993), pp. 125–126, citing Ronald Syme, *Roman Papers*, ed. E. Badian (Oxford, 1979–), IV: 19, and VI: 164, that "to become intelligible, history has to aspire to the coherence of fiction, while eschewing most of its methods."

45. Bowersock, *Fiction as History*, p. 12.

46. Charles William Fornara, *The Nature of History in Ancient Greece and Rome* (Berkeley, 1983), pp. 116, 152, 164–165.

47. Averil Cameron, "History as Text: Coping with Procopius," in *The Inheritance of Historiography 350–900*, ed. Christopher Holdworth and T. P. Wiseman (Exeter, 1986), pp. 53–54. Cameron here comments on Procopius's *Secret History*.

48. See T. J. Luce, "Ancient Views on the Causes of Bias in Historical Writing," *Classical Philology* 84 (1989): 16–20; T. P. Wiseman, "Practice and Theory in Roman Historiography," *History: The Journal of the Historical Association* 66 (1981): 387–388; Woodman, *Rhetoric*, pp. 73–74.

49. Sallust, *Bellum Catalinae* 4.2–3; Tactitus, *Historiae* 1.1, *Annales* 1.1. On Cicero's similar view, see Woodman, *Rhetoric*, chap. 2, especially pp. 73, 82. Arnaldo Momigliano notes that the *sine ira et studio* phrase was a convention of Greco-Roman historiography: "Tacitus and the Tacitist Tradition," in his *The Classical Foundations of Modern Historiography* (Berkeley, 1990), p. 113.

50. Finley, *Use and Abuse*, p. 12. Lucian's work is dated to *ca.* 165 C.E.

51. Lucian of Samosata, *De historia conscribenda* 38–40 (text and translation in M. D. Macleod, *Lucian: A Selection* [Warminster, 1991], pp. 232–234).

52. Eusebius is sometimes heralded as the first to develop this important innovation: see Finley, *Use and Abuse*, p. 83. Arnaldo Momigliano credits Persia's example for the use of documents; Jews (who had lived under Persian dominance) used historiographic documentation more readily than did the Greeks. Of the eleven documents that Thucydides quotes verbatim, five concern Persia ("Persian Historiography, Greek Historiography, and Jewish Historiography," in his *Classical Foundations*, pp. 13, 16).

53. For modern commentators' tendency to read ancient "rhetorical procedure" as "'scientific' historiography," see Woodman, *Rhetoric*, p. 23.

54. Finley concludes that both substance and wording of most of the speeches reported in ancient histories were fabricated—and gently tweaks his colleagues who posit that at least the ancient writers' "attitudes" were truthful ("The Ancient Historian and His Sources" [1983], in his *Ancient History*, p. 13); contrast Charles Fornara's claim that since ancient writers "unfailingly endorsed the convention that speeches must be reported accurately," they indeed did so (*Nature of History*, pp. 142, 168).

55. Luce, *Greek Historians*, p. 3. "Plausibility" thus stands as the major criterion of judgment for ancient historiography (Woodman, *Rhetoric*,

p. 93). Cicero recommended "the devising of matter true *or lifelike* which will make a case appear convincing" (Cicero, *De inventione*, 1.7.9, my emphasis).

56. Wiseman, "Practice and Theory," p. 389. Woodman compares the practice of *inventio* to the technique of modern newsreel-making, in which "real" shots are spliced in to give a sense of events as taking place (*Rhetoric*, p. 211).

57. See Finley's put-down of this view in "'How It Really Was'" [1984], in his *Ancient History*, p. 48, challenging the oft-cited opinion that von Ranke produced "scientific" history.

58. Woodman, *Rhetoric*, p. 17. Arnaldo Momigliano concludes that the debate over the veracity of Thucydides's speeches "must lie somewhere between the two opposed interpretations" (Momigliano, "The Herodotean and the Thucydidean Tradition," in his *Classical Foundations*, p. 42), adding that only Josephus mentions that some doubted Thucydides' reliability (45, no reference given).

59. Woodman, *Rhetoric*, p. 13. Woodman stresses the Sophists' influence on Thucydides, p. 14. For the Latin side, Woodman discusses such cases of *inventio* as Tacitus's account of the German campaigns of 15 C.E. (178–179).

60. Woodman, *Rhetoric*, p. 4. A much-cited study is Detlev Fehling, *Herodotus and His "Sources": Citation, Invention and Narrative Art* (trans., Leeds, 1989 [1971]). For Henri-Irénée Marrou, "Herodotus . . . now seems less like the 'Father of History' than an elderly grandfather lapsing into second childhood" (*Meaning*, p. 30).

61. Arnaldo Momigliano, "The Place of Herodotus in the History of Historiography," in his *Studies in Historiography*, p. 135.

62. Fornara, *Nature of History*, p. 163.

63. Finley, *Use and Abuse*, p. 26.

64. Finley, "The Ancient Historian and His Sources," p. 9.

65. Finley, "Epilogue," in his *Ancient History*, p. 104; idem, *Use and Abuse*, pp. 23–28: Finley here discusses "interest," rather than "ideology."

66. See my comments on Eusebius in "Rewriting the History of Early Christianity," in *The World of Late Antiquity: The Challenge of the New Historiographies*, ed. Richard Lim and Carole Straw (Turnhout, 2004), with numerous references.

67. Averil Cameron, *Christianity and the Rhetoric of Empire: The Development of Christian Discourse* (Berkeley, 1991), pp. 138–141, 143, 147.

68. Roger Chartier, "Introduction," in his *Cultural History: Between Practices and Representations* (trans., Ithaca, 1988), pp. 13–14; idem, "Intellectual History and the History of *Mentalités*" [1980], in ibid., p. 34.

69. Postcolonial theory informs Andrew Jacobs, *Remains of the Jews: The Holy Land and Christian Empire in Late Antiquity* (Stanford, 2003); Virginia Burrus's discussion of Sulpicius Severus's writings pertaining to Martin of

Tours, in Burrus, *The Sex Lives of the Saints* (Philadelphia, 2003); and my own "On Not Retracting the Unconfessed," in *Confessions,* ed. John D. Caputo and Michael Scanlon (Bloomington, 2004).

70. English translations of these writings can be found in *New Testament Apocrypha. Volume 2,* ed. Edgar Hennecke and Wilhelm Schneemelcher (trans., Philadelphia, 1965).

71. This is particularly the case with some Pelagian writings; see Georges de Plinval, *Pélage* (Lausanne, 1943), pp. 26–31.

72. For an overview of the debates, see Frederik Wisse, "Gnosticism and Early Monasticism in Egypt," in *Gnosis,* ed. Barbara Aland (Göttingen, 1978), pp. 431–440. Also see Michael A. Williams, *Rethinking "Gnosticism"* (Princeton, 1996).

73. My book, *Reading Renunciation: Asceticism and Scripture in Early Christianity* (Princeton, 1999), provides numerous illustrations of the problems that the contradictions and gaps in the *biblical* accounts gave to early Christian writers.

74. Cameron, *Christianity and the Rhetoric of Empire,* pp. 58, 181, 68. Also see Janice Martin Soskice, *Metaphor and Religious Language* (Oxford, 1985); Northrop Frye, *The Great Code: The Bible and Literature* (San Diego, 1982 [1981]), pp. 54–55.

75. Although traditional commentators such as T. Herbert Bindley blame Origen and his followers for introducing "the biological ideas current in Gnosticism" into Christian doctrine by their use of the word "begotten," it appears to have biblical precedent (see Bindley's discussion of phrases from the Creed of Nicaea in *The Oecumenical Documents of the Faith,* ed. Bindley, revised F. W. Green [4th ed.; London, 1950], p. 22).

76. For a contrast between the sexual exploits of the Greek gods and the Christian God, who is said to be above "lust, passion, and procreation," see, for example, Athenagoras, *Legatio* 21 (trans., *Athenagoras' Plea,* in the *Library of Early Christian Classics. Volume I: Early Christian Fathers* [Philadelphia, 1953], pp. 300–340).

77. See Athanasius, *De decretis* (trans., *Defence of the Nicene Definition,* in *A Select Library of the Nicene and Post-Nicene Fathers of the Christian Church* [Grand Rapids, n.d.)], pp. 150–172). Also see Eusebius's explanation of the Creed of Nicaea: "consubstantial" should not be understood on the analogy of parents and children, or of mortal creatures; the Son's generation by the Father is "inconceivable" (cited in Socrates, *Historia ecclesiastica* 1.8).

78. Virginia Burrus, *"Begotten, Not Made": Conceiving Manhood in Late Antiquity* (Stanford, 2000), pp. 7, 14, 57, 185, 190, 193.

79. Cameron, *Christianity and the Rhetoric of Empire,* pp. 155, 179, 172.

80. John Chrysostom, for example, promises the consecrated virgins that they will have Jesus the Bridegroom as a "lover more ardent than any man" (*Quod regulares feminae viris cohabitare non debeant* 12; trans., "On the

Necessity of Guarding Virginity," in Elizabeth A. Clark, *Jerome, Chrysostom, and Friends* [New York, 1979], pp. 209–248).

81. Greek text in SC 95; trans. by Herbert Musurillo (Methodius, *The Symposium: A Treatise on Chastity* [Westminster, Md., 1958]). See discussion in L. G. Patterson, *Methodius of Olympus* (Washington, D.C., 1997), chap. 1.

82. Methodius, *Symposium* 7.3, 8.13 (SC 95, 186, 234).

83. Ibid., 4.5, 6.2, 6.5, 7.3, 10.6 (SC 95, 138, 140, 166, 168, 176, 186, 302), and Thecla's hymnic refrain at the end of the treatise (SC 95, 310–320).

84. Plato, *Symposium,* from 206c1, passim, through 212a5; see discussion in David M. Halperin, "Why Is Diotima a Woman?" in his *One Hundred Years of Homosexuality and Other Essays on Greek Love* (New York, 1990), pp. 113–151; Methodius, *Symposium* 4.5 (SC 95, 136, 138).

85. Methodius, *Symposium,* Thecla's hymn (SC 95, 312, 314).

86. See, for example, Augustine, *De bono viduitatis* 6.8; John Chrysostom, *Hom. 23 II Cor.* 1; *Hom. 28 Hebr.* 16; *Hom. 2 In Eutropium* 14; *Hom. 24 Rom.*

87. For example, Jerome, *Ep.* 66.10; John Chrysostom, *Ad Theodorum lapsum* 13.4; Gregory of Nyssa, *De virginitate* 20; Origen, *Hom. 6 Iesus Nave* 4; John Chrysostom, *Hom. 23 II Cor.*

88. For a summary of issues, see Elizabeth A. Clark, "John Chrysostom and the Subintroductae," *Church History* 46 (1977): 171–185.

89. For fuller elaboration of this example with reference to metaphor theory, see Elizabeth A. Clark, "The Celibate Bridegroom: The Ambiguous Marriage of Jesus in Early Christian Ascetic Exegesis," forthcoming.

90. For the theme of metaphors that "hover over," see discussion in Georges Canguilhem, *La Connaissance de la vie* (2d ed.; Paris, 1969), p. 48.

91. Georges Bataille, *Erotism: Death and Sensuality* (trans., San Francisco, 1986 [1957]), p. 90.

92. See Averil Cameron on panegyric: "History as Text," pp. 53–54.

93. See Clark, *Reading Renunciation,* pp. 50–56; Cameron, *Christianity and the Rhetoric of Empire,* pp. 85, 179.

94. A special talent of Jerome: see his attacks on the styles of Jovinian (*Adversus Iovinianum* 1.31), of Rufinus (*Apologia contra Rufinum* 1.17, 3.6), and of Tertullian (*Ep.* 58.10).

95. Texts: Clement's *Quis dives salvetur?* in GCS 17; *De divitiis* in PLS 1. Clement explicates the parable of the rich young man (Matt. 19:16–30 = Mark 10:17–31 = Lk.18:18–30). For a helpful discussion of what now counts as "Pelagian," see Michael Rackett's Duke University dissertation (2002), "Sexuality and Sinlessness: The Diversity among Pelagian Theologies of Marriage and Virginity."

96. See L. William Countryman, *The Rich Christian in the Church of the Early Empire* (New York, 1980).

97. Methodius, *Symposium* 1.2–4; Lactantius, *Divinae Institutiones* 5.6.

98. See Michèle Barrett, *The Politics of Truth* (Stanford, 1991), pp. 1–17;

Jorge Larrain, *Marxism and Ideology* (Atlantic Highlands, 1983); Bhikhu Parekh, *Marx's Theory of Ideology* (Baltimore, 1982), pp. 33, 48. As Larrain notes (*Marxism*, p. 54), the first two generations of Marxist thinkers lacked access to Marx's *The German Ideology*, published only in 1923.

99. Anthony Giddens, "Four Theses on Ideology," *Canadian Journal of Political and Social Theory/Revue canadienne de théorie politique et sociale* 7 (1983): 19.

100. John B. Thompson, *Ideology and Modern Culture* (Stanford, 1990), p. 7.

101. Sometimes thought problematic in the early Althusser of *For Marx;* see Giddens, "Four Theses," p. 19; John Frow, *Marxism and Literary History* (Cambridge, Mass., 1986), pp. 26–29, 51; Bruce Robbins, "The Politics of Theory," *Social Text* 18 (1987/88): 15; compare Terry Eagleton, *Ideology* (London, 1991), p. 139. For critique, see Nancy C. M. Hartsock, "Louis Althusser's Structural Marxism," *Rethinking Marxism* 4 (1991): 10–40.

102. Jameson, *The Political Unconscious*, pp. 52–53.

103. Barrett, *Politics*, pp. 32–33, 158–159.

104. See Louis Althusser, "Ideology and Ideological State Apparatuses" [1970], in idem, *Lenin and Philosophy* (trans., New York, 1971), especially pp. 141–157. Indeed, Althusser so privileges the realm of superstructure that he can write: "in History, these instances, the superstructures, etc.—are never seen to step respectfully aside when their work is done or, when the Time comes, as his pure phenomena, to scatter before His Majesty the Economy as he strides along the royal road of the Dialectic. From the first moment to the last, the lonely hour of the 'last instance' never comes" ("Contradiction and Overdetermination" [1962], in his *For Marx* [trans., London, 1990 (1965)], p. 113).

105. Althusser abandoned the rigid claim that the material "base" entirely determines the cultural "superstructure," allowing that religious, legal (etc.) systems also work on the economic; see his "Ideology," pp. 134–136, 141–148.

106. Frow, *Marxism*, 76; Rosalind Coward and John Ellis, *Language and Materialism* (London, 1977), pp. 7, 68.

107. Louis Althusser, "On the Marxist Dialectic" [1963], in his *For Marx*, pp. 200–201, 210, 212; idem, "Est-il simple d'être Marxiste en philosophie?" *La Pensée* 183 (1975): 17.

108. Coward and Ellis, *Language and Materialism*, p. 2 (their discussion owes much to Lacan; see especially p. 7 and chap. 6); Althusser, "Ideology," p. 171.

109. Roland Barthes, *The Pleasure of the Text* (trans., New York, 1975), p. 40, and discussion in Coward and Ellis, *Language and Materialism*, p. 54; on "symbolic construction," see Thompson, *Ideology*, p. 60.

110. For "historical sedimentation," see Gayatri Spivak, "The Politics of Interpretation" [1982], in *The Politics of Interpretation*, ed. W. J. T. Mitchell (Chicago, 1983), p. 347. See Eagleton, *Ideology*, p. 59; for his list of ideol-

ogy's functions *("unifying, action-oriented, rationalizing, legitimating, universalizing* and *naturalizing")*, see p. 45.

111. John B. Thompson, *Studies in the Theory of Ideology* (Berkeley, 1984), p. 131, citing C. Lefort; also see Parekh, *Marx's Theory*, pp. 36, 49, 136. For a discussion of the "naturalizing" aspect of ideology as "the pre-constructed" ("what everyone knows"), see Michel Pêcheux, *Language, Semantics and Ideology* (trans., New York, 1982 [1975]), pp. 115–116, 121.

112. Karl Marx, *The German Ideology* 2.1B; compare 1.1.1.4; 1.1.22 in Marx and Frederick Engels, *Collected Works* (New York, 1976), V: 479, 36, 39.

113. Thompson, *Ideology*, p. 41; idem, *Studies in the Theory of Ideology*, p. 186. Also relevant is Karl Mannheim's comment: "It is no accident that whereas all progressive groups regard the idea as coming before the deed, for the conservative . . . the idea of an historical reality becomes visible only subsequently, when the world has already assumed a fixed form" (*Ideology and Utopia* [trans., New York, 1946 (1929)], p. 208).

114. Thompson, *Ideology*, pp. 61–62; idem, *Studies in the Theory of Ideology*, p. 11. Contemporary theologians, philosophers and feminists often *view* narrative more positively, stressing its role in creating "community": from the standpoint of ideology critique, that "community" is precisely founded on exclusion.

115. According to Hayden White, narrative carries with it a moralizing message ("The Value of Narrativity in the Representation of Reality," in his *Content*, pp. 14, 21–22). For disagreements and nuances, see Jameson, *Political Unconscious*, pp. 19, 283n.2; Steven Best and Douglas Kellner, *Postmodern Theory* (New York, 1991), p. 186; Nancy Fraser and Linda J. Nicholson, "Social Criticism without Philosophy: An Encounter between Feminism and Postmodernism," in *Feminism/Postmodernism*, ed. Nicholson (New York, 1990), pp. 34, 22 on Lyotard's critique of meta-narratives.

116. Michael J. Shapiro, *The Politics of Representation* (Madison, 1988), pp. 21, 51. Here, Althusser's claim that Marx was the founder of the "science" of history is striking; see his essay, "Philosophy as a Revolutionary Weapon" [1968], in his *Lenin*, p. 15.

117. Louis Althusser, "From *Capital* to Marx's Philosophy," in his *Capital*, p. 28. See also Shapiro, *Politics of Representation*, p. 22; Frow, *Marxism*, pp. 24–25.

118. Pierre Macherey, *A Theory of Literary Production* (trans., London, 1978 [1966]), pp. 155, 296.

119. Thompson, *Ideology*, p. 85.

120. Elizabeth A. Clark, "The Lady Vanishes: Dilemmas of a Feminist Historian after the Linguistic Turn," *Church History* 67 (1998): 1–31; idem, "Ideology, History, and the Construction of 'Woman' in Late Ancient Christianity," *Journal of Early Christian Studies* 2 (1994): 155–184.

121. Jerome, *Hom. 42 on Ps. 127/128* (CCL 78, 265); *Comm. Nahum.* (on Nahum 3.13–17) (CCL 76A, 569); *Comm. Is.* 2 (on Is. 3.16) (CCL 73, 55);

Ep. 130.17 (CSEL 56, 197–198): here used to explain why ascetic women should live in community.

122. Jerome, *Ep.* 54.13 (CSEL 54, 479).

123. Jerome, *Ep.* 50.1, 50.5 (CSEL 54, 388–89, 393–94).

124. Jerome, *Ep.* 66.13 (CSEL 54, 664).

125. John Chrysostom, *Laus Maximi* 2 (PG 51, 227); *De virginitate* 40.1 (SC 125, 232).

126. Hence the frequent claim that they ceased to be "women": see Elizabeth A. Clark, "Friendship between the Sexes: Classical Theory and Christian Practice," in her *Jerome, Chrysostom, and Friends,* pp. 54–57.

127. For patristic writers' use of the word "nature," see my essay, "Ideology, History, and the Construction of 'Woman,'" pp. 167–168. For the use of the word "nature" in roughly contemporary secular literature, see John J. Winkler, *The Constraints of Desire: The Anthropology of Sex and Gender in Ancient Greece* (New York, 1990), especially pp. 17–22, 38–44, 217–220.

128. For example, John Chrysostom, *Hom. 10 Col.* 1 (PG 62, 365–366); *Hom. 26 1 Cor.* 4 (PG 61, 218).

129. For example, John Chrysostom, *Serm. 5 Gen.* 1; 3 (PG 54, 599, 602); *Hom. 26 1 Cor.* 2 (PG 61, 215); *Hom. 9 1 Tim.* 1 (PG 62, 544).

130. See Elizabeth A. Clark, "Devil's Gateway and Bride of Christ: Women in the Early Christian World," in her *Ascetic Piety and Women's Faith* (Lewiston, 1986), pp. 31–32; for patristic texts on the subject, see Roger Gryson, *The Ministry of Women in the Early Church* (trans., Collegeville, 1976). Also see Karen Jo Torjesen, *When Women Were Priests: Women's Leadership in the Early Church and the Scandal of their Subordination in the Rise of Christianity* (San Francisco, 1993).

131. Tertullian, *De cultu feminarum* 1.1.2 (CCL 1, 343).

132. I borrow the word from Brian Stock (*Listening for the Text: On the Uses of the Past* [Berkeley, 1990], p. 164): "traditionalistic" ("the self-conscious affirmation of traditional norms" selected from the past "to serve present needs"), is contrasted with "traditional action," defined as "the habitual pursuit of inherited norms of conduct, which are taken to be society's norm." For examples, see my "Ideology, History, and the Construction of 'Woman,'" pp. 170–172.

133. Jerome, *Ep.* 107.10 (CSEL 55, 3). In *Ep.* 121.6 (CSEL 56, 22), Jerome praises Xenophon's *Oeconomicus,* which contains traditional household regulations. For Augustine, see *Ep.* 262 to Ecdicia (CSEL 57, 621–631). For Monica's wifely submission, see Augustine, *Confessiones* 9.9.19–22 (CCL 27, 145–147). Hearkening back to the "good old days" is characteristic of (pagan) Latin moralists and satire writers: see Judith Evans-Grubbs, *Law and Family in Late Antiquity: The Emperor Constantine's Marriage Legislation* (Oxford, 1995), chap. 2.

134. For works detailing the changes in Roman law pertaining to women by

late antiquity, see Clark, "Ideology," pp. 171–172n.86. For "consent" to marriage, see idem, "'Adam's Only Companion': Augustine and the Early Christian Debate on Marriage," *Recherches Augustiniennes* 21 (1986), especially 158–161, with numerous references.

135. On the Fathers' lack of success in influencing imperial law on such points, see the list of works in Clark, "Ideology," p. 172n.87. Such ideologies were largely established through textual interpretation (chiefly, but not exclusively, of the Bible) and by the appropriation and deployment of literary forms and rhetorical devices borrowed from earlier, often non-Christian, authors; see my book, *Reading Renunciation*.

136. For fuller elaboration of these texts, see Clark, "The Lady Vanishes"; idem, "Rewriting Early Christian History: Augustine's Representation of Monica," in *Portraits of Spiritual Authority*, ed. Jan Willem Drijvers and John W. Watt (Leiden, 1999), pp. 3–23.

137. Gregory of Nyssa, *Vita Macrinae* 18 (SC 178, 200); composed *ca.* 380 C.E. (pp. 57 ff.).

138. Ibid., 3 (SC 178, 148, 150); see Anthony Meredith, "A Comparison between the Vita S. Macrinae of Gregory of Nyssa, the Vita Plotini of Porphyry and the De Vita Pythagorica of Iamblichus," in *The Biographical Works of Gregory of Nyssa,* ed. Andreas Spira (Cambridge, Mass., 1984), pp. 191–192.

139. Gregory of Nyssa, *Vita Macrinae* 17 (SC 178, 198).

140. Gregory of Nyssa, *De anima et resurrectione* (PG 46, 24, 28, 76–79, 93, 96–97, 53, 32–33, 36–37).

141. Gregory records her tale so that it will not remain "useless" *(anôphelês)* for the chastisement and instruction of other Christians: *Vita Macrinae* 1 (SC 178, 140, 142).

142. Peter Brown, *The Body and Society: Men, Women, and Sexual Renunciation in Early Christianity* (New York, 1988), p. 153, borrowing a phrase from Claude Lévi-Strauss.

143. On the fate of Origenism in the later fourth and early fifth centuries, see Elizabeth A. Clark, *The Origenist Controversy: The Cultural Construction of an Early Christian Debate* (Princeton, 1992).

144. Lawrence R. Hennessey notes that Gregory had "tamed" his Origenism before he wrote De opificio hominis and De anima et resurrectione ("Gregory of Nyssa's Doctrine of the Resurrected Body," *Studia Patristica* 22 [Leuven, 1989], pp. 31–32). On male authors' appropriation of women's voices, see Gayatri Chakravorty Spivak, "Displacement and the Discourse of Women," in *Displacement: Derrida and After,* ed. Mark Krupnick (Bloomington, 1983), p. 190. Arnaldo Momigliano accepts the role of Macrina in the *Vita* and *De anima et resurrectione* at face value ("The Life of St. Macrina by Gregory of Nyssa" [1985], in his *On Pagans, Jews, and Christians* [Middletown, 1987], p. 208).

145. Gregory of Nyssa, *De anima et de resurrectione* (PG 46, 112–113, 85, 148–149).

146. Since humans are created in the image of the Prototype, the Son of God, in whom "there is no male and female" (Gal. 3:28), maleness and femaleness cannot be assigned to the original creation but emerge only at a second stage, when God, foreseeing the Fall with its resultant penalty of death, provides for sexual reproduction by differentiating males and females: Gregory of Nyssa, *De opificio hominis* 16 (PG 44, 181, 185). Note Verna Harrison's summation: "Gregory argues that there is no gender in the eternal Godhead since even within the human condition gender is something temporary" ("Male and Female in Cappadocian Theology," *Journal of Theological Studies* 41 [1990]: 441).

147. Gregory of Nyssa, *De opificio hominis* 16 (PG 44, 185).

148. As do virgins, according to Gregory of Nyssa, *De virginitate* 13 (SC 119, 422–426); idem, *Hom. in Canticum Canticorum* 15 (Jaeger VI: 439–440), on Song of Songs 6:2; according to Gregory's teaching here, we recover the image when we model ourselves on Christ. See Patricia Cox Miller, "Dreaming the Body: An Aesthetics of Asceticism," in *Asceticism*, ed. Vincent L. Wimbush and Richard Valantasis (New York, 1995), p. 288, analyzing Gregory of Nyssa's dream of Macrina's glowing bones in *Vita Macrinae* 15: "[t]he glowing body of his virginal sister was so important to Gregory because it was a sign that a momentous shift in the constitution of the human person with respect to time was possible."

149. Gregory of Nyssa, *Vita Macrinae* 1 (SC 178, 140).

150. Verna E. F. Harrison notes how Gregory also can allow "Wisdom" to change genders in his *First Homily on the Song of Songs* ("Gender Reversal in Gregory of Nyssa's *First Homily on the Song of Songs*" [*Studia Patristica* 27 (Leuven, 1993), pp. 35–36]).

151. Scholars now view the *Confessions* not as "autobiography," but as a literary construct that artfully (and retrospectively) builds its case through intertextual allusions to classical literature and Scripture. Pierre Courcelle's *Recherches sur les Confessions de Saint Augustin* (2d ed.; Paris, 1968), with its trenchant analysis of the "literariness" of the *Confessions,* provoked an uproar among historians and theologians who believed that Courcelle had erased the "historicity" of the work. On the problems of understanding Augustine as a "retrospective" self-creation, see Paula Fredriksen, "Paul and Augustine: Conversion Narratives, Orthodox Traditions, and the Retrospective Self," *Journal of Theological Studies* n.s. 37 (1986): 3–34. Scholars, James O'Donnell advises, should look to "the rhetorical and exegetical strategies of the *Confessions*" (*Augustine: Confessions* [Oxford, 1992], I: xxi).

152. For a discussion of the late ancient family, using Augustine's as an example, see Brent D. Shaw, "The Family in Antiquity: The Experience of Augus-

tine," *Past & Present* 115 (1987): 3–51. For the effacement of Patricius, Augustine's father, see Augustine, *Confessiones* 3.4, 3.6, 1.12, 1.18, 4.16, 8.3. (Note "family romance" themes: Augustine's own inadequate father is replaced with a wondrously adequate substitute.) For the effacement of Monica, see *Confessiones* 9.13, 12.16, 8.2.

153. Augustine, *Confessiones* 1.11.17, 9.9.18 (CCL 27, 9–10, 145–146); see Kim Power, *Veiled Desire: Augustine on Women* (New York, 1996), p. 76. His portrayal, it should be noted, is consistent with his approach to women's status elsewhere in his writings: see Elizabeth A. Clark, "Theory and Practice in Late Ancient Asceticism: Jerome, Chrysostom, and Augustine," *Journal of Feminist Studies in Religion* 5 (1989): 25–46; for a more positive view, see Gerald Bonner, "Augustine's Attitude to Women and 'Amicitia,'" in *Homo Spiritalis: Festgabe für Luc Verheijen OSA,* ed. Cornelius Mayer and Karl Heinz Chelius (Würzburg, 1987), pp. 259–275.

154. Augustine, *Confessiones* 2.3.7, 3.11.19, 6.1.1 (CCL 27, 21, 37, 73).

155. Augustine, *De beata vita* 2.10 (CCL 29, 70–71); Augustine notes that her understanding corresponds with that of Cicero in his (lost) treatise, *Hortensius.*

156. Augustine, *De beata vita* 4.27(CCL 29, 80).

157. Augustine, *De ordine* 1.11.32 (CCL 29, 105–106); compare Plato, *Phaedo* 9 (64A); *Confessiones* 9.10.26–11.28 (CCL 27, 148–149).

158. Augustine, *De ordine* 2.19.51–20.52 (CCL 29, 135–136).

159. Ibid., 2.18.48, 2.19.51 (CCL 29, 133–134, 135); *Soliloquia* 1.13.22–1.14.24 (PL 32, 881–882). See Paul Henry, *La Vision d'Ostie. Sa place dans la vie et l'oeuvre de Saint Augustin* (Paris, 1938), chap. 2; and discussion in Courcelle, *Recherches,* pp. 222, 156–157, referring to Henry, *Plotin et l'Occident* (Louvain, 1934), pp. 78–119, 128. For Augustine's qualification, see *Confessiones* 9.10. The debates over whether the Ostia experience was "mystical" are summarized by J. Kevin Coyle, "In Praise of Monica: A Note on the Ostia Experience of *Confessions* IX," *Augustinian Studies* 13 (1982): 87–90.

160. Augustine, *De ordine* 1.8.26, 1.11.31, 2.17.45 (CCL 29, 101–102, 105, 131–132).

161. Augustine, *De beata vita* 1.6 (CCL 29, 68); *De ordine* 1.11.31 (CCL 29, 105).

162. Power, *Veiled Desire,* p. 88.

163. Augustine, *De beata vita* 4.27 (CCL 29, 80).

164. Augustine, *De ordine* 2.17.46 (CCL 29, 132).

165. Earlier, Christian Apologists such as Origen had argued that the uneducateds' ability to grasp Christian truth showed Christianity's miraculous quality: see his *Contra Celsum* 1.9, 1.13, 1.27, 3.44–58 (GCS 2, 61–62, 65–66, 79–80, 239–253).

166. Even the very exclusion of women (as Virgina Burrus notes) may point to "actual subject positions and social relations available to women histori-

cally 'as women'": "absence" itself provides social data (Virginia Burrus, "Is There a Woman in the Text? Reflections on *Doing* 'Women's History' in the Field of Late Antiquity," conference on "Religion and Gender in the Ancient Mediterranean," Ohio State University, May 22, 1997, typescript, p. 7); also see Bernadette Brooten, "Early Christian Women and Their Cultural Context: Issues of Method in Historical Reflection," in *Feminist Perspectives on Biblical Scholarship,* ed. Adela Yarbro Collins (Chico, Calif., 1985), p. 66: "The lack of sources on women is part of the history of women."

167. Stephen Slemon, "The Scramble for Post-colonialism" [1994], excerpted in *The Post-Colonial Studies Reader,* ed. Bill Ashcroft et al. (London, 1995), p. 45.

168. Ibid., p. 49; compare Bart Moore-Gilbert, *Postcolonial Theory* (London, 1997), p. 9.

169. Laura Chrisman and Patrick Williams, "Colonial Discourse and Post-Colonial Theory," in *Colonial Discourse and Post-Colonial Theory,* ed. Williams and Chrisman (New York, 1994), p. 8.

170. Sara Suleri, "Woman Skin Deep: Feminism and the Postcolonial Condition" [1992], excerpted in *The Post-Colonial Studies Reader,* p. 274.

171. Edward W. Said, *Culture and Imperialism* (New York, 1993), p. 9.

172. Slemon, "The Scramble for Post-colonialism," p. 50. Gayatri Spivak is sometimes faulted for her position that the subaltern "cannot speak" (if he or she could, they wouldn't be subalterns, is Spivak's early view; later, she grants the subaltern more voice and agency); see discussion in Benita Parry, "Problems in Current Theories of Colonial Discourses" [1987], excerpted in *The Post-Colonial Studies Reader,* pp. 36–38.

173. Anne McClintock, *Imperial Leather: Race, Gender and Sexuality in the Colonial Contest* (New York, 1995), p. 12.

174. See Nicholas Thomas, *Colonialism's Culture: Anthropology, Travel and Government* (Princeton, 1994), pp. 8, 50, 60. Thomas notes that the emphasis on regional particularity and how it evolved owes more perhaps to Pierre Bourdieu's "located subjectivities" than to Spivak or Bhabha (8); likewise, Said's model is not adequate to other strains of colonial representation (27). Thomas explores what assistance Foucault might offer to post-colonial theory.

175. Gayatri Chakravorty Spivak, "Can the Subaltern Speak?: Speculations on Widow Sacrifice," in *Wedge* 7(8) (Winter/Spring 1985), pp. 120–30 (reprinted in *Colonial Discourse*); and Gayatri Spivak, "The New Historicism: Political Commitment and the Postmodern Critic" [1989], in her *The Post-Colonial Critic,* ed. Sarah Harasym (New York, 1990), pp. 158, 166. Nicholas Thomas notes that the original Subaltern Studies group emphasized subaltern resistance, in contrast to Spivak and Bhabha (*Colonialism's Culture,* pp. 55–57).

176. See Ranajit Guha, *Dominance without Hegemony: History and Power in*

Colonial India (Cambridge, Mass., 1997), discussed in Dipesh Chakra-barty, *Provincializing Europe: Postcolonial Thought and Historical Differ-ence* (Princeton, 2000), p. 15; Chakrabarty makes the rather strained argu-ment that "historicism" is in large part to blame for European colonialism (6–12, 22–23, and the epilogue).

177. Gyan Prakash, "Postcolonial Criticism and Indian Historiography," *So-cial Text* 31/32 (1992): 10–11; Simon During, "Postmodernism or Post-colonialism Today" [1987], excerpted in *The Post-Colonial Studies Reader,* p. 125; and Young, *White Mythologies,* pp. 3, 17, 71.

178. For example, Barbara Christian, "The Race for Theory" [1987], excerpted in *The Post-Colonial Studies Reader,* pp. 457–460; discussion in Moore-Gilbert, *Postcolonial Theory,* pp. 17–18.

179. Gayatri Spivak argues that postcolonial critique and the Derridean project here have much in common. Spivak claims that a Derridean analysis of texts countering the nostalgia for lost origins aligns well with postcolonialist cri-tique; in Derrida's work, she argues, there is no "first-world intellectual masquerading as the absent nonrepresenter who lets the oppressed speak for themselves," but a call to the *tout-autre* (Spivak, "Can the Subaltern Speak?" in *Colonial Discourse,* pp. 87, 89, 104). For a similar linking of postcolonial and deconstructive approaches, see Prakash, "Postcolonial Criticism and Indian Historiography," pp. 10–11.

180. Kwame Anthony Appiah, "Is the 'Post-' in 'Postcolonial' the 'Post-' in 'Postmodern'?" in *Dangerous Liaisons: Gender, Nation, and Postcolonial Perspectives,* ed. Anne McClintock et al. (Minneapolis, 1997), pp. 420–444, especially p. 440.

181. See the "presentist" description of postcolonial criticism in Homi K. Bhabha, "The Postcolonial and the Postmodern: The Question of Agency" [1992], in his *The Location of Culture* (London, 1994), p. 171. For an early "moment" in the history of postcolonial criticism that places the critique within anthropology, see Talad Asad, "Introduction," in *Anthropology & the Colonial Encounter,* ed. Asad (Atlantic Highlands, 1973), pp. 9–19.

182. Caution must be exerted against the "ahistorical" use of terms in post-colonial theory, warns Anne McClintock (*Imperial Leather,* pp. 11–13).

183. Neville Morley comments: "The main difference between the Roman Em-pire and the capitalist world-economy of Wallerstein lies not in the imbal-ance of power between core and periphery—that is clear enough in both cases—but in the different levels of demand in pre-industrial and industrial systems" (*Metropolis and Hinterland: The City of Rome and the Italian Economy 200 b.c.–a.d. 200* [Cambridge, 1996], p. 158). There have been debates over whether, with Lenin, imperialism necessarily involves monop-oly capitalism (V. I. Lenin, *Imperialism: The Highest Stage of Capitalism* [revised trans.; New York, 1933], especially chap. 10). For debates on the "fit," see Jane Webster, "Roman Imperialism and the 'Post Imperial Age,'" in *Roman Imperialism: Post-Colonial Perspectives,* ed. Webster and Nicho-

las J. Cooper (Leicester, 1996), pp. 2–4, citing W. R. Harris, *War and Imperialism in Republican Rome 327–70 BC* (Oxford, 1979), p. 4.

184. P. D. A. Garnsey, "Rome's African Empire under the Principate," in *Imperialism in the Ancient World,* ed. P. D. A. Garnsey and C. R. Whittaker (Cambridge, 1978), p. 241. Barbarism, Nicholas Thomas notes, generally signifies a "lack": "the absence of the civilized life of the *polis* which the Greeks regarded as distinctive to their own culture" (*Colonialism's Culture,* p. 72).

185. Said, *Culture and Imperialism,* p. 7; Said cites Conrad on p. 68 (see Joseph Conrad, "Heart of Darkness," in his *Youth and Two Other Stories* [Garden City, 1925], pp. 50–51).

186. Webster, "Roman Imperialism," p. 7.

187. D. J. Mattingly, "Africa: A Landscape of Opportunity?" in *Dialogues in Roman Imperialism,* ed. Mattingly (Portsmouth, R.I., 1997), p. 135; Greg Woolf, *Becoming Roman: The Origins of Provincial Civilization in Gaul* (Cambridge, 1998), pp. 19–20.

188. Martin Millett et al., "Integration, Culture and Ideology in the Early Roman West," in *Integration in the Early Roman West,* ed. Jeannot Metzler et al. (Luxembourg, 1995), p. 1. Older generations, lauding Rome's "civilizing mission," and perhaps themselves citizens of nation-states that had extended their appropriating reach to distant continents, freely utilized a vocabulary of "imperialism" and "colonization." See discussion in P. A. Brunt, "Reflections on British and Roman Imperialism" [1965], in his *Roman Imperial Themes* [Oxford, 1990], p. 124); M. I. Finley, "Colonies—An Attempt at a Typology," *Transactions of the Royal Historical Society,* 5 ser., 26 (1976): 169, 178; Mattingly, "Africa," p. 134; Woolf, *Becoming Roman,* pp. 55, 57; Garnsey, "Rome's African Empire," p. 223; Dick [Richard] Whittaker, "Integration of the Early Roman West: The Example of Africa," in *Integration in the Early Roman West,* p. 25. For comparisons of the Roman and the British Empires, see Steven K. Drummond and Lynn H. Nelson, *The Western Frontiers of Imperial Rome* (Armonk, 1994), pp. 173, 182–183; and Brunt, "Reflections on British and Roman Imperialism," pp. 110–111. On France in North Africa, Yvon Thébert, "Romanisation et déromanisation en Afrique: Histoire décolonisée ou histoire inversée?" *Annales E.S.C.* 33 (1978): 64–65; Marcel Bénabou, *La Résistance africaine à la romanisation* (Paris, 1976).

189. Freeman, "'Romanisation,'" p. 442; Martin Millett, "Romanization: Historical Issues and Archaeological Interpretation," in *The Early Roman Empire in the West,* ed. Thomas Blagg and Millett (Oxford, 1990), p. 37, Bénabou, *La Resistance africaine,* pp. 581–583. See L. A. Thompson, "Partnership and Integration in Roman Africa," *Phrontisterion* 4 (1966): 32; idem, "Settler and Native in the Urban Centres of Roman Africa," in *Africa in Classical Antiquity,* ed. Thompson and J. Ferguson (Ibadan [Nigeria], 1969), pp. 133, 143, 148.

190. Thébert, "Romanisation," p. 69. As the editors of *Integration in the Early*

Roman West write, "Romanization is . . . determined on the one hand by Roman imperialist policy . . . using culture and ideology as specific instruments, and on the other by native responses to Roman structures" (Millett et al., "Integration, Culture and Ideology," pp. 2–3).

191. Whittaker, "Integration," p. 30.

192. For Greece, see S. E. Alcock, "Greece: A Landscape of Resistance?" in *Dialogues in Roman Imperialism,* pp. 103–115, and her *Graecia Capta: The Landscapes of Roman Greece* (Cambridge, 1993).

193. Greg Woolf, "Becoming Roman, Staying Greek," *Proceedings of the Cambridge Philological Society,* n.s. 40 (1993): 121; idem, "The Foundation of Roman Provincial Cultures," in *Integration in the Early Roman West,* pp. 15–16.

194. Woolf, *Becoming Roman,* p. 11.

195. Millett et al., "Integration, Culture and Ideology," pp. 1–2.

196. Clifford Ando, *Imperial Ideology and Provincial Loyalty in the Roman Empire* (Berkeley, 2000), pp. 7, 66, 68, 77, 145, 160, 173, 337–338, and chap. 6.

197. Brunt, "British and Roman Imperialism," p. 132.

198. Freeman, "'Romanisation,'" pp. 443, 445; Mattingly, "Africa," p. 206.

199. For North Africa: Thébert, "Romanisation," p. 73; Millett, "Romanization," p. 36.

200. Brent D. Shaw, "Archaeological Knowledge: The History of the African Provinces of the Roman Empire" [1980], in his *Environment and Society in Roman North Africa* (Aldershot, 1995), pp. 32–35, 38, 45.

201. Jacobs, *Remains of the Jews,* pp. 14, 10.

202. Ibid., pp. 10–11.

203. Ibid., p. 9.

204. Ibid., p. 9. Jacobs cites Bart Moore-Gilbert's definition of postcolonial criticism: a "distinctive set of reading practices . . . preoccupied principally with analysis of cultural forms which mediate, challenge, and reflect upon the relations of domination and subordination—economic, cultural and political—between (and often within) nations, races or cultures" (*Postcolonial Theory,* p. 12).

205. Jacobs, *Remains of the Jews,* pp. 206–209.

Index

Alltagsgeschichte, 77, 195n9, 244n135
Althusser, Louis, 4, 43, 60, 68, 80, 81–82,
    83, 84, 97, 104, 174, 175, 176, 223n18,
    241n104, 246–247n166, 247n168,
    247nn170–171, 247nn173–174, 248–
    249n183, 257n94, 275n122, 276n134,
    280n180, 309n101, 309n105, 310n116
American Historical Association (AHA),
    13, 195–196n11, 204n62, 209n119
Analytical philosophy (Anglo-American
    philosophy), 3, 4, 29–41, 42, 70, 86, 87–
    88, 90, 91, 139, 140, 196n15, 206n84,
    211n139, 220n82, 221n1, 235n17,
    251n13, 253n38
Anderson, Perry, 55, 59–60, 82, 248n180,
    248n183, 249n184
Ankersmit, Franklin R., 27–28, 36, 87,
    101, 103, 111, 206n84, 214n176
Anthropology, anthropologists, 5, 6, 7, 24,
    44, 47–54, 55, 57, 79, 84, 94–95, 110,
    153, 154, 155, 158, 159, 160, 185,
    193n4, 222n12, 227n55, 228n57,
    229n75, 229n78, 231n102, 237n45,
    256n75, 266n34, 295n128, 297n159,
    298n170, 299nn180–181; and histori-
    ans, 70, 76, 94, 149–151, 160, 238n57,
    256n72, 299n173, 299n181; interpre-
    tive, 6, 76, 131, 135, 145–155, 161
Appleby, Joyce, 1, 18, 26, 40, 41
Archaeology (Foucauldian), 114, 117,
    272n84, 274n119

Aron, Raymond, 16, 20, 71, 204n70,
    205n71, 230n95, 231n96, 240n83
Augustine, 160, 161, 170, 178, 179–181,
    221n88, 313nn151–152
Austin, J. L., 138, 144, 289n61, 290n62,
    290n66, 294n119, 297n152
Authorial intention, 7, 8, 132, 133–134,
    136, 139–141, 142, 144, 150, 158, 162,
    163, 170, 253n35, 271n80, 290nn66–
    67, 290n69

Bachelard, Gaston, 81, 247n173, 273–
    274n108
Bakhtin, Mikhail, 74, 84, 162, 163,
    242n111, 285n10
Barthes, Roland, 4, 5, 6, 43, 44, 46–47, 84,
    86, 89, 95–98, 102, 122, 132, 133–134,
    149, 157, 175, 212n157, 222n6,
    226nn42–43, 232n130, 241n107,
    242n113, 256n81, 259n114, 260n134,
    274n113, 285n10, 286–287n21
Beard, Charles, 3, 13, 14, 20, 24, 37, 40,
    203n52, 203–204n57, 207n100,
    208n112, 210n128
Becker, Carl, 3, 20, 24, 40, 195n11,
    205n75, 206n88, 208n112
Begriffsgeschichte, 112–113, 194–195n9,
    268n53, 269n59
Benveniste, Emile, 45, 46, 221n1, 223–
    224n22
Berkhofer, Robert, 17, 27

Bevir, Mark, 140–141, 266n33, 290n67

Bloch, Marc, 16, 18, 20, 63, 64, 65, 66, 67, 68, 89, 114, 205n72, 226n46, 235n14, 235n23, 236n31, 237n40, 237n44, 239n69, 270n76, 304n38

Bourdieu, Pierre, 148, 282n208, 300n190, 315n174

Braudel, Fernand, 44, 66, 67, 68, 69, 72, 89, 91, 114, 231n107, 239n60, 242n109, 242n118, 254n48, 262n156

Brown, Peter, 160, 199n11

Burguière, André, 65, 66, 74, 239n69, 242n109, 277n142

Burke, Kenneth, 99, 139, 147, 260n125, 291n75

Burke, Peter, 14, 76, 93–94, 243n131, 244n141

Burrus, Virginia, 161, 171, 306–307n69, 314–315n166

Cameron, Averil, 167, 169, 171, 172, 208–209n116

Canguilhem, Georges, 81, 116, 119, 269n66, 273–274n108

Carr, E. H., 15, 16, 304n35

Chartier, Roger, 6, 7, 17, 57, 61, 100–101, 106, 113, 117, 119, 124–126, 152, 153–155, 157, 165, 170, 237n41, 259–260n121, 279n169

Christianity (early, late ancient), studies of, xi–xii, 7, 8, 86, 106, 129, 145, 150, 156–185, 193n1, 193n3, 246n160

Classicists, historians of antiquity, 165–169, 182–184, 246n160, 304n36

Collingwood, R. G., 29, 106, 108–110, 112, 150, 156, 166, 216n19, 265n19, 265n26, 267n48, 289n61

Contexts, contextualism, 6, 7, 20, 27, 101, 109, 128–129, 130–155, 157, 161, 162, 164, 170–171, 209n119, 213n165, 284n1, 289n57, 290n63, 291n73

Correspondence theory, 2, 7, 14, 18, 25, 35–38, 39, 40, 44, 46, 47, 62, 157, 164, 195n10, 196n12, 211n138, 217n42, 291n77

Covering-law theory, 32, 33–34, 90

Critical theory, xi, xii, 2, 8, 126, 161, 169–170

Croce, Benedetto, 20, 98, 109, 202n45, 207n106, 212n153, 237n42, 265n26

Danto, Arthur, 34–37, 40, 87–88, 197–198n5, 216n19, 217nn40–41, 217nn45–46, 218n49

Darnton, Robert, 7, 125, 152–155, 239n67, 243n130, 282n206, 299n178, 300n194, 301n200

Davis, Natalie Zemon, 76, 95, 149, 299n178

De Certeau, Michel, 6, 18, 68, 73, 92, 106, 113, 119–124, 156, 157, 162, 206–207n95, 214n3, 241n95, 241n98, 254n58, 257n90, 277n142, 279n161, 280nn179–181, 280n187

Deconstruction, 27, 92, 106, 128, 135, 141, 143, 150, 161, 165, 182, 210n132, 284n234

Denaturalization, 4, 62, 112, 117, 176

Derrida, Jacques, 6, 26–27, 55, 57–59, 79, 84, 102, 104, 127, 128–129, 131, 132, 134, 135–137, 138, 140, 142–145, 152, 157, 161, 163, 164, 170, 182, 194–195n9, 210n132, 213n167, 220n85, 232nn129–130, 233n136, 233n138, 260n134, 283n222, 284nn233–234, 285–286n13, 293n97, 316n179

Dewey, John, 20, 37, 38, 39, 40, 41, 207n105, 219n71, 219n74, 220n86

Dilthey, Wilhelm, 12–13, 64, 90, 135, 200–201n30, 201nn32–33, 201n36, 216n19, 240n82, 284n232, 286n17

Discontinuity, 4, 43, 61, 62, 228n62, 262n150, 273n104, 273n106. See also History, discontinuity in

Discourse, discourse theory, 55, 68, 92, 102, 104, 114–115, 117, 118–119, 121, 122, 123, 125, 134, 135, 152, 154, 165, 181, 185, 271n83, 275n123, 282n212

Dissemination, 129, 132

Dosse, François, 42, 43, 61, 74

Dray, William, 33–34, 36, 90, 105, 203–204n57, 205n80

Einstein, Albert, 16, 109

Elton, Geoffrey (G. R.), 17, 19, 21, 106, 209n121, 209n123, 220n88, 254n48

Episteme, 106, 124, 117, 254n56, 274n119

Epistemology, 2, 5, 17–25, 34–35, 39, 65, 70, 71, 73, 79–80, 81, 84, 85, 93, 98, 99, 113, 117, 122, 164, 200n30, 205n80, 206n84, 211nn140–141, 235n14,

240n78, 246n160, 247n171, 273–274n108
Evans, Richard J., 110–111, 208n109
Existentialism, Existentialists, 21, 42, 43, 47, 52, 54, 71, 72, 137, 228n68, 253n37
Experience, 7, 79, 81–82, 91–92, 120, 125, 137, 147, 148, 157, 201n39, 222n5, 249n186, 267n47, 300n190
Explanation, 25, 30–34, 37, 77, 87, 90, 92, 93, 99, 135, 218n58, 220–221n88, 250n5, 251n11

Febvre, Lucien, 20, 25, 51, 63, 64, 65, 66, 67, 68, 69, 114, 229n84, 234n3, 235n14, 237n40, 239n69, 274n118
Finley, Moses, 166, 168, 169
Foucault, Michel, 6, 21, 23, 27, 43, 44, 61, 73, 74–75, 84, 92, 102, 104, 106, 113–119, 121, 122, 123–124, 127, 133, 134, 156, 157, 165, 169, 170, 176, 195n9, 196n15, 196n17, 200n17, 223n19, 225n38, 231n113, 241n99, 242n109, 242n113, 254n56, 260n134, 269–270n67, 270nn70–71, 270nn74–76, 271n79, 272n86, 272n88, 273n104, 273–274n108, 274n113, 275n122, 276n132, 276n134, 276n138, 277n140, 280n187, 281–282n202, 282n207, 282n212, 301–302n2, 315n174
Frankfurt School, xi, 193n4, 276n134
French Revolution, 53, 75, 149–150, 203n52, 242n115, 300n183
Freud, Sigmund, 53, 60, 233n138, 272n91
Frye, Northrop, 99, 147, 260n125
Furet, François, 52, 66, 75, 89, 238n57, 240n77, 242n117

Gadamer, Hans-Georg, 111–112, 135–137, 156, 201n38, 267nn47–48, 290n69, 293n102
Gallie, W. B., 87, 90, 212n154
Gardiner, Patrick, 33
Geertz, Clifford, 5, 6, 24–25, 44, 47, 54, 76, 131, 135, 141, 145–155, 164, 165, 210n131, 243n119, 283n215, 295n126, 295nn128–129, 296n134, 297n148, 297n159, 299n182, 300n183, 300nn194–195
Gender studies, 156–157, 174, 249n188
Genealogy (Foucauldian), 73, 117–118, 275n128, 276n131

Genette, Gérard, 131–132
Ginzburg, Carlo, 7, 26, 76, 77, 79, 94–95, 212n157, 244n143, 252n31, 255n70, 256n71, 256nn75–76, 261n141, 273n41, 282n206, 299n178
Gregory of Nyssa, 178–180, 312n141, 312n144, 313n146, 313n148

Habermas, Jürgen, 2, 244n140, 268n52
Hadot, Pierre, 119
Harlan, David, 20, 84, 141–142, 210n131, 211n146, 260n123, 260n125
Hegel, G. W. F., 5, 49, 81, 98, 196n19, 217nn44–45, 223n18, 247n170, 265n23, 270n70,
Heidegger, Martin, 55, 111, 137, 141, 194–195n9, 267n43, 273n99, 289n51, 289n58
Hempel, Carl G., 31–33, 34, 37, 214n6, 215n16, 218n58
Hermeneutic circle, 12, 145, 151, 153, 300n183
Hermeneutics, 2, 12, 14, 40–41, 47, 106, 112, 119, 125, 136–137, 143, 147, 151, 194–195n9, 201n39, 253n37, 281n200, 284–285n3, 287n22
Hexter, J. H., 25–26, 195n11, 212n154
Hill, Christopher, 80, 245n158, 248n180
Himmelfarb, Gertrude, 21, 23, 26, 41, 209n123, 213n158–159, 255n66
Historicism, 9, 43, 111, 113, 114, 136, 141, 162, 181, 193n4, 197n4, 215n12, 223n14, 229n74, 291n70, 315–316n176
Historiography: *Annales, Annaliste*, 6, 20, 25, 30, 60, 63–69, 70, 71–74, 79–80, 86, 87, 88–89, 90, 92, 93, 99, 100, 101, 120, 122, 124, 156, 209n116, 233–234n2, 235n16, 235n25, 236n26, 236n32, 238n55, 240nn77–78, 240n89, 251n14, 255n65, 270n67, 271n83, 273–274n108, 279n161, 281n201; British Marxist, 6, 63, 79–85; French, 2, 6, 13, 30, 54, 63–75, 89–92, 101, 111, 113–126, 196n19, 234n4, 235n14, 235n25, 240n78, 240n88; German, 2, 9, 13, 14, 15, 64, 77, 111–113, 194–195n9, 197n4, 199n15, 200n16, 203n55, 210n136, 234n2, 243–244n133, 263n1, 269n59; Marxist, 19, 21, 23, 25, 43, 44, 60, 68–69, 71, 73, 75, 93, 97, 101, 118–119, 122, 148, 239n60, 241n99,

Historiography *(continued)*
242n115, 245n158, 246n160, 249n183,
263n3

History: causation in, 3, 109, 215n16; cultural, 6, 76, 102, 106, 111, 124, 126,
152, 153, 163, 243n130; deconstruction
and, 26, 27, 40, 75, 128–129, 141, 161,
164, 165, 220n85; de-familiarization in,
70, 116–117; demographic, 66, 67, 93;
discontinuity in, 6, 7, 54, 68, 87, 104,
116, 117, 121, 157, 175, 213n164, 264–
265n13, 273n104, 273n106, 275n121,
301n1; documentary, xi, 10, 11, 14, 72,
94, 95, 120, 127, 128, 130, 164, 165,
171, 210n124, 217n40, 237n44,
245n158, 253n35; economic, 3, 68, 73,
93, 94, 106, 110, 111, 127, 130, 163,
237n36, 239n70, 243n128; effective
(Wirkungsgeschichte), 136, 157; event
history *(histoire événementielle)*, 14, 66,
68, 71, 74, 86, 87, 88–89, 91, 94, 100,
236n29, 240n88, 250n7; explanation in,
3, 12, 15, 25, 31, 33, 44, 45, 72, 87, 92,
99, 215n6, 215–216n16, 218n58, 220–
221n88, 241n92, 254n57; feminist, 19,
21, 22, 175–178, 182, 208n115,
209n119; of ideas, 5, 6, 69, 106–129,
239n70, 266n33, 266n35, 289n60; intellectual, 1, 2, 5, 6, 7, 28, 41, 42, 62, 63,
69–70, 75, 106–129, 130, 138, 141,
150, 152, 153, 156, 159, 161, 163, 169,
185, 237n36, 260n123, 263n2, 266n33,
270–271n76, 271n80, 281n200;
mentalité, 67, 68, 69–70, 106, 124, 153,
237n45, 239n63, 239nn69–70,
243n130, 271n83, 278n149;
microhistory, 6, 25, 63, 75–79, 80, 94–
95, 243n120, 243nn130–131, 281n201;
New History, 3, 68, 89; objectivity in, 1,
3, 9, 10, 11, 13, 14, 15, 16, 19, 20–23,
25, 33, 36, 40, 67, 84, 88, 90, 91, 96,
97, 103, 111, 157, 199nn11–12,
203n55, 207n105, 208n111, 209nn119–
120, 210n131; philosophy of, 3–5, 13–
16, 29–37, 49, 65, 71, 81, 84, 100, 119,
196n19, 197n2, 260n128; political, 9,
65, 66, 68, 89, 100, 101, 106, 111, 112,
113, 130, 150, 163; positivism in, 3, 12,
13, 23, 25, 29, 31, 63–64, 65, 67, 71, 73,
78, 79, 92, 101, 108–109, 118, 127,
148, 201n32, 208n112, 211n151,
234n11, 234n13, 251n18; postmodern,
1, 23, 102, 162, 209n120, 213n158,
251n18; post-structuralist, 7–8, 19, 23,
26, 40, 54, 74–75, 94, 161, 163,
208n109, 209n123, 213n165;
professionalization of, 2, 5, 11, 14, 15,
17, 22, 122, 126–127, 166, 199n15,
204n63, 212n154, 212n157, 255n61;
quantitative, 3, 67, 69, 75, 76, 93, 121,
213n159; relativism in, 9, 16, 23–25,
40–41, 84, 98, 102; representation in,
17, 18, 28, 73, 80, 90, 97, 121, 124,
125, 170, 178, 179, 181, 183, 185,
261n139, 294n109, 303n20; rhetoric in,
3, 64, 65, 75, 86, 102–103, 113, 122,
125, 127, 159, 161, 167–168, 169, 173,
185, 250n2, 261n138, 312n135; science,
in relation to, 3, 9, 12, 16, 29, 30–34,
36, 41, 43, 54, 72, 74, 108, 197n3,
199n12, 205nn73–74, 216n23; serial,
66–67, 68, 69, 77, 121, 237n36; skepticism in, 23, 24, 34–35, 79, 92, 140, 167,
168, 256n75, 261n144, 283n218; social,
6, 63, 67, 75, 78, 94, 106, 110, 111,
112, 125, 126, 127, 130, 138, 153, 158,
163, 209n120, 256n76, 263n1, 273–
274n108, 299n176; social-scientific, 3,
64, 67, 68, 89, 98, 124, 126, 149–150,
158–159, 160, 163, 166; structuralist, 3,
71, 74–75, 77, 79, 91, 93–94, 95–96, 98,
100, 102, 115, 116, 222n13, 242n109,
260n130, 272n86; of women, 21, 175–
181, 209n121

Hobsbawm, Eric, 80, 83–84, 235n16,
248n180, 255n66

Humanism, humanists, 33, 36, 42, 43, 52,
53, 54, 57, 66, 72, 80, 81, 97, 115, 148,
221n2, 223n18, 229n74, 230n90,
247n170, 247n174, 272n94,

Humboldt, Wilhelm von, 12–13, 197–
198n5, 201n37

Hunt, Lynn, 1, 18, 26, 40, 41, 79, 151,
300n183

Ideology, ideology critique, 4, 6, 7, 8, 60–
61, 68, 69, 77, 81, 86, 94, 95–104, 110,
128, 138–139, 149, 150, 152, 157, 159,
161, 162, 165, 168–170, 173–178, 183,
184, 203n55, 236n30, 237n45,
245n158, 247n174, 257–258n94,
258nn95–96, 258n98, 258n101, 261–

262n145, 271n79, 280n181, 287n31,
288n40, 309–310n110, 310n111,
310n114, 312n135
Iggers, Georg, 1, 26
Internal realism, 38, 39, 40, 41, 157,
219n62, 219nn66–67, 220n79, 220n84

Jacob, Margaret, 1, 18, 26, 40, 41
Jacobs, Andrew, 8, 184–185, 306n69,
318n204
Jakobson, Roman, 48–49, 222n8, 227n50,
228n57, 228n60, 259n118
Jameson, Fredric, 101, 161, 174, 259n108,
260n130, 285n10, 300n183
Jenkins, Keith, 19, 22, 156
Jerome, 134, 170, 176–177, 184, 287n29,
308n94, 311n133
Johns Hopkins University, 10, 15, 221n1,
242n111
Jones, Gareth Stedman, xii, 18

Kellner, Hans, 3, 23, 69, 90, 93, 96, 99,
100, 101–102, 105, 217n45, 254n48,
255n65, 258n105, 293n101
Kloppenberg, James T., 40–41, 128,
220n85, 284n232
Koselleck, Reinhart, 22, 112–113, 251n13,
285n3, 288–289n51
Kristeva, Julia, 6, 74, 104, 132, 286n16
Kuhn, Thomas, 21, 139, 209n120,
291n77

Lacan, Jacques, 43, 104, 182, 222n8,
223n16, 223–224n22, 228n62,
231n113, 279n172
LaCapra, Dominick, 6, 7, 20, 57, 95, 100,
106, 113, 126–129, 141–142, 143, 152,
156, 157, 165, 246n164, 249n188,
256n76, 257n92, 272n94, 283n215,
284nn232–234, 285–286n13
Langlois, Charles V., 64, 234n11, 262n157
Le Goff, Jacques, 65–66, 69, 70, 89,
283n224
Le Roy Ladurie, Emmanuel, 66, 67, 68, 70,
77, 78, 88, 89, 226n46, 242n109,
244n139, 244n143, 251n31, 255n66,
282n206
Levi, Giovanni, 76, 94, 151, 153, 243n128,
299n178
Lévi-Strauss, Claude, 5, 24, 43, 44, 47–54,
55, 56, 57, 58–59, 60, 61, 70, 104, 121,

146, 147, 148, 150, 155, 205n74,
211n143, 222n8, 222nn11–12, 223n14,
223n19, 227n50, 227nn55–56, 228n57,
228n62, 228n64, 228n68, 229n70,
229n77, 230n90, 230nn92–93, 230n95,
231n102, 232n133, 233nn137–139,
259n118, 272n92, 274n113, 295n128,
296n143
Linguistics, 4, 5, 44–50, 55, 57–60, 61, 62,
68, 139, 146, 163, 164, 223nn21–22,
224nn24–25, 225n39, 226n42, 226n46,
228n57, 228n60, 228n62, 228n64,
232n130, 241n105, 258n95
"Linguistic turn," 1, 5, 75, 125, 126, 147,
166, 226n46, 282n212
Lovejoy, Arthur O., 6, 106, 107–108, 110,
156, 264n5, 264n7, 264n9
Lyotard, Jean-François, 105, 157, 161,
310n115

Macherey, Pierre, 55, 60–61, 157, 176
Macrina, 178–180, 181, 312n144,
313n148
Mandelbaum, Maurice, 24, 36, 196n12,
211n138
Markus, Robert, 159–160, 302n5
Marrou, Henri-Irénée, 64, 71, 160,
204n70, 205n73, 234n11, 265n26,
306n60
Marx, Karl, 43, 51, 53, 81, 83, 97, 98,
116, 174, 175, 223n18, 233n138,
236n34, 240n83, 242n115, 246n161,
247n170, 257n94, 273n104, 280n180,
308–309n98, 310n116
Marxism, 26, 74, 80, 81–82, 223n18,
238n47, 246n160, 247n168, 247n170,
247n174, 248n176, 272n88, 276n134,
301–302n2
Miller, J. Hillis, 91–92
Mink, Louis, 33, 87, 88, 91–92, 102, 105,
216n23
Momigliano, Arnaldo, 10, 21, 97, 168,
198n8, 199n11, 208n116, 257n83,
305n49, 305n52, 306n58, 312n144
Monica, 178, 179–181, 311n133, 313–
314n152

Narrative, "grand narrative," 3, 4, 7, 16–
17, 70, 71, 86–105, 120–121, 122, 125,
157, 161, 175, 177, 196n14, 250n10,
251n11, 251–252n18, 253n35, 253n41,

Narrative *(continued)*
  255n66, 258n101, 259n114, 262n150,
  262n152, 262n154, 262n156, 283n218
Nietzsche, Friedrich, 11–12, 13, 14, 98,
  102, 115, 116, 118, 137, 143, 144, 145,
  200n17, 272n88
Novick, Peter, 1, 2, 9, 14–15, 16, 17, 20,
  21, 37, 40, 41, 194n5, 204n62,
  208n111, 208n113, 208n115,
  209nn117–119, 260n123

Oakeshott, Michael, 19, 206–207n95,
  289n61
Objectivity, 1, 2, 9, 14, 15, 19, 20–23, 25,
  38, 39, 96, 133, 148, 149, 197n2,
  208n111, 209nn119–120, 210n131.
Origins, quest for, 43, 102, 114–115, 116,
  117, 120, 144, 157, 236n31, 288n41

Past, status of, xii, 2, 7, 18–19, 20, 35, 102,
  156, 162, 206–207n95, 207n101, 211–
  212n151, 217n45, 265n26
Peirce, Charles Sanders, 4, 37, 154,
  219n61, 225n40, 245n152
Phenomenology, 42, 43, 71, 90, 91–92,
  136–137, 228n68, 240n83, 241n102,
  253n37, 272n88, 288n50, 301–302n2
Plato, 61, 172, 264n9
Pocock, J. G. A., 7, 36–37, 113, 131, 138,
  139–140, 141, 142, 147, 157, 290n66,
  291n77
Popper, Karl, 30–31, 37, 214n6, 215nn9–
  10, 215n12, 215n14, 215n16, 218n58
Postcolonial theory, 8, 19, 22, 156–157,
  170, 181–185, 306–307n69, 316n179,
  316n181, 318n204
Postmodernism, 23, 84, 182, 209n123,
  220n86, 213n166, 221n89
Post-structuralism, post-structuralists, xi,
  xii, 5, 7, 9, 23, 26, 41, 42, 44, 60, 84, 91,
  92, 95, 102, 105, 119, 127, 131, 132,
  137, 139, 140, 144, 147, 157, 158, 162,
  163–164, 175, 181, 182, 209n123,
  236n30, 248n181, 249n184, 259n114,
  276n132, 278n155
Pragmatism, pragmatists, 30, 37, 38, 39,
  40, 41, 169, 219n72, 220n83, 220n86,
  247n174
Pre-modernity, studies of, xi, xii, 2, 5, 6, 7,
  28, 41, 63, 95, 105, 106, 111, 113, 126,
  129, 138, 155, 156–158, 161

Present, "presentism," 19–20, 22, 65–66,
  107, 108, 109–110, 111–112, 116, 119–
  120, 121, 156, 165, 201n39, 203n55,
  207nn100–101, 207nn105–106,
  208n110, 211n137, 264nn11–12,
  316n181
Production, conditions of, 114, 122–123,
  162
Psychoanalysis, psychoanalytical theory,
  21, 44, 68, 101, 120, 121, 193n1,
  224n22, 228n62, 229n83, 232n117,
  241n105, 278n149
Putnam, Hilary, 30, 37–39, 40, 204n69,
  220n79

Rabinow, Paul, 117–118, 149, 196n21
Ranke, Leopold von, 1, 2, 9–11, 12, 13,
  25, 39, 64, 98, 166, 168, 196n19,
  197n2, 197–198n5, 198nn7–9,
  199nn11–13, 200n16, 202nn45–47,
  203n48, 203n52, 203n55, 204n58, 206–
  207n95, 210n124, 234n4, 237n42,
  306n57
"Reality effect," 80, 86, 96–97, 149,
  257n90, 257n92, 286–287n21
Reference, 5, 7, 17, 38, 42, 43, 46, 55, 115,
  206n84
Relativism, 7, 23–25, 40, 84, 99, 157,
  196nn11–12, 205n71, 210n131,
  210n136, 211n137, 211n140, 211n143,
  211n145, 219n66, 219nn73–74,
  230n95, 245n158
Representation, 5, 7, 17, 28, 39, 73, 80,
  104, 121, 148, 170, 173, 178, 179, 181,
  272n88, 297n150, 303n20
Revel, Jacques, 64, 70, 75, 238n58,
  277n142, 278n149
Ricoeur, Paul, 55–57, 68, 86, 88, 89, 90–
  92, 135, 145, 146, 206n82, 225–
  226n40, 232n117, 238n55, 238n59,
  253n37, 253n41, 253n45, 254n48,
  254n57, 261n138, 262n156, 268n52,
  288–289n51
Robin, Régine, 92, 271n83
Romanization, 183–184, 318n190
Rorty, Richard, 24, 33, 37, 38, 39–40,
  206n84, 211nn139–142, 219n73,
  220n82, 284n232, 296n143
Rosaldo, Renato, 78–79, 248n181
Rüsen, Jörn, 194n9, 240n78, 244n140,
  259n118, 268n55

Said, Edward, 21, 47–48, 182, 183, 213n160, 221n1, 315n174

Sartre, Jean-Paul, 43, 50, 52–53, 223n14, 229n74, 230n92, 231n96

Saussure, Ferdinand de, 5, 44–47, 48, 57–58, 61, 62, 97, 146, 223n21, 224nn24–25, 224n28, 225n35, 225nn38–39, 226n42, 258n96

Scott, Joan Wallach, 21, 23, 27, 83, 105, 161, 209n119, 275n123, 300n190

Seignobos, Charles, 64, 234n11, 236n29, 262n157

Sewell, William E., Jr., 75, 149–150, 242n117, 282n212

Skepticism, 218n55, 221n88, 256n75, 261n144

Skinner, Quentin, 7, 131, 138–139, 140, 141, 147, 157, 292n86

Smith, Bonnie G., 22–23, 199n15, 210n128, 212n154

"Social logic of the text," 162–165, 172, 174, 178–181

Southgate, Beverley, 26, 27

Speech-act theory, 115, 135, 137, 138, 139, 142–144, 293n97, 294n119

Spiegel, Gabrielle, 8, 162–165, 178

Spivak, Gayatri Chakravorty, 182, 315n172, 315nn174–175, 316n179

Stone, Lawrence, 26, 86, 93, 100, 252n21, 252n29, 255n61, 255n64, 255n66

Structuralism, 4, 5, 6, 7, 42–62, 85, 89, 114, 115, 116, 117, 119, 123, 131, 132, 137, 146, 147, 155, 158, 205n74, 220n85, 221nn1–3, 222n8, 222nn12–13, 223n19, 228n57, 232n121, 236n30, 249n184, 275n122, 298n163, 300n190, 301–302n2

"Subject," 42, 43, 54, 55, 56, 66, 71, 74, 82–83, 115, 117, 119, 133, 134, 144, 175, 221nn1–2, 222n6, 227n52, 249nn185–186, 249n188, 276–277n38

Symptomatic reading, 60, 170, 176, 269n65

Text, textuality, xi, 6, 7, 27, 57, 62, 74, 94, 95, 101, 111–112, 113, 114, 124–126, 127–129, 130–155, 157–158, 159, 161, 162, 163, 164, 165, 193n2, 206n85, 209n119, 271n83, 284n1, 285n5, 285nn9–10, 285–286n13, 286n15, 286nn17–18, 288–289n51, 293n98, 294n121, 297n150; productivity of, 8, 131, 132, 133, 162–163, 286n15, 295n126

"Thick description," 25, 76, 78, 106, 141, 145–146, 151, 158, 212n153, 295n129, 301n200

Thompson, E. P., 80, 81–83, 246n161, 246n164, 248nn175–176, 248nn180–181, 248n183, 249nn185–186, 249n188

Thompson, John B., 174, 176

Todorov, Tzvetan, 89–90, 242n111

Turner, Frederick Jackson, 20, 207n103, 207n106, 208n114

Veyne, Paul, 6, 65, 70, 71–74, 89, 90, 92, 98, 101, 117, 118, 235n17, 241n95, 241nn98–99, 254nn56–58, 277n140

Vovelle, Michel, 69, 237n41

Walsh, W. H., 33, 34

White, Hayden, 4, 5, 15, 22, 23, 27, 36, 86, 88, 89, 97, 98–104, 105, 110, 111, 125, 130, 156, 157, 194n9, 200n29, 203n55, 204n63, 210n131, 212n157, 248n181, 251n11, 252n24, 255n61, 258nn104–105, 259n121, 260n123, 260n125, 260n127, 260n130, 260n134, 261n138, 261nn144–145, 264n4, 280n184

Wittgenstein, Ludwig, 29, 38, 39, 148, 196n15, 211n139, 214n3, 220n80, 284n1, 289n58, 289n60, 290n68, 291–292n84, 298n160, 298n162

Women, 174, 249n188, 312n144; and anthropology, 58, 227n56; in early Christianity, 8, 170, 172–181, 314n153, 314–315n166; as historians, 22–23, 199–200n15, 209nn117–118, 210n128, 263n1; in history, 22, 160, 170, 311–312n134; as metaphor, 25, 172, 206–207n95, 210n128, 212nn153–154